The
Essential
Guide to
Application
Service
Providers

ISBN 0-13-019198-1

90000

9 780130 191984

Essential Guide Series

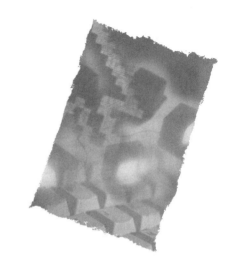

The Essential Guide to Application Service Providers

Jon William Toigo

Illustrations by Margaret Romao Toigo

Prentice Hall PTR, Upper Saddle River, NJ 07458
http://www.phptr.com

658.84
T64e

Library of Congress Cataloging-in-Publication Date

Toigo, Jon William
    The essential guide to application service providers / Jon William Toigo.
        p.   cm.
    Includes index.
    ISBN 0-13-019198-1
    1. Application service providers.   2. Electronic commerce.   3. Business
enterprises—Computer networks.   I. Title.

HF5548.32 T64 2001
658.8'4--dc21

                                                            2001026714

Acquisitions editor: *Tim Moore*
Cover designer: *Bruce Kenselaar*
Cover design director: *Jerry Votta*
Interior design: *Meg VanArsdale*
Editorial assistant: *Allyson Kloss*
Manufacturing manager: *Maura Zaldivar*
Marketing manager: *Tc Leszczynski*
Project coordinator: *Anne R. Garcia*
Compositor/Production services: *Pine Tree Composition, Inc.*

© 2002 by Prentice Hall PTR
Prentice-Hall, Inc.
Upper Saddle River, New Jersey 07458

Prentice Hall books are widely used by corporations and government
agencies for training, marketing, and resale.

The publisher offers discounts on this book when ordered in bulk
quantities. For more information, contact:

    Corporate Sales Department
    Phone: 800-382-3419
    FAX: 201-236-7141
    E-mail: corpsales@prenhall.com

    Or write:

    Prentice Hall PTR
    Corp. Sales Dept.
    One Lake Street
    Upper Saddle River, New Jersey 07458

Printed in the United States of America
10   9   8   7   6   5   4   3   2   1

ISBN: 0-13-019198-1

Pearson Education Ltd.
Pearson Education Australia PTY, Ltd.
Pearson Education Singapore, Pte. Ltd.
Pearson Education North Asia Ltd.
Pearson Education Canada, Ltd.
Pearson Educación de Mexico, S.A. de C.V.
Pearson Education—Japan
Pearson Education Malaysia, Pte. Ltd.
Pearson Education, Upper Saddle River, New Jersey

This book is dedicated to two persons: to my daughter, Mercedes, who dreams courageously, despite the fact that some dreams are inevitably nightmares; and, to my friend and father-in-law, Anthony Romao, whose decades of corporate management experience have taught him to temper enthusiasm with caution, but to embrace innovation courageously nonetheless. We will need both types of courage as business automation continues its advance into the next millennium.

Table of Contents

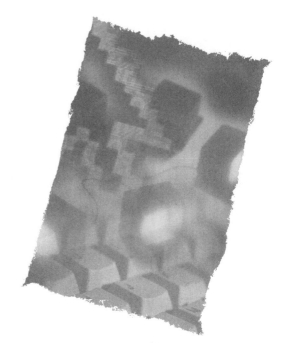

    DIFFERENT KINDS OF OUTSOURCING   101

    IN SITU OUTSOURCING   104

    OUT-TASKING   105

    BEYOND MARKET-SPEAK: ASPS AND OUTSOURCING   107

    LESSONS FROM OUTSOURCING   111

    CUSTOMIZATION AND ASPS   114

    APPLICATION SERVICE DELIVERY:
    THE NETWORK IS THE KEY   115

    CONCLUSION   117

5   The Contemporary ASP Market:
    Vendors, Intermediaries, and Aggregators   121

    INFRASTRUCTURE SERVICES LAYER   124

    APPLICATION SERVICES LAYER   135

    INTEGRATION SERVICES LAYERS   141

    ANALYTICAL SERVICES LAYER   143

    CONCLUSION   158

Preface
and Acknowledgments:
The Emerging ASP

Early one September morning in 1999, a Compaq Computer Corporation executive shuffled his notes, tested his lavolier microphone, and made other last-minute preparations to deliver a keynote address at the iForum Conference in Orlando, Florida. Individually and in small groups, attendees—still bleary-eyed and with first-of-the-day coffees in hand—filed quietly into the cavernous, dimly lit meeting room at the Walt Disney World Dolphin Resort. In near-complete silence, they found places among the neatly arranged rows of chairs, seated themselves, and stared blankly at the stage.

Oddly, the scene conjured to mind a would-be George Romero horror movie sequel—*Morning of the Living Dead*—in which zombies act out some sort of imprinted behavior without any real cognition or motive. Indeed, many attendees seemed to be using the session as a means to an end: as a justification for partaking in the delicious breakfast supplied by the host, an opportunity to plan their tee-times for golfing later in the day, or just a temporary respite from the uncomfortably bright Floridian morning sun. Few seemed to be attending the speech to actually hear the speaker's words.

The speaker watched, poker-faced, as the room filled with bodies. Most presenters would agree that the first-session-of-the-day is rivaled only by the first-session-after-lunch as the worst time to be scheduled to speak. Engaging the audience in the substance of the presentation is a greater challenge at those times owing to their characteristic grogginess. It requires that the speaker present his or her information with a greater degree of energy and originality than would be required at other times of the day.

On this occasion, the Compaq executive's demeanor was one of utter calm—implying either the cool confidence of a well-rehearsed speaker or the false confidence of a complete novice. An exciting, shocking, or humorous opening would decide the issue.

Instead, the speaker referred to his script and opened his talk rather pre-dictably—first, paying homage to the host, Citrix Systems, then extolling the merits of the Citrix approach to server-centric computing. Equally predictable was his asser-tion that his company's own server systems provided the optimal host platform for centralized application delivery. To support his claim, he asked that a digitized video of customer testimonials be played on the big screen behind him.

He stood to one side, preparing to bask in the pixelated glow and recorded praise of his customers. Without warning, the software-controlled playback abended in midkudo. A few awkward moments elapsed while technicians tried unsuccessfully to restart the hosted video clip.

The unplanned turn of events was perhaps the salvation of the presentation in disguise. The speaker forgot about his notes, journeyed away from the podium, and sauntered out to stage center. There, he began to deliver a more extemporaneous ver-sion of his talk.

Perhaps as much to jolt the crowd to a higher degree of alertness as to cover for the presentation *faux pas,* his pitch shifted from the even marketing drone of a corpo-rate mouthpiece to a much louder "shoot-from-the-hip" sort of rant. He opened with a blunt statement: Application Service Provisioning (ASP) is about to change the fun-damental dynamics of the business computing world in a way that has not been seen since the emergence of the Internet. He then proceeded to reiterate the key compo-nents of the ASP value proposition—a mantra chanted by virtually every speaker at the conference (and at the numerous ASP conferences that have occurred since then):

- With the ASP model, software is operated on an ASP's server computer, while the application user interface is delivered to the subscriber's client device—whether a desktop PC, thin computer, network computer, wire-less device, or other client—using a secure private network or public In-ternet connection. This model for application delivery eliminates the need for end users to purchase software and install it locally on their own PCs and servers. It prevents users from becoming enmeshed in the endless and costly downward spiral of patches and upgrades that have served software vendors like annuity programs.

- The ASP model moves the burden and expense for administering desktop software to a qualified service provider, the ASP itself, enabling IT re-sources to be reallocated to other meaningful tasks.

- ASPs enable medium and smaller companies to utilize "enterprise class" applications such as Enterprise Resource Planning (ERP), Materials Re-source Planning (MRP), and Customer Relationship Management (CRM) without incurring the expense and difficulty for application rollout that tends to make these applications the exclusive domain of the wealthiest and largest companies alone. In short, ASPs "level the playing field" between rich and poor, big and small.

- ASPs provide access to applications that are infrequently used and/or difficult to cost-justify for outright purchase. Why should companies buy software, if they are better served by using it on a "pay per drink" basis?
- ASPs provide an offset to the growing problem of limited IT staff resources. Instead of underwriting costly IT training programs or incurring the expense of locating and hiring increasingly scarce programmers, systems administrators, and network administrators, why not outsource the applications to a provider who already possessed these resources?

The best thing about ASPs, according to the speaker, was that the technologies that enable this model for application delivery were not experimental. Products such as Citrix Systems's MetaFrame were pedigreed and ready for use, enabling applications to be hosted on a centralized Windows NT or 2000-based server. Moreover, the Citrix ICA protocol enabled the user interface of a hosted application to be extended across low speed/low bandwidth networks. Thus, even the public Internet could provide a vehicle for ASP.

Quod erat demonstrandum. ASPs, he concluded, are poised to dominate the future of software distribution.

Without skipping a beat, the speaker shifted his tone from that of a visionary to that of an inquisitor. He asked rhetorical questions that mirrored an issue on the minds of many conference attendees: Why, given the inherent benefits of the ASP model for users and providers alike, was the ASP revolution not occurring more quickly?

Who was to blame for the hesitation of companies to subscribe to the offerings of a burgeoning ASP industry? What counter-revolutionary forces were at work?

He slowly turned to a section of the room where the representatives of the trade press were seated. Slowly and dramatically, he raised his hand and pointed an accusing finger.

"Despite what some malcontents in the trade press say," he grumbled, "the Application Service Provider model isn't just time-sharing* by a different name."

The ASP, he said, was an entirely new method of application delivery that stood on the threshold of revolutionizing the software industry. Only a few pessimistic pun-

---

*In the early days of corporate computing, "time-sharing" was a term used to describe processing by a service bureau provider that involved simultaneous use of a central computer by many users at remote locations. The term acquired some negative connotations as part of a backlash against information systems outsourcing in the late 1980s.

dits and naysayers stood in the way of the emergence of the ASP and all of the tremendous benefits that it would impart.

The assertion was rewarded by the enthusiastic applause of the audience, many of whom muttered grumbling agreement that they had seen many reports about ASPs—but few that actually endorsed the approach.

Although ASP-related events, such as the formation of ASP joint ventures by leading software, networking, and consulting companies, have been duly noted and reported, few publications have carried feature articles that might be viewed as "ASP positive." As with many other (but not all) technologies, the press has adopted a critical and cautious view of the ASP phenonmenon. Was the press shaping the popular view of ASPs, or merely reflecting it back to the vendors?

Many commentators and analysts have observed that, though the number of self-styled ASPs has been growing at a rate of more than 200 per month, the number of customers for these services has not proceeded apace with the growth of the vendor community.

Some have attributed this gap to conservatism on the part of prospective customers: unwillingness to trust third parties with important or critical information processing functions, concerns about the security of networked application delivery, or reluctance to deviate from established practices. Others have pointed to the lack of publicized industry standards and practices, and the absence of service level agreements (and of the means to monitor vendor compliance with them) as key impediments to the ASP revolution. Still others have noted that the ASP is a new concept and requires substantial consumer education before it can attain widespread industry acceptance.

Despite these challenges, leading industry analysts, including DataQuest, International Data Corporation, the Yankee Group and others, have released projections depicting the future of the ASP approach in bold lines that sweep high and to the right. Collectively, they hold that a compelling case is building, both for consumers and vendors, for application and infrastructure outsourcing. ASPs, they claim, will come to profit on these trends.

DEFINING TERMS

This book is about the evolving ASP phenomenon. It seeks to answer fundamental questions about ASPs: the who, what, where, when, and how of an emerging architecture that has seen substantial investment activity among recognized vendors of systems, network, and application technology.

It should be noted that the term "ASP" is not rigorously defined in this book. Strange as it may sound, establishing a hard definition of the term would likely create a point of contention rather than contributing meaningfully to the clarification of the term. Indeed, in performing the research comprising this book, it was common to find ASP spokespersons using some rarified (and usually self-serving) definition of an ASP as a "discriminator," that is, as a means for comparing one's service offering favorably to that of a competitor.

Some vendors added adjectives such as "pure play" and "self-sufficient" to the term ASP to suggest that a hierarchy existed among ASPs and that the inherent superiority or inferiority of any service could be discerned by reference to this hierarchy. Rightly or wrongly, some vendors emphasized their ownership of the application they were provisioning to minimize the offerings of vendors, who, themselves, leased applications from another company. Others suggested that their knowledge of complex systems integration and implementation placed them ahead of the pack of software vendors-turned-ASPs. Still others emphasized their expertise or ownership of system or network resources as a means to distance themselves from less competent or less well equipped competitors.

Considering the current shortfalls in customer subscriptions confronting virtually all ASPs, many interviews brought to mind the wisdom of Henry Kissinger's assertion that "the reason interdepartmental battles are so bloody is that the stakes are so small."

Suffice it to say that the term "ASP"—like the terms "integration," "e-business," and "middleware"—embodies more "marketectural" than architectural content. Marketecture is what happens when technology is "productized" by the sales and marketing and press relations organizations within the high tech industry.

The result of marketecture is that there are about as many definitions of ASP as there are vendors. Rather than defining the acronym, this book surveys the meanings attributed to ASP by analysts and practitioners and leaves to the readers the task of deciding which definition best meets their needs.

The origin of the term ASP is itself a sticky point. One analyst claims to have originated the term as a handy way to refer to a subset of a larger trend toward infrastructure outsourcing using web Technology. Her definition of the ASP acronym is Application Service Provisioning. By contrast, another prominent figure in the ASP world claims to have originated Application Service Provider (also abbreviated ASP) as a means to identify a cadre of companies that were offering rented applications via private networks or the public Internet. The use of ASP in this book encompasses both interpretations but will generally refer to the provider, rather than the process.

THE ORGANIZATION OF THIS BOOK

This is not to suggest that ASP is a wholly relativistic concept. Although there are a number of self-proclaimed ASPs in the market today that are little more than traditional outsourcing companies, or Web site hosting companies trying to capitalize on the current interest in ASPs by recasting themselves as application service providers, there are some characteristics that establish ASPs as a breed apart. These characteristics are covered in the first of three sections that comprise this book.

The first section comprises several chapters that cover ASP fundamentals. An optional first chapter, aimed at the nontechnical reader, sets the stage for the discussion by explaining a number of technical terms and by introducing a conceptual framework for understanding application delivery service. Both experienced and novice business technology planners can use this chapter to orient themselves to the material that is presented later.

In Chapter 2, the reader will be introduced to the many definitions attributed to the deceptively straightforward moniker, ASP. The basic components of an ASP will be identified, as will the central themes that constitute the business value proposition of the ASP. Application service provisioning is also discussed against the broader backdrop of infrastructure outsourcing using Web technology.

Chapter 3 continues this discussion by contrasting Application Service Provisioning with conventional corporate computing models that are currently used by most organizations. This chapter demonstrates how the ASP phenomenon is less a sudden and disruptive departure from the normal modes of corporate computing than a natural evolution of computing—a predictable outcome of corporate computing trends and directions, given their inherent costs and challenges.

Chapter 4 takes on the issue of whether ASPs can properly be termed another form of outsourcing. A brief historical tour will be offered of the traditional outsourcing approaches of the early 1980s. Deservedly or not, the outsourcing experience of that era left a set of negative impressions and attitudes in its wake which have come back to haunt the advocates of the ASP approach. These attitudes need to be reckoned with, both from the standpoint of their applicability to present ASP initiatives and for what they can teach about requirements for effective ASP service contracts in the future.

Chapter 5 provides an overview of the types of companies that are providing ASP services today:

- from Internet service providers and Web hosting companies who are seeking new business lines and revenue streams by fielding application service offerings

- to traditional outsourcing companies who are retooling service offerings to capitalize on the ASP craze
- to software companies looking for new distribution models and improved market share
- to more complicated alliances of network providers, integration consulting firms, and others who are endeavoring to make networks or data centers more profitable or to set the stage for future client work

Part of the confusion about the meaning of the term ASP derives from the mixture of objectives and approaches brought to bear by the very different entities offering ASP services. Trying to make sense of it all is the ASP Industry Consortium, a group of service providers interested in promoting the adoption of ASPs by business worldwide.

Chapter 6 concludes the Fundamentals section with an examination of the issues that must be addressed for the ASP model to achieve widespread use within the contemporary business setting. It sets the stage for a discussion of the current technical capabilities of, and the obstacles confronting, ASPs (the substance of Part Two of the book) and also examines the strengths and deficits in the management and practices of ASPs and their business models (Part Three) that are only today, as the hype around ASPs has begun to dissipate, beginning to receive serious attention from vendors.

Part Two covers the enabling technologies for ASPs. Chapter 7 begins with an examination of application software itself. An overview is provided of the languages and architectures that are commonly used to create modern software applications in order to describe how structures increasingly favor "Web technology–based" software delivery.

Chapter 8 introduces readers to the concept of "middleware" and its use in interconnecting distributed application components, which may be hosted on numerous levels or "tiers" of computer server platforms.

Chapter 9 tackles the often confusing and mysterious topic of application servers: software that integrates applications (and middleware services) that were not themselves designed for Web-based hosting, thereby enabling applications for distribution as an ASP service.

Chapter 10 explains what the airy term "Web technology" means in detail. There is a popular misconception that delivering application services via Web technology means that applications are themselves distributed via the public Internet and World Wide Web. This is not generally the case with most ASPs. Rather, Web technology is used with private networks to create "intranets" (or extranets) which facilitate the use of applications using common Web browsers as clients.

Chapters 11 and 12 move the discussion from software to hardware and networks. In Chapter 11, the hosting platform, the multitiered server platforms and storage infrastructure used by ASPs to host applications, is examined in considerable detail. The chapter covers basic hosting platform design, then identifies architectural enhancements that can improve the availability, performance and security of platforms.

Chapter 12 addresses the network provisioning requirements for successful ASP-hosted application delivery. Most ASPs do not provision their own networks, but utilize transmission and access facilities provided by public carriers or third-party service providers. The fact is that the further a company is from a metropolitan area that is well served by high bandwidth networks, such as fiber optic network rings, the more difficult it may be to derive the greatest value from current hosting models. The current state of the network is discussed in this chapter.

Having discussed the ASP value proposition, the current generation of ASPs themselves, and the underlying technologies that enable the delivery of software as a service, the final section this book covers ASP implementation. Chapter 13 begins this discussion by setting forth an approach for business planners who are interested in determining whether the ASP approach is right for their companies. Specific steps for acquiring an ASP solution may differ from company to company, but most approaches will entail the tasks described in the model introduced in this chapter and articulated in the remaining chapters of the book.

Chapter 13 provides an overview of the initial steps, including the formulation of objectives and the creation of an "in-house" application deployment alternative that can be used in comparing ASP solutions and setting criteria for their selection. The chapter also provides references to a number of information sources that the reader can consult to identify prospective candidates to deliver ASP services for the company.

Chapter 14 continues the process of ASP evaluation and selection by providing an overview of the structure of a request for proposal (RFP) that can be submitted to ASP vendors in order to solicit bids for the company's business. The chapter describes an RFP-based screening process that is increasingly used by companies to identify best-of-breed providers, winnowing the field of candidates to one or two that can be visited by the company planning team and evaluated per documented evaluative criteria.

Chapter 15 tackles the subject of ASP contracts and service level agreements. In the absence of generally agreed-upon industry standards and practices, a common-sense approach—drawing in part from other types of outsourcing agreements—is offered for structuring formal relationships with ASPs. The intent is to create a relationship that both meets customer expectations and facilitates ongoing cooperation between both vendor and consumer in the face of constant business and technological change: no easy task!

Chapter 16 concludes the book with guidance about the requirements for managing the ASP relationship over the long haul. The human factor—referring to the intelligent and thoughtful invocation of contractual remedies for ASP service problems—is just as important to determining the success or failure of an ASP solution as any technical component of the solution itself. The chapter examines successful and failed arrangements to derive a better understanding of the necessary ingredients of an ASP implementation that meets company needs.

CONCLUSION

Here then is *The Essential Guide to Application Service Providers*. The author wishes to thank the hundreds of ASP executives, analysts, and marketing personnel—and especially the many current ASP customers—who have shared their experiences, insights, and time to make this project a reality.

Thanks also to ASP Industry Consortium Chairman Traver Gruen-Kennedy, and to Christopher McCleary, chairman of the board for one of the earliest players in the ASP market, USinternetworking, for contributing their views to the book both in interviews and in a special foreword and afterword to the book.

Finally, the author wishes to thank those who labored to make this book the best it could be, including:

- The manuscript readers, expert editor Russ Hall, and Louis Columbus, formerly of ZLAND, for their time and effort in keeping this manuscript useful and to the point

- My good friends, Mike and July Linett, proprietors of Zerowait.com, who contributed freely of their knowledge and experience in engineering cuttingedge application hosting platforms for ASPs and for numerous Fortune 1000 companies engaged in "internal ASP deployments"

- My Prentice Hall PTR production editor and the production staff at Pine Tree Composition, who added clarity and visual appeal to the project

- My senior editor, mentor, and friend at Prentice Hall PTR, Tim Moore, who tolerated mind-bending schedule changes—necessitated in part by the serious ASP market shift that occurred in summer 2000—and who facilitated the project in so many ways

- Last but not least, my wife and partner, Margaret Romao Toigo, who served as illustrator, sanity check, and wall-off-which-ideas-are-bounced

The ASP, like all technology innovations, mixes old and new technologies. The author hopes that, having read this book, readers will be empowered with a clearer understanding of the capabilities and the limitations of ASPs so that they can better evaluate the suitability of the strategy against the backdrop of their own business requirements.

As a companion to this book, the author has also created a Web site at *www.eguideasp.org* that will serve as a respository for vendor neutral information about ASPs and a clearinghouse for information received after the publication of the book. Readers are encouraged to use the site and to suggest to the author any changes or additions that would make this book more useful in subsequent editions.

The Web site associated with this book, as well as the illustrations created by Margaret Romao Toigo for inclusion in this book, were developed using best-of-breed media development tools provided to the author by Corel Corporation (*Corel Draw 10*), Adobe Corporation (*Adobe Photoshop 6*), Microsoft Corporation (*VISIO*), and Macromedia, Inc. (*Dreamweaver 4, Dreamweaver UltraDev 4,* and *Fireworks 4*). We heartily thank these software vendors for their contributions and recommend their products to anyone interested in media-rich information delivery.

Foreword

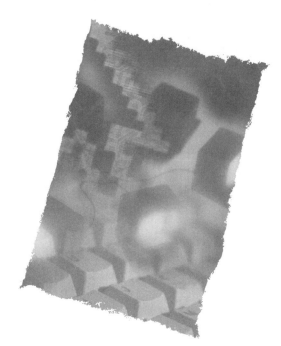

BY

CHRISTOPHER R. McCLEARY

Chairman of the Board

USinternetworking, Inc.

It's hard to believe that not too long ago the most common affiliation with the acronym ASP was Active Server Pages. Two years and 1,400 companies into the ASP industry later, it is safe to say that Application Service Providers have recoined the acronym and are in the process of revolutionizing an industry. As ASPs become more mainstream and the market continues to mature, one might wonder how it all began. . . .

Several years ago, I started including my home telephone number on my business card. I wanted clients to have the ability to contact me at any time to discuss matters of importance to our service delivery. When I was chairman and CEO of Digex, one of the recognized leaders in Web hosting, I received a call from a client that stands out for a very important reason—it helped lead to the creation of USinternetworking (USi), Inc., and consequently the ASP market.

The call came from a Web-hosting client concerned that their commerce site was not performing well under our management and required immediate action. After getting an earful, he allowed me to review the situation and call him back. A thorough evaluation determined that the application software deployed by their integrator partner, albeit loaded on a server at our location, had failed and had multiple conflicts with new features loaded the prior week .

I delivered a prompt, detailed report and offered advice on a solution to the customer. The proposed solution, however, could not address the root of the problem, because Digex was not responsible for the software application, and the split in responsibility between Web hosting responsibilities, system integrators, and software providers did not provide a clear chain of ownership.

The customer was furious, wanting us to assume total responsibility for the functionality of the application software in our network environment. To tell you the truth, I understood this frustration—there was a clear need for a total responsibility solution.

One year later, insight gained from this experience and a review of similar Web-hosting client satisfaction case studies served as the basis for the formation of USi. The thesis was simple: a company that would assume total responsibility and end-to-end application software which relies on wide area communications to provide underlying functionality should be provided as an extension of the communication service.

Stated another way, the best corporate email and collaboration software product in the world, Microsoft Exchange, has no utility or value to the corporate user if the T-1 is down. Similarly, a copy of BroadVision Commerce software has zero utility unless the communication infrastructure operates as well and in concert with the functionality of the application.

Yet, all the influencers in the software industry said this is the way the industry works: Corporate users buy high performance hardware and complex software, and they pay upfront for consultants to perform implementation and integration services. Additionally, they must subscribe to communication services for interoffice connectivity and connectivity to suppliers and customers, with the ideal end result being improved effectiveness of their business as a result of the rich functionality.

Even though this remains an accurate description of the current process development, it is not necessarily an accurate description of the result. In order to optimize effectiveness, all aspects of the application, including the ability to communicate interoffice, must work together and must work 24×7.

At this time, the USi team had a total of 30 employees, including my two cofounders, and we were learning the hard way that there was a reason software was not sold as a service: legacy momentum. Software companies and communication service providers both had Wall Street–driven business models; software companies were encouraged to sell new licenses each quarter (and collect the license fee during the quarter); and communication service providers were judged on number of lines or megabytes. Furthermore, providing the functionality of a software application, including the necessary elements to make it function and guarantee a service level agreement $7 \times 24 \times 365$, was hard work!

Today, just two years after the first venture funding, however, USi's corporate clients have subscribed to more than one-third of a billion dollars in ASP services, providing the rich functionality of leading software applications from Siebel, PeopleSoft, Microsoft, Plumtree, Broadvision, Ariba, Lawson, and others with literally no upfront capital investment in hardware, software, or implementation labor. A multiyear service contract, inclusive of all critical elements, which permits a client's employees, clients, or other authorized remote users to log on from anywhere at anytime, has forever replaced the complex integration morass and split responsibility of the past.

In all fairness, our industry has had some help. Billions have been invested to create the required network security and authentication systems. The price of a T-1 has dropped to $500 per month, and a dial account is free. Desktop computers and browsers are virtually free, and no one can find a good UNIX administrator anymore. Industry trendsetters began conducting seminars on the corporate need to push authority down to lower levels, which required more remote-to-company systems throughout the world. Finally, the marketing expenditure to educate the marketplace has also been of assistance.

In three years, ASP services will be the primary vehicle for deployment of companies' technology. The reasons for this massive shift are clear. First, companies are demanding that technology be pushed out to facilitate the ability of remote users to harness the power of the Internet—this is the defining value proposition of e-commerce. Second, networked software runs better and is more reliable if it is managed as an integrated service. Last, but most important, the ASP model allows the service provider and the customer to share the same goal—keeping the software running well, all the time. Delivering on this promise is the key to this maturing market. If the software is not running well, the ASP has not earned its monthly service fee.

Historically Management Information Systems (MIS) professionals exposed their companies to huge financial risk by making large upfront investments in numerous technology elements, fully expecting that the integrated system would perform and be internally manageable. Today that risk is forever averted by selecting the software application of your choice, signing a service contract, and logging on from anywhere; and, if the service does not work each and every month, don't pay. Period.

In our ongoing efforts to "make software simple," we have created an environment in which all software runs more effectively, with less downtime and at a lower total cost than a corporate internal-governed system. At USi, there have been no failed implementations of a software application instance, because we are all motivated to see our clients maintain their mission-critical enterprise software functionality. If the service does not work, USi does not get paid. At USi we are dedicated to making sure that each implementation of PeopleSoft, Siebel, and Microsoft Exchange works. Today, tomorrow, and beyond.

In closing, the ASP business model and many variants of service offerings will be introduced and available over the next several years, but the underlying element that continues to drive this maturing industry is extremely powerful and most basic in nature—the demand for better customer service. Service providers that assume long-term responsibility and can deliver on the demand for ubiquitous, yet secure access to information stores from anywhere in the world will be the winners. Other big winners will be the software companies that embrace the model, because it is their platforms that are utilized by the ASPs. But, far and away the biggest winners will be the clients of technology solutions.

Part 1

ASP Fundamentals

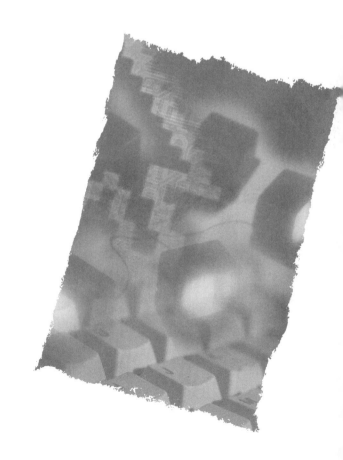

1 Setting the Stage

In this chapter...

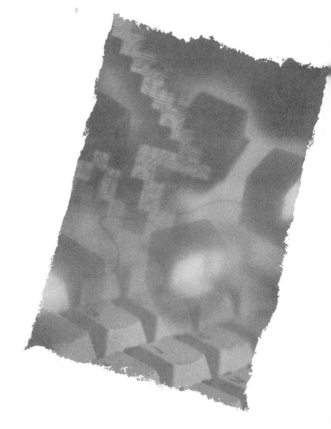

If you are in business today, chances are good you have heard about the business potential of the Internet and the World Wide Web. E-business is all the rage. An inexact term, e-business refers to virtually any application of the technologies developed for the Internet and the Web to meet business needs.

As you might suspect, e-business covers a lot of territory. It includes "informational" Web sites that are being fielded on an almost daily basis by companies ranging from the *Fortune 500* to local mom-and-pop knickknack stores. These sites are intended to provide current company information and, in some cases, to establish brand-name recognition among the growing population of people worldwide who "surf the Net." In effect, informational Web sites are the 21st Century equivalent of the Burma Shave sign.

E-business also includes e-commerce. E-commerce refers to the selling of goods and services across the Web. Online bookseller Amazon.com is an archetype of an e-commerce site, as are Bluefly.com and the host of other online catalog shopping venues offering everything from assemble-it-yourself furniture to pasta machines to sporting goods. For those with an Internet account, a Web browser, and a credit card, the World Wide Web is the world's biggest department store!

In addition to the sale of consumer goods, e-commerce also includes online banking, online stock trading, intermediation services (price comparison programs that tell consumers the lowest available price for a given product or service), electronic versions of print publications, and any other venture that earns money—in the form of sales revenues or advertising commissions—to its operators. Consumers worldwide spend billions of dollars annually at e-commerce sites. Getting a piece of this action is the primary incentive of the "dotcoms"—a jargon term for companies, many of which failed miserably in their efforts to use the Web for commercial purposes. Dotcom itself is derived from a system of domain names used to classify Web sites by their purpose. Domain Registration Services that control such matters use the designation *www.companyname.com* to identify organizational Web sites with an e-commerce bent.

E-business also encompasses Business-to-Business (B2B) arrangements. These are Web-enabled connections between the business processes of two or more companies. In many cases, B2B arrangements are established between business partners (e.g., a company and its key suppliers) and are intended to replace paper-based transactions (paper-based invoices, purchase orders, etc.) with electronic ones. Simplistically, each company uses the public Internet (or a private network) as a vehicle to provide its partner with controlled access to its internal business applications. The potential cost savings from such arrangements and increased productivity derived from effective B2B relationships are enormous. This proposition continues to drive revenues from the sale of B2B-enabling products and services toward the multibillion dollar mark over the next couple of years, according to industry analysts.

B2B is one example of how business is harnessing the technology of the Internet and World Wide Web to improve its bottom line of profitability. Another approach, which is the subject of this book, is Web-based service provisioning.

Service provisioning, while offering a potential boon to corporate efficiency and profitability in many ways, is less about business than about technology. This chapter is intended as an introduction to the concept of service provisioning for those who are not already steeped in technology matters. A reader who already understands the fundamental concepts of business information services may want to skip ahead to the next chapter. Readers who are a bit less technical in their orientation or who want a quick review will find this chapter helpful in orienting themselves to topics that are explored in greater detail later.

INFORMATION TECHNOLOGY AS A SERVICE . . . . .

Information technology (IT) entered the business world in the late 1950s as part of the computer revolution. Initially computers were used to augment or replace manual business functions, such as file keeping and accounting. Data processing units were established within most large firms by the mid-1960s.

Historically, IT departments—originally termed Data Processing (DP) or Information Systems (IS) departments—were corporate cost centers rather than "profit centers." That is to say, the technology departments performed tasks to support other profit-making business activities, rather than generating revenues and/or profits for the company directly.

The value of these services was linked initially to their consistency and availability. Business units were pleased to have access on an ongoing basis to the services available from corporate DP. When the honeymoon ended, however, simple availability was determined to be a poor measure of IT service value. Business units redefined the value of their corporate computing capability in terms of the timeliness and accuracy of the information provided to them as information consumers.

As service quality demands increased, many corporate data processing shops began to assign dollar values to their service. Charge-back systems—methods for billing business units for the data processing services they consumed—were implemented by DP shops in many companies. DP managers saw charge-back as a means to underwrite, or at least justify, operating budgets—the costs for personnel and technology resources, including computer hardware and software. Inadvertently, these charge-back systems also created opportunities for competition.

In the late 1960s, independent data processing service companies were created by entrepreneurs to advance the notion of obtaining IT services from providers outside of the company. These outsourcing firms and service bureaus contended that all corporate DP amounted to the same thing—computations of information expressed as binary 1s and 0s. If a company could obtain the same quality of DP services from an external service provider, and at a lower cost than doing it themselves, vendors were confident that the quiet logic of cost-efficiency would dictate that they do so.

Merits of this argument notwithstanding, the view of IT as a business-enabling service is well entrenched. In the years that have followed, technology services have become so integral to many business processes that they are almost inseparable from each other. Testimony to this fact can be found in numerous cases of IT disasters and their impact on business continuity.

Over the past 30 years, natural and man-made disaster events have repeatedly shut down corporate computers and networks. Their designation as "disasters" implies more than an interruption of IT operations: These events are disasters when they interrupt the business processes that are enabled by the IT service. When they do, business grinds to a halt.

Twenty years ago, the dependency of business on IT services was less profound than today. Most large companies could revert to manual processes in the event of a DP outage and continue operations for several weeks until systems and networks were repaired. Today the same companies would likely be out of business, or at least severely financially damaged, by an outage lasting only a few days—or, in some cases, a few hours!

The point is that mission-critical business processes and the software applications that support them are very closely entwined. Few business professionals can perform their work without the support of IT services—whether they themselves interact with computers and use software applications directly, or act on the basis of information derived from application services.

SERVICE PROVISIONING . . . .

Service provisioning is basically the means by which IT services are provided to support business processes. This book is about application service providers, or ASPs. However, there has recently been a boom in service provisioning that has led to a plethora of potentially confusing acronyms ending in "SP." To understand them and to sift through the literature intelligently, one needs a basic familiarity with business technology. Figure 1–1 provides a convenient point of reference.

As shown in Figure 1–1, corporate IT can be viewed as a series of layers or infrastructures that work together to provide service to business processes. The foundation layer of this model is the storage infrastructure. (Note that the position of any

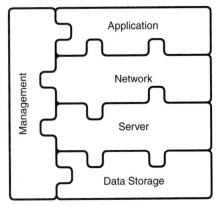

Figure 1–1
An intrastructural perspective of
IT service.

layer in this model does not connote its importance relative to the other layers. All layers working together efficiently determine the efficiency of IT service generally.)

THE STORAGE LAYER . . . .

The storage layer or infrastructure is an extremely important component of IT service. The storage layer provides space (capacity) for storing data, as well as stored data access and data sharing, and overall storage management, as depicted in Figure 1–2.

Computer data is typically stored on hard disk drives for fast retrieval, though tape and optical disc may be used to store older, less frequently accessed data, or copies of data for backup purposes. The storage infrastructure is designed, or architected, to ensure that the right mix of primary (disk) and secondary (tape or optical disc) technologies are provided.

To increase storage capacity beyond that of a single disk drive, multiple disk drives are often configured into a larger storage array. To a computer, the array may look like an extremely large disk drive, or it may be divided into several very large "virtual disks."

Arrays also frequently offer internal technologies for data protection through redundancy, as in the case of redundant array of independent disks (RAID) arrays. Some also provide additional technologies, such as array mirroring, used for copying data from one array to another as it is being recorded. Mirroring provides a stop gap against disaster: if one array fails, its mirror array, if properly configured, can replace it instantaneously, and IT services can continue to be provided.

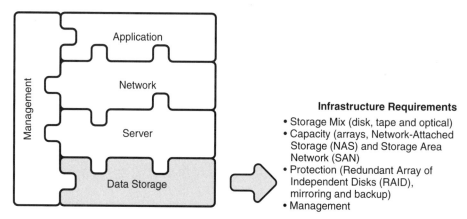

Figure 1–2
Data storage infrastructure functions.

Much more can be said about storage, including the application of technologies such as network-attached storage (NAS) and storage area networks (SAN), and the storage infrastructure is explored in greater detail later in this book. For now readers need to understand that the storage infrastructure is key to the performance of IT services, so much so that a class of service providers—Storage Service Providers or SSPs—have begun to appear in the marketplace. SSPs offer managed storage as a service. More on this later.

THE SERVER LAYER ....

Above the storage layer in our simplified diagram is the server layer or computing infrastructure. This layer consists of computer "servers"—a term that includes mainframes, minicomputers, and personal computer-based systems—that process data to produce useful information.

Simply explained, a server utilizes a central processing unit (CPU) to execute the programmed instructions submitted to it as software. For basic operations, the CPU acts in accordance with a software-based operating system. An operating system (OS) is the program that manages all the other programs in a computer. Popular operating systems range from OS/390 on IBM mainframes, to UNIX variants, Linux and Microsoft Windows NT or Windows 2000 on midrange and server systems, to Microsoft Windows or Apple OS on desktop systems.

The programs managed by the operating system are called applications. Applications range from complex and specialized business transaction processing systems to generic databases, spreadsheets, electronic mail, and word processors. A server is said to "host" the application it executes.

There continues to be a bit of a bias in the technology industry that places the server at the center of the "IT universe." This concept, which affords the server infrastructure precedence over other infrastructure layers, dates back to the earliest days of corporate computing and is reflected in the designation of the department responsible for corporate IT as "data processing" or "information systems." The bias is easily explained by the dominant architecture of early corporate IT shops: a mainframe typically sat at the center of the "glass house" of the data center, where it controlled data storage, hosted all applications, operated all peripherals (such as printers, tape drives, and other devices), and managed access through a network of dedicated user terminals. In this configuration, the server would seem to be the "king."

The arrival of personal computers (PCs) and of local area networks (LANs) changed this mainframe-centric universe, however. PCs enabled computing technology to be distributed beyond the confines of the mainframe data center, out into departmental settings and onto the desktops of individual users. LANs allowed the distributed computers (desktops, minicomputers, and mainframes) to be united into networks and to share resources with one another, if necessary. New applications were designed to capitalize on this distributed computing "platform," leading eventually to the observation by Sun Microsystems's CEO, Scott McNeely, that the network had become the computer.

The bottom line is that the server layer or computing infrastructure today comprises a key component, but by no means the only or most significant component, of IT service provisioning. The functions of this layer are numerous, as summarized in Figure 1–3. First and foremost, architects need to evaluate the appropriateness of operating environments and platform hardware to meet specific application requirements.

According to Dan Kusnetzky, vice president of Systems Software Research for International Data Corporation (IDC) in Framingham, Massachusetts, approximately 5.7 million operating environment shipments were made to consumers worldwide in 1999. Microsoft Windows NT shipments commanded approximately 38 percent of all shipments, while the open source UNIX operating system "look-alike," Linux, accounted for 25 percent. The balance of operating system environments comprised a mix of Novell Corporation's Netware, various versions of UNIX, and a small percentage of other OS products. A summary of IDC's findings is provided in Table 1–1.[1]

[1]From Jon William Toigo, "Open Systems: Web-Basing Leads Linux to Forefront," Washington Technology, Vol. 15 No. 7 (July 3, 2000). Kusnetzky goes on to say that the Linux market share could be much larger, owing to the fact that only purchased (as opposed to freely distributed) software is included in IDC estimates. The Linux operating system can be downloaded free-of-charge from numerous Web servers and File Transfer Protocol-accessible (FTP) sites on the Internet, in addition to being purchased as shrink-wrapped software from Red Hat (Research Triangle Park, North Carolina), Corel Corporation (Ottawa, Canada), and others. It is also included on many servers shipping today, including all platforms from Dell Computer Corporation.

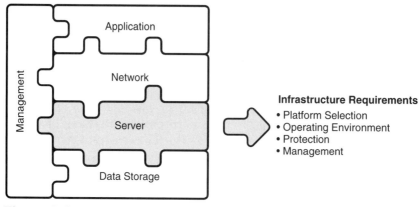

Figure 1–3
Systems infrastructure systems.

Kusnetzky clarifies a popular misconception that all operating environments are general purpose in nature. Based on IDC research, he observes that organizations "tend to use different operating environments for very different purposes."

According to Kusnetzky, the four uses most often cited by companies deploying Microsoft NT and Novell Netware operating environments "are file and print services, electronic messaging, communications services, and database support—in that order." By contrast, companies fielding UNIX servers rank "database support as their number one use for the operating system," followed by electronic messaging and custom application development. "While functionally similar," he points out, "different operating environments fill very different application niches."

Table 1–1   1999 Operating Environment Shipments Worldwide

Microsoft NT Server	38%
Linux	25%
Novell Netware	18%
UNIX	15%
Other	4%
Total Shipments:	5.7 million copies

Source: Dan Kusnetzky, International Data Corporation (Framingham, Massachusetts), quoted in Jon William Toigo, "Open Systems Web-Basing Leads Linux to Forefront," Washington Technology. Vol. 15 No. 7 (July 3, 2000).

For example, Kusnetzky observes that Linux, although certainly capable of supporting a broad range of applications, "is primarily used to support Web servers. In contrast to UNIX, less than 10 percent of companies use Linux to host databases."

Sorting through the options for server architecture(s) and OS environment(s), then fielding a well-managed server infrastructure that can scale as company needs dictate, remains a key determinant of an effective systems layer in corporate IT services. Also, like the storage infrastructure, the server infrastructure needs to be designed with acceptable levels of redundancy, failover capabilities, physical security, and other disaster avoidance technologies to protect the operation of servers and to provide availability at desired levels. A sturdy server management capability is also required to monitor thresholds of server performance so that problems can be identified early and resolved before they cause avoidable downtime.

THE NETWORK LAYER . . . .

No less critical than the server infrastructure is the local and wide area network infrastructure that is deployed by a business organization—the next layer in the simplified diagram. Networks, as previously discussed, enable the interconnection and interoperation of distributed servers, and provide access to applications and data for distributed users.

LANs began to appear in the 1970s as an enabler of distributed computing. Their wide area networking (WAN) counterparts, it can be argued, date back to the earliest days of telegraphy. The world's largest WAN, the Internet, continues to make use of the core networks established by telecommunications companies for telephony services.

Whether a LAN or a WAN, networks serve the function of interconnecting "nodes"—computers, peripheral devices, storage arrays, and so forth—so that they form an organized, manageable, and secure whole. Data traverses networks in the form of analog or digital packages represented by audible tones or electrical, infrared, microwave, radio, or laser emissions. Many standardized techniques, or protocols, exist for encoding and decoding data to facilitate its transmission across the network media—the generic name given to the wire, cable, or wireless carrier used to link nodes together.

LANs are usually networks that are deployed within a corporate premise, whereas WANs are used to move data between geographically remote locations. Increasingly popular is the acronym, MAN, which refers to a metropolitan area network—a variety of WAN used to interconnect nodes within the boundaries of a city or other regional area supported by a MAN vendor.

Within the corporate premise, LANs provide the equivalent of a roadway for moving information. Servers and other devices interconnected via the LAN may exchange information in the form of file transfers, share each other's resources on a peer-to-peer basis, or they may share access to server-hosted applications. Based on the characteristics of data traffic traversing the LAN, media bandwidth (capacity) and quality of service requirements may be deduced.

Many organizations deploy high-capacity networks, such as Gigabit Ethernet (with its 1,000 bits per second throughput), as "corporate backbone" networks, and utilize lesser capacity networks (Fast Ethernet at 100 bits per second or 10BaseT Ethernet at 10 bits per second) to interconnect nodes within a department or work group. This is roughly analogous to the idea of providing a six-lane superhighway (the enterprise backbone network) to which four-lane highways (departmental networks) and/or two-lane streets (work group networks) interconnect.

Of course, there are other networks besides Ethernet, but Ethernet—developed by Xerox Corporation, Digital Equipment Corporation, and Intel Corporation in 1976 and ratified as a standard by the Institute of Electrical and Electronic Engineers (IEEE)—enjoys the most widespread adoption within modern corporations. Ethernet so eclipsed its most popular LAN rival, Token Ring, that numerous analysts have discontinued the tracking and analysis of the Token Ring market completely. One analyst's rationale for this move was that Ethernet had become ubiquitous. In 1999, according to analysts, Ethernet accounted for 98% of the switch and hub ports shipped by vendors and 90% of the revenues within the LAN.

Ethernet supports a broad range of media options, including numerous wire and cabling standards and radio frequencies. It can be used to enable both *peer-to-peer* data and resource sharing, when deployed in conjunction with protocols such as NetBIOS Extended User Interface (NetBEUI) from IBM, and also more robust *Internet working communications*, when used with protocols such as the Novell-inspired Internetwork Packet Exchange (IPX) or the Internet Engineering Task Force's (IETF) Internet protocol suite. This suite of 20-odd protocols is typically known by the acronyms for the two best-known core protocols: Transmission Control Protocol/Internet Protocol or TCP/IP.

TCP/IP, which has the distinction of being the official protocol of the Internet, is a set of communications protocols specifically designed for Internet-working heterogeneous networks. The protocols—which were developed under the aegis of the U.S. Department of Defense (DOD) Advanced Research Projects Agency (DARPA) to interconnect DOD's diverse collection of systems and networks—took hold in the business world as a means to stitch together LANs and WANs based on different network technologies, including Ethernet, Token Ring, Fiber Distributed Data Interface (FDDI), X.25, Frame Relay, Switched Multimegabit Data Service (SMDS), Integrated Services Digital Network (ISDN), and, most recently, Asynchronous Transfer

Mode (ATM). The Internet protocols are widely regarded as the most proven approach to Internet working a broad range of LAN and WAN technologies.

Network and communications protocol selection are only part of network infrastructure design. Implementing the modern network typically entails the deployment of networking devices that will facilitate the efficient movement of traffic among and between departments, work groups, data centers, and external networks. Building blocks of modern networks are numerous, but four general categories of network devices are commonly used, as summarized in Table 1–2.

According to Cisco Systems, a leading vendor of switches and routers, network designers are moving away from bridges and concentrators and primarily using switches and routers to build "Internetworks." The design of a modern network utilizes the capabilities of routers and switches to forward data efficiently to its destination, prevent data loss, avoid bottlenecks and chokepoints that might impede performance and throughput, ensure necessary quality of service requirements as dictated by the application, and provide security and management.

LANs are increasingly connected to WANs to facilitate communications between a company headquarters and its branch offices, customers, partners, and/or suppliers. WAN gateways may be employed to establish these interconnections

Table 1–2   Network Devices

Device	Description
Hubs (concentrators)	Hubs (concentrators) are used to connect multiple users to a single physical device, which connects to the network. Hubs and concentrators act as repeaters by regenerating the communications signals as they pass through them.
Bridges	Bridges are used to logically separate network segments within the same network.
Switches	Switches are similar to bridges but usually have more ports. Switches provide a unique network segment on each port. Today, network designers are replacing hubs in their wiring closets with switches to increase their network performance and bandwidth while protecting their existing wiring investments.
Routers	Routers are used to connect different networks, directing network traffic based on network addresses rather than machine identifiers. They are protocol dependent.

Source: Cisco Systems, Inc., "Internetworking Design Basics," 1998.

(TCP/IP provides an external gateway protocol for connecting to non-IP nets), or internal networks may be simply attached to the Internet or to WAN services offered by public carriers, most of which support TCP/IP connections directly.

In supporting LAN-WAN communications, the network infrastructure needs to attend to two practical matters: cost and security. Costs accrue to WAN links (and bandwidth) which are generally quite a bit greater than LAN connection costs. Considerable planning is often required to obtain exactly the right WAN facilities which will meet company needs within budget-imposed limitations.

Security is another consideration that requires close attention by network infrastructure designers. Exposing internal networks, systems, data, and applications to outsiders via a WAN is risky business. Hackers intrusions, computer virus and other malicious software, electronic espionage, and other threats are increasingly prevalent. The responses of some 273 organizations collected by the Computer Security Institute (San Francisco, California) and the Federal Bureau of Investigation's Computer Intrusion Squad as part of the *2000 Computer Crime and Security Survey* revealed several alarming facts:

- Ninety percent of respondents (primarily large corporations and government agencies) detected computer security breaches within the last 12 months.
- Seventy percent reported a variety of serious computer security breaches other than the most common ones of computer viruses, laptop theft, or employee "net abuse"—for example, theft of proprietary information, financial fraud, system penetration from outsiders, denial of service attacks, and sabotage of data or networks.
- Seventy-four percent acknowledged financial losses due to computer breaches.
- Forty-two percent were willing and/or able to quantify their financial losses. The losses from these 273 respondents totaled $265,589,940 (the average annual total over the last three years was $120,240,180).

According to the Computer Security Institute, survey results illustrate that computer crime threats to large corporations and government agencies come from both inside and outside their electronic perimeters, confirming the trend in previous years. Seventy-one percent of respondents detected unauthorized access by insiders. But for the third year in a row, more respondents (59%) cited their Internet connection as a frequent point of attack than cited their internal systems as a frequent point of attack (38%).

The point is that networks frequently provide the point of entry for security threats. Thus, provisions must be made within the network for preventing unauthorized access both to the network and to the systems connected to it. Common risk re-

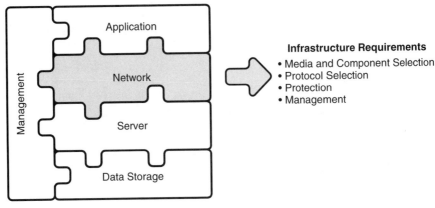

Figure 1–4
Network layer functions.

duction methods include the deployment of network firewalls, the use of data encryption, the creation of virtual private networks, and the implementation of access control and user authentication technologies.

These security measures must be balanced against other considerations, such as cost of deployment and the user-friendliness of the resulting security capability. That is to say, none of the methods are perfect shields against dedicated attacks. Thus, many organizations add intrusion detection capabilities to their prophylactic measures for intrusion prevention. Taken together, these measures constitute an important part of the infrastructure requirements of the network layer, as depicted in Figure 1–4.

THE APPLICATION LAYER . . . .

The top layer in our model refers to the application infrastructure. Applications are programs used to support business processes either directly, as in the case of a financial bookkeeping application, or indirectly, as in the case of a spooler program that manages the orderly printing of documents.

There are many ways to categorize application software that reference such criteria as

- How the software is used: multiuser versus single user
- Degree of customization: customized versus "vanilla" or "shrink wrapped"

- Fit with the requirements of a specific industry: vertical software used by medical clinics versus horizontal software used across all industry segments
- Degree of "integration": an integrated software suite versus a "point" product or standalone application

Application software may also be divided into functional groups:

- Utility application software assists in coordinating or managing the operation of system processes or extends the operating system.
- Communications software facilitates the connection to and use of communications "facilities" such as electronic bulletin board systems, email systems, the Internet, and so on.
- Graphics software provides the means to draw pictures, create graphs and charts, develop electronic slide shows, capture and manipulate electronic photos, and so on.
- Business application software enables, supports, or augments a business process.

Yet another classification method refers to "enterprise" application software—products designed for companywide supply chain management (SCM), enterprise resource planning (ERP), customer relationship management (CRM), manufacturing resource planning (MRP), or decision support (data warehousing and data mining)—to distinguish software of this type from less comprehensive application software packages.

Most of these taxonomies serve less to enlighten than to obfuscate, which is one reason why they are used extensively in the marketing literature of vendors. From a coding perspective, all applications are the same. They are all programs written in a programming language that is either compiled, then executed, or interpreted when executed, by a server.

Structurally applications may be quite different. Some applications are architected for use on a single server by a single user: Most PC-based applications are of this type. Some are designed for use by many users but reside on a single server host. Many database-driven products are of this type.

Application architecture may establish a "client-server" relationship in which the application itself is divided into discrete components that may be hosted on two or more distributed servers. In operation, these components send messages to one another across the network. Middleware may be used to facilitate this messaging. In such client-server applications, users access applications using a software "client" that may provide a user-friendly interface that conceals from them the complexity of the distributed application altogether.

The term "Web-enabled" has recently become connected with application software to describe software that, at a minimum, has been enabled to work with a Web browser application familiar to anyone who has used the Internet and World Wide Web. In connection with this description, the Web browser is frequently referred to as a "universal client."

The purpose here is not to teach how application software is designed, but to provide some insight into the ways that application selection or development influences the overall IT service. Application software provides the direct interface between the business user and the IT infrastructure overall. It also dictates to a large extent the requirements—including capacity, bandwidth, throughput, security, and quality of service—that must be met by the network, server, and storage infrastructures. There is a time-honored dictum among systems developers that applications software should be selected (or designed) before platform design and acquisition commences.

The application layer must also be secured and managed. Application layer security consists of access and authentication routines, such as application-specific logins and user identifications (IDs), which are implemented to prevent unauthorized access to applications themselves.

In some cases, organizations elect to perform authentication checks at the network or system layer, then to grant authorized users with the necessary access to storage and applications automatically. For sensitive applications, the application itself may be designed to challenge the user for an additional proof of identity before granting access. In some cases, application layer security may control the time of day that a user can access the application, or it may rechallenge the user on a periodic basis for additional validation information. Permutations of these approaches are numerous and are dictated by the perceived sensitivity of the application and of the risk that its unauthorized use represents to the organization.

Application management is also a key infrastructure requirement. Applications are designed to initiate processes, perform instructions, and deliver results. From time to time, it is possible for a process to abend (to quit working), or to continue running after it was programmed to cease operation. Application-related errors—whether due to "bugs" in the program itself, or problems with the server hardware or operating system software, or network-based problems—need to be identified quickly and rectified as proactively as possible to avoid both erroneous output and expensive downtime.

Figure 1–5 describes the functions of the application layer. It can be argued persuasively that the application infrastructure is what makes the other layers of IT purposeful. Application services are the heart of corporate IT, though they are impossible to provide without a sound and capable platform provided by the other layers.

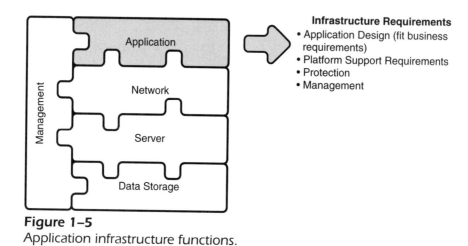

Figure 1–5
Application infrastructure functions.

THE MANAGEMENT LAYER ·················

For every layer described earlier, there is a discrete management function. Storage management consists of such low-level functions as storage device status monitoring to higher-level functions such as proactive capacity planning based on usage. Server and network management each entail similar low- and high-level functions, including server and network device configuration, performance threshold setting, threshold monitoring, and trend analysis for capacity planning. Application management, as described earlier, includes process monitoring, resource consumption monitoring, response time monitoring, and the proactive detection and resolution of potential problems.

With all of this layer-specific monitoring and management going on, one might wonder why a separate management layer exists on the figures contained in this chapter. It is a good question.

IT services, as discussed in the preceding pages, are enablers of mission-critical business processes with which they are increasingly intertwined. As such, IT services need to be held to the same performance standards as business processes themselves. They need to be managed for the quality of service that they provide to the organization, quantified and measured, subjected to guaranteed service level minimums, then monitored to ensure that service levels are met.

The management layer in this model embodies more than layer-specific management functions. A business manager is not particularly interested in the heat generation of a specific disk drive in a specific array located in a specific zone of a storage area network. Nor is the manager anxious to see a report on the number of Internet protocol (IP) packets dropped by a particular port of a network switch, or the CPU utilization of a specific server in the "server farm."

What does interest the business manager, ultimately, is how much improved productivity has been realized as a consequence of IT services. What percentage of customer requests are being handled within the first 24 hours of receipt? How many customer inquiries are being addressed via automation as opposed to requiring expensive "live" conversations with a customer support operator? How much have sales revenues increased as a result of the new e-commerce site? How has just-in-time manufacturing, augmented by automated supply chain management, reduced inventory costs and improved market share?

These questions, and myriad others, cannot be asked of infrastructure-level management resources. A management layer thus appears in the diagram to symbolize the tools and techniques emerging within IT services over the past several years that aim to distill platform and application management data into reports, analyses, and online representations that depict the impact—and hopefully the payoff—of the organization's IT investment.

At a minimum, capabilities should be provided to enable business management to view IT services on a business process by business process basis, so they can readily see whether the IT services supporting a specific process are doing the job. Performance measures, carefully defined, must be harnessed to provide a snapshot of the quality of service that is being provided at any given time. Historical data about performance needs to be wedded to service level agreements and to budgets to identify the compliance of IT services with both and to quantify cost differentials between planned and actual IT service performance.

IT services are not complete until the requirements of the management layer have been fulfilled, as shown in Figure 1–6.

CONCLUSION . . . .

The layered model of the infrastructure components comprising the modern IT service as described in this chapter is, of course, a simplified one. The model and its supporting narrative are not intended to address all the technical complexities of corporate computing in this burgeoning era of e-business. Rather, they are intended to orient readers to the subject of this book, application service provisioning, and to provide a business context for understanding the ASP phenomenon.

This chapter has introduced concepts and terminology that are explored in greater detail later in the book. By now, readers should have a general appreciation of

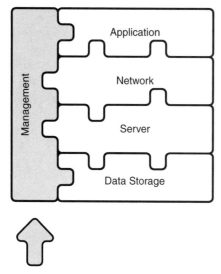

Infrastructure Requirements
- Measure IT Driven Productivity
- Establish and Track Service Levels
- Provide Business Process Views of IT Services

Figure 1–6
Management infrastructure requirements.

what is meant by the terms "platform," "server," "network," "application," "Web enablement," "service level agreement," and so forth. Some acronyms have also been decrypted, such as LAN, WAN, ERP, CRM, and so on. Additionally, some important standards-making organizations have been identified, including IEEE and IETF. A glossary at the conclusion of this book is also available to the reader to assist in keeping up with terms, acronyms, and entities.

A second purpose of this discussion is to assist the reader in conceiving of IT as a set of services. With most business people, the mention of IT conjures to mind a complex computer or some other high-tech gadget whose inner workings are shrouded in mystery. IT staff are those people who live in the data center, keep odd hours, drink lots of caffeine, speak in an alien language, and form impenetrable cliques at corporate gatherings. They seem to march to a different drummer, have a different sense of fashion, and, in a few cases, a different concept of personal hygiene. It is easy for a businessperson to conceive of the corporate IT department as a different kind of business unit, not subject to the same rules as other business units.

More and more, IT is being subjected to familiar business criteria. IT managers and chief information officers are being held to budgets, and they are being told to show results: consistent—and improving—service levels and measurable contributions to the bottom line of corporate productivity, efficiency, and profitability. If they can't demonstrate their value, options are becoming increasingly available. ASPs are an example of one such option.

From a strictly business perspective, application services (and their enabling infrastructure) need not be the product of an internal corporate IT organization. ASPs can be harnessed to augment, or, in some cases, to completely replace, comparable, internally provided services.

Now that some of the basic context has been provided, it is time to get on with this exploration of ASPs.

2   What is an Application Service Provider?

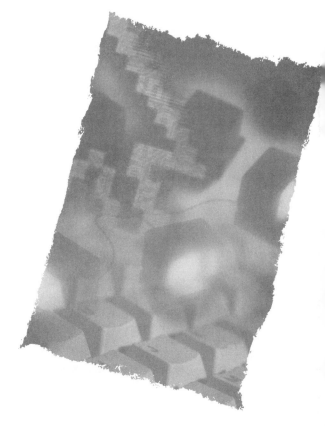

In late 1997, a press release appeared in the in-boxes of technology news magazine editors announcing that a new service would be offered via the Internet in 1998. This service would enable individuals to prepare their U.S. federal income tax returns online and to file them electronically.

In the minds of most editors, the release simply underscored the growing utility of the Public Internet and World Wide Web. New uses were being found almost daily for the emerging medium.

In the press release, the vendor said that its new offering provided an alternative for the millions of consumers who flocked annually to their local computer stores to purchase the latest year's PC-based tax accounting programs. Rather than purchasing and installing a new tax program each year, the user could simply use the service—a tax preparation software application hosted on the vendor's server somewhere in the ether of the Net—for a small subscription fee.

In addition to convenience, several other advantages accrued to this approach, said the vendor. For one, using the service eliminated the need for users to perform last minute software patches or upgrades, a common practice with PC-based tax preparation software. Developers of tax software, the vendor explained, are subject to a product delivery cycle that requires them to ship products to stores well in advance of final decisions on pending tax regulations. To ensure that these products properly calculate balances due or owed once tax laws are finalized, the software vendor must send out a program update or patch program at a later date.

Patching sometimes caused program failures or resulted in data corruption or data loss that necessitated a second round of hair-pulling data entry, the vendor commiserated. With the subscription service, patch problems would simply go away, the release claimed.

The press release went so far as to offer a cost argument for the new service: Why should a consumer pay several times the price of the subscription service to purchase software that would be used once, then discarded for next year's version? Although customers having more complex tax returns could expect higher subscription costs, the vendor expressed confidence that most returns could be handled under a basic subscription rate yielding a much reduced cost to the consumer.

Between the lines, the vendor was making a case for an approach to software delivery that would later be called application service provisioning. The basic tenants of the case included the following:

- Software applications can be loaded on a remote server and access can be offered to an end user client device, such as a browser-enabled PC, via a network.

- Delivery of an application's user interface (the means by which the end user interacts with the application software) to the end user client device can be provided as a service to which the user subscribes.

- Subscription-based application service delivery can have advantages over traditional—that is, user-purchased, installed, and operated—application software implementation. These may include:

  - Lower cost—owing to the fact that the service is shared among many subscribers

  - Efficient application maintenance and support—the service provider's own trained IT staff supports the application, server platform, and network

  - Improved application timeliness—owing to reduced product marketing life cycle lead times

  - Reduced user training requirements (browser-based programs feature common operating principles) and access to extensive online help and qualified support personnel (at an additional cost)

It is worth noting that the announcement did not address issues of information security. For example, it did not address the unasked questions of how the private financial information of the user would be protected from prying eyes or how information integrity and nonrepudiation would be assured. These questions have only now begun to be addressed by many application service providers based on numerous surveys indicating that security concerns are a major impediment to ASP adoption. Security is discussed in greater detail later in this book.

Even though the online tax preparation service was probably not the first implementation of an ASP approach to application delivery, it provides a simplified example that can serve as a starting point in this discussion of ASPs.

ASP: DEFINITION OR DESCRIPTION . . . .

What is an ASP? Some say that the term originated with industry analyst Clare Gillan of International Data Corporation (IDC) in October 1998. Gillan accepts credit for the acronym, which originally translated to "application service provisioning." The analyst admits that the term has since been stretched, warped, and skewed to embrace a broad range of meanings and implementations. ASP is now commonly used to describe a provider of application services, rather than the action of provisioning an application for a service customer.

According to IDC, an ASP provides a contractual service offering to deploy, host, manage, and rent access to an application from a centrally managed facility. ASPs are responsible, either directly or indirectly, for providing all of the activities and expertise required to manage a software application or set of applications. Additional defining characteristics of ASPs are also set forth by the analyst. (See the text box.)

IDC analysts describe, rather than define, what is meant by the term ASP—and with good reason. There are many types of ASPs. The variations are depicted in a diagram (see Figure 2–1), which arranges applications on one axis and services on the other.

As depicted in Figure 2–1, there are many variables involved in delivering application services. Applications offered by ASPs vary in complexity, from single user applications designed to operate on a personal computer, to "enterprise-class" applications such as resource and supply chain management and business intelligence applications.

Additionally, the types of services offered to a customer by the ASP may range from "core functions," such as managing the core application environment

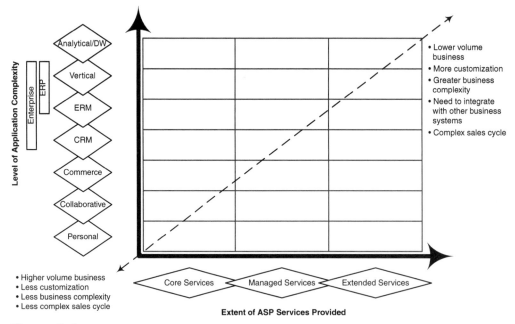

Figure 2–1
The ASP market landscape. *Source:* IDC, Framingham, MA, 1999. Reprinted by permission.

....

DEFINING CHARACTERISTICS OF AN *ASP*

According to analysts at IDC, the defining characteristics of an ASP are:

- Application centric. ASPs provice access to, and management of, an application that is commercially available. This service is different from business process outsourcing, for instance, where the outsourcing contract encompasses the management of entire business processes such as human resources or finance. It is also different from basic hosting services, where the focus of the service is management of the network and servers, with minimal applications management involvement.

- "Selling" application access. ASP services offer customers access to a new application environment without making up-front investments in the application licenses, servers, people, and other resources. The ASP either owns the software or has a contractual agreement with the software vendor to license access to the software. In an ASP model, the service provider rents access to the application on a shared basis.

- Centrally managed. ASP services are managed from a central location rather than at each customer's site. Customers access applications remotely, such as over the Internet or via leased lines.

- One-to-many service. ASP services are designed to be one-to-many offerings. The ASP often partners with other vendors to package standardized offerings (providing for minimal or no customization) to which many companies will subscribe over a specific contract period.

- Delivering on the contract. The ASP is the firm that is responsible, in the customer's eyes, for delivering on the customer contract, ensuring that the application service is provided as promised. ASP services will often involve several partners. If a problem arises, however, it is the ASP that is responsible for closing the loop on the trouble ticket, even if the ASP works with other companies to provide the actual support.

Source: "The ASPs' Impact on the IT Industry: An IDC-Wide Opinion," IDC, Framingham, MA, 1999.

and providing a base level of customer support, to include "extended" services, such as application customization and consulting/training services. As application complexity increases and services become more extensive in nature, service provider arrangements begin to deviate from the basic description of an ASP and assume characteristics that have more in common with traditional outsourcing arrangements.

The point is that within this broad spectrum of possibilities there is considerable "wiggle room." Companies that do not fit neatly into a particular definition or description of the term "ASP" do categorize themselves as ASPs—if only to capitalize on the current buzz of interest surrounding the term.

For a company shopping for an ASP solution, this situation can be confusing. It can also add a measure of difficulty to an already complex process of comparing the offerings of one or more service providers as a prelude to selecting the one that offers the best fit for a specific set of business requirements.

A SURVEY APPROACH . . . .

To convey the diversity of meanings that have come to be associated with the ASP concept, a survey of some of the current vendors offering ASP services* may be useful. As these boxed-text vignettes reveal, ASPs differ widely in terms of the types of software applications they offer, the manner in which the software is delivered, the extent of services provided, ownership of software, the hosting platform, network resources, and even customer support.

The vendors also differ in terms of the customer population that they target with their services. Some offer desktop applications to individual consumers or small businesses, whereas others offer highly customized ERP, MRP, CRM, or e-business applications to large- and medium-sized businesses. Some providers target specific industries or markets with vertical application services; others offer horizontal services—intended to serve consumers across all industry segments.

In addition to the specific application services offered, ASPs are often differentiated from one another based on the capabilities they bring to a service engagement. IDC has articulated a Venn Diagram depicting the disciplinary domains that are required for ASP service delivery. As shown in Figure 2–2, the analyst identifies three areas of skills and expertise that the ASP must provide (either through its own resources or by proxy) in order to begin fielding a viable service.

(text continues on page 42)

---

*Readers should note that a random sampling of vendors has been used in this chapter. The author does not endorse or recommend any of the vendors described herein.

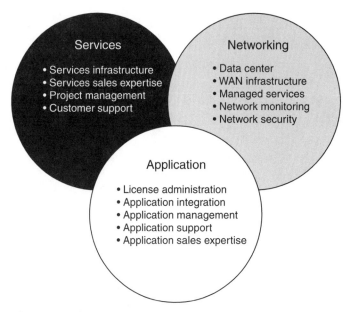

Figure 2–2
ASP required skills sets. *Source:* IDC, Framingham, MA,
1999. Reprinted by permission.

ASP SNAPSHOTS

Agilera, Englewood, Colorado

Agilera is a full-service, pure-play application service provider (ASP) that offers a flexible hosting platform for IT and e-business operations. Agilera's interdependent business model enables customers to expand efficiently and scale their level of enabling technologies without significant ongoing investments in infrastructure. Agilera, headquartered in Englewood, Colorado, was founded by CIBER, Inc., the 27-year international systems integrator; Verio Inc., the world's largest Web hosting company; and Centennial Ventures, Colorado's largest venture capital firm. Agilera provides its customers the velocity for faster time to market, as well as "dot.com agility and Fortune 500 stability™."

The ASP is targeting vertical markets, including manufacturing, retail, and financial services with e-business and enterprise resource management software products from top-tier vendors.

Says Todd Sterrenberg, Vice President of Channels, "In today's volatile market, businesses are looking for ways to drive cost out of their business model and ensure their established and future budgeted IT dollars and enterprise applications are being optimized. Effectively doing both can ensure success long-term, but determining the best method to achieve it can be daunting. Agilera understands the needs of today's businesses and the potential risks they face when implementing new technologies. Agilera's ASP business model is built on mitigating risk—financial risk, technology risk and human capital risk—enabling companies to effectively manage their enterprise applications."

According to Sterrenberg, clients leverage Agilera's enterprise application management skills and expertise to outsource the necessary skills and technology to gain full advantage of the emerging new technologies. He notes, "Customers are feeling the demand for 24/7 availability and the need to leverage their internal IT personnel on strategic, core business initiatives. Agilera fulfills both requirements by providing a proven, high-availability hosting environment and viable outsourcing alternative to the application management skills needed to augments a company's key IT and application personnel."

Sterrenberg says that important differentiators are appearing in the ASP marketplace, "Although there are a growing number of companies interested in an ASP providing the full gambit of services including managed services [hosting], Agilera doesn't limit its market to only hosted clients. Comprehensive, cost effective application management knowledge is the key differentiator and true value-add in our market whether it's provided remotely or as part of a hosted solution. Another key differentiator for Agilera is its ability to manage multiple enterprise applications for a client. This ability is growing in importance as a majority of mid-market clients and above now have multiple enterprise applications deployed ranging from CRM, ERM, ERP to B2B. True full-service ASPs need to be able to integrate, support and manage multiple enterprise applications, not a single application like the ISV ASPs who only provision, manage, and support their own application."

Sterrenberg says that he is "truly convinced" that over the next several years, the market will view enterprise applications as "solution utilities" paid monthly to provide the necessary applications "to most effectively meet the applications needs of their ever changing markets and business dynamics."

AristaSoft Corporation, San Jose, California

Launched in November 1999, AristaSoft has been "working in stealth mode ever since," according to CEO and co-founder Drew Hoffman. The objective of the firm is to provide a "subscription IT service" by integrating, implementing, operating, and supporting a portfolio of business applications to high-tech electronics companies.

According to Hoffman, the business software offering, delivering "just-in-time" support for integrated business processes within the enterprise and its value chain, is complemented with a managed services offering described as a "tightly meshed network of technology partners [providing] business-critical solutions you can depend on 24 hours, 365 days a year." Components of the managed services include "a desktop access environment, high-speed DSL local network access, a virtual private network for solution delivery, and Class A data center facilities." Hoffman refers to the solution as a "one-stop-shopping resource for Tier-1 enterprise IT solutions."

"By focusing on a particular market segment, AristaSoft gains a high-level understanding of each market's specific needs," Hoffman explains. "This knowledge lets us enter a company's business environment at a sprint instead of a crawl." In addition to a small direct sales force, Hoffman reports that the "word travels fast in Silicon Valley" regarding the solvency and quality of service providers. He notes that AristaSoft has already signed up over 20 customers, including Turnstone Systems, Inc., a vendor of telecommunications products.

Hoffman notes that the OneWorld product is "about 90 percent ASP-ready," but adds that the company uses Citrix Systems MetaFrame with the product "as an interim delivery mechanism." He says that the real value of ASPs is the integration of applications that they can provide and notes that the building blocks of integration and web enablement are steadily improving. In short, the idea of an ASP may pre-date the availability of applications that have been developed with the ASP mode of delivery in mind, but this is changing quickly. "XML, DCOM, CORBA will enable higher levels of integration in the near future," says Hoffman, "and every software vendor is now working on web enabling their products."

Corio, Inc., Redwood City, California

"Corio is a follow-on to DSCI," reports founder, Jonathan Lee. "DCSI was a virtual IT management team-for-hire, serving Silicon Valley companies." Lee says Corio provides a similar service: high-growth technology firms once hired DCSI to deploy IT systems used to manage the company while their own personnel focused on bringing company products to market. Lee says that the experience acquired in the consulting firm drove the "enterprise ASP" that Corio is today and helps them service mid-market and large enterprises.

Corio leverages its experience in fielding enterprise applications such as PeopleSoft, SAP, and Oracle Enterprise Resource Planning apps, Seibel Customer Relationship Management software, Commerce One and SAPMarkets e-market software, and E.piphany Business Intelligence software. In January 2000, Microsoft purchased a $10 million equity share in the company, joining long-time equity shareholders and partners, PeopleSoft, and Sun Microsystems.

Corio builds neither its own data centers nor networks. Instead, the company leases the data center facilities from XO Communications (previously Concentric Network) and iStructure, and networks from best-of-breed network providers, Sprint, and InterNAP.

Lee says that Corio brings to its customers "Quick implementation using our Fast Lane methodology, which incorporates 17 years of rapid implementation knowledge and experience." He also emphasizes the investment that the company has made in developing platforms that facilitate the sharing of multiple instances of applications on the same server. These "Orion integration platforms" is a valuable feature of the service, he says, because "some of the top-tier enterprise applications are not host-centric, multi-tenant ready."

Crossrun, San Jose, California

Chuck Moreland, CEO of Crossrun, views his ASP as a facilitator of "companies that want to put software on line as a service." His firm offers "infrastructure compentency" that is often lacking in software companies—his target customers.

Crossrun enables software vendors to offer "business class subscription services" as a means for delivering software to their customers. Thinter.net hosts the software and offers additional security, availability, and support services which combine to provide a Web-enabled software delivery system.

The vendor utilizes Windows application serving technology from Citrix Systems and became a member of the Citrix iBusiness Partner Program in January 2000. According to Moreland, Citrix MetaFrame makes it unnecessary for Crossrun's clients to rewrite their applications for the Web, enabling faster time-to-market.

According to Al Stirpe, president of an enterprise resource planning software vendor (and Crossrun's client), Qube Connections, "Thinter.net had our software up and running in a couple days. We didn't have to rewrite a single line of code. The performance over the Internet is very impressive."

Electronic Data Systems (EDS), Plano, Texas

Electronic Data Systems (EDS), well known in the traditional outsourcing world, is one of the most successful application service providers in the market today. According to Royce P. Resoso, Global Offering Manager, Applications Hosting, the organization is succeeding by adapting as the ASP revolution works through several phases.

In the first phase, says Resoso, the focus of service provisioning was on reducing the cost of managing desktops, "Small, medium, and large enterprises were looking for ways to reduce their costs to deploy and manage desktop applications. The technologies used in this phase were Windows Terminal Services, Systems Management Server, and other products from other vendors. This approach worked but it didn't address the broad mass of consumers or business users. The value to the organization was significant, but it was not high up on the value chain of what a CIO thinks about."

In phase two, ASPs adds additional value, Resoso says, "by taking charge of messaging and mission-critical, line-of-business applications."

He notes, "Beside reducing costs, the impetus here comes from trying to overcome a skill shortage, trying to achieve faster deployments, and reducing initial investments—in other words, from trying to achieve higher revenues, not just cost savings."

Resoso observes that these first two phases "have already happened and are still ongoing today." He adds that ASPs appear to be entering a new phase.

"Almost four years later—in mid-2001, the ASP market has dramatically lost its verve," Resoso notes. "The market has gone from a climate of excitement to one of despair. Bankruptcy, lack of venture capital, mergers, an over-abundance of competition, the inability to execute, and poorly developed business models have forced ASPs to pull themselves out of the race. All markets go through cycles, from development, to explosion of growth, to consolidation and reorganization. Consolidation has already started, as service providers look to assemble an effective combination of applications expertise, infrastructure and operational skills, in search for that 'Second Wind' to keep up with the pace of those who are still running along."

Extending the metaphor, Resoso explains that EDS has always been "the marathon runner" in delivering IT services. He adds, "This is no different, as we have strategically entered into this race to be in a position as one of the forerunners. EDS has enormous strength in this space by building upon what we do best—managing IT services for our clients. EDS has the ability to leverage a global-wide investment in hosting and provisioning infrastructure and applications expertise. EDS assets poised for application hosting services include over one million square feet of data center capacity, a global network, 35,000 application specialists, established relationships with Independent Software Vendors, varied sales and marketing channels around the world, and established relationships with current customers for cross/up sell in the BASP space. In fact, EDS was profitable and was recognized as the 10th largest ASP provider in the world within a year of entering into this market."

What differentiates EDS from other ASPs is the vendor's "application centric elements of service: application maintenance and operations, application management, and extended enterprise services." Says Resoso, these are essential services that many small suppliers cannot offer, such as integration, customization, and application functionality support.

Resoso positions EDS ASP services at arm's length from those of competitors offering "boilerplate applications," noting, "There was nothing inherently magical in the ASP concept that eliminated the need to tailor the "rented" applications to the individual needs of clients—especially large clients that need the ASP applications to integrate into their legacy databases and other applications. Today, EDS offers new and existing business this integrated ASP solution delivered to the organization at large or segmented to target only certain functions within the organization."

Says the Manager, a new paradigm is emerging, "a third phase in which ASPs move [away] from delivering monolithic applications to offering Web services—'components' of solutions delivered as services through the Internet. Engineered for easy integration with each other, these Web services will afford speed and flexibility in creating solutions for changing business needs."

EDS has adopted this emergence of a new software architecture and delivery/management model—Web native software. According to Resoso, "Software as a service" will be the mantra where open Internet standards, XML and J2EE will pervade the Independent Software Vendor landscape. These net-native solutions will be designed from the ground up, specifically to leverage network-based architecture and integrate with legacy, existing and future applications. Interoperable, integrated applications across the Internet will improve services over the Web and enhance the ability of businesses to work together with their partners, suppliers and customers.

EDS intends to take "the inside track" on these developments, says Resoso. "EDS Hosting Services Portfolio is strategically redefining its offerings to espouse this paradigm shift. EDS' vision is predicated on the widely-held assumption that, eventually, the Internet's reach will extend to every part of the world; that high-speed bandwidth, both wired and wireless, will be ubiquitous and cheap; that all public media will be converted into digital; and, that the World Wide Web will be the massive pipe through which all data travels."

Emagisoft, Inc., St. Petersburg, Florida

Aimed at organizations seeking to develop their own e-commerce sites on the World Wide Web, Emagisoft offers a suite of software development tools on a subscription basis "that would cost in excess of $150,000 to purchase individually," according to President and CEO Kyle E. Jones. Clients use the software and a back-end database to create interactive catalogs for customer use in purchasing products via the Internet. Applications can also be integrated with processing systems at the client site to support back-end order processing and fulfillment.

Emagisoft owns and supports the software it provides to client subscribers, an important discriminator between Emagisoft and other e-commerce software ASPs, Jones observes.

Moreover, the company's origins as a business Web hosting firm, Jones says, account for the expertise of his staff in the operation of two host data centers (in the United States and Eastern Europe) and a redundant-leased line network connecting Emagisoft to the Public Internet (and its data centers to each other).

Prentice Technologies, Denver, Colorado

Shawn Richmond, chairman and CEO of Prentice Technologies, claims that his company has had the ASP vision for years. "ASP is just a new word for it. We call it application outsourcing."

Richmond says that numerous consulting engagements for JD Edwards's enterprise management software demonstrated the need for a service provider that could take a business from a complex client-server application platform to an application service provider delivery model. Beginning in 1994, the company built a core competence in application hosting and developed its own methodology for deploying the software which was of enormous use when the firm began offering its own enterprise ASP services, "akin to those of Corio and Usinternetworking."

At the time of this writing, Richmond could talk about eight customer contracts, comprising 14 companies, including the first "live" user of J. D. Edwards OneWorld, but he claims to have implemented over 100 solutions.

Prentice Technologies provides hosting and management services for its clients based around a data center facility in Denver. "We lease a three million square foot facility from a facility provider, Level 3, and we lease our software from J. D. Edwards [and some add-on package vendors], then we rent the software to the customer."

The other details of the service are described by Richmond as "a menu pick." Customers can designate the number of hosting platforms ("cabinets") they want. The platform can be mirrored at an alternate site, "if the customer is willing to pay for it." Prentice will even lease data center space closer to the client location, if required. Software, including Microsoft Office applications delivered via Citrix Systems MetaFrame, can be rented or purchased.

Richmond says that one key to ASP success is for the vendor to understand his core competencies. Most ASPs, in his view, do not possess the expertise in applications, hardware platforms, and networks to do it all for their customers. Recognizing his own firm's limitations has helped Prentice Technologies to thrive, he says.

"We don't man the data center 24-by-seven, though we will go there if the need arises. Instead, we get a professional data center and staff from Level 3. We could build a data center ourselves, but why would we want to? We also don't do business process consulting. We leave that to people are are good at it. We have reduced our people costs."

Richmond describes his firm as "a total solution general contractor." He notes that his firm provides software rental and hosting services. "We dedicate hardware and T-1 lines to the customer, because there is no way to deliver a Service Level Agreement over the Internet. We provide technical support, but J. D. Edwards provides the software help desk to address the software-related 'how to' questions."

Richmond describes his marketing approach as a "late sales cycle deal." Although many referrals come from Deloitte & Touche and other sources, he says that J. D. Edwards deal makers typically bring in his company toward the end of a software sales negotiation, providing the prospective customer with an option to rent the application. "We are brought in to reduce the customer's fears about deploying enterprise resource planning software."

TeleComputing, Fort Lauderdale, Florida

Jeff Hagins, Chief Technology Officer (CTO) for TeleComputing, states that the ASP model is currently undergoing a significant realignment, in which providers are beginning to segment into retail and wholesale providers.

Says Hagins, "Many early ASPs have dropped out of the market, while major Network Service Providers are just now entering the ASP marketplace, driven by a need to provide additional higher-margin services and to increase customer retention."

However, he notes, Network Service Providers (NSPs) are frequently unwilling to commit to the significant investment required to build a carrier-class application services delivery platform, and need to get to market quickly with new services in order to differentiate themselves, preventing further commoditization of existing services in a weakened economy.

To address this burgeoning requirement, TeleComputing has launched a private-label or wholesale ASP offering in response to market demand from the NSPs. TeleComputing is leveraging it's own investment in TECOS, a complete service delivery platform for application services, that automates operational and business support processes, resulting in increasing reliability, and lowering total cost of service delivery.

Says Hagins, "Many early ASPs have failed due to a lack of standardization and automation in the delivery environment. NSPs recognize the value in a highly standardized and automated delivery environment, but don't have the expertise or want to make the capital investment today to develop their own platform. TeleComputing's development of TECOS over a 4-year period was designed to accomplish three things: improve time-to-market, improve reliability, and improve contribution margins."

Using TECOS, TeleComputing is offering private-label services to NSPs in which TeleComputing owns and operates the platform, either in a TeleComputing data center or the NSP's data center. TeleComputing then wholesales the service to the NSP on a subscription basis (per user, per month). The NSP provides the sales, marketing, and level-1 customer support, while TeleComputing provides a fully managed service along with second and third tier support. "The net result for the NSP," observes Hagins, "is faster time-to-market, a highly reliable and available service, and a guarantee of profitability as long as minimum user levels are reached."

"We believe that the Network Service Providers will ultimately be the distribution point for all web-based application services for the enterprise," says the CTO, "but the NSPs can't deliver all of the services by themselves, resulting in a natural segmentation into retail and wholesale domains."

"TeleComputing has 5 years of operational experience in delivering application services to over 450 customers." Hagins says, "We've proven that the business model works by achieving profitability in Europe—a fact largely attributable to the automation provided by TECOS—and now we can leverage the business, technology, and operational expertise to enable the NSPs to succeed in delivering these services."

Hagins tends to characterize TeleComputing not as an ASP, but as a .NET ("dot-net") Service Provider. "Our business focus has always been on delivering Microsoft-based applications," says Hagins, and with the introduction of Microsoft's .NET strategy, TeleComputing is positioned to become the premier provider of wholesale .NET services."

Transchannel, Atlanta, Georgia

Another PeopleSoft-consulting-firm-turned ASP is Transchannel. According to CEO George Valentine, the company saw the opportunity in 1998 to support its customers more efficiently by focusing their services not only on hosting their customer applications, but more importantly providing world class functional and technical support. "We also realized the importance of providing application maintenance and upgrade services. Over overall goal is focused on allowing our customers to optimize their ERP investment.

Says Valentine, "We were able to host a PeopleSoft ERP application centrally and deliver the interface to the end user's PC. However, our experience quickly led us to the conclusion that the biggest problem was the PC client itself. About 60 percent of our customers' problems were difficulties with the PC. When the PC had a problem, users weren't sure whether it was their client software, their PC hardware, the network or the server that was causing the fault."

The solution to that problem was to use Citrix Systems MetaFrame, Valentine reports. Rather than loading client software on the PC, the end user's desktop is maintained on a Transchannel application server. This arrangement limits the hardware requirements for the desktop system.

The Transchannel ASP model differs from the approach of other ASPs, such as Corio, that offer ERP software in several ways, notes Valentine. "For one, we do not provide the customer with a vanilla copy of the application software. Our customers already have the software, and have, in most cases, already customized it to meet their needs. We take on the complexity of managing the application by re-hosting it in our data center."

USinternetworking, Annapolis, Maryland

Michele Perry, vice president of marketing for Usinternetworking (USi), belives that there are two types of ASPs, distinguished by the type of applications they offer. The categories she prefers are "enterprise" and "utility."

"IBM, Corio, Qwest Cybersolutions, Oracle Business On-Line, and USi are all examples of enterprise ASPs. We provide enterprise applications—financials, human resources, supply chain, procurement and so forth, while the utility ASPs, such as TeleComputing, provide utility software, such as Microsoft Office applications."

Perry says that USi has standardized on Hewlett-Packard and Sun Microsystems hardware platforms and leverages the Cisco Powered Network (named for network technology giant, Cisco Systems) to build its own USi Global Network to interconnect its four Global Enterprise Management Centers in Annapolis, Maryland; Milpitas, California; Tokyo, Japan; and Amsterdam, the Netherlands with customer sites.

The organization fields a direct sales force to cultivate customer contracts and offers only "the best software brands, so that we don't have to sell the application itself." The firm offers Seibel Customer Relationship Management packages; Ariba business-to-business e-commerce tools; BroadVision One-to-One management software; Oracle, Lawson, and PeopleSoft enterprise management applications; Niku professional services management applications; and Exchange messaging solutions from Microsoft. To ensure effective support of these applications, says Perry, USi has developed capabilities in-house and acquired other firms specializing in integration of the applications in the USi portfolio.

Perry says that the USi model for application delivery can be distinguished from competitors by the fact that the organization offers the hardware, network, integration services, and support organization as a one-stop shop. Obtaining these capabilities from multiple sources in the manner of a general contractor, she says, "would be silly."

"Imagine asking customers to plunk down money with a hardware vendor, software vendor, and integrator in order to buy a car. Our key difference is that we do it all."

One of the first ASPs in the marketplace, Perry adds that USi held a market leadership position early on. According to market analysts, USi's market share in 1999 was 34 percent, which represents a commanding lead over competitors.

Says Perry, "We have had a lot of advantages. Chris McCleary, USi's founder and chairman, had considerable experience as chairman and CEO of Digex, Inc. (a national Internet carrier) and knew how to capitalize the company early on."

ZLAND, Costa Mesa, California

Bret Hassler, Vice President of Product Marketing for Zland.com views ASPs as a natural evolution of the business use of the web. The trend began with the fielding of "brochureware" by businesses seeking to stay competitive. Hassler cites analysts to support the claim that the brochureware/web hosting market has reached 80 to 90 percent saturation. He says that the next trend in the evolution of business use of the web was characterised by shopping cart applications providing basic e-commerce functionality. That market, he says, is at 30 to 40 percent saturation.

The next stage is "e-business," Hassler claims, which is the realm of ASPs. It is the integration of all business functions on the web, creating efficiencies in functions from sales to fulfillment. He believes that the Return on Investment promise of ASPs is as compelling as the challenges. Says Hassler, "ZLand.com provides a suite of proprietary, hosted business applications that enable a client to place company, product, and employment information on the web, sell products on-line, and automate a wide range of operational activities, such as human resources, sales, payroll, or purchasing—all for a fraction of the cost and effort associated with the internally-developed solutions found in Fortune 500 companies. Essentially we've leveled the playing field for the SMB market."

New to the ZLand.com suite are contact sharing and commitment management applications, to facilitate internal sales and marketing collaboration and enhanced customer relationship management via the Web. "Trace any business process and you'll find that the stand alone application simply does not exist. e-Business requires an integrated approach to moving business functions to the web. The addition of contact management and opportunity management was a natural evolution for us". Moreover, the ASP is furthering the development of "a new class of integration solutions for connecting ZLand.com web-based business software with a company's existing back-office business systems."

Hassler sees the suite integrated solutions as "necessary, but not sufficient" for clients to take advantage of the promise of e-business. "Our client companies require more than tools, they require experienced local support." Zland uses a franchise model to both garner a customer base in this emerging market and provide the local services and support required by their clients. "A key to our success has been qualified franchisees and operators who guide clients through the implementation process."

As depicted in the diagram, ASPs must combine skills in services, networking technology, and management (including data center operations in IDC's characterization), and applications administration, integration, management, and support. Early ASPs have endeavored to leverage specific capabilities in one or more of these domains to discriminate themselves from their competitors.

Based on this delineation of skills set domains, IDC has gone one step further to provide a high level model of an ASP, as shown in Figure 2–3. This model adds to the basic or "core services" skills sets additional components that the analyst views as practical requirements for delivering ASP solutions to customers. These additional components include third-party software tools and infrastructure, hardware vendor-supplied servers, networks and storage platforms, and the ASP's own sales and marketing force, which increasingly includes distributor and reseller sales channels.

The IDC model was the first to introduce the concept of a "pure play" ASP, that is, an ASP that provides its own software, supported by its own personnel, using its own hosting platforms and networks, and marketed via its own direct sales force. In

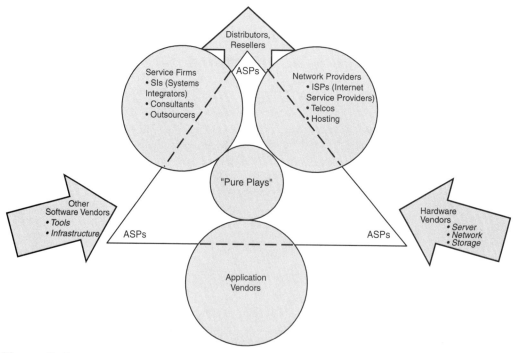

Figure 2–3
ASP model. *Source:* International Data Corporation, Framingham, MA, 1999. Reprinted by permission.

theory, customers are best served by a pure play ASP because the vendor exercises a greater measure of control over its service and can manage and resolve breakdowns in service more efficiently. By contrast, ASPs that rent "components" of their service from one or more third-party providers are thought to have less control over their services to their own customers.

There are about as many vendors who embrace the pure play model as a paragon or ideal as there are vendors who decry the pure play model as a myth. As one might expect, a vendor's position on this issue often has much to do with its own model for delivering services and how far afield it takes them from the pure play definition.

As a rule, ASPs that obtain service delivery components from third parties describe these arrangements as strengths rather than weaknesses of their service. Why, many vendors argue, should a provider create and staff a data center when a fully operational data center can be leased readily from an experienced, disciplined vendor?

At least one vendor, Prentice Technologies, openly embraces a "general contractor" approach to service delivery. In this model, the ASP application and virtually all resources required for its delivery are obtained from third parties, who are managed by the ASP provider.

For analytical purposes, the pure play model and the general contractor model may be viewed as the opposite ends of a continuum along, which most ASPs logically fit. Table 2–1 identifies some of the positives and negatives vendors themselves have ascribed to the pure play versus general contractor ASP operational models in their marketing materials and other commentary.

As of this writing, there is no evidence that customers are better served by a pure play or a general contractor ASP model. The fact is that the service delivery models of most ASPs are a mixture of owned and leased resources.

USinternetworking, for example, hosts its customers on its own platforms and often acquires (i.e., purchases) third-party consulting firms outright to support new applications that it adds its portfolio of offerings from time to time. By contrast, Emagisoft provides its own applications on its own hosting platforms, but invites franchise partners to provide integration, customization, and support services to its customers.

Strictly speaking, pure plays do not exist. Even if a provider owns its own software, operates its own hosting platform, and maintains a staff of service personnel, one does not need to dig much below the surface to discover numerous relationships that the service provider maintains with companies such as operating system providers (Microsoft, Sun Microsystems, Red Hat, etc.); server hardware providers (Sun Microsystems, Hewlett Packard Company, IBM, Compaq, Dell, etc.); network equipment providers (Cisco Systems, Lucent Technologies, Nortel Networks, etc.); providers of networks themselves (Qwest Communications, UUNET, AT&T, etc.);

Table 2–1   *Pure Play versus General Contractor ASPs*

Criteria	Pure Play	General Contractor
Descripton of service	ASP is "one-stop-shop"—a software company that provides its own ASP implementation, hosting, networking, and management services.	ASP is "one-stop-shop"—a manager of numerous, best-of-breed, third-party software, hosting, networking, and service providers.
Application expertise	Ownership of the application by the ASP is critical. The application represents the core value to the customer. Supporting the customer's deployment and use of the application requires a depth of skills and knowledge possible only from the application developer itself.	Application expertise can be obtained from experienced integrators or consultants with track records in the deployment and management of the application. When adding an application to the portfolio of applications offered to ASP customers, the engagement or outright acquisition of a consulting/integration firm specializing in the application compensates for the fact that the application is not owned.
		In any case, with most current applications, software vendors have not designed applications for delivery via the ASP model, so their intimate knowledge of their own applications is of little value.
		Finally, a software vendor rarely possesses the skills required to deliver a network/systems infrastructure to support ASP operations.

Table 2–1   *Continued*

Criteria	Pure Play	General Contractor
Hosting expertise	The pure play owns its hosting platforms and can capitalize on this control to provide a tighter integration of hardware and software-components. Ownership of the delivery platform enhances management of its operations. No finger pointing will result when tracking the causes of service interruptions.	Hosting platforms are commodity offerings. Numerous data center and network providers exist who have specialized in Web hosting services. Why reinvent the wheel? Hosting operations are best managed by experts who deal exclusively with day-to-day operations of systems and networks. Commitments can be obtained from third-party hosting service vendors that will properly vest management responsibilities with those who are best qualified to deliver them. No finger-pointing will result.
Service expertise	Application and hosting expertise enhance the quality of service that can be delivered by the ASP. Pure plays do not require the support of external providers for implementation, customer support, management, billing or sales. The fewer the number of third parties involved, the better the service to the end user.	The use of third-party providers for services reduces the number of personnel that the ASP must hire, train, and maintain and the overall cost of service to the customer. With proper management of third-party service contracts, the ongoing monitoring and review of service quality, and the constant quest for alternative service providers who can deliver required capabilities at lower cost, the ASP customer will see the advantages (*continued*)

Table 2–1 *Continued*

Criteria	Pure Play	General Contractor
		of this approach in both the quality and the cost of the services delivered.
Customer requirements	Defined by license agreement. Direct relationship between service provider and customer.	Defined by service contract. General contractor coordinates all component contracts and licenses.
Risks of arrangement	Software vendor ASP offering usually a business unit of the software company. Software subject to the same risks as standard, license-based software acquisition. Availability of other services contingent upon decisions affecting ASP business unit.	Substitutions available for services (other than software) to mitigate risk. Software availability subject to decision making and financial health of software company.
Sales	Handled via traditional sales channels of software company—typically direct sales force supplemented by distributors and value-added resellers.	Same, but may be supplemented by sales force of service partners.

vendors of enabling technologies (Citrix Systems, Marimba, Epicon, Progress Software and others); or numerous other infrastructure providers. These relationships, which are integral to delivering ASP services, void any claims that a vendor can make to the pure play moniker.

Most current ASPs are "composite organizations" owing to how they have been created (or evolved). Those providing "enterprise class" applications such as ERP, MRP, or CRM can often trace their pedigrees to traditional systems integration and outsourcing companies.

Qwest Cyber.Solutions, for example, is based upon a relationship between an established "Big Five" management consulting firm (KPMG) and an established network/data center provider (Qwest Communications). According to the announcement of the joint venture in June 1999, KPMG contributes "selected methodologies, templates, software and help desk facilities, and more than 450 applications specialists" and Qwest provides its "secure, broadband networks and industry-leading Cyber-centers."

Elsewhere, Agilera.com, was founded as a partnership between an established systems integrator (CIBER, Inc.) and a well-known Web hosting service provider (Verio). Today it can be safely assumed that virtually every established systems integrator and traditional outsourcing company is looking at the ASP model with the intent of capitalizing on existing industry enthusiasm to enhance its revenues.

In addition to these "enterprise-class" players in the ASP revolution, the ASP landscape is also becoming crowded with smaller players catering to small- and medium-sized businesses. Many of the companies comprising this "revolution from below" are local and regional Internet Service Providers (ISPs) who have seized upon the ASP model as a logical next step within a lines-of-business diversification trend that has been witnessed in the ISP community for about a decade.

Many ISPs have grown their businesses over time to deliver more than basic Internet on-ramp services to their clients. Most have added Web hosting services for their business customers, followed by e-commerce "shopping cart applications" for local entrepreneurs. Some offer VPNs to enable secure communications through the fabric of the public Internet. Many view application hosting as a straightforward extension of ISP offerings.

Today, by licensing and deploying Web-enabled office application software suites, such as StarOffice from Sun Microsystems, or Web site development products such as the Idetix REVIZE Web Site Content Delivery System (see Figure 2–4) that have been enabled for shared use over Internet connections, ISP and smaller Web hosting companies have discovered that they can "hang out an ASP shingle" overnight. This view is being fostered not only by software companies but also by network and system hardware vendors.

Technically speaking, traditional ISPs have been delivering application services since the inception of email. Indeed, there are those who argue that email was the original hosted application service. Moreover, many ISPs have provided online Hyper Text Markup Language (HTML)-based editors for many years to aid novice customers in the creation of "home pages" on the World Wide Web. These and other applications offered by ISPs set the stage for a broader range of applications to be delivered using the ASP model in the future.

Today, ISPs are being courted by software and hardware vendors alike to become full-fledged ASPs. In some cases, this is a side effect of marketing campaigns by vendors, whose objectives have little to do with encouraging ASP proliferation.

For example, Sun Microsystems's August 1999 acquisition of Star Division, and its subsequent announcement that it would make the German software company's Java-technology based office automation suite (e.g., word processor, spreadsheet, etc.)—called Star Office—available without charge to anyone who wanted it, contributed to

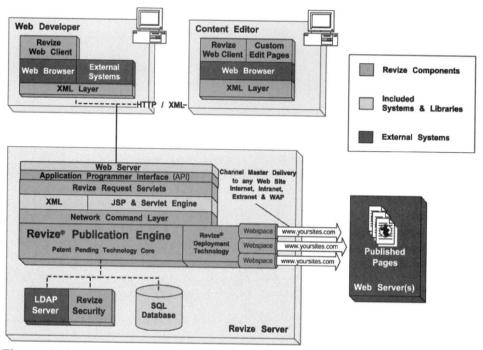

Figure 2–4
A flexible and robust website content delivery System, REVIZE is designed for ASP deployment. *Source:* Idetix Software Systems, Troy, MI.

the ISP-to-ASP evolution. Sun's servers already enjoyed preeminence in the ISP market, and Star Office products, including a server-centric ASP-ready Star Portal, were viewed as complimentary software to the existing hardware platform.

The Star Office announcements, however, were less targeted at encouraging ISP-to-ASP evolution than at unseating long-time rival Microsoft, the market hegemony in the desktop office automation software segment. Although Microsoft Corporation, vendor of the leading desktop computer-centric Office applications suite, claimed to be unconcerned about the Star Office offering, it began changing its public message about hosted applications soon after the Sun announcements. In November 1999, the company articulated a plan to enable ISPs to rent its desktop software to their customers online.

Microsoft expanded its ASP-enablement play in July 2000, when the company announced that part of its .NET initiative would be a suite of tools and programs, including new technical resources, partnerships, and licensing and certification programs, which were tailored to enable independent software vendors (ISVs) and Microsoft Certified Solution Providers (MCSPs) to bring hosted solutions to market on the Microsoft® platform, including Microsoft Windows® 2000, SQL Server™ 2000, Exchange 2000 and Office 2000. In its press announcements, the vendor boasted that over 65 ASP, ISV and systems integrator partners had announced support for Microsoft's platform and applications. The vendor nailed the growing availability of hosted application services as a mechanism for broadening customers' choices in addressing their IT needs.

In addition to enabling Microsoft and Windows–compatible applications for ASP delivery, the move also signaled an effort by the vendor to advance its own Web-based hosting platform and its own implementation of XML—a language intended to facilitate communications between two or more organizations and their applications—called Biztalk. According to senior spokespersons, ASPs, developers and channel partners can participate in the .NET vision today by building, customizing and reselling XML-based, programmable Web services, integrating .NET building block services and customizing and reselling bCentral™ small-business services.

The company also targeted to the needs of "ASP enablers," including DIGEX Inc., Data Return Corp., EDS, Hewlett Packard Company, and Cable and Wireless plc, who provided infrastructure services ISVs, ASPs, and MCSPs, alleviating "the need [for these organizations] to build and manage their own infrastructure, including communication and datacenter facilities."

Tom Ament, vice president of EDS, reported that his large outsourcing and services company had been working with Microsoft to "launch our Windows DNA- and Exchange-based on-demand services. We will enable channel partners to jumpstart their application service offerings with minimal investment and leverage their core competencies."

Microsoft filled out its ASP play with an ASP Certification Program, "developed to provide market recognition to ASP partners that demonstrate consistent, high-quality delivery of specific hosted or outsourcing services built on Microsoft technology," and new software licensing arrangements for ASPs to reduce entry level costs for its key products when used in their ASP delivery models.

Microsoft and Sun are not alone in their efforts to leverage the popularity of ASPs as an additional vehicle for marketing. Other office productivity software vendors, including Corel and Lotus, have also begun pursuing a Web-based delivery model for their products.

In addition to software companies, hardware companies, including Cisco Systems, Hewlett Packard Company, and Nortel Networks, have been actively courting ISPs with ASP-enabling technologies. At a January 2000 gathering of members of the Internet Service Provider Business Forum (ISPBF) in Austin, Texas, traditional network hardware firms presented application hosting models that promised to take ISPs "to the next level"

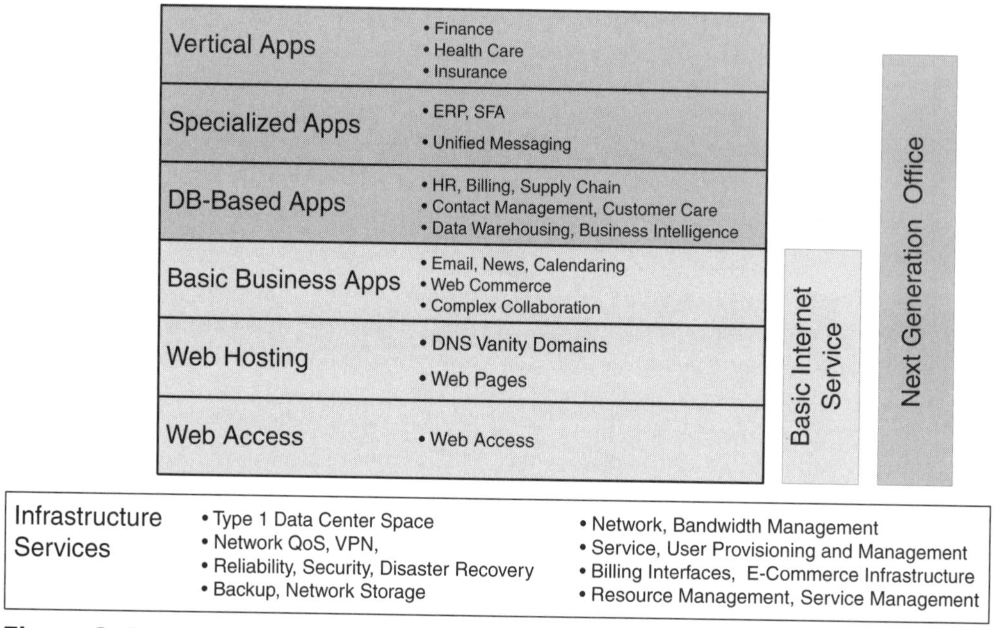

Figure 2–5
Hewlett Packard's application hosting business model. *Source: "Application Service Providers: Issues, Trends, and Enablers." A presentation delivered by Paul Voelker, director, Business Development Service Providers, Hewlett Packard Company, January 2000.*

in terms of services and revenues. Shown in Figure 2–5 and 2–6, Hewlett Packard spokespersons suggested that ASP services were well within the grasp of forward-looking ISPs, especially with Hewlett Packard platforms and support programs.

Similarly, spokespersons from other network equipment vendors, made the case that ISPs needed to begin thinking about becoming ASPs. He stated that connectivity had become a commodity and that ISPs had to begin offering value-added services as a means of product differentiation. Bundling value-added services, such as application hosting services, would reduce expensive customer "churn" (customers changing from one ISP to another) and solidify the "ownership" of customers for ISPs.

Leveraging industry research, speakers made the case that the "sweet spot" in the ASP market comprised small- and medium-sized businesses, representing 98 percent of all U.S. businesses and accounting for IT expenditures of more than $445 billion annually.* Internal vendor surveys suggested that demand for ASP services could

*This estimate of IT spending by small- and middle-tier companies is generally considered inflated within the market. No doubt, however, the actual number is staggering.

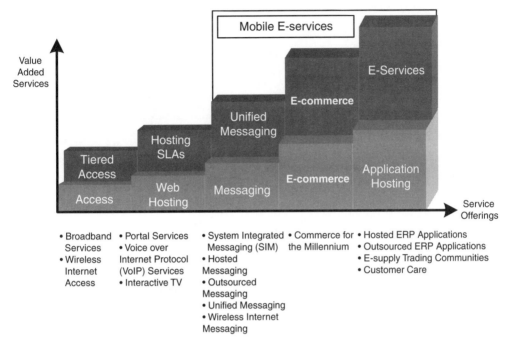

Figure 2–6
"Service provider evolution—can you keep up?" *Source: "Application Service Providers: Issues, Trends, and Enablers." A presentation delivered by Paul Voelker, director, Business Development Service Providers, Hewlett Packard Company, January 2000.*

grow by 50 percent by 2001. The familiarity of the ISP with its customers could enable much of this business to accrue to the ISP, which had built the infrastructure to enable the ASP delivery model in the first place.

Cisco Systems added its voice with an emphasis on the capabilities of Cisco products to support the application performance requirements of ASP service delivery. At the end of the day, said the company spokesperson, application performance, supported by virtual private networks, security, and other service level guarantees, would determine the success of ASPs. Citing various analysts (see Figure 2–7), the vendor offered that market opportunities for ISP-turned-ASPs catering to small office home office (SOHO), small businesses, and medium businesses were profound.

Cisco Systems went to great lengths to describe different configurations and topologies for delivering application services before introducing its own "Hosted Application Initiative" and "ASP Partner Ecosystem." The future, in the vendor's view, would likely comprise numerous pure plays and partnership-based ASPs supported by disciplined data centers and hosting services.

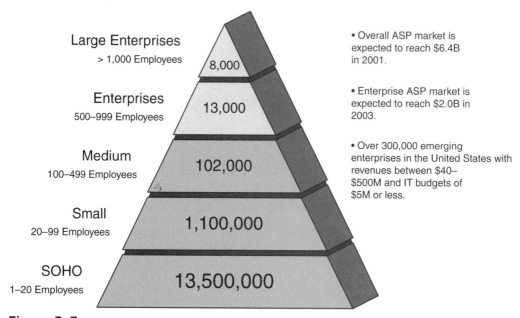

Large Enterprises
> 1,000 Employees
8,000

• Overall ASP market is expected to reach $6.4B in 2001.

Enterprises
500–999 Employees
13,000

• Enterprise ASP market is expected to reach $2.0B in 2003.

Medium
100–499 Employees
102,000

• Over 300,000 emerging enterprises in the United States with revenues between $40–$500M and IT budgets of $5M or less.

Small
20–99 Employees
1,100,000

SOHO
1–20 Employees
13,500,000

Figure 2–7
ASP market opportunity. *Source:* "Application Service Provider Market Overview, January 2000." A presentation by Cisco Systems, January 2000.

BUSINESS VALUE PROPOSITION OF AN ASP: COST REDUCTION, RISK REDUCTION, AND NEW CAPABILITIES FOR BUSINESS . . . .

The survey of ASPs discussed earlier demonstrates the diversity of meanings attributed to the concept. Some firms use the ASP moniker to describe application hosting services simply; others reserve the term to describe a vendor who hosts an application and makes available individual instances of the application for use by multiple, independent subscribers.

Some ASPs cater, through the applications and services they provide, to different classes of subscribers: large enterprises, medium-sized businesses, small businesses, SOHOs, or even individuals. Some ASPs distinguish themselves from others by fulfilling the needs of a vertical market, that is, by delivering applications specifically tailored for high-technology start-up firms, medical doctors' offices, and so forth. Others offer basic productivity applications used across all industry segments.

All these differences, however, share to some extent a common business value proposition to the end user, namely, that it is more cost-efficient and/or less risky to obtain application services through an ASP than to purchase, deploy, manage, and maintain applications on in-house servers or desktops. In a few cases, though not many, the ASP value proposition also includes the delivery of business capabilities that did not previously exist and that could not exist without the use of an ASP.

As several case studies provided by USi and reprinted throughout this section illustrate, cost reduction and risk reduction are familiar themes in virtually all ASP value proposals. In this respect ASPs borrow much from their "cousin" service arrangements within the realm of traditional outsourcing. This fact has lead to considerable confusion within the trade press and elsewhere regarding the difference between ASPs and traditional outsourcing. Table 2–2 summarizes the meanings attributed to cost and risk reduction in the literature of both traditional outsourcing firms and their modern ASP counterparts.

ASPs may "enhance" their cost- and risk-reduction arguments by referencing specific characteristics or components of their delivery method or by restating benefits in terms that are more familiar or germane to their prospective customers. For example, TeleComputing uses technology from Citrix Systems together with its own TECOS service delivery platform to deliver a hosting solution for Microsoft Windows-compliant application services to its customers: Network Service Providers (NSPs) or large enterprises.

According to Chief Technology Officer, Jeff Hagins, TeleComputing's offering enables NSPs to add application services to their list of service offerings using a platform (see Figure 2–8) that is already proven through TeleComputing's highly successful direct ASP practice in Europe. "In the US market, we offer our own hosting platform as a private label service that NSPs can re-brand easily in order to go to market quickly and realize benefits in the shortest possible timeframe."

The strategy builds on TeleComputing's experience as a direct provider of ASP services and on a sales model that emphasizes "simplicity over complexity." Says Hagins, potential customers are seeking a way to meet IT resource requirements that does not distract their business managers and staff from core business activities.

Industry insiders observe that effective ASPs tailor their value proposition messages to the priorities of their clientele. An ASP that hopes to cater to large corporate clients must offer a value proposition that emphasizes rapid delivery and reduced risk, especially with respect to ERP applications. Most agree that an ASP that possesses a true understanding of corporate requirements and a tested integration model can dramatically reduce the time and expense of rolling out enterprise applications. The cost of implenting ERP has been about five to ten times the price of the software license. ASPs that can deliver rapid implementation of ERP can reduce the costs to where the customer wants them—a maximum of two times the cost for the software license.

Table 2–2 *Common Cost And Risk Reduction Claims Of ASPs*

Business Value	Value Statement
Cost reduction—reduced acquisition cost	Using an ASP-delivered application enables applications to be acquired on a fee basis. New versions of applications need not be licensed separately thereby reducing costs. Some companies that would be unable to afford the costs to license and roll out complicated enterprise software can acquire access to the software much more cost effectively through an ASP.
Cost reduction—reduced application deployment costs	Companies do not need to allocate personnel and time to rolling out applications on in-house platforms. ASP-hosted applications are available immediately, or with minimal delay for customization, enabling them to support key business processes virtually upon ASP contract signing.
Cost reduction—total cost of ownership reduction	The true cost of owning an application consists of the costs to manage and maintain the application, the costs for maintaining application hosting environments, the costs for user training, the costs for operations and support personnel, and many other costs that go well beyond the software license or purchase price. Many of these costs are eliminated or dramatically reduced when an ASP is used.
Cost reduction—application support personnel	Qualified applications support staff are in short supply in many parts of the country despite the fact that they comprise the fastest growing segment of the job market in terms of demand. The result is a growing gap between qualified workers and companies seeking their services. This gap is leading to enormous growth in salaries, driven by the simple law of supply and demand, for database administrators, computer support specialists, computer engineers and scientists, systems analysts, and system administrators. With ASP-provided applications, companies do not need to expend resources in candidate searches nor incur the costs for salary and benefits that new hires will demand.
Risk reduction—reduced risk of application deployment failures	ASPs have established methods and models for delivering service that reduce the risk of an application deployment nightmare.

Table 2–2 *Continued*

Business Value	Value Statement
Risk reduction—mirroring, fault tolerance, disaster recovery, security	Technologies for mitigating the possibility (or consequences) of an unplanned interruption of application services are often built-in components of an ASP service offering. Companies often find that they would need to spend an unacceptable amount of money to deliver the safeguards and business continuity provisions already present in ASP hosting platforms.
Risk reduction—investment protection	One of the greatest technology risks confronting companies is the exposure they face to changes in application software and support hardware made by their vendors. These changes can necessitate unplanned, expensive, and potentially disruptive forklift upgrades in computing platforms. With an ASP contract, the ASP assumes responsibility for maintaining software, hardware, and services in line with technology changes.

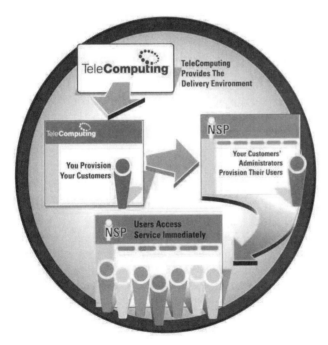

Figure 2–8 TeleComputing offers wholesale ASP service platforms to clients. *Source:* Telecomputing, Ft. Lauderdale, Florida.

Corio founder Jonathan Lee agrees with the value of rapid implementation, but points out that the real source of pain in organizations today is "IT indigestion." Says Lee, "Companies lack the personnel and the expertise to roll out enterprise resource management and e-commerce applications. Over 340,000 jobs went unfilled [in 1999]. If IT experts were abundant, the value of ASPs would go away."

These examples may explain why many business and IT professionals experience a sense of déjà vu as they listen to the value proposition of ASPs. In terms of cost- and risk-reduction benefits, the business case of the modern ASPs seems very similar to the business case used by IT outsourcing vendors nearly a decade ago.

ASPs themselves are split on the issue of whether this is a good thing. Some seek to distance themselves from traditional outsourcing—particularly those seeking to cultivate customers who have had a bad experience with outsourcing in the past. Other ASPs, whose customers have no negative recollections of past outsourcing experiences, actually endeavor to portray their services as the next wave of outsourcing. It needs to be clearly understood that an ASP's positioning in this matter has more to do with the prospective customer's views and attitudes toward outsourcing generally than with any meaningful differences in the inherent cost- or risk-reduction benefits provided by service alternatives.

As discussed in a later chapter, ASPs differ meaningfully from traditional outsourcing arrangements not in terms of their cost- or risk-reduction benefits, but because of the new business opportunities they enable. ASPs are unique and separate from traditional outsourcing service contracts because of their potential to enable new, or to improve existing, business processes.

Former chairman of the ASP Industry Consortium, Traver Gruen-Kennedy, notes that ASPs, although "a subset of traditional outsourcing" (a "blasphemous characterization," he notes, in some ASP circles), differ from their counterparts in the outsourcing/service bureau/timesharing world in one key way. By leveraging Web technology and WANs, says Kennedy, "ASPs are uniquely positioned to support business-to-business and business-to-consumer transactions over virtually any network from wired to wireless. Any application over any network to any user is a substantially different value proposition from that of traditional outsourcing offerings."

Yet this differentiator, which has the potential to yield completely new business opportunities to ASP customers, is typically overlooked in ASP sales and marketing pitches. Rarely, if ever, do customer case studies demonstrate benefits accruing to ASP contracts that go beyond cost savings and risk reduction. (The Hershey Foods Corporation case study from USi is one exception.) Perhaps this can be attributed to the comparative adolescence of e-business generally. Analysts say that a nascent industry forming around e-business currently will likely blossom into a $4 trillion industry within five years.

(text continues page 65)

....

ASP Arrangement with Usinternetworking Delivers New Business for Hershey

Hershey Foods Corporation, Hershey, Pennsylvania, is the leading North American manufacturer of chocolate and nonchocolate confectionery and chocolate-related grocery products. One of the divisions of Hershey Foods is Hershey Direct. Hershey Direct is a small, entrepreneurial outfit that has historically been focused on delivering Hershey products through mail order catalogs. The unit has recently sought to expand the sale of its goods through electronic commerce.

Rebuilding Its E-Commerce Site

Hershey Direct elected to use USi to build its ecommerce site. Even though Hershey Direct was an early entrant onto the Web (with a site dating back to early 1996), the company paid very little attention to its site. Consequently, Hershey's Direct had a site that it describes as not being consumer friendly and not up to the Hershey standards. However, the impetus for rethinking its Internet strategy was that Hershey's hosting provider (AMP) decided to get out of the hosting business. When AMP alerted Hershey it wouldn't be able to host the site any more, Hershey Direct decided to initiate a program to redo the entire site. Hershey goal for the new site was to create a site that:

- Addresses consumer and business issues more directly than had been done by the other site.
- Serves as a pioneer program for all of Hershey's. (The new site was to be the first major electronic commerce foray by Hershey.)
- Matches the quality and timeliness of customer service for which Hershey is known.

Hershey Direct's Decision-Making Process

Hershey's e-commerce efforts were led by a committee that consisted of the catalog direct marketing manager, the general manager from the direct marketing division, a person from finance, two people from the IT department, and a person from business development who served as the project manager. Mark Potter, the business development manager, was chosen to be the project manager because he had expertise around Internet technology.

The committee quickly decided that it didn't make sense to develop the e-commerce site in-house. "It was really an economic decision," says Potter. "If you consider the hardware, the software, and the personnel required to manage this kind of site, it's extensive." What really concerned Hershey Direct was the redundancy that was required for an e-commerce site. Hershey Direct felt that it couldn't be assured of sufficient uptime with one system, and that it would need redundant systems. However, in Hershey's mind, it didn't make sense to try to run redundant systems in-house. After an exhaustive analysis, Hershey's Direct decided to use an external service provider.

The committee made a request for information from 30 companies, including Internet service firms. It reduced that number to five. The five received a full request for proposal and were invited to make a presentation. One of the companies Hershey's Direct considered was BroadVision, an e-commerce application vendor, and a USi partner. BroadVision proposed an application solution with USi as the service provider. According to Potter, "when BroadVision made their initial bid in the request for proposal (RFP), it was clear that they were working in a different ballpark than we were." Potter notes that Hershey Direct is a small entrepreneurial division of Hershey that doesn't have a lot of money to throw around. According to Potter, the BroadVision solutions seemed suited for a larger enterprise.

Hershey Direct declined the BroadVision proposal. However, Potter says that the sales representative from USi was persistent and wanted to offer Hershey another solution—one that was based on Microsoft Site Server Commerce Edition 3.0.

Hershey Direct ultimately decided upon USi. According to Potter, USi was the only company that offered full end-to-end service. "There were companies that had pieces of the package/solution," said Potter, "and most of them had some affiliation with somebody that could do some of the other pieces." But Hershey Direct didn't want to manage multiple partners. The primary benefit it saw in working with USi was that USi was a single source for the entire solution.

USi's e-commerce solution for Hershey's Direct was the proposed creation of an Internet version of Hershey Direct's direct mail catalog. The Internet site was built using Microsoft's Site Server. The contract called for USi to develop the site, and then host and support it for two years.

E-Commerce in Five Weeks

Hershey Direct signed a contract with USi in March 1999. Hershey Direct's RFP defined an extensive list of features that the company wanted in the site. USi came up with a plan to deliver against this list. First, USi designed and built the various features of the site, and then built the infrastructure. Hershey provided the creative input. Hershey also provided the creative overlay, did the copyrighting, and had an art director oversee USi's creative work. Before the company went live, USi provided Hershey Direct with some customer service-oriented training that focused on the diagnostics of the site. The creation and implementation of the site took about five weeks. Hershey Direct went live at the end of April 1999. USi added more features to the site in the fall of 1999.

Operating Environment

Hershey Direct says the special provisions it needed to make in order to prepare for its e-commerce project were minimal. Integration with back-end systems has been achieved, so the order automation system pushes orders from the site into the back-end order fulfillment system four times per day. This task had been done manually twice a day in the past. In December 1999, just eight months into Hershey's contract, the site had already surpassed its revenue targets by 60 percent. Due to the overwhelming popularity of the site, Hershey's Direct sold out of products during the holiday season.

Hershey is now working out contract details to add an order fulfillment system to Hershey Direct, allowing sales representatives to order product in bulk (for large customer accounts such as Safeway Foods) directly through the Internet.

Currently Hershey Direct uses the Internet to connect to its e-commerce site, which is located at USi's data centers. However, when the company automates its order collection process, it is likely that Hershey's will move to a dedicated line.

Monthly Payment Model

USi priced the project by making an estimate of the total effort required to get the site up and running and then to maintain it for two years. This amount was amortized over two years in monthly payments.

Therefore, Hershey Direct pays a monthly payment that represents the site development and management work. Neither USi nor Hershey Direct will discuss the specifics of the pricing.

Service Assessment

Overall, Hershey Direct is satisfied with USi. Potter says he would recommend USi in any outsourcing discussion. Because the site was deployed, the company did face what it describes as a modest security issue. Potter explains that the potential problem, which was announced by Microsoft, related to the SQL server. Hershey Direct didn't actually have a security problem; however, it had some downtime and wrestled through a few bugs in the Microsoft platform.

Hershey Direct says it calls USi if it notices any problems with the site. There have been a couple of instances where Hershey Direct has not been able to resolve problems that consumers had with the site. On these occasions, Hershey Direct passed the problems along to USi's client care line. Hershey Direct says it has been very happy with how the calls have been handled by USi.

Assessment of Benefits and Risks

Some of the benefits Hershey Direct says it sees with the e-commerce outsourcing solution it selected from USi include:

- Access to a data center that Hershey Direct does not have to build in house This makes this project sound like a colocation arrangement; no one at Hershey has physical or root access to the data centers or servers.
- Access to IT talent that Hershey Direct does not have to recruit and retain.
- A pricing model that involves no up-front investment, but rather a flat monthly fee. It made the USi solution a proposition that Hershey could sell internally. Hershey also notes that this model provided benefits from a cash flow standpoint.
- Access to software and infrastructure that will scale with Herhsey's business.

Despite these benefits, Hershey does note that the newness of USi's e-commerce solution was a concern to Hershey Direct, primarily because it was unproven. The company did a risk-benefit analysis with

USi. "USi did such a good enough job of mitigating the risks that they successfully eliminated our concerns," says Potter.

Hershey Direct's IT department shared no objections to the e-commerce outsourcing proposal. Potter says the IT department was on board from the beginning because they did not consider the project to be within their area of expertise. "Our core competency is making chocolate and our IT department is very good as a service organization but this is not what we do for a living," says Potter.

Source: USi.

USi Provides ASP Medicine for Knoll Pharmaceutical Company

Knoll Pharmaceutical Company, headquartered in Mount Olive, New Jersey, is the U.S. pharmaceutical unit of BASF Corporation and part of BASF Pharma, the global pharmaceutical business of the BASF Group of affiliated companies. The parent company, BASF Aktiengesellschaft, is a $30.7 billion transnational chemical company based in Ludwigshafen, Germany. Knoll generated approximately $811 million in revenue in 1998 and employs more than 1,500 people in North America, 600 of whom are sales representatives. Knoll develops and markets prescription medications for central nervous system disorders and pain management.

Automating a Sales Force in a Changing Industry

Over the past 10 years, both the health insurance and pharmaceutical industries have undergone drastic changes. Changes in the distribution of medication have changed the method by which Knoll account representatives need to track their data and maintain relationships with their customers. For a start, Knoll's previous system was written in DOS and was not Y2K compliant. The system lacked the scalability and flexibility necessary to adapt to frequent industry changes. Because these factors were forcing Knoll to make a change, members of Knoll senior management decided they'd like to find an expanded system, one that could handle increased strategic complexity, and combine marketing, account management, and the ability for remote representatives to coordinate with one another on joint accounts. Siebel Systems Enterprise Relationship Management package looked like the right choice because a single-source vendor model (software and services) would minimize risk and provide the highest probability of a successful implementation.

Why USi?

Once Knoll settled on the Siebel product, Rick Ofeldt, director of information systems for Knoll, asked their account manager what Siebel's plans were for hosting and implementation. Siebel recommended USi.

Not only was Knoll overdue for a new sales force automation system, but they were under a time crunch. Y2K was not that far away, so a quick implementation was a requirement for the hosting company that would hired by Knoll. "USi allowed us to implement the system faster because they had the infrastructure in place already," said Ofeldt. Knoll Pharmaceutical's Siebel application was implemented in 45 days, as compared with the typical six- to nine-month time frame.

Ofeldt also wanted the vendor Knoll chose for this implementation to be fully responsible for every piece of the project. "I'm a firm believer in a single source vendor model. . . . I also feel that if someone's going to have responsibility for a project, they have to control all aspects of it," he said. After evaluating other ASPs, Ofeldt returned to USi. It was the only ASP he found that provides true end-to-end service and takes full responsibility for its clients' solutions.

Today, Knoll Pharmaceutical has an enterprise-class customer relationship management solution that's secure and scalable to meet future growth of the company. Because SiebelNet allows data to be transmitted over the Internet, Knoll believes that it will eventually save 50 percent of their previous costs in data transfer and communications.

"Our overall mission at Knoll is to provide innovative health care solutions that improve people's lives. Siebelnet's innovative approach is helping us fulfill this mission with our sales representatives and the customers they interact with," Ofeldt concluded.

Source: Usi.

Sunburst Hospitality Obtains Large Company Enterprise Management Solution at Medium Company Price via ASP USi

Sunburst's Enterprise Problem

Maintaining a large portfolio of full-service hotels and maintaining enterprise software are two very different business operations, yet doing both was a recent challenge facing Sunburst Hospitality.

Sunburst Hospitality is a leading hotel owner and manager of nationally recognized full-service, limited-service, and extended stay hotels. These hotels include MainStay, Clarion, and Comfort Inns, among others. They were recently spun off from their parent company, Choice Hotels International, who had been providing PeopleSoft Financial Management software to automate Sunburst's critical business functions.

The PeopleSoft product was an integral part of Sunburst's business foundation and success. They needed a strong and reliable financial application to buttress the flexibility needed in the hospitality industry.

"We need systems and procedures in place to be able to respond to the market," comments Chuck Warczak, vice president of financial systems for Sunburst Hospitality. "We're in a very dynamic industry and are subject to a lot of cyclical phases."

After separating from their parent company, Sunburst was left to reestablish the infrastructure that ran the PeopleSoft Financials enterprise application.

"We were facing two options: either do it in house or outsource it," says Mark Elbaum, director of information services for Sunburst Hospitality. "We watched our parent company build the solution and the structure internally. They increased their staff by 15 to 20 people, constantly installed new hardware, and budgeted huge capital expenditures for the hardware and software. We were looking to try and control these costs."

Another Challenge: Retaining IT Talent

Building the infrastructure is one challenge, but Sunburst noticed another problem, just as large. Finding and keeping the right people to build and maintain the enterprise solution is an entirely different headache.

"When our parent company was doing their in-house solution, they hired some very talented people," says Warzak. "And during the implementation, when they got ready to go live, these people got picked off by other companies."

Sunburst concluded that outsourcing to an ASP was clearly the best route. The attraction was they could continue to have the use of a leading enterprise application without hiring new IT talent or replicating a large corporate infrastructure.

Why Sunburst Chose USi

Sunburst considered several outsourcing vendors, in the end choosing USi, headquartered in Annapolis, Maryland.

"USi was the only ASP who came to us providing a detailed solution for the complex problems that we had," says Warzak. "We talked to other outsourcing companies but they didn't measure up. USi took the time to examine our situation, investigate our environment, and provide us with a comprehensive plan that we felt very comfortable with."

Sunburst Hospitality is a midsized company, and high costs of hardware infrastructure, software licenses, ongoing maintenance, and spiraling IT consultant salaries all threatened their budget. USi's end-to-end enterprise solution and fixed monthly fee suit Sunburst well. Sunburst does not have to focus on IT concerns, nor did they have to outlay large up-front funds.

"It really almost was a no-brainer," says Elbaum. "USi was the only ASP who offered a total solution that fits all our needs. Other companies offered more of an à la carte menu. They still charged up-front costs for hardware and up-front costs for implementation. If you wanted disaster recovery or needed a help desk, they charged more for those add-ons. With USi we got one flat price for everything we needed."

Sleeping Better

USi's CLIENT care, providing a single point of contact for USi's clients, is an added benefit for Sunburst.

"Having one place to go for support has been great," says Elbaum. "I think I talk to my account manager once a day to discuss what's going on or just for reassurance. It's relaxing to go home on the weekend and know my beeper won't go off. I sleep pretty well now."

Finally, Sunburst was happily surprised by the outcome of USi's rapid implementation methodology. "They exceeded all our expectations," says Elbaum. "I recall a lot of pain with the in-house implementation when we were with Choice Hotels International. It was drawn out over two years, and we had a number of implementation problems. We experienced none of that with USi. The solution was up and running within 90 days, and we've had no problems with it."

As a midsized company, Sunburst has found they can utilize an enterprise solution and still focus on their core competency: running a full-service hotel chain.

"Going forward, we'll be doing a lot more outsourcing," says Warzak.

Source: USi.

THE BOTTOM LINE ·

The variability of content that burgeoning ASPs have vested in the term "application service provider" has led to considerable confusion in the industry. For business people interested in evaluating ASP alternatives for software delivery and service, the lack of a clear definition of what ASPs are and how they deliver services continue to complicate decision making.

Analytical models, such as those provided by IDC and others, provide a framework for thinking about ASPs and facilitate the understanding and interpretation of ASP marketing messages. Of course, reviewing actual case studies helps to ground theoretical models in reality. Business leaders need, more than anything else, to read about ASP solutions that have been deployed in order to glean an approach to an ASP that might work well for them.

For business decision makers, the assessment of the business value proposition of ASPs should be based, as with all technology investments, on measurable benefits to the company in terms of cost reduction, risk reduction, and new business enablement. Business managers need to evaluate ASP offerings in sane, straightforward terms: Will using an ASP save money on IT staff or application management? Will using an ASP reduce the risks of unplanned outages or unsuccessful application deployments? Will using an ASP make a business process more efficent? Will it shorten time to market for products? Will it enhance competitiveness?

In the final analysis, cost benefits may not be the most significant benefit from utilizing an ASP. Depending on the business, cost and risk reduction may be only peripheral issues.

A spokesperson for one provider of enterprise application services observes that his clients are "mostly large firms with $1 billion-plus in revenues," and are not driven to utilize his company's services based on costs alone. He notes that "cost is fourth or fifth on the list for doing something in large companies, though it may be second or third on the list for medium-sized firms. Most [of these firms] are clueless about total cost of ownership."

Businesses may be driven to the ASP model by other business values. They may see the ASP model as a means to dedicate internal resources to core competencies. In other cases, ASPs may represent a fast track for developing an e-business opportunity. Still other firms may wish to utilize an ASP to facilitate the rapid deployment of automated supply chain management.

For all of the hyperbole and confusion surrounding a nascent industry, ASPs are finding a place in the market. They are likely to become a fixture on the business information technology landscape for years to come.

3 How Does an ASP Differ from Traditional Computing Models?

In this chapter...

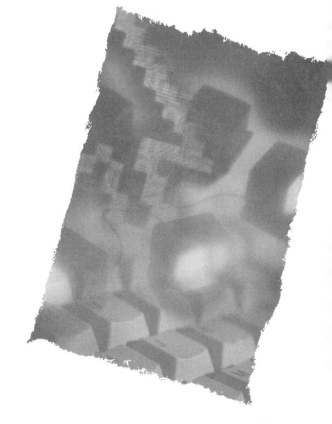

IDC refers to the APS model for software delivery as a "disruptive innovation," a concept borrowed from Clayton Christensen's *The Innovator's Dilemma*.* Simply stated, disruptive innovations consist of the repackaging and delivery of established or known technologies or solutions in a new or unique manner that proves to be simpler for end users than were prior approaches.

Christensen and numerous interpreters observe that, when disruptive innovations occur, industry-leading technology solution providers need to transition to the new model. If they fail to do so, they risk losing share in the competitive marketplace.

Whether ASPs constitute a "disruptive innovation" (or a "paradigm shift"—to cite another phrase sometimes used to describe ASPs, especially by those who position the ASP model as the antithesis of the established PC-centric desktop computing model) is a subject for debate. As discussed in the previous chapter, ASPs represent a "new" model for application delivery. The model takes familiar products and services—including application software, server technology, Web technology, network technology, integration services, customer support, and so on—and repackages them for delivery to end users and corporations in a potentially more convenient, potentially less expensive and risky, and potentially more business-enabling way. But, are ASPs truly a new phenomenon?

A survey of the widespread coverage of the ASP phenomena in both the IT trade press and in popular business publications suggests two diametrically opposed answers to this question. Press accounts have, alternatively, hailed the ASP model as a radically new phenomenon or decried it as a simple recasting of the familiar outsourcing methodologies of the 1960s and 1970s.

This chapter evaluates the first claim: that ASPs are a unique and entirely new phenomenon. The next chapter evaluates the second claim: that the ASP model is merely a relabeling of traditional outsourcing approaches.

EVOLUTION IN BUSINESS INFORMATION SYSTEMS

ASPs are deemed by many to be an innovation because they deviate from the typical software delivery models used in most organizations. It follows that, to understand the differences between ASPs and traditional computing models, it is useful to begin with a consideration of traditional models.

Figure 3–1 depicts, in simplified terms, a typical "pre-ASP" process by which software is delivered to an end user. In this diagram, an ISV creates a product, which

*Christensen, Clayton M., *The Innovator's Dilemma* (Boston, MA: Harvard Business School Press, 1997).

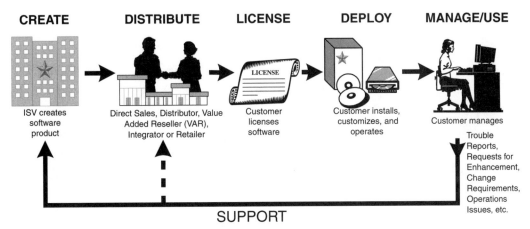

Figure 3–1
A common software delivery model.

is then packaged for distribution and sales via a direct sales force or various intermediaries such as distributors, value added resellers, integrators, retailers, and others.
The consumer purchases a license for the software product, installs the software on a
computer, customizes the software to meet his or her unique needs and preferences,
and operates the software to perform useful work. The user also manages the application software by applying fixes, patches, and upgrades supplied periodically by the
ISV in accordance with the terms of the existing license or a new license. The customer may also solicit support from the ISV or the distributor to resolve problems and
issues that arise in operations and maintenance.

The software delivery model represented in Figure 3–1 is probably familiar to
anyone who has ever used a PC, popularlized by Apple Computers, IBM, and Intel
Corporation beginning in the late 1970s. It continues to be a dominant model for delivering and deploying single-user software and is sometimes referred to as the WINTEL
model, referring to the efforts of Microsoft Corporation (makers of Windows operating
system and application software) and Intel Corporation to define a common platform
for delivering application software functionality to users of desktop computers.

The WINTEL model grew to dominate the corporate desktop in large part because of the purported ease of deployment and operation of applications using this
delivery mechanism. Prior to the personal computing/Windows "revolution," other
application delivery models, which may be collectively referred to as a centralized
computing model, were prevalent in business organizations. Figure 3–2 depicts, again
in a simplified way, the centralized application delivery model.

The model in Figure 3–2 may be familiar to readers—especially to those who
have worked in a business environment that featured a centralized information system

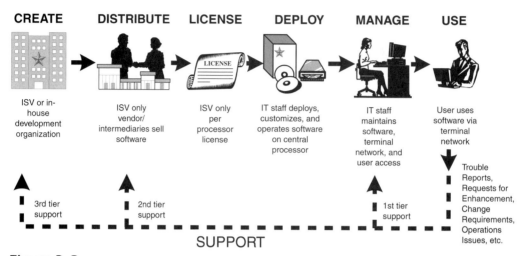

Figure 3–2
Centralized application delivery model.

(IS) or IT department tasked with delivering application services from a centralized corporate data center.

In this model, applications are either developed by in-house program development staff or licensed from third-party ISVs and are deployed on a centralized mainframe computer or large minicomputer. Application maintenance and management is provided by disciplined IS or IT department technical staff in accordance with operational procedures. Typically, end users access and use the centralized applications via "dumb" terminals connected to the central computer via a network.

In the centralized application delivery model, end user application access is controlled by policies and protocols established by IT administrators. This is to ensure the security and integrity of both the data and processes. IT departments often establish service level agreements (SLAs) with end user departments, in part to "justify" the allocation of operating expenses to their "departmental customers" based on their application access.

SLAs also cover procedures for handling end user support issues. Structured, "multitiered" problem reporting and resolution mechanisms are often devised with IT administrators providing "first-tier" support to end user trouble reports. Problems that cannot be resolved at this tier are commonly "escalated" to upper tiers of the IT organization or, in the case of licensed software, to ISVs and their intermediaries directly.

The perceived inadequacies of this centralized application delivery model helped to drive the PC revolution, discussed earlier. In many organizations, bureaucratic IT departments became backlogged with support requests from end users. In some cases, IT organizations were villianized for their failure to provide timely responses to requests for new program functionality. In other cases, centralized DP produced information products that were erred or that lacked the timeliness required to support business-critical decision making. PC makers and later client-server computing advocates seized upon these complaints to offer new software delivery models.

The PC revolution's "business value proposition," articulated by advocates of decentralized computing (including more than a few PC software and hardware vendors), held that some information processing tasks, then assigned to centralized IT organizations, could be handled more efficiently by end users themselves—provided that users were equipped with platforms and application software that was designed for deployment, maintenance, and use by nontechnical personnel.

Advocates argued that mixing PCs with mainframe computing enabled a more efficient use of computing functions and greater end user productivity. They proposed the replacement of dumb terminals with more intelligent and capable PCs. Doing so would allow end users to continue to access "enterprise" or centralized applications (via terminal emulation software installed on their PC), but would also permit them to perform other tasks using "productivity" or single user applications (such as spreadsheets and small databases) supported by the local resources of the PC itself.

Many of the same themes advanced by PC/decentralized computing advocates were co-opted in the mid-1980s by ombudsmen for new client-server or distributed computing approaches. Client-server computing leveraged the decentralized computing model embraced in the PC revolution and capitalized on the emergence of LANs, which were rapidly replacing proprietary terminal networks.

Vendors of client-server products, seizing upon the cost-benefit calculus of the earlier PC revolution, argued that centralized data centers could be replaced entirely by much less expensive networks of distributed micro- and minicomputer *servers*. Operating in concert across a LAN, these distributed server networks could provide the "horsepower" previously thought possible only from "big iron" mainframes.

Moreover, advocates claimed, by unifying standalone PCs (decried as unmanaged "islands of automation") into networks and by building applications so that their tasks could be distributed across multiple processors, the resulting economies of scale would enable even smaller firms to avail themselves of mainframe-class applications. Some even argued that the lesser complexity of client-server applications and platforms would enable the disbanding of centralized IT organizations altogether, removing an expensive cost center within most corporate environments. Ultimately, they said, client-server technology could be maintained by end users.

Despite the generally acknowledged failure of client-server computing to realize all of the vendor claims of reduced cost and increased efficiency, its underlying model for software delivery (see Figure 3–3) did catch on. Client-server computing changed commercial software licensing schemes. Software went from being sold on a

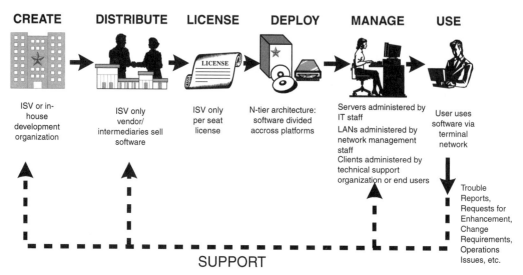

Figure 3–3
Client-server application delivery model.

"per processor" basis to being licensed on a "per user" or "per seat" basis. Moreover, the client-server computing model distributed responsibilities for software deployment and maintenance among server, LAN, and client administrators (either end users individually or end user technical support organizations).

In modern client-server parlance, PCs became known as "fat clients" to application software distributed across one or more "server hosts." That is, the desktop system hosted an application's client component that was used to access and operate the application's server components.

Client-server software matured over the course of a decade from applications featuring a simple, two-tier architecture—in which part of the application executes on the client PC and part executes on a server host—to more complicated designs. By the late 1980s and early 1990s, three-tier and eventually *n*-tier software architectures began to appear. As the number of tiers increased, these architectures required "middleware"—software designed to manage the processing and delivery of client requests and server tasks—to facilitate complex interactions between components. Figure 3–4 depicts an integrated *n*-tier client-server configuration, circa 1995.

Early client-server applications were created by programmers within the corporate environment itself. However, a full-fledged software industry—comprised of integrators, value-added resellers, and even many mainframe software vendors—soon developed around client-server computing.

Some mainframe software vendors, seeking to capitalize upon the popularity of the client-server value proposition, reengineered their financial applications, human

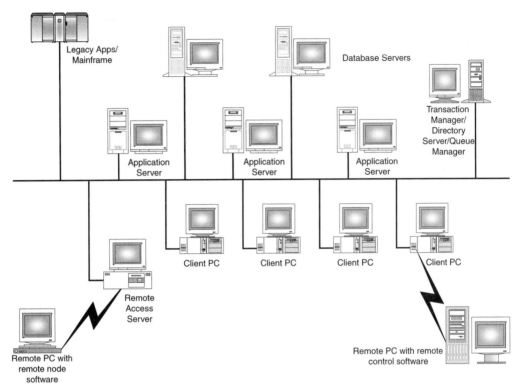

Figure 3–4
n-Tier client server architecture, ca. 1995.

resources management applications, materials and supply management applications, and so on, into "shrink-wrapped" software packages tailored to client-server deployment. Most of the current generation of ERP, MRP, and CRM client-server software suites trace their origins to earlier mainframe products.

In addition, many of today's leading relational and object-oriented database software vendors can trace their origins to the client-server revolution. Database-driven applications flourished in the distributed client-server platform because of the synergy between software and hardware architectures. In a database-driven application, the database software (or engine) is typically hosted on a dedicated server, which is accessed by a number of distributed application servers, which are themselves accessed by numerous client desktop systems. This simple three-tier architecture proliferated in the client-server environment.

Although it did have a significant impact, client-server computing never fully replaced the centralized computing environment. Despite repeated vendor claims that the mainframe was dead, the "legacy" mainframe did not fade away into the pages of computer lore. Some of the factors that contributed to the perpetuation of the centralized software delivery model, despite the challenges from desktop and client-server computing, include the following:

- Spectacular failures of multitier client-server system deployments: Many firms that endeavored to field large-scale client-server systems met with dismal, expensive, and well-publicized failures. Although some of these outcomes were probably due to poor management or faulty designs, a significant number of projects traced their failure to the inability of the underlying technology to scale. Whatever the explanation, business managers grew reluctant to risk the red ink of cost overruns and the black ink of negative press. By industry analyst accounting, as late as 1997, less than 30 percent of mission critical applications had migrated to client-server platforms; 70 percent or more continued to reside on mainframes.

- Greater awareness of management costs: With the rollout of client-server applications, the cost arguments of client-server advocates began to fray. Even though hosting platforms—mini- and microcomputer servers—were substantially less expensive than mainframes from the standpoint of acquisition costs, operating applications across a distributed platform quickly pointed up "costs of ownership" issues. Contrary to the hyperbole of client-server advocates, management and administration of distributed computing could not be accomplished effectively by end users themselves, supported by a few system administrators. Managing a large number of distributed clients and servers, including their storage components, security components, performance, network interconnections, and so forth, required a cadre of expensive technical staff, as well as hardware/software resources. In short, migrating applications off of the central computing host platform and onto a distributed client-server platform entailed additional requirements to re-create the disciplined IT staff of the data center and to replace the convenient set of management tools previously provided by the mainframe operating system with third-party management products—an expensive proposition.

- Pace of technological change: Client-server may also have become the victim of the rapid pace of technological change. Most large-scale application development projects proved to be iterative ventures. That is, application functionality was rolled out over time—sometimes over a period of several years. During the same period, the underlying technology of server platforms, PC clients, middleware, networks, and other hardware and software components steadily advanced. The pressure that technological change exerted upon application design was tremendous. Often the end results were applications that were either based on outmoded technology or represented a kluge* of multiple technologies, compounding difficulties in management and administration and driving up the cost of ownership. This, in turn, inhibited the scaleability of applications or impaired their flexibility to changing business requirements.

- Changes in mainframe technology directions: Client-server computing's challenge to the mainframe was also diffused, in part, by the mainframe vendors themselves. To a certain extent, vendors such as IBM co-opted the client-server value proposition by releasing mainframe operating systems that were more network friendly and by adding functionality that supported their use as "super servers" in distributed networks.

At the end of the day, client-server, centralized, and single-user computing models came to share, rather than dominate, the IT landscape in many corporations. By the mid 1990s, one did not need to look too far to find efforts within these organizations to make the best of this situation.

Some firms struggled to integrate these disparate models into *n*-tier client-server architectures comprised of PCs as the client tier, distributed application servers and database servers as middle tiers, and legacy systems as the top tier. Complicated middleware and data interchange protocols and application programming interfaces (APIs) were leveraged to provide the connecting "glue" between the tiers. Hampered by a lack of nonproprietary standards that were both well defined and practical to implement, most firms continued to cobble together "integrated" enterprise computing solutions, which would avail themselves of centralized management and not impair the business processes that they were fielded to support.

TOWARD POST–CLIENT-SERVER COMPUTING . . . . .

Although it can be argued that client-server computing largely failed to deliver on its value proposition, it did set the stage for other important software delivery models, including the ASP delivery model. Three significant trends in client-server computing, witnessed at the end of the 1990s, helped to usher in the ASP: server recentralization, application recentralization/thin client computing, and the advent of Web technology.

---

*The *New Hacker Dictionary* defines a kluge /*klooj*/ [from the German `klug,' clever; poss. related to Polish `klucz' (a key, a hint, a main point)] 1. n. A Rube Goldberg (or Heath Robinson) device, whether in hardware or software. 2. n. A clever programming trick intended to solve a particular nasty case in an expedient, if not clear, manner. Often used to repair bugs. A crock that works. 3. n. Something that works for the wrong reason. 4. vt. To insert a kluge into a program. "I've kluged this routine to get around that weird bug, but there's probably a better way" (*The New Hacker's Dictionary,* by Eric S. Raymond, 3rd ed. (1996: MIT Press).)

Server Recentralization

In an effort to reduce management costs, some organizations have moved database and application server platforms back into the "glass house" of the centralized corporate data center. There, the "server farm" can be managed by a smaller number of IT administrators, share a common storage infrastructure, and derive other operational benefits.

Although this server recentralization phenomenon did not impact software licensing or end user application access, it did breathe new life into client-server architecture from a total cost of ownership (TCO) perspective. Recentralization enabled more servers to be more efficiently maintained by fewer IT staff.

In addition to reducing costs, the strategy also helped to reduce perceived risk. Centralized servers, for example, were subject to the disciplined data backup schedules that are part of the IT staff's operational routine. Thus, the possibility of disastrous downtime due to data loss was mitigated by such a strategy.

Finally, server recentralization established a mind-set—a way of thinking about IT—that was important for ASPs later on. Basically, recentralization demonstrated what had always been known about distributed computing, though rarely acted upon. Specifically, recentralization demonstrated that the location of servers relative to end users in a distributed computing architecture didn't matter. Given a dependable network infrastructure, servers could be placed well outside of a department or work group that used them and could still provide the necessary application access for performing useful work. Later, ASPs leveraged this mind-set to argue that servers could be positioned anywhere in the larger network—even outside of the company premises—and still provide a dependable means for corporate computing.

Application Recentralization and Thin Client Computing

While some client-server total cost of ownership issues were being addressed through server recentralization strategies, businesses and analysts alike sought other cost areas to conquer. Ultimately this quest turned attention to the corporate desktop and "fat client" PCs.

The late 1990s computer trade press was filled with discussions of the costliness of WINTEL PCs. Analysts, including the Gartner Group and others, released startling desktop TCO reports theorizing that each PC deployed by a company represented an annual maintenance and administration expense of $5,000 to $13,000. Multiplied by the numbers of PCs deployed in business organizations, the resulting TCO tally was staggering.

Seizing upon the "findings" of prominent analysts, a group of WINTEL PC competitors—nicknamed *SONIA* for its prominent participants: Sun Microsystems, Oracle Corporation, Netscape Communications, IBM, and Apple Computers—

posited a new desktop device to replace the traditional PC: a thin client or network computer. Although each SONIA member had its own reasons for promoting a thin client approach, the fundamental argument was compelling: Many users did not require the complex and expensive WINTEL PC platform in order to perform useful work. They might be better served by a less complex, less costly, more manageable, terminal-like device.

The first generation of the thin client devices failed to catch on for a number of reasons. Primary among them was a lack of applications available to exploit the "new" architecture. Moreover, the PC industry responded with less expensive desktop PCs offering "zero administration" options that made them highly competitive with thin computer devices, while maintaining end user access to local applications. In the end the Gartner Group, which had started all of the desktop TCO fuss in the first place, conceded that the whole matter had been something of a red herring.

What persisted from the debate, however, was a view that servers, rather than clients, were the logical focal point for systems scaling. Citrix Systems, Santa Cruz Operation (SCO), and a few other vendors seized upon the notion of recentralizing desktop applications—both single user "productivity" applications and the client software of client-server applications—onto application servers. The result was an "thin computing, server-centric" application delivery model (see Figure 3–5) that delivered

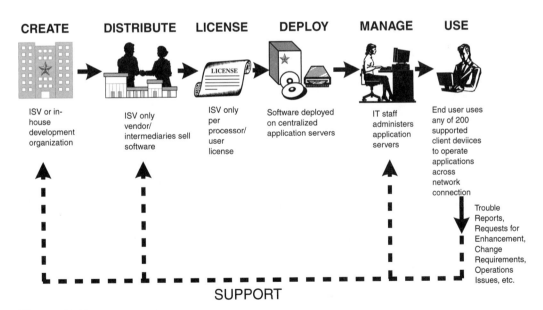

Figure 3–5
The Citrix Systems application delivery model. *Source:* Citrix Systems, Inc., Ft. Lauderdale, FL.

cost-reduced application management, while providing a flexible, high-performance desktop computing solution.

Both the thin client initiative and the server-centric application hosting technologies from Citrix and SCO, which are discussed in greater detail in subsequent chapters, helped to set the stage for the ASP delivery model.

WEB TECHNOLOGY: THE INTERNET, INTRANETS, AND EXTRANETS . . . .

Client-server computing architecture is also at the heart of what has come to be called the World Wide Web. The World Wide Web is a system of servers interconnected via a public network (the Internet) which supports the exchange of information specially formatted into what are commonly called Web pages. Interaction between Web servers and end users on the Web is facilitated through the use of a "universal" client known as a Web browser.

The technologies supporting the operation of the Web—from its underlying network protocol, TCP/IP, to the Web page creation language, HTML, to the protocol for exchanging Web pages, the HyperText Transfer Protocol (HTTP)—are based upon standards adopted and approved by the IETF. It is the rigorous attention to standards that accounts for part of the appeal of Web technology for business.

As the World Wide Web (and the public Internet generally) caught on in the mid-1990s, the idea of utilizing Web technology for delivering applications and information to end users within the corporate enterprise generated enormous interest within business organizations. The notion of a single, universal, standards-based client—the browser—sounded like a godsend to companies coping with "client proliferation" resulting from the deployment of numerous and disparate client-server applications.

Early on many companies sought to apply the Web model used in their public Web site development efforts to their internal systems. *Intranets*, the application of Web technology–based client-server models to internal applications, and *extranets*, the extension of Web Technology–based client-server applications to external entities (business partners, investors, supply chain providers, etc.) via the Internet or private networks, appeared virtually overnight.

Although these early efforts demonstrated the promise of standards-based client-server computing to expedite systems implementation, facilitate systems management, normalize transactions, and provide access to end users regardless of their client device and connection speed, they also pointed up the limitations of first-generation Web technology. In short, developers quickly discovered that Web technology provided an excellent means to publish information, but not applications. A few people discounted Web technology altogether as too superficial to support much more than the interchange of static data within a stateless network environment.

The perceived limitations of Web technology as an interactive medium suitable for application delivery generated responses from both the standards-making community and from the community of vendors that had coalesced around the Internet. In 1998 proposals for "next generation" Web technology standards began to circulate that promised to enhance the speed and functionality of the medium in ways that would enable greater business-to-business and business-to-consumer interaction. One target for improvement was HTTP.

First-generation HTTP was called a stateless protocol because of its inherent command processing method: Each command is executed independently, without reference to any of the commands that came before it. This limitation accounted for the difficulty Web designers confronted when seeking to implement Web sites that reacted intelligently to user input.

Early efforts to address this shortcoming involved the enhancement of HTTP with technologies such as Microsoft's ActiveX, Sun Microsystems' Java and JavaScript, and Netscape's persistent client state cookies. Of course, competing approaches invited disagreements among vendors, which impacted browser capabilities to support the technologies (such as the Java Virtual Machine). This, in turn, limited the accessibility of all Web pages by all Web browsers.

Efforts are underway to implement a new set of standard capabilities in HTTP to enable persistent connections and to support interactive applications without proprietary add-ins. In 1998 several members of the World Wide Web Consortium (W3C), which develops standards for referral to the IETF, proposed the formation of a special working group to spearhead this effort. Upon review a decision was made by W3C in 1999 to break up the issues involved into smaller parts for development by other W3C working groups. Within the next few years, these working groups are expected to produce standards proposals for updating and improving HTTP. In a W3C activity status report regarding HTTP-Next Generation (HTTP-NG), a summary of the situation is offered:

> By breaking down the HTTP-NG Activity into smaller more manageable pieces we expect to better be able to interact with other Activitites both in the W3C and in the IETF. We still believe that HTTP-NG is a significant step forward in the W3C's [pursuit] of realizing the full potential of the Web. There are today so many applications that we would like to see on the Web which either can not be implemented or simply are too complex to deploy in the current infrastructure. We hope to be able to change that!*

*W3C Architecture Domain Activity Statement, HTTP-NG, Copyright© 1994–2000 World Wide Web Consortium (Massachusetts Institute of Technology, Institut National de Recherche en Informatique et en Automatique, Keio University). All Rights Reserved. *http://www.w3.org/*.

In addition to enhancements to HTTP, the W3C has also introduced the Extensible Markup Language (XML) as a successor to the HTML. XML is expected to convert Web technology from "a fancy fax machine" into a medium for intelligent application-to-application messaging.

Several organizations are working on the development of common business schemas for XML messages, which will facilitate direct electronic information interchange between the applications operating on servers located in different organizational locations. In practice XML-based interserver application messaging via Web connections will be a boon within vertical industries—law firms, health care organizations, insurance providers, and so on, that wish to integrate their systems with those of their partners.

Although XML and HTTP-NG dominate the future-oriented thinking of application designers and vendors, corporate IT professionals have continued to pursue the Web enablement of applications—leveraging standards-based mechanisms (e.g., HTTP 1.1 and Dynamic HTML), as well as available proprietary schemes, to establish persistent sessions between servers and clients capable of delivering high-performance, interactive applications across both private and public Webs. Figure 3–6 depicts a simplified topology used by many companies to Web enable their legacy systems.

The absence of standards-based, next-generation Web technology enhancements has curbed neither the interest nor the activity of corporate developers seeking to deploy applications on intranets, extranets, or the Internet. It has instead challenged firms (and vendors) to discover ways to work around deficits in Web technologies while leveraging technology strengths. These efforts have taken many forms.

In some cases, companies (and software vendors) have opted to develop entirely new applications using Web technology itself. Early efforts to field Web-ready applications harnessed the Common Gateway Interface (CGI), a standard method for transferring information between a Web server and a CGI-compliant program. CGI programs could be developed using common programming languages such as C, Perl, Java, or Visual Basic.

Typical implementations of CGI processing involved the use of fill-in-the-blank forms, whose data was processed by CGI programs upon submittal by the end user. This approach provided basic application interactivity, but at a price: Every time a CGI script was executed, a new process was started on the server. For busy servers, server-side execution could result in serious performance degradation.

This consideration led to other approaches for "server-side" application development, albeit more complicated and difficult ones to implement, including the use of server APIs and Java "servlets." It also drove the development of another class of applications which featured "client-side" execution, including Java "applets," Java scripts, and ActiveX controls.

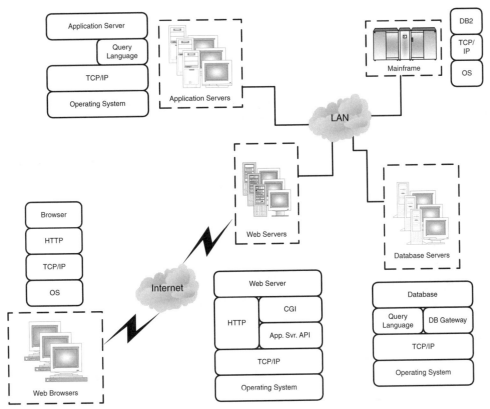

Figure 3–6
An infrastructure for Web-enabled legacy applications.

Over time these techniques have become integral parts of applications, both "home grown" and "shrink wrapped," aimed at Web-based e-commerce. Vendors of ERP, MRP, and CRM applications are slowly integrating these techniques and methods to Web enable their commercial software offerings as well, setting the stage for ASPs.

For all their value, however, these new, Web-ready applications are not a panacea for the "application publishing" requirements of businesses. Given the investments that many firms have already made in their existing applications—both "legacy" applications (e.g., mainframe applications, sometimes called "stovepipe" systems) and client-server applications—application replacement is less economically feasible. Instead, Web enablement, often facilitated by a new breed of "Web integrators," has become the strategy of choice.

Numerous techniques have evolved for connecting non-"Web-ready" applications to Web servers. Some borrow from earlier efforts to integrate legacy and client-server platforms.

One example is "screen scraping," a comparatively simple method for Web enabling "legacy" applications which involves the emulation of a "dumb terminal" within a standard Web-browser screen. Screen scrapers, which have been in the mar-

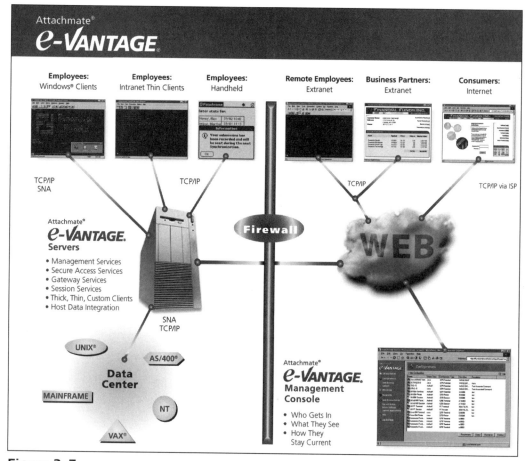

Figure 3–7

Attachmate e-vantage host-to-Web architecture. *Source:* Illustration is provided by 2nd copyright of Attachmate Corporation. All rights reserved. Attachmate and the e-Vantage logo are registered trademarks of Attachmate Corporation in the United States and/or other countries.

ket for nearly 15 years to enable the delivery of a mainframe application interface on a Windows PC, have been rapidly retooled and enhanced by vendors to support legacy-to-Web integration efforts.

Screen scrapers contain instructions for separating textual information from terminal interface data streams and presenting them in another format, such as HTML. In operation, browser-equipped users interact with mainframe applications just as they would if sitting at a terminal.

The ease of deployment and use of screen scrapers and related technologies from vendors such as Attachmate Corporation (see Figure 3–7), Wall Data (now NetManage; see Figure 3–8), Mozart Systems (now a subsidiary of SEEC), and others have sustained their popularity as tools to facilitate the Web-enablement of legacy apps.

Application interface extension products mentioned in the previous section from Citrix Systems, SCO, and a few other vendors comprise a somewhat different take on the screen scraping approach. These products combine a server-based application hosting or gateway component with an application networking protocol component and a client component to deliver the interface of an application to a diversity of client devices, including Web browser-equipped devices.

Most of these products trace their origins to the late 1980s and early 1990s, when they sought to address the needs of small companies for inexpensive application sharing and remote access. Today these products provide the means of extending the

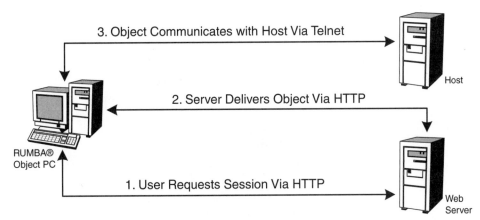

Figure 3–8
NetManage's RUMBA® Architecture for Web to host integration. *Source: NetManage, Inc., Cupertino, CA. www.netmanage.com*

"presentation layers" of mainframe, UNIX, and Windows-based applications to end users connected via browsers to intranets, extranets, or the public Internet.

Citrix Systems, known for some years for its extensions to Microsoft's NT Server operating system which enabled multiuser access to server-hosted applications (a technology that has been licensed by Microsoft and integrated into subsequent editions of their operating system), began offering MetaFrame in the late 1990s as a means to facilitate the delivery of server-hosted applications to a diversity of client desktops, including those equipped with Web browsers. Lately the company has been offering "NFuse" technology within MetaFrame, providing an easy-to-use "wizard" program which enables administrators to select the server-hosted applications that are to be Web enabled and to configure them into application "portals" customized to end user requirements. (See an operational overview in Figure 3–9.)

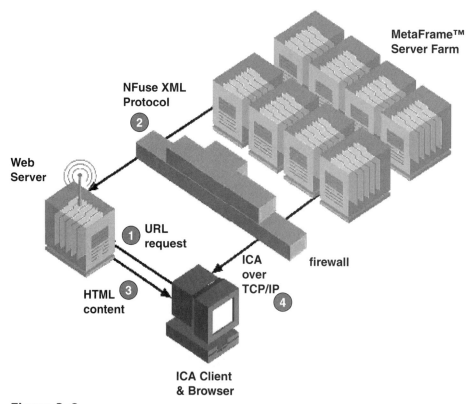

Figure 3–9
Web Enablement with Citrix Systems MetaFrame and NFuse. *Source:* Citrix Systems, Inc., Ft. Lauderdale, Florida.

Like Citrix Systems MetaFrame, SCO's Tarantella derives from an earlier effort to manage the sharing of UNIX applications among multiple and mobile users. The functionality of the product has since been enlarged to support mainframe and Windows-based application extensions, as well. According to analysts, Tarantella competes with Citrix Systems's MetaFrame, despite numerous architectural differences, and both technologies are already finding their place in both corporate and ASP Web technology–based application delivery platforms.

Conceptually similar to the screen scraper/terminal emulation approach is a technique called graphical user interface (GUI) extension. Like screen scrapers, GUI extenders first made their appearance in the early 1990s, described by vendors as tools for "beautifying without replacing" legacy applications and for taking advantage of the GUI capabilities of Windows client desktops. Applied to Web enablement, GUI extenders allow developers to create custom-coded screen generation programs that "process" textual elements of a legacy (or client-server) application screen for presentation in a browser.

Depending on the product, each legacy application screen can be converted to a Web browser "screen" on a one-for-one basis, or multiple legacy screens can be combined through the selective inclusion or exclusion of screen fields. With some products, data from other sources can be included with the application GUI, or legacy data can be captured into data objects for use by other programs.

The most advanced GUI extenders begin encroach upon the realm of a third category of Web-enabling technologies known as "application wrappers." Application wrappering entails the "capture" of legacy application processes into function-oriented data objects ("JavaBeans" for example), which are then stored on a specialized server or in a database. These objects can be called by scripts or programs either individually or in combination, creating "new" composite applications for Web delivery.

Wrappering technology aligns well with the object-oriented database architectures that have been adopted by leading database software makers, including Oracle and InterSystems Corporation. Object support varies from vendor to vendor, with most offering support for Java, XML, COM/DCOM objects, as well as objects created from proprietary sources (such as middleware products) and those of the vendor's own design.

Ultimately, wrappering technology can be used in connection with an integration framework to Web enable entire business enterprises, according to vendors such as Bluestone Software and Level 8. Hewlett Packard's (formerly Bluestone's) Total-E-Server (see Figure 3–10) may be thought of as an enterprise wrapper framework and is designed to support the integration of applications and distributed objects with its Universal Business Server.

Numerous vendor-supplied case studies, three of which are reprinted in this section, demonstrate the value of corporate application Web enablement and describe the

(*text continues on page 93*)

hp bluestone
total-e-server

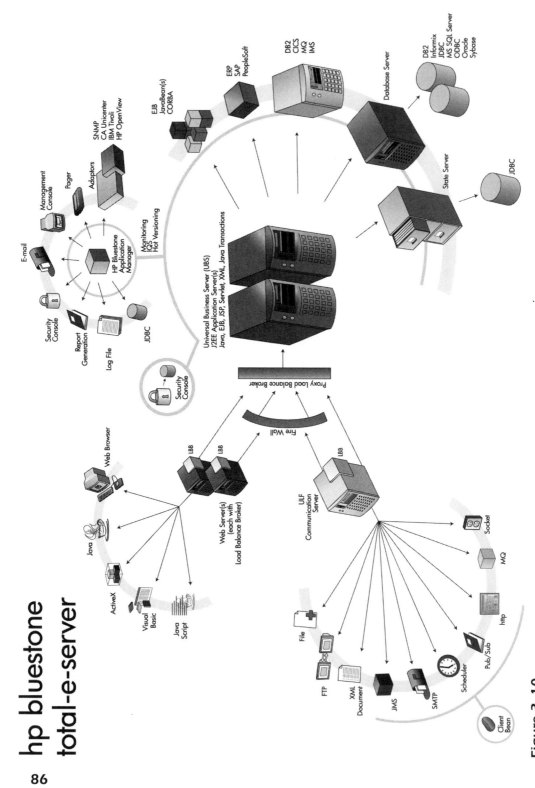

Figure 3-10
HP Bluestone Total-E-Server Framework. *Source:* HP Bluestone, Philadelphia, PA.

PROTEGRITY SERVICES, INC. EMPLOYS CLIENTBUILDER WEBPACK TO DRIVE ITS BREAKTHROUGH WORKCOMPNOW.COM SITE

Protegrity Services Inc., Longwood, FL, is a premier provider of insurance products and related services to insured and self-insured business clients located in the South, Mid-Atlantic, Midwest, Mountain, and Southwest regions of the United States. The company distributes and administers these products and services through multiple channels and strategic relationships. Protegrity is also one of the largest privately held workers' compensation service companies in the nation.

In 1999, Protegrity foresaw an excellent opportunity to be a pioneer in making workers' compensation insurance underwriting and rating information available in real time to licensed property & casualty agents via the Internet. Such a leadership position would in fact be in keeping with Protegrity's ongoing strategy to develop products and services that enhance and simplify customer interaction while reducing transaction costs.

The key challenge the company faced in achieving this "first to market" objective, was finding an efficient way to seamlessly integrate its Web-based front-end called Workcompnow.com™ with its existing IBM AS/400™ legacy system that contained a storehouse of underwriting, rating, policy and claim-related data. Moreover, it was particularly critical that the agents visiting the site be provided with quick, secure and transparent access to that legacy-based information.

To address these challenges, Protegrity's IT staff undertook a comprehensive search for some type of "middleware" link that could connect the new Web-based network with its established AS/400 systems.

After reviewing a number of alternatives, Protegrity ultimately selected ClientSoft's ClientBuilder WebPack™ for its ease-of-use and the speed with which it could be implemented. Protegrity also appreciated WebPack's scalability, as the company's aggressive expansion plans for Workcompnow.com required an application that could easily adjust to support increasing visitor sessions.

"To make Workcompnow.com a reality we needed a proven tool that would allow us to transparently connect our existing legacy system with a new Web-based network, and ClientBuilder WebPack was truly the ideal solution to meet that need," according to Greg Kerrebrock,

Senior Vice President for E-commerce, Marketing & Communication, Protegrity Services, Inc., in Longwood, FL.

Through the use of WebPack, Protegrity was able to create a seamless, end-to-end solution, one that facilitates quick and easy Internet-based access to the wealth of underwriting and rating information stored on its legacy systems.

The WebPack-powered Workcompnow.com site provides licensed insurance agents with a sales edge in a very competitive marketplace. By pricing and binding workers' compensation coverage from A-rated insurers on-line through Workcompnow.com, agents can replace existing paper-intensive, time-consuming processes with the speed, efficiency, and power of the Internet. What took days to complete, now takes minutes.

According to Kerrebrock, "Thanks to ClientBuilder WebPack, we were able to pioneer Web-based access to workers' compensation-related underwriting and rating information, and it also helped to provide us with yet another way to increase our premium revenues and improve CRM while simultaneously reducing our administrative costs."

First launched during the fourth quarter of 2000, the Workcompnow.com site had, by the close of the first quarter of 2001, already received more than 600,000 hits, hosted over 9,000 visitor sessions, and processed more than 800 quotes representing in excess of $5 million in premiums. Moreover, during that same time over 1,100 insurance agents had successfully completed the straightforward registration process required to gain access to the various tools provided by the site.

Source: ClientSoft, Inc., Hawthorne, NY.

CLIENTSOFT SUPPORTS BLUE CROSS BLUE SHIELD OF SOUTH CAROLINA'S WEB TRANSFORMATION

Blue Cross and Blue Shield of South Carolina (BCBSSC) serves more than one million South Carolinians, offering health care insurance to the individuals, families, and businesses of South Carolina. BCBSSC has more than 10,200 employees with offices throughout South Carolina, as well as in Virginia, Florida, Texas, and Maryland, largely due to the growth of their government program operations. The company consistently ranks as one of the top Blue Cross plans in the nation, and is continually researching new products to increase efforts to offer South Carolinians with secure, cost-efficient, health care coverage.

In 1998, Blue Cross Blue Shield of South Carolina, determined to leverage technology to build its customer base, called on ClientSoft to help break the constraints imposed by its in-house mainframe-based systems. Their goal was to begin offering information directly to the public through the Internet.

This project was a success, and BCBSSC wanted to expand its Internet capability even more to include a broad range of targeted information for members, providers, benefit coordinators, and agents.

ClientSoft originally programmed its proprietary software Web-Pack2000 to help customers with Internet access get online, real-time information about participating doctors. Customers could log on and find doctors by specialty or location—and they could do it any time of the day, any day of the week. To BCBSSC, the move represented a step into the future and paved the way for the eventual transfer of a wide range of its consumer and business-to-business operations from mainframes to the Web.

"Our goal is to make technology transparent to the user, so that what chimes through the Web is the content and the data," said Bry Curry, BCBSSC's Web systems manager.

> The easier we make it for our members to find the information they want and need, the stronger and more trusted we become as their insurer—and the more we distance ourselves from our competitors. We not only maintain our customer base; we build on it. Since our information is simpler for customers to use and understand, and easier and cheaper for us to administer, everyone wins.

The Solution

In November 1999, once again relying on WebPack2000, BCBSSC customized its "Insurance Manager" Web software to offer customers online access to such information as authorization status, claims status, deductibles and out-of-pocket status, benefit booklets, and other health insurance. In addition, members are being given the option of ordering ID cards online. This improves customer access to important data while decreasing phone requests to BCBSSC for the same information.

The Benefits

BCBSSC's Curry said that in just a few months, the company is already starting to experience a decrease in the number of phone requests. BCBSSC is convinced this will translate directly into a decrease in personnel costs and general overhead. "We're just beginning to take advantage of the opportunities that the Web offers," Curry added. "ClientSoft has given us systems that are leading edge in quality and effectiveness, and yet easy to use. We'll be integrating other functions online over the next year. Our goal is to develop Web sites for all lines of business that reach out to our customers—and let them reach back—24/7."

Source: ClientSoft, Inc., Hawthorne, NY.

DREYFUS PUTS $90 BILLION IN MUTUAL FUNDS ONLINE WITH HP BLUESTONE TOTAL-E-SERVER

With more than $90 billion in assets under management, Dreyfus is a Wall Street powerhouse. So, moving the system that tracks thousands of mutual funds to an intranet was no small matter. Dreyfus dealers, brokers, sales advisors, and financial consultants need to provide customers with instant information and the ability to complete 140,000 transactions per day.

Customers expect Dreyfus representatives to be able to provide quotations on how their mutual funds are fairing. These representatives have to be able to provide daily pricing, pricing history, five- to 10-year yield information, Morningstar ratings, holdings and any other information on the fund that would be of interest to the fund holder. With the new Web-to-database application, Dreyfus representatives have the information needed at their fingertips, enabling them to respond to customer queries immediately.

Taking Advantage of the Web

Subsequent to this new mutual fund operation application, Dreyfus was utilizing a client/server model, including a client/server application that tracked mutual fund problems. When the company began to add other applications, including email and an intranet link, they wanted and needed something more scalable than what was in place. Dreyfus needed to standardize on one platform but had problems with applications working together. They wanted to rearchitect applications to increase scalability and accessibility across the enterprise, eliminating software distribution issues and desktop compatibility problems.

Dreyfus needed a Web development and deployment solution to build their most important mission-critical Web-to-database application. They needed an open solution that would work across the enterprise handling transaction processing while providing speed and performance and something they could roll out and maintain easily across their U.S. locations and abroad.

Choosing Total-e-Server

"We considered a number of application development solutions before choosing HP Bluestone Total-e-Server (formerly known as Bluestone's

Sapphire/Web), but found that other systems had proprietary limitations and could not meet the speed and performance of HP Bluestone Total-e-Server," said Joe Sclafani, manager of application interfaces, Dreyfus. With the product, Dreyfus was able to establish a consistent connection to the database and reuse and integrate JavaScript code in less than a week.

With Web technology changing so quickly, Sclafani said that HP Bluestone Total-e-Server's plug-and-play architecture ensures that Dreyfus can leverage technologies of today and tomorrow without missing a beat.

Application Success

"This is the most widely used application in Dreyfus," said Sclafani. "It is absolutely a mission-critical system. This application handles more than 140,000 queries daily and is the information pipeline to our customers. We wouldn't be able to do business without it.

"It took two years to build our old client/server applications and only six months to replace it with HP Bluestone Total-e-Server," said Sclafani. "Time and again Bluestone has proven that they can incorporate new technology incredibly fast. . . . With HP Bluestone Total-e-Server our deployment costs have been cut in half. And reduced development cycles let us concentrate on additional projects."

Sclafani maintains that Dreyfus could not handle business without this solution. "If the application fails, we fail. That's why we're committed to HP Bluestone Total-e-Server," said Sclafani. "Bluestone is the clear leader in developing and deploying enterprise-class Web applications."

Continually Improving Customer Service

The next phase of the Dreyfus mutual fund operation application will enable Dreyfus account holders to conduct business from their own PCs. Customers will be able to order additional checkbooks and duplicate statements and send for prospectuses or request applications.

Work has also begun on a HP Bluestone Total-e-Server application that will allow access of public marketing information, portfolio tracking, and stock quotes from self-service kiosks in Dreyfus Financial Centers.

Source: HP Bluestone, Philadelphia, PA.

techniques employed by organizations and their integrators to support end user application delivery via the public Internet and across private intranets and extranets. The case studies suggest the surge of interest that was generated by the the World Wide Web and explain the rapidity with which a broad array of Web-enablement tools appeared on the market.

The important point to draw from the case studies of Web-enablement methods is simple: For many firms, the replacement of legacy mainframe and client-server applications with new Web-ready applications is not an option. Instead, developers and integrators have sought to employ low-cost, minimum-effort approaches, such as screen scraping, GUI extension, and wrappering, to deliver legacy application access to end users via Web technology. These efforts are ongoing and provide the basis for much of the application delivery services offered by current ASPs.

THE PAST IS PROLOGUE: SOFTWARE DELIVERY VIA WEB TECHNOLOGY . . . .

This historical perspective concludes with a brief discussion of the efforts by companies in the late 1990s to enable their applications for delivery to end users across corporate intranets and extranets, as well as the public Internet. It should come as little surprise that discussions of the ASP model for software delivery began at around the same time.

The ASP model owes a substantial part of its heritage to the business "e-commerce" and intranet development initiatives that were in full swing in many businesses by the end of the millennium. In fact, ASPs cannot be understood without considering the broader canvas of e-business.

In the late 1990s, the widely heralded (and, in many cases, exaggerated) success of "dotcoms"—companies founded exclusively for operation on the Internet and World Wide Web—encouraged many established "brick-and-mortar" companies to investigate how they could become part of the "new economy" of the Web. Many firms created new business units within their organizations tasked with harnessing Web technology to extend business services or to expand business markets across the public network.

In some cases, these business units were supported by Web technology–based IT infrastructures developed and maintained by internal personnel. In other cases, the business units utilized external service providers to "host" their "Web presence" and to manage its underlying IT infrastructure. Both approaches contributed to the development of the ASP concept in meaningful ways.

Companies that elected to "grow their own" Web technology–based platforms—whether to exploit the business potential of the public Internet or to support internal information distribution and application access requirements—created, intentionally or inadvertently, "laboratories" for innovation. Their experimentation with various hosting technologies and with techniques for integrating existing systems and applications with newer Web-based hardware and software platforms helped to point up the deficits and limitations of Web technology so they could be addressed by vendors.

Similarly, firms that elected to use outside contractors to provide their Web technology infrastructure and support helped to define, through these evolving relationships, both the capabilities requirements and the procedural requirements that Web hosting providers (and ultimately ASPs) would need to fulfill. Early Web hosting offerings consisted of little more than an IP address, a registered domain name, a few megabytes of disk storage space for Web page data, a couple of email accounts, and an allocation of bandwidth deemed adequate to facilitate visits to the customer Web site by Internet users. Later, in response to business customer requests, hosting firms added access to CGI forms processors, support for secure sessions, and primordial e-commerce applications—so-called "shopping cart" programs—which enabled companies to do more with their Web sites than simply publish data.

Today, new capabilities seem to be appearing daily on the menu of services offered by hosting providers, including:

- Varying levels of support for connections to a customer's "backend systems and databases" to facilitate the integration of Web-based ordering and company-based fulfillment systems

- Site mirroring and data replication services to ensure uninterrupted operation of the customer site

- Load balancing and other capabilities to reduce congestion-related slowdowns of sites due to large traffic loads and to enhance the visitor's experience when visiting the site

- Support for the dynamic presentation of Web page data in formats suitable to wireless devices, as well as wired desktop computers

- Support for Internet-based telephony, and

- Integration of third-party services, such as credit card and check processing services

All the above features, and many others, have come about as the result of competition among service providers. By and large, this competition has been generated by customers who have defined their expectations of a Web hosting service and are willing and able to switch to whichever service provider best meets their needs.

ASPs have profited from advancements in business Web hosting services both from a technological and a business practice standpoint. In some cases, the relationship is a direct one: as observed in the preceding chapter, many ASPs utilize the platforms of a Web hosting provider to deliver applications. However, even those ASPs that "host their own" applications have learned a great deal from Web hosting companies about the infrastructure requirements for fault-tolerant, performance-optimized, and well-managed service platforms. ASPs have also capitalized on the operational procedures and best practices that have made successful Web hosting companies, such as Verio and Exodus Communications, the industry leaders that they are as of this writing.

CONCLUSION . . . .

Returning to the question asked at the outset, whether the ASP model for software delivery represents a revolutionary break with traditional models for application delivery, one would have to answer in the negative. Given the evolution of traditional computing models to date, the ASP software delivery model can be seen as a logical outgrowth of continuing corporate efforts to deliver applications and information to decision makers regardless of their location.

Having said this, it is also important to note that application software itself is in a state of transition. Few applications today have been developed expressly for delivery via Web technology. This is changing, of course, and soon "Web-ready" versions of popular applications will likely become available, strengthening the portfolio of solutions that ASPs will be prepared to deliver to their customers. Until then, ASPs will continue to leverage Web-enabling technologies, such as those described earlier, to facilitate the requirements of their business clients.

4

ASP Arrangements and Traditional Outsourcing

In this chapter...

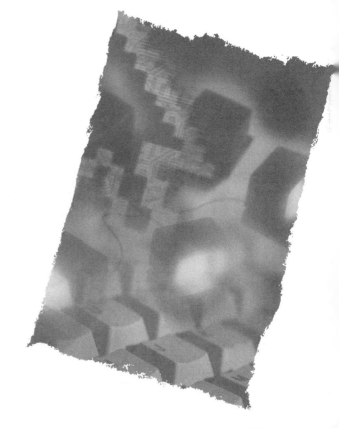

In the previous chapter, it was argued that the ASP software delivery model is not, as some suggest, a sudden or revolutionary departure from tradition. Nor is it a "paradigm shift," or even a "disruptive technology" in the Christensen sense of the term. Contrary to marketing hype, the ASP model builds on established techniques, methods, and architectures of traditional business computing. It is properly viewed as an evolutionary, rather than revolutionary, development.

This position is not intended to minimize the importance of ASPs, or to question their utility. In fact, some users might actually be more inclined to embrace ASP service offerings if vendors were to emphasize how much this model builds on existing technology, rather than deviating from it.

Ultimately, ASPs promise to become the means by which many companies and end users—perhaps the majority—will obtain application software services. According to analysts, the ASP industry will grow from revenues in the range of $300 million in 1999 to about $8 billion by 2004. This growth will be facilitated by improvements in broad bandwidth, high-speed networks, the increasing readiness of applications for delivery via the ASP model, and by a mounting record of well-publicized success stories that will reinforce user confidence in the overall strategy. If the analysts are correct, the future of the ASP model—to paraphrase the song lyric—is so bright, vendors will need to wear "shades."

Another view of ASPs, advanced by numerous commentators in the trade press, is that they are merely traditional outsourcing arrangements by another name. As noted in the introduction, making such assertions at an ASP conference or trade show is a sure way to trigger an argument—and possibly a physical altercation—with many advocates of the model.

Why do so many ASPs resist the association of their software delivery model with outsourcing? One explanation, mentioned in the introduction, is that the term "outsourcing," for many IT professionals, is loaded with negative emotional content.

Outsourcing conjures to mind arrangements in which corporate organizations dissolve their internal IT departments and contract out the entire kit-and-kaboodle to third-party service providers. These arrangements have come into and gone out of style at different times in the history of corporate computing. When in vogue, outsourcing arrangements were entered into for a variety of reasons—most of them "bad" from the standpoint of corporate IT professionals.

Often, when senior management opted to outsource their IT functions, this decision was based on the assumption that outside contractors could deliver the same (or better) value as the internal IT organization at less cost and/or with less hassle. To senior managers, outsourcing was a pragmatic choice between two more-or-less equivalent alternatives—a decision based on a simple cost-benefit calculus.

Typically, upon learning of management's consideration of the outsourcing option, corporate IT professionals adopted a contrary position. They argued that external agents did not share in the objectives and vision of the company and were less likely "to go the extra mile" to facilitate corporate goals. Internal IT personnel, sharing the corporate culture (and depending on the payroll) of an organization, had more at stake in the success of the business than a third-party service provider.

Outsourcing vendors responded that such arguments were without merit and that they made client priorities their own. Failing to do so, they observed, would be self-destructive—losing them both clients and contracts. Plus, outsourcing IT to a vendor ensured that the latest technologies would be brought to bear to meet corporate requirements—at no additional cost to the client company.

Often the entire debate fell on deaf ears within the comfortable, smoke-filled board rooms of senior management. In many cases, management expressed the desire to use outsourcing as a means to "get out of the technology business." They asserted that hiring an outside contractor to provide IT services would enable them to focus on core business values. More often than not, such statements were little more than rationalizations barely able to conceal the actual reason most firms had for outsourcing: to cut budgets.

Especially in periods of general economic adversity (high inflation or recession), off-loading IT responsibilities to an external agent was part of corporate "downsizing" or "right sizing" strategies. The corporate IT department was, after all, an "overhead expense" (at least, in terms of corporate accounting) and not a "profit center" for the company. In lean years, senior management was likely to regard corporate IT as an indulgence of companies that could afford to capitalize technology investments and underwrite IT operational costs.

Reinforcing this view were the persuasive arguments that could always be made (and frequently were, by a number of critics) that corporate technology investments evidenced no correlation—no demonstrable relationship whatsoever—to company share value. Although it was true that modern information processing technologies were part of the "price to play" in an increasingly competitive business marketplace, to senior managers it made little difference whether these enabling IT services were "home grown" or secured from an outsourcing agent.

Considering the "embattled state" of mainframe-centric IT departments in many business organizations in the late 1970s, 1980s, and early 1990s—IT managers were striving to deliver promised service levels to business units while dealing with threats to the mainframe data center posed by the PC, then the client-server "revolution," and by the fast pace of technological change itself—it is easy to see why many IT professionals were hostile to outsourcing. The possibility that senior management, which often lacked technology savvy, would opt to dissolve the data center and outsource mission-critical application processing on the basis of an accounting report or *Wall*

Street Journal article only reinforced the "bunker mentality" that had developed in more than a few corporate IT shops. Many of today's IT professionals remember vividly the feeling that they were living on borrowed time.

When management settled upon outsourcing as an appropriate strategy for the business, they sometimes sought to make the decision more palatable to corporate IT staff by providing for their transfer to the outsourcing vendor as part of the contract. In general, however, personnel transfers were not long-lived. Personnel who had served as computer operators, tape librarians, and in other low-level staff positions were often released shortly after the deal was finalized. In many cases, application experts, systems programmers, and others further up on the IT department hierarchy had only a slightly longer tenure. Many were turned out by their new employers to seek jobs elsewhere before the end of the first year of the outsourcing contract.

In more than a few cases, outsourcing contracts contained no provisions whatsoever for internal IT personnel futures. Outsourcing was equated to unemployment.

Many IT professionals still recall past outsourcing-related dismissals with fear and loathing. Some continue to regard the jobs lost to outsourcing contracts as personal affronts, an insult to their skills, experience, and contributions. Many are still delighted by the irony of trade press accounts of outsourcing failures. Despite IT skills shortages that have increased demands for qualified professionals and created a seller's market for technology expertise, outsourcing still carries with it a good measure of negative baggage.

Thus, although ASPs are clearly a form of outsourcing, according to ASP Industry Consortium Chairman Traver Gruen-Kennedy and others, many ASP advocates prefer to steer well clear of any assertions to that effect. In addition to the negative connotation of the term in the minds of many technology professionals, ASP advocates are afraid that nontechnical business decision makers may also be put off by the outsourcing moniker. Their reasons are twofold:

- ASPs are marketed as a "new economy" technology, while outsourcing is "old economy" technology. ASPs capitalize on Web technology to deliver their value proposition. In so doing, they are innovative, new, and fresh. A substantial percentage of early adopters of the ASP model (and most ASPs themselves) are "dotcoms"—firms that have no history of entrenched IT establishments. They are "virtual" firms that often lack any brick-and-mortar facilities. Their business processes are mapped to the Internet, and their technology infrastructure is provided through the ubiquitous network, not by a "glass house" data center in the basement of a corporate headquarters building. Old technology is anethema to these businesses. To be successful, in the eyes of many advocates, ASPs must represent themselves as an entirely new model for business process support.

- In marketing ASPs to traditional firms, describing ASPs as outsourcing arrangements is a bit like showing a stranger a tattoo. Some might find tattoos an attractive form of self-expression, whereas others may regard them as self-mutilation. So too with the ASP-outsourcing nexus: Companies that have had positive experiences with outsourcing contracts may regard "ASP-as-outsourcing" descriptions without so much as a blink. In fact, vendors may benefit from the prospective customer's familiarity with the ways and means of outsourcing: less "hand-holding" and customer education may be required to close a deal. By contrast, if the prospect has had a negative experience with an outsourcing arrangement in the past, it may be advantageous to avoid using the term when discussing the potential benefits to be derived from ASP services.

One thing that is missing from most of the debates over ASPs and other outsourcing arrangements is a clear definition of outsourcing itself. As the following survey suggests, outsourcing has, over time, adopted many different forms and meanings. In some cases, it is an arrangement encompassing all corporate IT functions; in other cases, outsourcing involves only certain applications or functions. A brief review may be useful to readers as they endeavor to sort out the issue of ASPs versus outsourcing.

DIFFERENT KINDS OF OUTSOURCING . . . .

Early in the annals of business computing, when systems were extremely expensive to acquire and qualified IT management and staff were in short supply, firms that were anxious to capitalize on technology to support business processes often utilized the services of outsourcing companies. Early outsourcing providers used different names to describe their services. Somewhat confusingly, they described themselves either in terms of function (service bureaus) or method (time-sharing).

From an operational perspective, however, these providers delivered a common service in the form of a shared application environment. Methods of sharing computing resources changed over time.

As depicted in Figure 4–1, the earliest providers typically leveraged the capability of mainframe host operating systems to schedule and manage sequential processing tasks. In general, early providers offered a single application software product to their customers. The application was shared among numerous firms by dividing the processing schedule of the mainframe among multiple, rigorously managed jobs. This was the origin of the term "time-sharing."

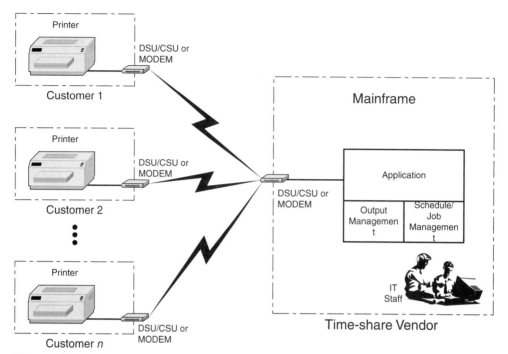

Figure 4–1
Sequential task time-sharing.

In time-sharing arrangements, various methods were used to "input" data (or to submit "jobs") to the outsourcing vendor's processing schedule or job queue. In some cases, outsourcers employed a cadre of data entry operators who input data from copies of customer source documents. Alternatively, customers prepared data volumes for storage to magnetic tape, often using simple data entry systems located on-site. The customer then forwarded the tapes to the vendor for input.

The results (or output) of customer data processing activity were typically returned to the customer via reports and other printed matter. Sometimes documents were printed at the outsourcer's site, then couriered to the customer. In other cases, output was printed (or recorded to tape) at the customer site using equipment purchased by the customer, leased to the customer by the provider, or simply provided as part of the outsourcing agreement.

When a printer (or tape unit) was located at the customer site, a dial-up or dedicated telephone line was usually provided to connect the local printer to the outsourcer's off-site data processing facility. Mainframe data output was directed to a device, such as a modem or digital service unit/channel service unit (DSU/CSU), then transmitted via the dial-up or dedicated communications link to the customer facility. This data was, in turn, received at the customer site using a modem or DSU/CSU and directed to locally installed peripheral devices (e.g., printers, tape drives, etc.).

The sophistication of mainframe operating systems and hardware increased over time, as did the requirements of customer data processing. Although many firms elected to build their own internal data processing facilities and IT departments, others continued to outsource their data processing requirements—but added increasingly complex requirements for vendors to fulfill.

Vendors harnessed the increased capability of mainframes in the 1970s to respond to increasingly sophisticated customer demands. One innovation in the mainframe operating system, logical portioning, enabled vendors to establish multiple "virtual" partitions or domains within the operating environment, thereby enabling the application(s) and resource requirements (data storage, etc.) of each individual customer to be segregated from those of other customers on the same platform. In effect, multiple customers could be supported on a single processing platform, each running in its own "logically partitioned" application environment. (IBM coined the acronym, LPAR, to describe its technology for diving the mainframe operating system into logical partitions. The term is used generically in this discussion, rather than referring exclusively to IBM product capabilities.)

Depicted in Figure 4–2, LPAR-based sharing appeared at about the same time as more sophisticated forms of mainframe channel extension and WAN technologies. Delivery of application services via this type of communications link provided the customer with a data processing capability that, in many cases, rivaled that of a local, on-site data center and terminal network.

The rise of environment-sharing capabilities also enabled outsourcing firms to diversify their offerings from a single, shared application to a more diverse, and often highly customized, portfolio of applications. Many vendors were quick to seize upon the business model of the full-service-IT-department-for-hire, sensing that significantly greater revenues would accrue to offering customized application environments as opposed to single purpose, or commodity, application services. Based upon current worldwide outsourcing market information from analysts such as IDC and others, the full-service outsourcers appear to have predicted the future with some accuracy.

According to industry analysts, companies worldwide spent approximately $99 billion on outsourcing services in 1998, a figure that the firm expects to grow to more than $151 billion by 2003. Of the broad range of services offered by contemporary outsourcing vendors, single application outsourcing (such as payroll processing, credit card processing, and claims processing) accounts for the greatest share (60 percent) of corporate outsourcing expenditures, but the fastest growing segment is full-service IT outsourcing, which is expected to grow at a compound annual rate of 12.2 percent through the first few years of the new millennium.

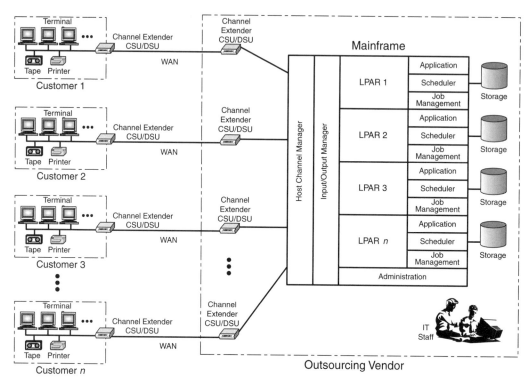

Figure 4–2
Environment or LPAR sharing.

From the earliest time-sharing and service bureau arrangements to today's full service "megadeals," outsourcing remains a fixture on the modern business computing landscape. Two additional innovations in outsourcing technology are important to consider before continuing to the issue of ASPs and outsourcing. These are in situ outsourcing and out-tasking.

IN SITU OUTSOURCING . . . .

The "full service" IT outsourcing approach has traditionally leveraged channel extension and WAN technologies to deliver service across a "split" technology infrastructure. The mainframe platform (or other host system) resides at the outsourcer's facility, while peripheral devices, such as terminals, printers, tape devices, and so forth, are installed at the customer location. One evolution of this model was seen during the outsourcing boom of the late 1980s.

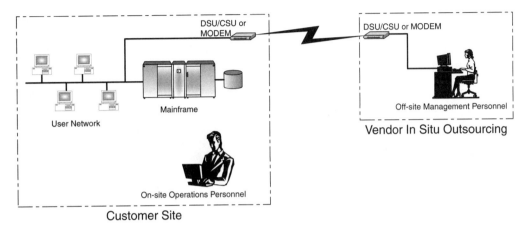

Figure 4–3
An in situ service model.

Weary of supporting their own data centers and IT departments—especially during the difficult financial climate of the day—many prominent companies instead elected to contract out with third parties to provide their internal IT operations. However, under a novel arrangement, IT resources (applications, hardware, networks) remained on-site at the company. Only the *management* of these systems was outsourced.

In these in situ outsourcing contracts (in situ refers to the fact that systems are left in their original place—in the data center environment of the company hiring the outsourcer), IT staff often became employees of the outsourcing agent. As depicted in Figure 4–3, a cadre of operations personnel (often former customer employees) ran the on-premise data center for the customer, while additional outsourcing vendor personnel monitored and managed networks and systems remotely.

It is worth noting a variation on the in situ scheme. In a few cases, companies spun off their IT departments into new companies, then contracted back with them for services. In a few cases, these spin-offs went on to become outsourcing providers for other firms in addition to their parent company.

OUT-TASKING . . . .

Another variant of the traditional outsourcing arrangement is referred to as "outtasking." Popularized in the early 1990s by analysts such as The Yankee Group, outtasking involved the allocation of certain IT processes or functions to outsourcing agents, while retaining internal control of other tasks. According to many industry observers, the use of such "selective outsourcing" can secure increasingly scarce expertise, while surmounting concerns among IT staff regarding layoffs that usually accompany outsourcing discussions.

Outtasking can cover a broad range of services. In some cases, it has become synonymous with a return to the practice of outsourcing a single application. Companies "rediscovered" payroll processing outsourcers, for example, in the late 1990s and began using them again in droves to offload an important but "nonvalue added" task. Doing so cleared the IT schedule of a task that could be performed reliably and cost-effectively by an outside agent, enabling new tasks to be added to the schedule.

In other cases, firms have outtasked resource-intensive functions such as desktop management. Often this is done following an investigation into desktop total-cost-of-ownership (TCO). The TCO analysis reveals that costs could be cut through tighter management, but firms lack the human resources to allocate to the task. The solution is often to hire a contracting party to perform this straightforward, but nontrivial work.

One area in which companies have been quick to use the out-tasking model is Web hosting. According to numerous analysts, the cost savings accrued to utilizing a Web hosting company to implement and host a high-end Web site are significant, as shown in Table 4–1. Other advantages include access to skills that may not exist in-house, improved security, and rapid deployment capabilities that allow companies to "jumpstart" their e-business initiatives. About the only negative aspect of the arrangement that has been cited by companies quoted in the trade press is a lack of flexibility or responsiveness to change. Outtasking Web site design, development, and hosting introduces a layer of bureaucracy that can become a barrier to change. However, few companies are willing to forego the value of outsourced hosting arrangements and to bring Web operations in house just to shave a few days (or hours) off the change management life cycle.

Table 4–1   First-Year Costs for a High-End Web Site

	In-House	**Outsourced**
Hosting fee	—	$42,000
Hardware and software	$27,000	Included
Connectivity	$31,000	Included
Off-site storage	$3,000	Included
Labor	$160,000	Included
Total	**$221,000**	**$42,000**

Many critics of traditional outsourcing have been much more friendly to out-tasking. Some suggest that this variation on the outsourcing theme resolves the inherent problems with the multi-year, all-encompassing, outsourcing agreements of the late 1980s and early 1990s—many of which failed to yield their promised value and, in some cases, led to spectacular failures.

The problems cited with traditional outsourcing arrangements are numerous, but can be distilled into one point: traditional outsourcing has been used by many companies as a cost-cutting strategy that almost invariably failed to produce in practice the theoretical value promised by vendors. One commentator of note, Paul Strassmann, writing in a 1995 *Computerworld* column, "Outsourcing: A Game for Losers," reviewed large-scale traditional outsourcing contracts and determined that advertised benefits simply could not be found in the results experienced by the companies. He said of outsourcing,

> I am in favor of outsourcing to take advantage of somebody else's capacity to accumulate know-how faster than if it remains homegrown. But it shouldn't be applied as an emetic. I will be encouraged about the prospects for outsourcing services when I get a large list of prosperous and growing organizations that have picked this option as a way to enhance their mastery of information management.

Outtasking might just deliver the list of successes that Strassmann and others are seeking, if press accounts are to be believed. Unlike many traditional outsourcing arrangements, outtasking efforts are linked to specific, carefully defined, business goals. Companies do not relinquish control over their "destinies" to their outsourcing providers, but instead share risks and rewards with the providers, utilizing an established, well-defined business objective and well-defined methods for its measurement to monitor progress toward stated goals. Table 4–2 further illuminates the differences between traditional outsourcing and outtasking.

BEYOND MARKET-SPEAK: ASPS AND OUTSOURCING . . . .

The brief survey provided should demonstrate that outsourcing, like ASP, is an imprecise term that describes a spectrum of service offerings. Part of the variability of the term relates to the diversity of corporate computing elements that are most frequently targeted for outsourcing. According to a circa 1997 publication of the Information Technology Association of America (ITAA), these include:

Table 4–2   Traditional Outsourcing and Outtasking Compared

Traditional Outsourcing	Outtasking
DESCRIPTION: Typically a multiyear contract in which a vendor is contracted to manage and operate corporate IT either from a dedicated or shared platform located at the vendor site or in situ at the customer location	**DESCRIPTION:** Variable length contracts with external vendors to provide specific functions, tasks or application services as an adjunct to, or replacement for, internal IT processing
VALUE PROPOSITION STATEMENTS: Yields infrastructure/operations cost savings; resolves staffing issues; enables focus on core business; streamlines management ("one throat to choke"); improves IT quality of service; reduces downtime; and shortens time to market	**VALUE PROPOSITION STATEMENTS:** Enables targeting of internal resources to business-value-add projects Provides enabling solutions keyed to specific objectives and metrics Offloads non-value-add tasks, functions, or applications Supplements capabilities on an as-needed basis
PRIMARY OBJECTIVE: IT budget reduction	**PRIMARY OBJECTIVE:** Realization of a business goal determined by customer
TYPICAL MANAGEMENT VEHICLE: Multiyear contract with service level agreement	**TYPICAL MANAGEMENT VEHICLE:** Risk/reward contract tied to measurable business results
IMPACT ON EXISTING IT ORGANIZATION: Staff layoffs	**IMPACT ON EXISTING IT ORGANIZATION:** Staff retasking

- Operations at data processing facilities, from basic facilities to network services
- Software application development, maintenance, and management
- Business recovery and disaster recovery capabilities
- Desktop management
- Help desk services
- Program management services
- Telecommunications and network operations

Today this list could be appended with at least two additional bullets: Web site hosting, and, with the advent of ASPs, applications hosting and delivery.

In the taxonomy of business technology, ASPs must be classified as members of the "phylum" of outsourcing vendors. ASPs, like their other outsourcing kin, offer to replace certain services typically delivered by in-house IT resources with comparable services delivered from an external source under some sort of contractual arrangement.

Some ASPs share much in common with the single-application processing services—specializing in payroll, credit card, and claims processing—that comprised the earliest forms of outsourcing and that persist today. In other cases, ASP vendors have positioned themselves as the "new economy" cousins of traditional, full-service outsourcing firms, offering comprehensive managed application portfolios (MAPs) or "application infrastructure outsourcing" services, dedicated platforms and resources, and dedicated staff professionals—your basic IT service for hire.

Many observers and analysts claim that, if the latter "infrastructural" ASP model gains customers and credentials, it will compete directly with the offerings of established, full-service outsourcing providers. To many traditional outsourcing vendors, such an assertion constitutes "fightin' words."

ASPs, in the view of some traditional outsourcers, are just that: a kind of snake. From the beginning, some vendors bristled privately at the upstart companies that were steadily encroaching on their turf. Publically, the responses of traditional outsourcing firms to ASPs ranged from philosophical detachment to cautious regard to outright disdain.

As late as 1999, some outsourcing vendors were comforting themselves with the fact that ASPs were not on the "radar" of their client base. "It comes down to a simple point," said Paul Shaughnessy, senior vice president and general manager with Syntacom IT Services in an article appearing in *Solutions Integrator* magazine*. "Of the dozen or so RFPs we [are bidding] right now, I don't see any ASPs in 'best of finals' evaluations. The old, traditional outsourcing model is not going away."

In the same article, John Haworth, vice president of business development and corporate strategy with the business consulting firm KPMG LLP, acknowledged that ASPs did not yet garner the outsourcing "megadeals" that were the mainstay of traditional outsourcing providers, but believed that the time was right for ASPs to begin offering complex products such as ERP. Formerly the head of outsourcing for People-Soft, Haworth worked with KPMG to develop a business plan for its ASP business. "What was missing was the telecommunications backbone for IP switching and the data center components." A joint venture with Qwest Communications in June 1999 filled in the missing pieces of the plan.

Said Haworth, Qwest Cyber.Solutions LLC combined resources from Qwest Communications—including seven "new age" data centers, a fully provisioned net-

*See Jon William Toigo, "Web-Enabled Applications: The Next Wave," *Solutions Integrator,* May 1, 1999.

work IP switching network, and license rights obtained from SAP, PeopleSoft, and Oracle Corporation to host and provide application services to sublicensees—with KPMG's expertise in deploying client/server application suites. This enabled the ASP to deliver, Haworth claimed, "the first example of an end-to-end, go-to-market strategy [for ERP and CRM]."

Haworth noted that Qwest Cyber.Solutions customers are able to "sublicense SAP, PeopleSoft or other applications and obtain the telecommunications and data center services on one monthly bill." He expected the "middle market to be the primary uptake" for the service and observes that the needs of that customer base are served adequately by the templates and methodologies that have been developed by KPMG.

Added Haworth, "The market is bifurcated. [Middle-sized companies] need a rapid implementation scenario: the right amount of [application functionality], and not more than necessary. At the higher end of the market, there is more complexity and a need for more customization. We are capable of playing at the high end, as well, and can leverage our privileged position to compete with high end [traditional integrator/outsourcers] like EDS and IBM."

Syntacom's Shaughnessy, for one, wasn't convinced that ASPs could play in the same space as traditional integrators, "Can you have multiple customers sharing one SAP license? I haven't heard of that. PeopleSoft and Oracle are putting together licenses around the ASP concept. If it makes money, it will drive SAP to do the same.* But even if you have a license to do it, can you do it technically? Can you put multiple customers on one client/server product. We don't think so."

Shaughnessy agreed that the underlying theory of infrastructure outsourcing via the Web is very similar to the traditional outsourcing model, with the key difference being a dependence on a WAN, or the Internet, to provide the interconnect between customer and remote data center. In his view, the test of the viability of complex application outsourcing using an ASP would be application response time and privacy guarantees, "I have big questions about service levels and security."

He noted that the template-based implementation strategy of ASPs offering ERP, MRP, and CRM applications is commonplace in traditional outsourcing arrangements, facilitating rapid application deployment. However, he compared the use of this method as an ASP service offering with "a bait-and-switch tactic." He observed that most companies, presented with a "pure vanilla" ERP implementation, would quickly discover the need for more customized features and functions.

"Once they begin asking for the customization they need," Shaughnessy argued, the original value proposition—"a fixed monthly fee including hardware, software, installation, hosting, and so forth"—would go right out the window.

---

*SAP announced at CeBIT in February 2000 that it planned to field an "application hosting" business unit by second quarter 2000.

Jeff Wagner, director of product management with SunGard Computer Services, Inc., agreed with Shaughnessy's assessment in the 1998 article, but was not as quick to dismiss the issues associated with service delivery via the Web. "In a traditional outsourcing model, we have more control over the performance of the network. We can detect problems and commit to a service level agreement. Even with private transit paths through the Internet, you are talking about a lot of hops. You can lose control over network performance and applications can take a hit."

Even in late 1998, however, Wagner foresaw that the ASP model offered potential benefits that SunGard might "want to offer eventually." (SunGard did, in fact, enter the ASP market as a service provider in 2000.) He pointed out that his company joined the ASP Industry Consortium in order to participate actively in the standards development process. The lack of standards and best practices in ASP services, noted Wagner and many other observers, had to be addressed before ASPs will be truly ready to compete with traditional outsourcers.

Then Consortium chairman Traver Gruen-Kennedy observed that standards-making efforts within the Consortium focused on management methods and best practices, "There is a need for the certification of ASP practices. Ernst and Young and Deloitte and Touche are already offering best practice audits. We will be looking at selection criteria, quality of service agreements, availability guarantees, and service level agreements. In time, we'll take it up another notch to the level of an ISO standard."

Until this happens, Shaughnessy said, "ASP [infrastructure outsourcing] is just another new, different and sexy concept. I don't think that the CIO is going to bet his mission critical applications on the ASP model."

The criticisms of the ASP model raised by outsourcers in the late 1990s have largely disappeared from discussions surrounding current generation ASPs—mainly because most outsourcers have themselves gotten into the ASP business. However, the concerns raised by outsourcers—regarding the functional adequacy of applications offered by ASPs, about the security and service levels available from the ASP model, about the dearth of best practices and real standards for delivering applications as a service, and about the efficacy of the ASP model as a means to service customers not blessed with close proximity to high bandwidth networks—remain central to the debate around the viability of ASPs going forward.

LESSONS FROM OUTSOURCING . . . .

From the earlier discussion and from the viewpoints expressed in this chapter, it is clear that traditional outsourcing and modern ASPs share many characteristics in common. This, in turn, supports the contention that the past experience of companies who used traditional outsourcing arrangements may yield insights of value to businesses that are considering the use of ASPs today. Some recurring axioms about outsourcing generally that have special relevance to ASPs include the following:

- *Outsourcing is rarely a long-term cost-saving solution.* Among other things, there is a management cost that must be borne by companies choosing to outsource: between 7 to 9 percent of the outsourcing contract amount annually, according to one analyst. Companies that have been successful with outsourcing are those that have leveraged the option to achieve other goals than simple cost savings. Companies embracing ASPs might be best served by looking beyond purported cost savings to justify and set expectations for the relationship.

- *Outsourcing is not a "fire-and-forget" strategy.* Contract management is required to ensure that guaranteed service levels are being provided and that the outsourced services are constantly adapted to meet changing business requirements. Service level agreement monitoring is extremely important in ASP arrangements as well, but mechanisms for effective performance monitoring are still in their nascent stages. Moreover, changes made by customers to more complex ASP solution offerings may dramatically restructure contract pricing. These points are acknowledged by most analysts and are viewed as an impediment that must be surmounted before ASPs are truly ready for business "primetime."

- *Just as out-tasking is preferred to full-service IT outsourcing in many cases, so too might companies profit from utilizing ASP services to provide "point replacement" for selected applications—at least, initially.* Outsourcing processes (such as payroll) that are reasonably straightforward, but that have high internal maintenance requirements to qualified service providers, have proven beneficial to many organizations. This approach to ASP contracting may provide comparable benefits: enabling IT organizations to focus staff resources on other productive work, while building confidence in, and testing the adequacy of, ASP services.

- *Outsourcing has never proven to be the panacea that advocates (particularly vendor marketing organizations) claimed.* An inefficient or ill-defined business process is not improved through outsourcing, nor does the underlying process simply go away. Veterans of outsourcing arrangements agree universally that only those processes that are known to deliver on their underlying business value proposition should even be considered for outsourcing. So, too, with application outsourcing via ASPs: depending on an ASP to provide an application does not fix underlying problems in either the application or how it is used to deliver value within an organization.

- *Outsourcing can capitalize on capabilities of the vendor that do not exist in the business IT organization or its technology infrastructure.* In the past, companies have benefited tremendously from the outsourcing vendor's high-availability provisions, for example. They are able to leverage the outsourcing vendor's disaster recovery capabilities, such as network and system redundancies, mirroring across multiple data centers, and so forth, to achieve higher levels of uninterrupted processing than they could achieve with their own resources. Good outsourcing vendors also provide redundant and fault-tolerant networks, sophisticated internal and external security provisions, and other features that, though important to corporate IT organizations, are often beyond their budgets. In some cases, these services are offered to customers as an additional feature of their existing contracts; in other cases, they must be purchased separately as "add-ons." An old saying, popular among carpenters, holds that the craftsman always purchases the best tool he can afford. The same holds true for outsourcing and ASP deals: if value-add capabilities are available, companies should purchase all the capabilities that they can afford.

- *The trend in outsourcing agreements is toward "shared risk and reward."* In such arrangements, contract performance and vendor payment is tied to clearly identified and measurable results. Few (if any) of today's ASPs feature "shared risk and reward" agreements, though some vendors do offer compensation in the form of billing adjustments if stated performance guarantees are not met (this is small consolation if downtime or reduced performance loses the client customers or market opportunities!). Before utilizing the services of an ASP (or any other outsourcing company), business decision makers must weight the risks, identify suitable indicators of contract performance, then haggle for the best possible deal with the provider keyed to the benefits expected from the arrangement. (A more detailed discussion of ASP contracts is provided later in this book.)

Most of these are commonsense observations drawn from the record of traditional outsourcing that can be applied to ASPs, as well. They reflect the common heritage of traditional outsourcing and ASPs in time-sharing and resource sharing architectures and offer a way of thinking about ASPs that builds on experiential wisdom rather than marketing hype.

However, ASPs are also substantively different from other types of outsourcing arrangements. Other lessons for utilizing ASP services effectively to achieve business goals will need to be derived over time from the actual experience of companies with ASPs themselves.

A key area of difference between ASPs and traditional application outsourcing is, according to Oracle.com Pesident, Timothy Chou and others (see sidebar), the software offered by the ASP itself. In Chou's view, traditional outsourcing and systems integration has sought to "cobble together" multiple software products into a customized platform suited to the specifications of an individual client. "True" ASPs, by contrast, endeavor to deliver a more "generic" solution—one that meets the needs of most businesses without significant customization to the needs of any one customer.

What constitutes "significant customization" is a much-debated point and merits some additional discussion here.

CUSTOMIZATION AND ASPS . . . .

A current dictum of many ASP advocates is that the greater the extent to which applications are customized, the less suited they are to ASP delivery. This is the basis of the sharp distinction drawn by Chou and others between "true" ASPs and many of the current generation of "self-styled" ASP vendors.

The true ASP, according to Chou and others, takes an approach that departs significantly from traditional full-service outsourcing (or even modern Web hosting) solutions. If comparisons must be made to outsourcing at all, advocates grudgingly prefer the correlation of true ASP services to older time-sharing/service bureau outsourcing arrangements, rather than full-service IT "megadeals."

True ASPs enable the sharing of an application among multiple customers (or tenants), rather than offering the custom development of an application and hardware platform for each individual client. Armed with "multitenant" software, true ASPs can capitalize on the economies-of-scale that this delivery model enables. In fact, the true ASP vendor derives profit as a function of reducing "operational overhead costs" by reusing staff and platform resources (e.g., systems and networks) in supporting multiple customers.

Even though per contract pricing information is not forthcoming from ASPs, it may be assumed that the closer an ASP comes to delivering services under a multi-tenancy, shared-platform model, the greater its profit margin. This assumption is supported in the public discussions within the ASP community regarding business profitability. Numerous analysts and vendors have repeatedly stressed that those ASPs that do not capitalize on the shared resource approach will see profits decline as more and more customers are added to their service. This is the logical outcome, familiar to traditional outsourcers, of having to add staff and resources (with all of their managerial requirements) each time a system is built for a new customer.

According to Chou and others, many first generation ASPs have not embraced the multitenancy, shared resource model and operate instead using a dedicated resource model that is very similar to full-service IT outsourcing. As a result, they must dedicate staff and infrastructure to customized solutions offered on a per client basis, increasing costs of operation significantly with each new customer.

This explains why many early ASPs are realizing limited profits from their efforts. Like the traditional full-service outsourcing vendor, many early ASPs operate a "margin" business: once all costs to support the customer are calculated, the traditional outsourcing vendor seeks to realize a marginal profit in the range of 7 to 12 percent on a contract. ASPs that must dedicate staff and hosting platforms to each customer account—and, more importantly, that customize applications to each client's specifications—have seen their profit margins decline as more customers sign up for service.

To what extent can applications be customized without disrupting the ASP business model? Vendors are currently struggling for a definitive answer. Much has to do with the design of the software itself. One ASP offers a simple guidance, which it applies in its own service offering: Any customization is too much customization if it causes a disruption of service when routine software patches and upgrades are applied. This definition is problematic at best, according to critics. Not only are "routine" patches and upgrades notorious for causing system disruptions, whether applications have been customized or not, but also the only way to test the potential disruptive impact of customization is to apply the software patch or upgrade. Moreover, each patch or upgrade can pose an entirely different set of conflicts within the customized environment of the client.

It should also be pointed out that comparatively few ASP software offerings are designed for ASP delivery in any case. Only through the use of middleware and operating system extensions can many applications be shared on a multitenancy basis. Applications fielded to customers by ASPs in this way are, by their nature, "customized environments."

Over time, as the requirements for offering application services via the ASP model become better understood, the software industry will deliver products that are increasingly ASP-ready. For now, however, the ASP industry continues to struggle with the question of customization and with the limitations, familiar to traditional outsourcers, that it imposes on profitability.

APPLICATION SERVICE DELIVERY: THE NETWORK IS THE KEY . . . .

From the end user's perspective, the shared versus dedicated resource approaches of current generation ASPs, and the importance of customization of applications, may yield important criteria for choosing between the services of different vendors.

Another component that cannot be ignored—and one that separates ASPs from their traditional outsourcing cousins—is the network.

Communications links have always served a role in outsourcing. For the most part, data communications established the information "umbilical" between the business and its outsourcing vendor. Durable point-to-point WAN connections provided the means for delivering input to and/or receiving output from the vendor service platform.

Data communications links were originally one of the most expensive components of the outsourcing arrangements. For obvious reasons, companies sought redundancy in these links so that data processing support would not disappear as the result of a line cut or other natural or man-made disruption.

Even when vendors began to avail themselves of shared, third-party network services (such as Frame Relay services from major interexchange carriers) or built their own networks (typically using facilities leased from telephone companies), the costs for fault tolerant data communications remained high. As a result, most firms contented themselves with a simple data communications networking capability. They focused on establishing fault-tolerant connections between the home office and the outsourcing vendor, sometimes with additional connections to a large branch office and/or an external entity, such as the Federal Reserve Bank in the case of certain financial institutions.

The point is that prohibitive networking costs and limited network service availability through much of the latter half of the 20th Century helped to limit the scope and focus of business-related networking generally and the networking component of outsourcing in particular. The "arrival" of the Internet in the late 1990s changed everything.

There is substantial evidence that business desired to do more with data networking prior to the advent of the Internet and World Wide Web. There were numerous, mostly unsuccessful, efforts to define standards for *electronic data interchange* (EDI), which would enable the information systems of two or more businesses to interoperate with little or no human intervention. The promise of such a technology for improving the efficiency of manufacturing supply chain processes was enormous. EDI was touted by advocates as a replacement for redundant data entry functions, a major step toward the paperless office, and even as a bulwark of the environmental movement and the preservation of rain forests. The high cost of networking, however, was as much an inhibitor of EDI as were the conflicts between groups advancing different EDI methods.

With the arrival of Web technology, on which the ASP model is based, many networking alternatives considered too expensive in traditional outsourcing are now becoming increasingly available. Although some current ASPs utilize the Internet, or virtual private networks (VPNs) "tunneled" through the Internet, as a means to deliver application interfaces to end users, many continue to use private networks to connect vendors to customers. Regardless of the physical medium employed, it is important to keep in mind that the underlying technology for application delivery is almost always Web technology.

Web technology enables the use of both public and private networks to connect users to an ASP service. One significant outcome of this fact is that it facilitates business-to-business data communications on a broader basis and at a lower cost than were previously possible or practical with traditional outsourcing arrangements. In the future, ASPs will leverage these capabilities on an increasing basis to realize the vision of the EDI advocates of a decade ago.

Traditional outsourcers, too, will likely harness Web technology to diversify the networking possibilities for their clients. Many are already doing so in response to the "e-business" trend and the influence it has had on client requirements. For now, however, "new economy" ASPs can (and do) distinguish themselves from most "old economy" traditional outsourcers by virtue of their network-based delivery model and Web technology-based infrastructure. The ability to streamline business-to-business communications between a client company and its business partners is, in the final analysis, a key component of the business value proposition of ASPs and, for now at least, a key differentiator between ASPs and other outsourcing models.

CONCLUSION . . . .

The song lyric "everything old is new again" may be used to describe ASPs. In one sense, the ASP model is very similar to time-sharing and resource sharing outsourcing models, which have existed for decades. That this pedigree has generated so much pointless debate and umbrage at industry conferences and in the trade press may be testimony to the triumph of marketing spin over reasonable discourse, or it may be something else.

By all accounts, ASPs are a form of outsourcing and business decision makers can capitalize on the experience of companies that have used outsourcing service providers in the past to help them evaluate the fit for ASP services with their IT strategies. This conclusion is, at the same time, straightforward and complex.

Obviously, ASPs bring to the table a value proposition that is similar in many ways, but not all, to traditional outsourcing arrangements. However, the increasing availability of ASP-ready software and Web technology–based business-to-business networking capabilities enable significant improvements over earlier full-service IT outsourcing offerings.

Although important, this distinction does not justify or explain the reproach of some vendors at the suggestion of commonality between ASPs and other outsourcing arrangements. Could it be that some ASPs resist the comparison for another reason altogether?

ORACLE.COM PRESIDENT TIMOTHY CHOU: THE FUNDAMENTAL ISSUE OF ASP IS SOFTWARE DELIVERY

Timothy Chou, President Oracle.com, Oracle's Online Services business, views ASPs as a significant departure from traditional outsourcing services. The confusion between the two, he says, is the result of how some early ASPs have tried to adapt applications that were not designed for delivery via the ASP model for delivery across a network. For the ASP model to succeed, he notes, several requirements must be met.

"First, the software itself must be reliable," Chou notes, stating that software defects and delivery interruptions have the potential for becoming front-page news that could bode ill for the ASP industry as a whole. Reliability, says Chou, results from reducing the number of "moving parts" in the software. "Cobbling reduces reliability, so the less cobbling together of different software components, the more reliable the application is."

Chou summarizes the second requirement for successful ASP software delivery as "more utility and less chrome." In the past, he notes, the software business was "a feature/function business"—in effect, vendors emphasized the broad array of functionality that enabled software to be heavily customized to an end user's requirements. Chou says that the movement needs to be away from feature/function and toward "utility." "People need to think about reliability and scalability," he says.

A third requirement for ASP success, he says, is related to the above. "Software itself must be architected for delivery in this model. People have been taking old client-server software and trying to cram it into an Internet delivery model." New ASP applications need to be highly manageable, and they need to take advantage of the economies of scale derived from shared resources.

Customizing each and every application to meet the needs of individual customers is prohibitively expensive for vendors in the long run, according to Chou. It also slows solution delivery to the customer. Chou borrows the fourth requirement for ASP success from the *Star Trek* movie dictum: "The needs of the many must outweigh the needs of the few or the one." The software offered by ASPs must be roughly the same for every customer, so that "a fix that is made to the software benefits everyone, not just an individual customer." Chou admits, "this is hugely different from what software vendors have done in the past." It is also different from the mind-set of traditional outsourcing, which approached service delivery with a consultative approach intended to facilitate customization.

Chou contrasts Oracle.com, Oracle's Online Services business, with USinternetworking (Usi), suggesting that the competitor is closer to being a traditional outsourcer than an ASP.

> Let's say that a customer wants to rearchitect for the new economy. USi, with its consultative background, will work with the customer to identify software components for a solution. They look like a traditional consultant, offering a cobbled solution following a consulting engagement of 50 to 100 days. Their expertise in resolving any problems or questions that arise is problematic. How do they identify and fix software bugs? They take fix requests from the customer and send them to the software companies. The customer waits while the software companies attempt to resolve the issues. [The cobbled solution approach] lacks systems management functionality and substitutes problem reporting.

Chou contrasts the approach to Oracle.com services, "We offer the customer an ebusiness suite from Oracle. The components of the suite are good enough to meet customer needs, plus they are integrated, which solves many problems. When the customer has a problem, we offer one call support: the customer is talking to the guy who built the software. Bugs are resolved more quickly."

Chou says that the benefits of this approach to application software delivery far outweigh its purported deficits, "We tell our customers that they might be able to get better pieces (individual applications), but not a better overall solution. We are integrated inside, not by a consultant."

Oracle.com is currently considering relationships with vendors of data center facilities to host its applications, noting that there is no shortage of "commoditized, high-quality real estate available." Chou says that the company will ultimately offer between 10 and 20 data centers—"the sweet spot for ASP service delivery."

He says that Oracle Business OnLine's formal introduction in late 1998, which has since been renamed Oracle.com, does not reflect Oracle's interest in ASPs, which dates back four years to the company's work in developing a reference standard for the Network Computer, an unsuccessful thin client replacement for WINTEL PCs. "People mistook the Network Computer as the architecture. The architecture is where we are today: fat servers and thin clients. People named the architecture ASPs about two years ago."

Given their long heritage, traditional outsourcing providers have developed to a mature form a set of best practices and procedures that are currently absent in nascent ASPs. These standards and practices, as much as underlying technology infrastructures and resources, make possible the formulation of measurable service guarantees that form the basis for well-defined service level agreements (SLAs). Meaningful SLAs are also largely missing from ASPs in this early stage of development, as are techniques for measuring service levels and reporting them to customers.

SLAs do not guarantee performance, of course. But, they hold the vendor's "feet to the fire" and provide a legal basis for the redress of customer complaints in the event that service levels decline over time.

The somewhat excessive objections registered by some ASP advocates at the mention of traditional outsourcing in connection with the ASP model brings to mind a Shakespearean observation about those who protest too much. Often the noisy protest is intended to distract attention from other significant matters.

Ultimately ASPs will need to provide a body of standards and practices and a set of service level guarantees similar to those that have evolved within the traditional IT outsourcing space if they are to obtain the widespread acceptance of the business community.

5

The Contemporary ASP Market: Vendors, Intermediaries, and Aggregators

In this chapter...

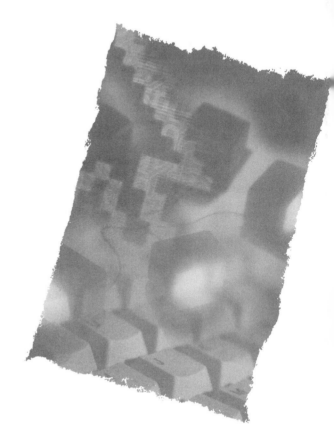

Understanding the Application Service Provisioning model can be an enormous challenge for business persons—especially given the often confusing trade press reports and inconsistent marketing claims made by ASP vendors, both when describing their own services and when differentiating them from the services of competitors.

The preceding chapters sought to address this challenge by examining the historical and technological context from which ASPs have emerged. Major themes and conclusions included the following:

- ASP is not a rigorously defined concept. Within the somewhat self-serving definitions set forth by analysts and vendors, there is plenty of room to maneuver. The essential proposition of the ASP model is straightforward: ASP vendors deliver applications to corporate and individual end users via a network for a contracted fee. The type of application, the architecture of the hosting system and network, and the terms of the service agreement vary widely from one ASP to another. This variability can lead to considerable confusion about ASPs from an end user perspective, and can make the selection of an ASP a complicated procedure.

- Despite claims to the contrary, ASPs are a logical evolution of traditional application delivery models that have been employed within business since the inception of corporate DP. ASP vendors are harnessing the same technologies and architectures that have developed over time to serve application delivery requirements within corporate IT. The ASP is merely providing the service on an outsourced basis.

- ASPs are part of a spectrum of service offerings collectively referred to as outsourcing services. ASPs may be differentiated from other outsourcing arrangements in two ways. First, they increasingly utilize "ASP-ready" applications: applications designed for "multi-tenant" or "shared use" operation—with a minimum of customization per tenant. Second, they typically harness Web technology, both in their hosting environments and in their network-based delivery approach. These characteristics help to distinguish ASPs from other outsourcing methods, but do not represent a revolutionary break with the past. Much of the experience of companies that have utilized traditional outsourcing arrangements in the past is relevant to the evaluation of ASPs, as well. Moreover, ASPs can learn much from their traditional outsourcing "cousins" with respect to business practices and SLAs.

Having established a context for understanding the ASP phenomenon, this chapter turns its focus toward a more detailed examination of ASPs themselves and of the industry that has emerged around the ASP value proposition. The objective of this chapter is to enable business readers to formulate criteria for comparing and selecting ASP services that are appropriate to a company's needs from among a field of competitors.

The current who's who of ASPs comprises a wide range of companies that include:

- ISPs and Web hosting firms that seek to generate additional revenue by offering software services
- Traditional outsourcing companies that are "hanging out an ASP shingle" in order to capitalize on the attention surrounding ASPs in the trade press
- ISVs that are seeking new distribution models and improved market share

These firms offer application and, in some cases, other *infrastructure* services—such as desktop management, help desk outsourcing, or remote storage services—on a subscription basis to their corporate and/or individual clients. Infrastructure services correlate to the IT service model introduced in the first chapter of this book. (If you skipped the chapter, which was aimed at those who possess a limited knowledge of IT, and you do not understand what an IT infrastructure is, it might be beneficial to go back and to scan the chapter quickly before proceeding.)

The list of players in the ASP industry can be expanded readily to include two additional groups. One group comprises a cadre of analysts and consultants who represent themselves as *intermediaries* between business and the ASP market. For a fee, these firms assess corporate requirements and recommend the services of specific ASPs to meet company needs. In some cases, they may be involved in the actual integration of the ASP with business processes.

A second group, which has appeared comparatively recently within the ASP industry, expands upon the intermediary role. These firms, sometimes referred to as *aggregators*, endeavor to "package" the offerings of multiple ASP vendors into a readily accessible form, such as a *portal* service. These portals "integrate" the service offerings of several ASPs in ways that are believed to meet a set of application service requirements that are common to a subset of prospective business customers.

Aggregators may focus their offerings on a particular vertical market—health care, for example—and offer a set of ASP services from different vendors to provide a "one-stop-shop" for their target customer base.

No overview of the ASP industry would be complete without including a reference to the various organizations that are engaged in efforts to create standards and to define best practices for the industry as a whole. The ASP Industry Consortium, as well as vendor-specific ASP certification programs, is contributing much to the effort to obtain for ASPs the credibility and presence that are required for ultimate success.

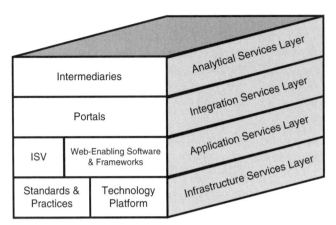

Figure 5–1
A model of the ASP industry.

Figure 5–1 provides a simple model of the current ASP industry. Even though various analysts and observers may assign different names, acronyms, segmentations, and meanings to the components of this model, this chart enables a straightforward basis for discussion here.

INFRASTRUCTURE SERVICES LAYER . . . .

The infrastructure services layer of the model presented in Figure 5–1 is the foundation of the ASP offering. It has two primary building blocks: a technology platform—including storage, servers, networks, and a cadre of experienced operations personnel—and a set of industry standards & best practices—a less tangible, but equally important component.

The technology platform of an ASP may or may not be under the direct control of the ASP vendor itself. As previously explained, some ASPs obtain their storage, server, and network infrastructure—collectively referred to as the ASP platform—on a contract basis from third parties. Those that do typically stress the value of leveraging the capabilities and skills of seasoned infrastructure providers as a guarantor of quality. ASPs that do not utilize third-party infrastructure providers tend to decry the practice as an invitation to calamity and a sure road to "finger pointing" if a service interruption of some sort occurs.

Figure 5–2 depicts a simplified technology platform for application hosting, one used by many ASPs. The details of this infrastructure are examined in greater detail

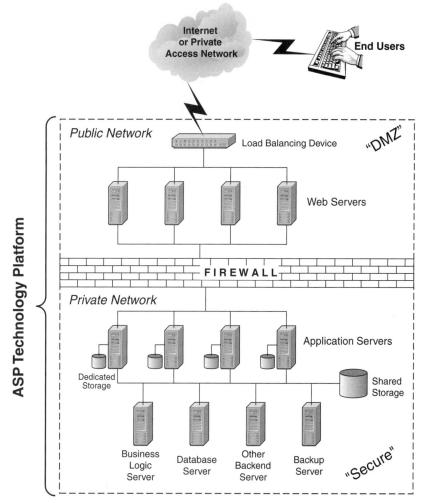

Figure 5–2
Simplified ASP platform.

later in the book. For now, it is useful to see the functional contributions provided by the various components.

As shown in Figure 5–2, a simple application hosting environment consists of public and private network components. Private network components are shielded from access by the public network (whether the Internet or a private network connecting the ASP to end users) by being placed behind "firewalls"—devices that mask internal server addresses from the outside world. On the public side of the firewall, called the demilitarized zone or DMZ, Web servers present the application interface from the protected application servers to the end user. That is, the Web server receives input from the end user, forwards it to the application server, then receives responses from the application server, and forwards application responses to the end user.

To facilitate multiple, concurrent accesses to, sometimes called "sessions" with, the hosted application, several "mirrored" Web servers may be set up in the DMZ. In such a configuration, the distribution of end user sessions (called collectively "the load") among the Web server may be managed by a Web load balancing device. Requests for sessions by end users are received by the Web load balancing device, which checks to see how busy each of the Web servers are, then routes the traffic to the least busy server. This technique is often used to enhance the end user experience with the hosted application.

The ASP Web servers typically are not the actual hosts of the applications to which they are providing access. The application hosts are often placed behind the firewall in the private network of the ASP. There, the application servers can work to process application requests in relative safety from malicious attacks by virus programs and hackers.

The application servers, too, may be replicated and/or mirrored and load balanced to facilitate multiple, simultaneous end user sessions. Moreover, the application servers may be interconnected with database servers, business logic servers, or other "back end" systems, depending on the nature of the application that is being hosted.

Also, the application hosting environment may feature either a dedicated or shared storage infrastructure. Dedicated storage means just that: a disk drive, array of disk drives, or network of disk drives are associated with a particular application server exclusively to store the application itself and end user data. In a dedicated configuration, this data storage is not shared among multiple application servers or by multiple ASP customers.

Shared storage infrastructures, by contrast, comprise large disk drive arrays or storage device networks that are configured to be shared among multiple applications or ASP customers. The advantages and disadvantages of shared and dedicated storage are discussed in a later chapter.

Additional servers may be present in the private network of the ASP technology platform to provide specific functions such as data backup, application server management, or security. Management and administration servers, like storage, may comprise a shared or dedicated service of the ASP.

Figure 5–2 depicts the ASP platform as a collection of standalone system and network devices. This is done only to add clarity for a functional evaluation. In point of fact, ASP platforms may be entirely contained ("rack mounted") within a 19-inch wide cabinet about as deep as a home refrigerator. Rack-mounted hosting platforms resemble, to a great extent, a component stereo system, elegant and simple from the front view, but a morass of many short patch cables (used to interconnect components) when viewed from the back.

It should also be mentioned that some of the individual components depicted in the drawing may actually be integrated within a single unit. Web servers, for example, may be equipped with integral firewalls.

Companies that visit a modern application hosting data center are often shocked by the fact that their most business-critical applications can be hosted in a space no larger than a walk-in closet. Many ASPs offer hosting in a "cage"—a raised-floor area surrounded, literally, by wire mesh or chain link fencing—rather like a small lock-up at a local self-storage rental facility!

Of course, the spartan design of the application hosting data center typically conceals a great deal of shared technology ranging from a complex, high-speed, internal network; a set of technologies to support access to the data center via the Internet, VPNs, or dedicated access lines; and, in some cases, a back-end storage area network or other networked storage infrastructure. These shared infrastructure technologies, plus the trained personnel who maintain both the shared infrastructure and the customer-specific hosting platforms, provide a significant part of the value proposition of ASP.

While on the subject of personnel, it should be noted that some ASPs dedicate a cadre of support personnel to a specific customer, others to a specific application software offering, and still others share personnel across all customers and applications. The closer an ASP is able to move to a "share everything"(e.g., personnel and infrastructure) model, the more it realizes economies of scale (and profits) in its own operations. If resources are dedicated by the ASP on a customer-by-customer basis, the ASP itself may soon encounter the staffing resource constraints that have driven many customers to its doorstep.

Much has been made by various ASPs of the shared-versus-dedicated resources model issue. Vendors frequently use their resource model as a discriminator by linking it to service quality. For example, if a vendor offers a "dedicated resource solution" to its customers (i.e., provisions a separate hosting platform for each customer, with separate storage and separate support personnel), it may argue that customers receive a higher quality of service than they would from a competitor who shares platforms and personnel among multiple customers. On the surface, this argument makes sense to many business decision makers, who view the business value of the solution in terms of:

- *Affinity:* Dedicated support staff are more knowledgeable about the customer's special requirements.
- *Security:* The share-nothing solution seems to afford greater safety to the customer's mission critical applications, protecting data from corruption

by another company's errant processes or potentially virus-laden data transfers.

- *Accountability:* Resolving any problems that arise should be more straightforward in a share-nothing environment.

The facts, however, may not align with these assumptions. Most ASPs, in fact, share critical network resources, management and monitoring functions, and administration tasks across multiple customers even when hosting platforms are located in separate cages. Moreover, there is an increasing trend within ASPs to build shared storage configurations that offer virtual, as opposed to physical, segregation of the data of one company from the data of another. This configuration is much easier to manage and represents, in the case of USinternetworking and others who have embraced it, a value to the customer. Also, if sharing affords greater economies of scale to the vendor, some of this savings may be passed along to the customer.

The point is that shared-resource environments can offer just as much customer affinity, security, and accountability value as segregated environments. In addition to numerous technology-based justifications for this view, there is also a case to be made that standards and practices provide the actual value of any service solution.

Standards and practices are the second building block of the infrastructure services layer shown in Figure 5–1. What are standards and practices?

Standards come in three types: formal, de jure, and de facto. Formal IT standards comprise detailed technical guidelines, usually articulated and codified by some recognized industry standards body, and are used as a way to establish uniformity in an specific area of technology development. Table 5–1 provides a partial list of formal technology standards organizations and their key interest areas.

Numerous formal technology standards may apply to an ASP solution. For example, the cabling assemblies used to interconnect servers in the ASP vendor's network may comply with formal standards specified by EIA, ANSI, and IEEE, while the servers themselves may comply with standards articulated for computer systems by ACM and IEEE.

The standards "alphabet soup" becomes even more dense where networks are involved. The ASP vendor's internal TCP/IP network may use an IETF-compliant software stack and operate across an ANSI-compliant Ethernet network interconnect. The WAN that is used to connect the end user to the ASP service may be provided by the public Internet (IETF-governed), or it may use any of a number of signaling protocols standardized internationally by the ITU.

Not all technology standards are finalized in time for their use. In some cases, de jure standards are created based on the work of a cooperative group or committee of experts to serve until such time as formal standards are available.

Table 5–1   Partial List of Technology Bodies

Standards Body	Areas of Interest	Web Presence
American National Standards Institute (ANSI)	Founded in 1918, ANSI is a voluntary organization composed of over 1,300 members (including all the large computer companies) that creates standards for the computer industry. In addition to programming languages, ANSI sets standards for a wide range of technical areas, from electrical specifications to communications protocols. For example, FDDI, the main set of protocols for sending data over fiber optic cables, is an ANSI standard.	*www.ansi.org/*
Association for Computing Machinery (ACM)	Founded in 1947, the ACM is an organization composed of U.S. computer professionals that publishes information relating to computer science, holds seminars, and creates and promotes computer standards.	*www.acm.org/*
Electronic Industries Association (EIA)	A trade association representing the U.S. high-technology community. It began in 1924 as the Radio Manufacturers Association. The EIA sponsors a number of activities on behalf of its members, including conferences and trade shows. In addition, it has been responsible for developing some important standards, such as the RS-232, RS-422, and RS-423 standards for connecting serial devices.	*www.eia.org/*

(continued)

Table 5–1   *Continued*

Standards Body	Areas of Interest	Web Presence
International Organization for Standardization (ISO)	ISO is not an acronym; instead, the name derives from the Greek word *iso*, which means equal. Founded in 1946, ISO is an international organization composed of national standards bodies from over 75 countries. For example, ANSI (American National Standards Institute) is a member of ISO. ISO has defined a number of important computer standards, the most significant of which is perhaps OSI (Open Systems Interconnection), a standardized architecture for designing networks.	*www.iso.ch/welcome.html*
International Telecommunication Union (ITU)	ITU is an intergovernmental organization through which public and private organizations develop telecommunications. The ITU was founded in 1865 and became a United Nations agency in 1947. It is responsible for adopting international treaties, regulations, and standards governing telecommunications. The standardization functions were formerly performed by a group within the ITU called Comité Consultatif International Téléphonique et Télégraphique (CCITT), but after a 1992 reorganization the CCITT no longer exists as a separate body.	*www.itu.int*

Table 5-1 *Continued*

Standards Body	Areas of Interest	Web Presence
Internet Engineering Task Force (IETF)	The main standards organization for the Internet, the IETF is a large, open international community of network designers, operators, vendors, and researchers concerned with the evolution of the Internet architecture and the smooth operation of the Internet. It is open to any interested individual.	*www.ietf.org/*
Institute of Electrical and Electronics Engineers (IEEE)	Founded in 1884, the IEEE is an organization composed of engineers, scientists, and students. The IEEE is best known for developing standards for the computer and electronics industry. In particular, the IEEE 802 standards for LANs are widely followed.	*computer.org/* and *www.ieee.org/*

In some cases, the absence of a formal standard is viewed by hardware and software vendors as a license to field their own technologies, and by virtue of market adoption trends, to declare their proprietary technologies to be a de facto standard in the industry. A notable software de facto standard throughout the 1980s and 1990s was Microsoft's Windows operating system, which, at its high point, was installed on nearly 89 percent of corporate PCs.

Except for when a de facto standard derives from the legitimate market share leadership position enjoyed by a vendor, formal "open" standards are preferred to de facto or de jure standards. The use of open standards-based technologies facilitates integration and interoperation between the components offered by different manufacturers. The use of standards-based technologies should be stressed in the evaluation of ASP service offerings.

In addition to standards compliance, ASPs technology infrastructure services can also be discriminated from one another based on their adherence to industry "best practices." Best practices identify the optimal implementation and uses of particular technologies. These practices, which are a focal point of development currently within the ASP Industry Consortium and elsewhere, are eventually documented and shared among technical experts involved in operational use of technologies.

It should be mentioned that, since 1987, the International Standards Organization has been working to formalize best practices in the area of management and quality assurance. Although the vast majority of ISO standards are highly specific to a particular product, material, or process, ISO 9000 is known as a generic management system standard.

According to ISO, "generic" means that the same standards can be applied to any organization, large or small, whatever its product of service, and whatever the sector of activity in which the organization operates, including business or government. The term "management system" refers to what the organization does to manage its processes or its activities. The larger the organization, and the more people involved, the greater the likelihood that documented procedures exist, and that forms and records are used to provide a definition of tasks and of those responsible for performing them, and of the technique or method for performing and verifying the completion of tasks.

Typically such management systems are developed by companies to superimpose order in the manner by which the organization goes about its business, so that time, money, and other resources are utilized efficiently.

Management system standards provide the organization with a model to follow in setting up and operating the management system. This model incorporates the features that experts in the field have agreed upon as representing the state of the art. Thus, a management system that follows the model—or "conforms to the standard"— is built on a firm foundation of state-of-the-art business practices.

Large organizations, or ones with complicated processes—including ASPs— would probably not function well without management systems. ISO, through the 9000 series of standards, has endeavored to capture these best practices in the form of generic standards that are made available to all organizations.

Various data center outsourcing organizations, including IBM, have obtained ISO 9000 certification for their operations management approach. This certification suggests that the vendor's operations have met criteria established by ISO in the 9000 standards family, and have been deemed, therefore, to be of high quality. However, this connection may not have much meaning within the context of vendor selection.

The operations of an "ISO 9000 certified" ASP may or may not be of high quality, and the ISO stresses on its Web site that it isn't backing vendor claims either way. ISO itself does not carry out assessments to check that its standards are being implemented by users in conformity with specified requirements. "Conformity assessment—as this process is known—is," according to ISO, "a matter for suppliers and their clients in the private sector, and of regulatory bodies when ISO standards have been incorporated into public legislation."

There are, of course, many testing laboratories and certification bodies that offer independent (also known as "third party") conformity assessment services to provide confirmation that products (including hardware, software, and processed materials), services, or systems measure up to ISO standards *as they interpret them* from guides published by ISO. According to ISO, such certification authorities may perform these services "under a mandate to a regulatory authority, *or as a commercial activity, the aim of which is to create confidence between suppliers and their clients* . . . ISO itself has no authority to control these activities."

ISO goes to great pains to stress that

> it is false to describe a company as "ISO-certified," "ISO-registered," or to use phrases such as "ISO certification," "ISO certificates," and "ISO registration." ISO operates no system for assessing the conformance of organizations' management systems with standards in the ISO 9000 family. ISO itself does not conduct ISO 9000 audits and awards no certificates attesting to conformity with the standards. There is no such thing as "ISO certification," or "ISO registration," whether in relation to ISO 9000 . . . or any other ISO standard.

Not to belabor the point, ISO cautions consumers against viewing ISO 9000 certification as a service guarantee. If a legitimate ISO 9000 certification is provided to a vendor by a scrupulous auditor, it merely means that the auditor may have checked that the processes influencing quality ISO 9000 conform to the relevant standard's requirements. Going further, the ISO states

> The objective is to give the organization's management and its customers confidence that the organization is in control of the way it does things. While this confidence may logically extend to the things it makes, ISO 9000 does not contain requirements for specific products or services. Therefore, certifications to these standards should not be presented as product or service guarantees. (*Publicizing Your ISO 9000 or ISO 14000 Certification,* ISBN 92-67-10278-8)

ISO 9000 compliance is not the only certification that has surfaced within the ASP field. Some vendors, notably Sun Microsystems, with its SunTone(SM) Certification and Branding Program, have set about the problem of ASP certification with an eye toward encouraging sales of proprietary servers and software. According to press accounts of Sun CEO Ed Zander's announcement of the Sun certification program, he likened the program to a "Good Housekeeping Seal for Service Providers."

According to Zander, SunTone Certification identified applications that were designed to run effectively on a SunTone certified service platform. He said that the program specified how to architect, develop, implement and deploy software in order to achieve increased availability, reliability and performance. The SunTone program for applications focused primarily on solutions that ASPs offer via the Web to their customers, but it also encompassed other software, middleware and tools that an ASP might use to create Web-delivered business services.

If one asks Sun to identify the specific criteria that are used to award certification to an ASP, the response is that one must first become a member of the program to learn about the details. Keeping secret the criteria for awarding the certification calls into question its similarity to the Good Housekeeping Seal of Approval.

The Good Housekeeping Seal, established in 1909, has, according to spokespersons for the company, been a highly recognized statement of Good Housekeeping magazine's renowned Consumers' Policy. The Good Housekeeping Consumers' Policy, published in every issue of the magazine, states that if a product bearing the Seal proves to be defective within two years of purchase, Good Housekeeping will replace the product or refund the purchase price.

Obviously the publication only stands behind products that have been subjected to testing within its laboratories, and only after a careful review of the advertising of the product vendor, which is performed to ensure that the vendor is not making unsubstantiated claims about its product's utility.

To the extent that the certification programs of Sun Microsystems and Good Housekeeping are similar at all, it is in the realm of marketing rather than standards and practices. Both stress that certification will likely help vendors sell more products by increasing consumer confidence.

Queried about the actual utility of the SunTone Certification program to business decision makers who are evaluating ASP services, Sun spokespersons almost always adopt an indignant posture: "if Sun Microsystems says that the platform is of the highest quality, you can trust us."

The SunTone Certification and Branding Program is described officially as a collaborative effort with industry-wide support led by Sun Microsystems. It is intended to make 7-by-24 service and reliability the norm for consumer and business Internet-based services. Under the SunTone Program, service providers and application service providers must endure a rigorous specification process that examines the infrastructure, operational practices, hardware, software, and overall service delivery of service providers and application service providers, ensuring that the services or applications provided meet the program's high standards.

SunTone certification, according to the vendor, is designed to give customers the confidence that every aspect of the SP's operations and infrastructure has been evaluated and judged to be reliable and high quality. The Program currently has more than 300 member service providers, independent software vendors, and network equipment providers working with Sun, spokespersons say.

The follow-on to the above description is a strong sales message. The certification is meant to drive the sales of Sun Microsystem hardware and software in the ASP space. According to one press account of the January 2000 program launch, Zander acknowledged that the standards laid out in the SunTone program were contingent upon substantial use of Sun products, but he did not completely rule out participation from other vendors, such as IBM or Hewlett Packard Co., in the future. The objective of the program from Sun's perspective is to bring Web-based applications and services to market quickly and support the growth of the service provider and the ASP industry. Rather than wait around and figure out what competitors are doing, Zander suggested that ASPs needed to demonstrate their vision in order to provide customers with a sense of assurance.

Traver Gruen-Kennedy, then chairman of the ASP Industry Consortium, notes that industry best practices have not yet been fully articulated for ASPs. Most ASPs have their own modus operandi and platform preferences for delivering services to their customers. He indicates that audit/consulting firm Ernst & Young is working to develop a best practices guide as of this writing, but contacts at Ernst & Young could confirm only that they have such a practice and that they are not at liberty to share their information to anyone but paying clients.

Thus, in the absence of uniform and industry standard practices, business decision makers must—for the time being at least—depend on a mixture of on-site visits, conversations with ASP operatives, and contractual service level guarantees to select an ASP vendor to meet their requirements.

APPLICATION SERVICES LAYER . . . .

Stacked atop the infrastructure services layer in Figure 5–1 is the application services layer. Applications are what set ASPs apart from the other "SPs"—Internet service providers (ISPs), business service providers (BSPs), enterprise service providers (ESPs), storage service providers (SSPs), management service providers (MSPs), and so on—that have crowded onto the stage recently.

Applications, as stated in a previous chapter, may be either designed for Web hosting and sharing—"Webified" is the latest buzz phrase, or they may be Web enabled through the use of enabling software and middleware. Either way, the business is able to utilize ASP application software remotely and on a subscription or pay-per-use basis.

The list of software companies developing ASP-ready or Webified versions of their products is growing almost daily. The drivers encouraging this trend are numerous and include:

- Ability to sell products into new markets: ASPs provide a new way for ISVs to sell application software into markets that may not have adopted shrink-wrapped products with hefty associated deployment costs. For example, Enterprise Resource Planning software, once the exclusive domain of large businesses with large IT staff and large IT budgets, can be offered on an ASP basis to medium-sized companies on a more affordable and less resource-intensive basis. Moreover, software that cannot be rationalized for purchase because of its low frequency of use can be obtained on an as-needed basis from an ASP.

- Ability to sell products at a different level of customer decision making: ASP-delivered software is more solution oriented than technology oriented. Although the "middleware" components (Enterprise JavaBeans, Java Servlets, XML, etc.) of a Webified product may be quite complex, the decision maker is shielded from this complexity through ASP application delivery. Thus, ASPs enable acquisitions to be handled by business rather than information technology decision makers—a potential advantage for software delivered via ASPs.

- Ability to exploit trends: Hitching a software product to the e-business bandwagon is good business for the ISV. The ISV and its products gain instant recognition as players in the next generation of business technology. This, in turn, encourages investors, garners increased (and hopefully positive) trade press interest, and gets ISV CEOs invited to join all the best industry collaborations and initiatives, to speak at the best colloquiums and conferences, and, only partially tongue-in-cheek, to attend all the best parties, golf tournaments, and so on.

- Increased control over software licenses: ISVs have been using just about every technique they can think of to encourage the use of their software, including the generous and expensive practice of providing evaluation copies of code on disk, or for download via the Web. This so-called "soft licensing" enables customers to use the product without formally registering or paying for it. Although some firms have implemented controls in their demonstration products—including self-destruction after a set period of use, limitations on productive use (for example, the report can be created with the software demo, but printing is disabled), or "annoy ware features" (for example, lengthening the time required for loading the software over time or popping up messages on the end user screen every few keystrokes reminding them to register and pay for the product)—these generally discourage, rather than encourage, the software sale. Thus, "soft licensing" cannot be trusted as a gauge of future "hard licensing"—a fact that some companies, including Citrix Systems, have learned to their dismay. ASPs provide a way to rectify this situation. In most cases, the ASP itself is the software licensee. Customers who wish to demo the software offerings of the ASP are served by the ASP directly, whether through demoware, downloads, or other soft license trials. If, after reviewing the software demo, the business elects to use the ASP service, the contract between the ASP and the customer simply adds "seats" or instances of the software code to the ASP's hard license with the ISV. Most ISVs are encouraging ASPs to use their software with attractive per seat licensing schemes tracked by means of some sort of session tracking and reporting system (sessions are instances of use of the software by individual end users). If more seats are required than a license permits, ISVs can enable additional seats in the ASP's purchased software readily, often through the use of a downloaded code. Thus, much as in the manufacturing space, where vendors have sought to push inventory and inventory-related expense down into the supply chain, ASPs provide a mechanism for offloading the ISV's soft licensing costs to the ASP.

- Greater control over intellectual property: ISVs, including Microsoft, are plagued by software bootlegging (e.g., unauthorized copying and distribution) and theft. Frankly, there are few, if any, effective ways to prevent a software distribution disk or CD from being copied by unscrupulous third parties, who then resell it without passing royalties back to the ISV. For every scheme that has been tried, protection breaking schemes have been developed by hackers and others and posted to electronic bulletin board systems and to the Internet's newsgroups. In extreme cases, ISVs report that their software code has been reverse-engineered or otherwise adapted into the code of competing products. ASPs appeal to software vendors as a mechanism to safeguard code from unlicensed copying and reengineering. Because the software is not distributed into the "anarchical world" of end users, but is, instead, accessed across networks from carefully managed and controlled ASP hosting platforms, the opportunity for unlicensed copying is dramatically reduced.

ISVs may also receive benefits such as partnerships and Original Equipment Manufactures (OEM) arrangements with major players in the hardware and software market by embracing the ASP model. Virtually, all the industry-leading IT companies, from IBM, Hewlett Packard Company and Sun Microsystems to Microsoft Corporation and Oracle Corporation, have initiated programs intended to support the development of full-service ASPs and e-business solution providers—emphasizing their own hardware and software offerings, of course. They endeavor to gain credibility for their initiative, while filling out their menu of offerings, by establishing relationships with third-party "best of breed" software and services. This packaged solution is then marketed to organizations, ranging from large corporations to outsourcing companies to ISPs, as a one-stop shop approach for getting into the ASP business.

The benefits to the ISV for participation in these initiatives are several. Arguably, the most important benefit for the ISV is the ability to leverage the relationship, which is usually accompanied by some sort of knowledge exchange (technology and sales training, etc.) to improve the ISV's internal intellectual capital and to provide an additional sales channel for its products.

ISVs must be wary, however, of vendor lock-ins, in the form of exclusive partnerships or noncompetitive sales arrangements, imposed by such relationships and requirements to enhance existing products with vendor-preferred technologies (support for Active X or Java Servlets, for example) when such enhancements would be too expensive to implement or would impose too great a support requirement or are simply deemed as nonstrategic within the ISV itself.

In addition to ISVs, the application services layer also includes software products designed to enable non-ASP-ready software for distribution via the ASP model. In a previous chapter, a few Web enabling software products, including Citrix Systems WinFrame and MetaFrame and The Santa Cruz Operation's Tarantella, were discussed. These represent server-based tools for Web enabling custom and packaged software applications residing on Microsoft Windows desktops or UNIX servers.

In addition to these tools, there is a growing cadre of Web application integration, content management, and content distribution. Package providers provide a comprehensive software framework for supporting the integration and delivery of complex software services via an ASP. These tools enable ISVs to remain in their core competency of technology development, rather than working to build customized, Web enabled solutions from their applications.

A list of Web enablement framework product vendors includes the following:

- The Progress Company—One of the first efforts to provide an enterprise class ASP-enablement framework for application development was delivered by The Progress Company. The Progress Company, a global supplier of software technology and services for developing, deploying, integrating, and managing e-business solutions, provides a suite of products that includes application development tools, application servers, messaging servers, and the industry's most widely used, lowest-cost-of-ownership embedded database. There are more than 2,000 independent software vendors (ISVs) and application service providers (ASPs) who supply annually over $5 billion in Progress®-based applications and related services. Over 40,000 organizations across more than 100 countries-including 70% of the Fortune 100-rely on Progress-based applications. The Progress Company's ASPen[SM] (ASP-enablement) Program provides the educational tools, business planning assistance, design and development services, and managed hosting services to assist Progress ISVs in rapidly delivering their applications through the ASP model. The ASPen Program supports hundreds of members that have deployed Web enabled vertical applications that serve over 70,000 end-users globally. For more information about the ASPen Program visit *www.ASPconnections.com.*

- IBM's WebSphere—While players such as Sun Microsystems, Oracle Corporation, and Microsoft Corporation continue to develop a consistent ASP-enablement framework offering that ties together their many, often excellent, Web enablement, integration, and middleware products, IBM is arguably the closest to bringing this task to fruition. WebSphere is described by IBM product literature as "a new, universal Internet software platform that can support any kind of e-business." Foundations for the framework are twofold: IBM's WebSphere Application Server and the vendor's highly regarded middleware product, MQueue. The vendor describes the WebSphere Application Server as "an e-business application deployment environment built on open standards-based technology. It is the cornerstone of WebSphere application offerings and services. The Standard Edition lets a company use Java servlets, JavaServer Pages and XML to quickly transform static Web sites into vital sources of dynamic Web content. The Advanced Edition is a high-performance Enterprise Java Beans (EJB) server for implementing EJB components that incorporate business logic. The Enterprise Edition integrates EJB and CORBA components to build high-transaction, high-volume e-business applications. IBM supplements the WebSphere Application Server with MQSeries middleware—"the market leader in commercial messaging, provides a key element of enterprise systems, and enjoys rich support from business partners. It also provides flexible, rapid application integration offering unparalleled business flexibility." To these foundation products, IBM adds a raft of "Foundation Extensions," including a comprehensive Java development environment, and a number of IBM-branded "application accelerators"—ASP-ready software by IBM and third-party ISVs that already work with the IBM WebSphere framework. The company offers an very readable white paper covering its application framework for e-business on the Web at *www.ibm.com/software/ebusiness.*

- Microsoft.NET—When Microsoft introduced Windows 2000 in 1999, the underlying architecture, called Windows DNA, was heralded as the future of Microsoft computing. Utilizing an application development model known as Distributed Component Object Model (DCOM), supported by Microsoft's Transaction Server, Internet Information Server, and Message Queue middleware, Windows DNA was intended to support the extension of Windows into the enterprise data center and ultimately into the Internet. Windows 2000, it should be noted, already embodied Citrix Systems WinFrame technology, enabling its use to host Windows applications so they could be made available for use by multiple concurrent users. DNA architecture expanded upon this capability to make any application designed to work with Microsoft DCOM services a candidate for ASP delivery. The latest advance in this direction by the company is its .NET Enterprise Server offering. As stated by the vendor in its marketing literature,

> the .NET Enterprise Servers let you integrate and Web-enable your enterprise today while building the foundation for the next-generation of Internet applications. Designed with mission-critical performance in mind, .NET Enterprise Servers are built from the ground up for interoperability, using open Web standards such as Extensible Markup Language (XML). The .NET Enterprise Servers, along with the Microsoft Windows® 2000 platform, supply the foundation for developing and managing applications for the .NET platform. Microsoft .NET enables the third generation of the Internet, where software is delivered as a service, is accessible by any device any time from any place, and is fully programmable and customizable. Microsoft designed the .NET Enterprise Servers specifically to help companies rapidly integrate and orchestrate services and applications into a single comprehensive solution.

- It remains to be seen whether this initiative will be any more successful than Microsoft's other efforts to become the framework provider for ASPs and e-business generally. Learn more about Microsoft .NET at *www.microsoft.com.*

- Oracle Corporation Application Server—Oracle Corporation, a market share leader in the database field, has articulated an e-business framework strategy as part of its release of Oracle 9i Database and Application Server. In the past, the company was arguably constrained by the requirement to continue support for customers running earlier application development tools licensed from the vendor. With 9i, the vendor became more aggressive in the face of competition in the e-business framework space from IBM and Microsoft. Oracle has even gone so far as to post a $1 million "guarantee" that applications will operate faster over its framework than over its competitor's. Oracle's offering includes a database engine and application server that supports application delivery via XML or Java. The company also offers to provide the framework and Oracle's own suite of Web-ready applications to organizations interested in getting into the ASP business and willing to join the Oracle iHost Community. More information is available at *www.oracle.com.*

- Hewlett-Packard—Not to be omitted from the list is Hewlett-Packard Company's Bluestone business unit, formerly Bluestone Software, one of the first application server vendors. According to John Capobianco, General Manager of Strategic Marketing for Hewlett-Packard, HP Bluestone's work with application integration and Web enablement predates the flurry of activity that is currently being seen in the industry. Capobianco notes that his company's Netaction Internet Operating Environment is an outgrowth of work performed over many years for customers and clients to provide application integration across distributed supply chains. "We didn't start out as a Web site provider, then grow into the ASP space. We started with an enterprise focus—an application built around the idea of scalability." The Web enablement of applications was a natural extension for the HP Bluestone technology, which offers an application server, integration server, transaction server, syndication and messaging capabilities. Copabianco is quick to distinguish the HP Bluestone solution from competitors offering a portal (loosely defined as an access point to a hosted application or set of hosted applications). "Portals are not enough," Capobianco observes. The infrastructure must be bidirectional to enable business-to-business integration. HP Bluestone utilizes Enterprise Java Beans and XML for interapplication messaging and content generation and supports virtually any kind of end user client device. More on the solution is available at *www.bluestone.com.*

Frameworks like the HP Bluesone Total-e-Server or IBM's WebSphere are slowly finding their way into the ASP space. Says HP's Capobianco, most first generation ASPs "have focused on getting some pretty basic applications up and running in order to get money through the door. This is somewhat shortsighted from the standpoint of future growth, but understandable from the perspective of income." He notes that ASPs will need a more robust infrastructure framework for integrating customer back-end systems to ASP hosted applications and for facilitating the B2B requirements of current and future customers.

INTEGRATION SERVICES LAYER . . . .

Many of the framework vendors discussed are also busily adding portals to their service offerings. Portal is a much used and often confusing term which merits further explanation.

A portal may be defined as an aggregation point for ASP software offerings. Although a few ASPs provide access to a single application, most ASPs offer a menu of applications that may be accessed in any combination from a single—typically Web browser accessible—screen. This is one, admittedly simplistic, definition of a portal.

An example of such a portal that may be familiar to Internet users is Yahoo! (*www.yahoo.com*). Originally, a search engine for seeking information on the World Wide Web, Yahoo! now offers to end users the capability to set up a personal portal that provides, in addition to the search engine application, access to newsfeeds, mail services, specialized user message groups, storage services, a calendar application, an image sharing application, a travel agent application, a weather information service, and so forth. The Yahoo! portal is a primordial ASP service, free to subscribers, supported by advertising sales.

Some framework vendors offer portal services to ISVs who join their particular cadre or initiative. Their applications added to a portal service maintained by the vendor. Alternatively, the vendor may facilitate the creation of portals by introducing ISVs in the same industry area to one another so they can create a common portal that provides customers with a one-stop shop.

An original idea for a vendor supported portal is Progress Software's ASPEN-related AppsAlive!^{SM} offering. This portal provides visitors with access to ASPEN partner applications, organized by market area, so that they can demo the application or take a "test drive." The offering both demonstrates the power of Progress Software's enabling technology and provides a nifty method for handling ISV software demonstrations.

Portals also have a different meaning. A portal is a window or opening enabling information exchange between the internal systems of two or more businesses. This is the meaning of portal alluded to by Bluestone Software's Capobianco. This type of B2B portal is arguably much more complex than the portals described earlier because of its integration requirements, including message exchange formats, security requirements, access provisioning requirements, and other necessities of intersystem interoperation.

As companies begin to depend on ASPs to deliver more complex solutions, portal development, part of the integration services layer, will likely become an increasingly lucrative component of the ASP model. What type of application could require such a solution? The answer is many.

Here's an example. A small silk screen T-shirt vendor gets an order from a customer for 500 shirts of various sizes and colors that are to bear the logo and name of the customer's company. Order processing is a straightforward application, handled readily by any present-day ASP providing such an application. However, the vendor wants to survey the closeout, discontinued and overstock T-shirt inventories of several suppliers, then place an order for the quantity, quality, type, and color of T-shirt needed to fulfill the customer's order.

This function requires linking to the inventory systems of several suppliers, looking up their stock of shirts and pricing information, and placing an order (or several orders) for shipment to the vendor at the right price and within the proper time frame.

This task is a candidate for a portal application that enables the necessary B2B transactions so that the stock is in-house in time for the vendor to silk-screen the shirts and to fulfill the customer's order. An ASP that is capable of offering this type of B2B portal service, either directly or as a service of a third-party portal provider, would add tremendous value to the services that it sells. Many in the industry believe that this is the level of service to which ASPs should aspire and that the true profitability of ASPs will not be realized without an extensive integration service offering and support for such functionality as B2B portals.

Conversely some commentators have suggested that traditional ASP offerings will become components—someone has coined the term "ASPlets"—to a future generation of portal service providers (audible author groan: "PSPs"). For reference, a list of portal creation software providers and portal services (at the time of this writing) is provided in Table 5–2.

As Table 5–2 suggests, numerous experiments in the design and operation of portals are underway at present. They are termed experiments not in any sort of derisive context, but as an indication of the still-growing body of technology, standards, and best practices that surrounds B2B and e-business generally. The descriptions provided in the table should provide the reader with a surface-level appreciation at least of the scope, breadth, and depth of the e-business transformation that is currently underway. Integration services, whether to support B2B portals or to customize ASP solutions to better fit business consumers, will likely grow in scope and value as the ASP model matures.

ANALYTICAL SERVICES LAYER · · · · · · · · · · · · · · ·

Atop the Integration Services Layer of the model provided in Figure 5–1 is the analytical services layer. No evaluation of the ASP market would be complete without a brief examination of the industry that has grown up around the ASP market that portends to serve in an intermediary role between the consumer of ASP services and the provider.

Something like a "food chain" develops around any new technological innovation. After watching the IT industry for a time, one can sense the gathering of peripheral players before their names are even known. It is akin to the groups that coalesce around an up-and-coming motion picture star, signaling his or her rise, and ultimate fall, from general popularity.

Intermediaries strive to influence technology adoption by disseminating information, whether factual or not, or, in some cases, strive to influence the milieu in which the technology must flourish or disappear.

Primary sources of information about ASPs are, of course, the providers and their customers (or prospective customers). In the first years of the ASP model, a

(text continues on page 155)

Table 5–2   *Partial List of Portal Software and Service Vendors*

Portal Software or Service Vendor	Description
2Bridge	2Bridge provides Web ware that allows companies to communicate, collaborate, and compete on the Web. Used by leading enterprises to transform their businesses, 2Bridge's solutions are functional in days, with lower up-front costs, and are optionally available as a managed ASP service. The company's award-winning technology enables the creation of portals, hubs, and interactive work spaces where customers, partners, suppliers, and employees can simultaneously interact and exchange ideas, access disparate business information, integrate business processes, and conduct commerce—all in real time.
AlarmX	AlarmX is a vertical portal for the security alarm industry.
arcadiaOne	arcadiaOne's eSyndication solution, built on standards such as XML, HTTP, and Java, makes it possible to have automated exchange networks where vertical portals, commerce hubs, and distributors become content subscribers.
B2Bgalaxy.com	B2Bgalaxy.com creates industry specific B2B e-commerce portals, linking buyers and sellers through competitive on-line exchange. The company targets industries where small- to medium-size business and local or regional distribution are dominant and where cost of goods is significant. B2B Galaxy plans to generate revenue through a subscription service for software, advertising, and commission revenue for aggregated services, and auction and catalog functions. FoodGalaxy.com was B2Bgalaxy's first marketplace.
b2bnow.com	b2bnow.com was launched in January 2000 as a member of the ShopNow.com network and serves as an on-line B2B portal site that enable merchants to promote, sell, or buy products from other member merchants. Other services include a comprehensive database of merchants, everything from venture capitalist to warehousing.
Band-X	In July 1997 Band-X launched the first independent virtual market for international wholesale telecom capacity. The Internet-based exchange provides a portal for buyers and sellers of bandwidth and related wholesale services. Band-X has an international membership of over 10,000 people and includes most communications service providers worldwide.

Table 5-2 *Continued*

Portal Software or Service Vendor	Description
Biospace.com	Biospace.com is a vertical portal for the life science industry. The goal of BioSpace is to facilitate informed and timely decision making by providing critical and organized bioscience information in one location on the World Wide Web. BioSpace.com operates 11 hotbed communities where news, company profiles, jobs, events, and resources are made available on a regional basis.
Biz2Biz.com Inc.	The Biz2Biz portal network provides small- and medium-sized businesses with Internet-based applications needed to help sell their B2B products and services on-line, run their companies more efficiently, and compete on an equal playing field in the global marketplace.
Bizee.com	Bizee.com, Inc. is an e-solutions provider of portal and procurement technologies. The company believes that its portal technology would facilitate the opening of businesses to a network of customers, partners, and employees.
BuildersPlanet.com	BuildersPlanet.com is a portal site for the construction industry. Through their portal, the company distributes real-time information, Web enabled tools and new Internet services client companies.
BusinessHere.com	BusinessHere.com provides dynamic pricing and exchange solutions for Web sites and Web portals.
CargoReservations.com	CargoReservations.com^{TM}, the first functional module of Zulunet.net^{TM}, is an open, neutral Supply Chain Management Internet portal. CargoReservations.com was conceived and implemented to provide an Internet-based real-time exchange for buying and selling charter aircraft flights.
CattleinfoNet.com	CattleinfoNet.com is a portal site for the cattle industry. The company provides users with up-to-date beef prices, as well as information on weather, grain, and related industry issues.
CHINAnUSA.com	CHINAnUSA.com is a one-stop B2B full-service portal for all trading and sourcing between China and the United States. The company's goal is to be the number one personalized Web platform, providing a vast import and export information pool.

(continued)

Table 5–2   *Continued*

Portal Software or Service Vendor	Description
	Facilitated by on-line and off-line services, subject matter experts in both countries can efficiently increase their trade leads at lower cost.
CMGI, Inc.	CMGI, Inc. uses its deep and broad management expertise to grow, develop, and invest in a diverse network of Internet companies. The company has a tightly targeted strategic focus, operating companies (both B2B and Business to Consumer or B2C) that fall into five core technology disciplines—marketing services, e-commerce and fulfillment, portals, Internet professional services, and infrastructure applications and enabling technologies. The company also has an affiliated venture capital firm, CMGI @Ventures, which maintains a portfolio of investments in more than 50 Internet companies.
CNET Networks, Inc.	The company is an informational and new-media portal site for businesses and professionals. CNET's content includes news, computer goods and services, and technology-oriented publications. CNET's old-media presence includes CNBC, national syndications, and CNET Radio.
CyberElan	CyberElan is the leader in providing highly manageable security software and services to the world's largest e-business portals. The company's access control solution, eCerberu, is based on PKI technology, featuring extensive scalability and manageability. CyberElan's nonrepudiation solution, enTACT, is based on PKI technology and XML standards. enTACT features digital signatures and receipts, as well as real-time receipt matching. eCerberus and enTACT work in concert to provide a comprehensive and highly manageable security solution for e-commerce portals. CyberElan provides consulting services to complement their leading edge software solutions through its subsidiary: CyberElan Global Servicesâ (CGS).
DataChannel	Founded in 1996 and headquartered in Bellevue, WA, DataChannel is a provider of powerful and flexible intranet and extranet portal solutions designed with open-standards based XML technology. DataChannel's enterprise information portal (EIP) solutions ensure the reliable, personalized exchange of data, keeping people connected to business-critical information wherever and whenever it's needed.

Table 5–2 *Continued*

Portal Software or Service Vendor	Description
EarthWeb, Inc.	EarthWeb is a business portal for the global IT industry. The company serves each of the major vertical markets in the IT industry, including enterprise management, networking and telecommunications, software and Internet development, and hardware and systems.
EC Cubed	EC Cubed is a provider of e-business solutions such as e-marketplaces and B2B portals. EC Cubed builds and continually evolves customized e-business applications and offers them as a managed service to Global 2000 and dotcom organizations.
EcomXML	EcomXML is a product developer for B2B e-commerce solutions, offering products that manage and control the secure exchange of information and transactions. EcomXML provides the enterprise interface solution to link buyers, suppliers, and e-commerce portals together to facilitate their e-business relationships in real-time through the Internet. EcomXML utilizes open XML technology to achieve both intercompany and intracompany integration regardless of existing technology infrastructure.
eConstructors	eConstructors is a B2B marketplace and vertical portal exclusively for the Web design and development industry.
eMake Corporation	eMake provides Internet-based real-time production applications, e-business and supply chain portals for the small to mid-sized, make-to-order manufacturer.
Enterworks	Enterworks, Inc., develops and markets software for the real-time cataloging and business process automation that drives e-marketplaces and information portals. The company's advanced solutions improve time-to-market for customers in health care, manufacturing, government, financial services, and telecommunications worldwide, including Boeing, IBM/Tivoli, and the Department of Defense.
Entrust Technologies	Entrust Technologies, Inc., brings trust to e-business relationships by securing and managing the transactions that constitute e-business. The company enables customers to secure their B2B, B2C and internal enterprise transactions and communications, as well as to manage the e-business portals through

(continued)

Table 5–2   *Continued*

Portal Software or Service Vendor	Description
	which these transactions take place. Entrust Technologies pioneered the public-key infrastructure (PKI) and digital certificate solutions that provide security for business transactions and communications over the Internet. Entrust Technologies is based in Silicon Valley, Ottawa, Canada, and Plano, Texas, and has offices around the world.
Epicentric	Epicentric helps mainline corporations and dotcoms to launch integrated and customized Internet portal networks for B2B e-commerce. Epicentric's offerings include a portal server, a hosted service, and a syndicated service that provides prenegotiated content, applications, and commerce services.
EquipmentLeasing.com	EquipmentLeasing.com offers a leasing portal in the fragmented leasing market, where small- and medium-sized business can obtain leasing on-line quickly and efficiently. Equipment Leasing.com earns a transaction fee for each closed lease.
e-STEEL	e-STEEL is a neutral B2B e-commerce marketplace for the steel industry. Through its proprietary STEELDIRECT technology, both buyers and sellers can initiate, specify, fully negotiate, and close transactions on-line for prime and secondary steel products. eSTEEL is also a vertical portal of industry news and information. They receive 0.825 of a 1 percent fee for each transaction processed via its exchange, paid by the seller.
EverythingAircraft	EverythingAircraft is a B2B portal for the aircraft and aerospace industry. EverythingAircraft is in the business of putting buyers and sellers together via the Internet without any special software requirements. Manufacturers and distributors can list their catalog of parts on-line where potential buyers can enter the Web site, click and buy their required parts, and expect prompt delivery.
Evolve	Evolve provides Internet-based end-to-end solutions for automating professional services organizations. Evolve's ServiceSphere software suite integrates and streamlines the processes that are critical to professional services organizations: managing project opportunities, professional resources, and service

Table 5–2 *Continued*

Portal Software or Service Vendor	Description
	delivery. Evolve's Services.com on-line applications portal enables smaller professional services providers to rapidly and cost-effectively access the benefits of Evolve's technology to manage their businesses.
Farmbid.com	Farmbid.com is a vertical portal in the agricultural sector. The company provides farmers with an infomediary site designed to meet their specific needs. In addition to the content service, the company offers an auction site that services numerous categories, including farm equipment, livestock, grains, and other farm-related items.
FuelSpot.com, Inc.	FuelSpot is an on-line exchange and e-commerce portal for the energy products industry. The Web site is an independent trading/supply platform that combines integrated logistics, back-office systems, and e-commerce for use by major oil suppliers, downstream oil companies, commodity traders, wholesalers, and major chain retailers.
Global TeleExchange Inc.	The Global TeleExchange Inc. (GTX) operates a full-service, Internet-based portal, and real-time applications exchange. The GTX enables member telecommunications companies to buy and sell products, access information, and perform telecom research on-line. Trading members have access to real-time trading floors, broker-assisted trading floors, and facilities management services.
GOwarehouse.com, Inc.	By Web enabling logistics providers, GOwarehouse makes real-time end-to-end commerce collaboration possible between manufacturers, merchants, and vertical market exchanges. The GOwarehouse logistics network and management portal form a transparent hub that enables trading partners to automate transactions and control inventory for maximum supply chain efficiency.
Integral Corporation	Integral Corporation provides a B2B e-commerce portal for capital markets. Through their Web site CFOWeb.com, Integral serves the needs of two major constituencies. First, fund managers and CFOs use the site to trade, process transactions, obtain independent valuations, and perform risk analysis. Second,

(*continued*)

Table 5–2 *Continued*

Portal Software or Service Vendor	Description
	the financial instituions use the site to increase their reach to a selected audience and reduce operating costs. CFOWeb.com generates revenue from a number of sources, including transaction fees, subscription fees, and advertising.
match21, Inc.	match21™ provides Web portals with the back-end technology to transform their communities into on-line marketplaces, matching buyers and sellers of products and services.
Medinex Systems, Inc.	Medinex Systems Inc. is the developer of MedMarket, Medinex E-Store, and the Medinex physician's office management system. MedMarket is the Internet's oldest and largest vertical medical portal. MedMarket is the premier place for buyers and sellers of medical equipment and supplies and fully integrates the many varied components of the e-commerce health care industry. Medinex E-Store is a secure Web site that provides discounted medical equipment and supplies to medical professionals, clinics, and hospitals.
MeetChina.com	MeetChina.com, a B2B portal for sourcing products from China, provides buyers worldwide with a set of tools to search, negotiate, and procure products directly and on-line. The Web site's comprehensive database lists detailed information on approximately 70,000 Chinese manufacturers and allows users to search products by Harmonized Code or from 12 broadly defined industry sectors. A third-party implemented rating system for suppliers allows buyers a time-saving tool to evaluate MeetChina.com database entries and quickly evaluate which suppliers come closest to fulfilling their needs. MeetChina.com offers its users an on-line Request for Quote (RFQ) function along with the added benefit of China-based "Industry Specialists" who help moderate communications and negotiations between buyers and suppliers.
NexTag, Inc.	NexTag is an e-commerce ASP specializing in building highly customized marketplaces. Offering turnkey solutions, NexTag provides manufacturers, retailers, portals, and net market makers the ability to quickly build unique, branded, flexible, and scalable marketplaces. NexTag's comprehensive solutions are delivered via a hosted model, allowing fast-moving companies

Table 5–2 *Continued*

Portal Software or Service Vendor	Description
	to launch dynamic- or fixed-priced marketplaces with millions of new and used products and hundreds of sellers within weeks.
NVST.com, Inc.	The company is a portal site for the financing and venture capital market. Through its site, entreprenuers can interact with potential investors and other sources of equity. Other services include a comprehensive research database, private placement library, an on-line academy, business plan services, and professional journals.
Persistent Web	Persistent Web provides customized Internet and intranet solutions, databases, information portals, and applications. The company specializes in high-volume, data-intensive sites ranging from e-commerce to n-tier network applications.
PharmiWeb	PharmiWeb is a portal for the life sciences sector, established in October 1998, and sponsored by many leading players, such as Roche, Novartis, Pfizer, Glaxo Wellcome, and Merck Sharpe & Dohme. In addition to providing sector-specific news, information, advertising, and marketing services, PharmiWeb offers a sophisticated range of e-commerce solutions, including on-line trading and ASP-driven e-procurement functionality via the PharmiWeb Net Market. UK–based, PharmiWeb focuses directly on the European marketplace, and is establishing partnerships to reach other territories.
PlazaVertical.com	PlazaVertical.com is a B2B multisector portal for Latin America. It allows companies to buy and sell products, stay informed and exchange opinions. It has five plazas: PlazaSalud.com, PlazaAlimentos.com, PlazaInformatica.com, PlazaSectorPublico.com, and PlazaIndustrias.com.
Polygon.net, Inc.	Polygon.net is a portal site for the retail jewelry business. Polygon has helped more jewelry companies make money on the Web than have all other Internet firms combined. Polygon has been chosen by virtually every major publication, trade association, and organization in the industry for Web site services.
ProcureNet Inc.	ProcureNet Inc. provides solutions that support the procurement process from end-to-end. The company generates revenue through a combination of software license and

(continued)

Table 5–2   *Continued*

Portal Software or Service Vendor	Description
	maintenance fees, margin and goods purchased through the buying portal, and fees for procurement services and system implementation.
ProduceOnline.com	ProduceOnline.com is a vertical portal for the $150 billion global fresh produce industry. The company's services have two major components: a transaction engine and an information and community segment. Using the transaction engine, buyers and sellers can complete end-to-end Web-based electronic purchases, reducing costs for both buyers and sellers. ProduceOnline charges a percentage fee for each produce transaction taking place on the site. This fee is paid by the seller.
Project.net	Project.net provides project collaboration and on-line project management for large corporate portals, vertical exchanges, and extranets.
PyBiz, Inc.	PyBiz is a provider of XML-based B2B solutions. Services and solutions include content management, flexible XML repository, and search engine and collaboration framework aimed at improving the integration and collaboration between Web sites in a portal, community, or a marketplace.
Radnet, Inc.	Radnet is a provider of B2B portal solutions.
S1 Corporation	S1 Corporation, formerly known as Security First Technologies Corp., develops integrated, brandable Internet applications that enable companies offering financial services to create their own financial portals. S1 targets organizations that view providing their products and services on the Internet as a strategic competitive advantage and an integral component of their business. S1's Virtual Financial Manager, known in the marketplace as VFM, integrates banking, investment, loan and credit card accounts at an institution, with content such as news, weather, and sports personalized by the end user. S1 licenses its Virtual Financial Manager software, provides installation and integration services, and offers outsourced Internet transaction processing through its data center. Current applications within S1's VFM product suite include banking, investments, relationship management, and customer care.

Table 5–2 *Continued*

Portal Software or Service Vendor	Description
SageMaker, Inc.	SageMaker is an EIP vendor that provides mission-critical portals containing high-value, high-volume internal and external content and powerful e-business applications integrated into a flexible, open, scalable XML-based platform. These portals are designed and targeted exclusively to strategic vertical markets, including oil and gas, power, financial services, insurance, pharmaceutical and biotechnology, and telecommunications. SageMaker brings together more than 9,000 high-value publications through strategic partnerships with, among others, McGraw-Hill, Reuters, and Financial Times Electronic Publishing, to give their integration portals comprehensive external content in the EIP market.
SciQuest.com, Inc.	SciQuest provides a neutral e-marketplace for scientific laboratory products in the biotechnology, university, clinical, and industrial sectors. SciQuest supports the entire life cycle of scientific products, from selection to procurement to ownership and disposal. The SciQuest science portal offers access to over 800 suppliers and almost a million products. SciQuest also conducts auctions of scientific equipment and delivers both information resources and industry news. SciQuest has signed exclusive contracts with industry suppliers including Alltech, Ambion, Amersham Pharmacia, BioWhittaker, Endogen, Nen Life Science, PerkinElmer, Pierce Chemical, Qiagen, and Shimadzu. SciQuest also has multiyear purchasing agreements with Dow Chemical, Dupont, Merck, and Monsanto.
Sequoia Software Corporation	Sequoia Software Corporation is a provider of XML-powered e-business software. Sequoia's flagship product, the XML Portal Server™ (XPS), gives users a Web-based, single point of personalized access to distributed information, along with the capability to publish, edit, change, or update content.
SOFTCARE	Founded in 1989 and headquartered in Vancouver, BC, SoftCare deploys vertical specific portals allowing companies to conduct B2B e-commerce. SoftCare is quickly building its U.S. presence with current offices in Seattle, San Francisco, and Los Angeles. SoftCare has transitioned itself from being a

(*continued*)

Table 5–2 *Continued*

Portal Software or Service Vendor	Description
	developer of EDI software, to a solutions provider of B2B electronic commerce portals. SoftCare's OpenEC® e-commerce platform integrates the business processes using knowledge gained from years of experience delivering EDI based e-commerce solutions to 150 clients worldwide with the tools and capabilities provided by Internet technology.
TIBCO Software Inc.	TIBCO Software Inc. is a provider of real-time e-business infrastructure software. TIBCO's three product lines—TIBCO ActiveEnterprise®, TIBCO ActiveExchange™, and TIBCO ActivePortal™–enable businesses to integrate enterprise applications, interact with other businesses in B2B commerce, and efficiently deliver personalized information through enterprise portals.
Trycos	Trycos is a developer of eCommerce solutions that dynamically link and adapt to companies' back-end ERP systems. Trycos offers four essential e-commerce solutions—BuyCentral™, SupplyCentral™, SellCentral™, and MarketCentral Portal™—all based on its proprietary object-based "Adaptive Technology Integrators"™ technology ("ATI"). ATI™ successfully addresses all e-business market-solution parameters.
Viador, Inc.	Viador's E-Portal Framework integrates application components and provides a scalable, customizable delivery vehicle for deploying e-business solutions.
WebEx, Inc.	WebEx provides real-time, interactive multimedia communication services that meeting-enables the Web sites of their clients, including corporations, portals, communications service providers, Web application vendors and on-line marketplaces. The company's services are delivered using their globally distributed network and scalable platform, ensuring predictability, reliability, and security.
Webridge	Webridge specializes in packaged, customizable e-business application software built on reusable enterprise-class infrastructure. In addition to its e-commerce solutions, Webridge focuses on partner relationship management (PRM) and knowledge portals.

Table 5–2   *Continued*

Portal Software or Service Vendor	Description
WorkExchange	WorkExchange is a B2B hub for clearing and facilitating the sale of project-based services via the Internet. The WorkExchange Network is comprised of on-line job sites, off-line staffing firms, business portals, and content sites that create a clearinghouse for companies to buy and sell professional services. WorkExchange currently receives a percentage fee for each transaction processed through the WorkExchange Network, paid for by the service provider.

considerable amount of evangelism was required of vendors by virtue of the fact that there were few customers to be queried and few customer success stories to demonstrate the ASP value proposition. ASP vendor evangelists were assisted early on by some milieu-level "scene setting" by IDC. IDC, followed in short order by others in the technology analysis services field, provided a name for the application hosting model, a high-level analysis of the ASP value proposition, and an operational definition of a generic ASP.

Unlike other technology fields, there was no industry association promoting ASPs to which all vendors subscribed. There was even a noticeable absence of "coopetition" (competitors agreeing to cooperate to achieve a common goal) among early vendors. They seemed at odds even in their efforts to create general, widespread adoption of the application delivery model.

Most vendors came onto the scene with marketing fists clenched, ready to do battle with their peers. Whether the result of personal animosities, inflammatory statements, or considered business decisions, current leading companies were set immediately against each other in their marketing literature and in the public statements of their executives. The vituperation did have the advantage of attracting the interest of the trade press, which sought to understand what all the fuss was about so they could report about it to their readers.

Somehow, against this ignoble backdrop, the ASP Industry Consortium was formed. Although not technically a creature of Citrix Systems, a company with much to gain from the realization of the ASP model given its application hosting software products, the vendor did much to support the development of the organization in its earliest stages. During the organization's first two years of operation, former ASP Industry Consortium Chairman Traver Gruen-Kennedy carried two business cards: one identified him as a Citrix executive; the other as the chairman of the Consortium.

In May 1999, Gruen-Kennedy was named by *Network World* as one of the 25 most powerful people in networking. Although he modestly declines comment on the kudo, he has become an international advocate of ASP and has cultivated the development of the Consortium to its current strength of more than 1000 companies.

The ASP Industry Consortium has sponsored or cosponsored hundreds of ASP Summits around the United States and the world, providing an educational forum for the discussion and debate of ASP utility and value. While side-stepping potentially devisive issues (including a specific definition of what is and what is not an ASP), the organization has worked to increase the popular perception of ASPs as a viable mechanism for application delivery. The organization has future plans to develop working groups to formulate best practices and to devise industry-standard SLAs—a preliminary document on SLAs published by the group is examined later in this book—and the organization is now recruiting ASP consumers for a customer council.

The Consortium has also been instrumental in working out a specification, if not a solution, for dispute avoidance and resolution best practices in cooperation with the World Intellectual Property Organization Arbitration and Mediation Center, based in Geneva, Switzerland. This step is important as a pragmatic and proactive effort to address the concerns of software vendors about their intellectual property as ASPs begin to operate on a global basis.

Some ASPs, including several of the largest players, have chosen not to join the Consortium. These include some international software companies, as well as some first-generation vendors who have defined their own ASP strategies.

Against this backdrop, analytical services come into play. Numerous information brokers, delivering content mostly on-line, provide the latest insights, news, and gossip about specific vendor offerings. These are listed in Table 5–3.

In addition to trade press and on-line resources, numerous industry market research companies have developed specialized practices around the ASP phenomenon, including IDC, The Gartner Group, Dataquest, The Yankee Group, Enterprise Management Associates, and several others. Many of these organizations have both general market reports and assessments of specific ASP vendors for sale to decision makers engaged in vendor assessments.

At least two "Big Five" audit/accounting firms are also developing specialized consulting practices around ASPs. Ernst & Young is reportedly working on a definition of best practices, and KPMG has partnered with Qwest Telecommunications to support ERP deployments using a joint venture ASP: Qwest Cyber.Solutions.

Table 5–3 Sources of Information About the Asp Industry

Information Source	Type of Information
a-com magazine (www.a-cominteractive.com/)	A monthly publication delivering focused analysis of business and technology developments in the ASP industry. Audience: application service providers and developers, ISPs, ISVs, IT consultants, and value-added resellers.
Alentis (www.alentis.com/)	Through the Alentis site, ASP buyers seeking solutions can access comprehensive, impartial information on hundreds of sellers, their solutions, and the ASP industry. Searching for buyers is free, and Alentis reviews all seller content prior to posting to help ensure accuracy. There is no cost for listing in the seller directory.
ASP Advisor (www.idc.com/aspadvisor)	A free newsletter offered by IDC, a leading provider of IT industry analysis and market data.
ASPConnection.com (www.aspconnection.com/)	Current industry news updated daily, plus on-line forum to interact with others in the industry.
ASP-Directory.com (www.asp-directory.com/)	A directory service dedicated to providing a comprehensive resource for connecting ASPs with the markets they serve.
ASPInsights.com (www.aspinsights.com/)	A new Web site that covers the ASP space from the vendors' perspective (mergers, acquisitions, product announcements, original analysis, features, and interviews and trend pieces).
ASP Island (www.aspisland.com/)	An on-line community forum aimed at a diverse audience, including sales executives, systems engineers, MIS managers, and CIOs.
ASPnews.com (forum.aspnews.com/news/ newsdigest/index.htm)	Breaking news releases, plus detailed news and analysis of the top global ASP news stories.
ASP News Review (www.aspnews.com/)	This newsletter, available by paid subscription only, is a monthly news summary and analysis of material in ASPnews.com.
ASP Outsourcing Center (www.asp-outsourcing-center.com/)	A collection of resources on ASP outsourcing. Includes the quarterly *ASP Outsourcing Journal*, which presents timely trends in the worldwide ASP outsourcing market

(continued)

Table 5–3   *Continued*

Information Source	Type of Information
	from at least three distinct perspectives: the customer, the supplier, and the analyst.
aspRegistry.com (www.aspregistry.com/)	Provides a personalized portal to access news, information shared knowledge, products, and services tailored specifically to the needs and interests of ASP users and suppliers.
ASPStreet (www.aspstreet.com/)	A collaborative portal featuring the latest trends, analysis, and information available about the ASP industry. ASPs and ASP-enablers can find and form fruitful partnerships. For ASP-buyers and ASP-sellers, it is an on-line marketplace, featuring "solution-search," "solution-matching," and RFP capabilities.
Network World Fusion ASP Newsletter (www.nwfusion.com/focus/)	A weekly commentary on key companies and technologies.
SearchASP.com (www.searchasp.com/)	An ASP-specific search engine delivering daily news tailored to visitor's preferred topics, plus execution tips for ASP customers, with editorial content from veteran IT journalists.
TheASPExchange.com (www.theaspexchange.com/)	A neutral B2B hub creating a marketplace for rented software applications by matching small/medium businesses with ASPs.
Web Harbor.com: The ASP Industry Portal (www.Webharbor.com/)	A comprehensive independent publication covering the ASP market and promoting the ASP model to corporate customers nationwide.

CONCLUSION . . . .

This chapter thus concludes, as of early 2001, that the ASP industry has evolved beyond the preliminary phase of self-definition and has begun to take hold as a valid model for software service delivery. The numbers of companies utilizing ASP services are growing steadily, though still at a much slower rate than the rate of proliferation of ASP vendors themselves. If recent Gartner Group projections are accurate, however, the industry may be on the verge of a shakeout.

According to Gartner analyst Audrey Apfel, of the 480 retail ASPs operating today in the $3.6 billion industry, only 20 will survive as enterprise-class, full-service, retail ASPs by 2004.

Apfel justifies this prognostication with reference to ASP market performance. "The barriers to entry into the ASP market are very low, and many ASP vendors are chasing the billion-dollar market projections, but many aren't taking the time to fully bake their business models."

Apfel predicts fewer than 100 ASPs will offer viable point and product solutions by 2004, joining the remaining 20 full-service companies in sharing a projected $25.3 billion industry. Most current generation ASPs will fall victim to bankruptcy, lack of venture capital, mergers, or traditional competition.

Gartner suggests the shakeout in the ASP market will have far more dramatic impact than did the early 2000 downturn in the business-to-consumer retail market on the Web. According to the analyst, the biggest difference is that dotcom companies have tended "to implode with little effect on their customers, while a bankrupt ASP providing business systems like ERP and accounting systems could leave their customers in a real bind."

The Gartner Group projection, issued in August 2000, took on special meaning, coming, as it did, in the wake of the shutdown of Pandesic, a joint venture of Intel and MRP software vendor, SAP AG, in July 2000. The decision of Pandesic owners, based on low profits realized from the venture, left more than 100 customers urgently seeking ASPs. Most customers, though embittered by the experience, chose to stick with the ASP model and were forced to negotiate new SLAs with new providers "on the fly" and to bear the significant costs for relocating their data and preparing their new hosts for use.

The event illustrated the vicissitudes familiar to many companies that have outsourced applications, and in some cases entire IT departments, to third parties over the past three decades. It underscored the necessity of understanding the limitations of contractual service arrangements and preparing ways and means for coping with the risks.

However, in the case of the nascent ASP industry, the event also created a credibility gap that did not help the business cases of smaller service providers. Although larger players, including Qwest Cyber.Solutions, announced lucrative contracts (with different customers than those abandoned by Pandesic) shortly after the Pandesic incident, concerns continued to linger about the viability of smaller ASPs over the long haul.

The Gartner projection of an industry shakeout, announced shortly after the Pandesic shutdown, stimulated a grassroots debate about the ASP community's ability to regulate itself. "What's needed," wrote one *Computerworld* columnist, "is an industry-based oversight body that will force the ASPs to meet certain functionality and quality requirements." The column went on to observe

ASPs have been compared to banks because a company's data is very valuable, and the company trusts the ASP to keep its data safe and provide experts who have experience supporting and managing the applications. But there's no standard for what an ASP must provide to its customers. The service parameters are decided by the IT, marketing and legal departments of both companies involved in working out an agreement. . . . It's not enough for a software vendor to approve of several ASPs to host its applications, because the vendor doesn't assume any liability if these ASPs fail. If the ASPs don't form a regulating group that can step in during crises to protect business data, it's only a matter of time before the federal government becomes involved. (Barbara Myles, "Message to ASPs: Regulate, or Be Regulated," *Computerworld*, October 2, 2000)

The columnist concluded that a representative group of vendors, whose software is commonly hosted by ASPs, "should begin working with successful ASPs and their customers to determine the essential qualifications, ethical responsibilities and requirements of ASPs and how to certify or license them. The group should also draw up penalties such as disbarring and fining ASPs that don't meet these standards. The primary benefit to ASPs that meet these requirements is that companies will be more willing to do business with them." No formal move toward regulation, whether industry- or government-imposed, has been detected as of this writing.

In the final analysis, the ASP industry has evolved from a concept to a practice, but it is still a practice undertaken in the "Wild West" environment of a young and burgeoning industry. In such an environment, consumers would be wise to observe the classic legal dictum, caveat emptor.

Or, stated in Wild West parlance: "Never trust nobody."

6

So, What is Holding Up the ASP Revolution?

In this chapter…

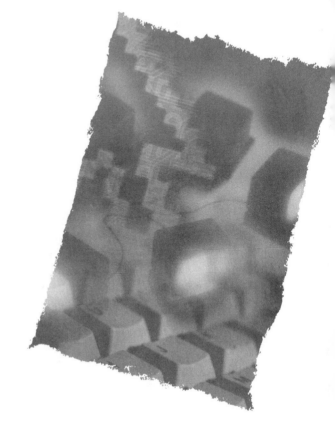

As stated in the author's preface, the ASP service model has demonstrated viability but does not yet enjoy widespread adoption among business. To conclude the first part of this book, it is useful to survey the obstacles that are impeding the realization of the ASP vision.

It would be an easy assumption to make, and many have, that ASPs are not yet in widespread use because the "pain threshold" within companies that would favor moving to an ASP model has not yet been reached. Elements of this "pain threshold" include:

- The increasing expense and scarcity of IT staff
- The increasing cost of traditional fat client desktop computing (e.g., PCs utilizing the Intel/Microsoft architecture for desktop computing), including the maintenance of distributed applications
- The increasing frequency of downtime due to distributed systems management inadequacy
- Increasing pressure to focus company resources on core functions
- Increasing pressure to outsource as a cost-savings measure
- Increasing requirements to extend application access beyond traditional enterprise boundaries
- Decreasing perception of value of in-house application delivery
- Increasing risk of IT obsolescence given unmanageable costs for upgrades

This list, which is essentially the value proposition of ASPs in reverse, could go on virtually ad infinitum. Basically there are many detractors who view the ASP as a solution in search of a problem. Until the problem presents itself squarely before a business decision maker, or until the pain of sticking with the status quo becomes greater than the fear and perceived risk of trying an alternative strategy, the ASP option is unlikely to be considered.

This observation has the value of simplicity and may even be true for some companies. However, it is not a comprehensive explanation for the paucity of customers that are signing up for services in a market that analysts project will enjoy revenue growth of more than 1,000 percent between today and 2004.

This chapter attacks the question of obstacles to ASPs from several directions. As depicted in Figure 6–1, there appear to be many hurdles that must be overcome before the ASP solution finds mainstream utility:

- The economy must favor ASPs.
- Customers must be willing (or compelled) to overcome inertia and to depart from customary IT approaches.

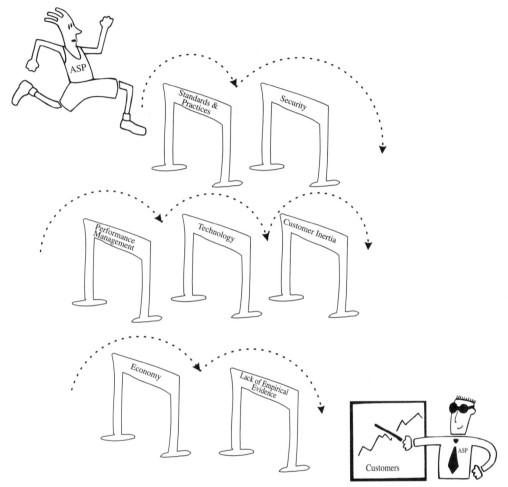

Figure 6–1
Potential obstacles to ASPs.

- Empirical evidence must support the ASP value proposition.
- Some nontrivial technical hurdles must be overcome.
- An effective performance measurement scheme must be developed to back-stop service level agreements.
- The customer must believe that data and application access is secure in an ASP.
- Standards and best practices must be fully articulated.
- Applications offered by ASPs must be the applications that the customers want and need.

Although this list may not be comprehensive, it does capture the observations and insights gathered from numerous IT consumers, analysts, and journalists who follow the ASP market. Regardless of its comprehensiveness, the author is aware that any discussion of impediments to ASP adoption is likely to invite the ire of ASP advocates, who, like advocates of any nascent technology proposition, tend to have little tolerance for naysaying.

The point of this chapter is not to suggest that the obstacles are insurmountable or that they apply to all companies with all their varied needs and interests. With all technologies, two cardinal rules apply: First, information technology is very seldom purchased for its own sake, but as an enabler of some other business goal; and, second, technically superior IT has no greater likelihood of succeeding (selling) in the business market than technologically mediocre information technology. These sobering dictums, when kept in mind, can help to check emotion and facilitate rational business decision making.

OUTSOURCING AND THE ECONOMY . . . .

When one maps the rise and fall of outsourcing activity against the general condition of the U.S. economy, it becomes immediately apparent that some sort of relationship exists. It would appear that periods of economic boom are often accompanied by technology acquisitions and in-house system deployments and integration efforts, whereas lean times have traditionally been accompanied by increased use of outsourcing services.

To be certain, too little data exists to substantiate the claim that a causal relationship exists between outsourcing and economic conditions. Business IT has not been around long enough, and certainly not in its current manifestation, to justify making such a claim. However, with the available data, it is clear that some relationship exists and that it may play a role in ASP adoption rates, as ASPs are properly regarded as part of a continuum of outsourcing arrangements.

Has outsourcing in the past been keyed to economic hardship within the companies who chose to use it? The answer is no—at least, not directly.

In the mid to late 1980s, a period in U.S. economic history characterized by high inflation and economic recession, mergers and acqusitions became the order of the day in many market segments, and outsourcing vendors were often the clear beneficiaries of these activities.

In the financial market of the day, for example, mergers and acquisitions among banks produced many of the large banking conglomerates we have today. When an acquisition occurred, institutions often turned to outsourcing companies to enable the acquired bank to maintain branch operations while its information systems were being absorbed into the DP operations environments of the acquiring bank. In such cases, economic conditions may have set the stage for the bank acquisition, but the outsourcing arrangements may be properly viewed as a by-product of the situation.

The point is that economic conditions may have only an indirect effect on outsourcing adoption rates. Not all companies that turned to outsourcing did so because they were "feeling the pinch" of economic hard times. Some did, of course; but, it can be argued persuasively that most companies chose outsourcing for other business reasons keyed to the business value proposition of outsourcing itself.

So, the question persists whether economic factors are impeding the adoption of current ASP services. Doubtless, they are a factor. Many ASPs advance economic arguments to sell their service to prospective customers:

- Expensive to maintain fat client desktop computers can be replaced by thin client, browser-based devices communicating with applications hosted at the ASP.
- IT staff are not only difficult to find, but expensive to recruit and retain. ASPs can solve the problem.
- Software expense (or the expense of rolling out enterprise-class solutions) can be reduced with an ASP.

Such arguments may find a more receptive ear in periods of economic belt-tightening than during a time of plenty. According to Michele Perry, senior vice president of marketing for ASP Usi, the company has always "shied away from the economic justification for ASPs."

> We push the values of faster deployment and better technology and try to deliver a solution that is as cost-effective as possible, without necessarily stressing the cost-cutting aspects. We try to cultivate customers who need strategic solutions available on a 24-by-7 basis—secure, reliable, and available. We find that those who are turning to ASPs to cut costs are just as inclined to outsource their applications to [a Third World country].

Perry notes that the preponderance of companies that utilize USi are Fortune 5,000 firms interested in enterprise applications such as ERP and CRM. USi has attracted a veritable who's who of clients, growing to a $300 million-per-year company in about two years: the quintescential ASP success story.

Although the general condition of the economy has not affected USi's client adoption rates to date, Perry is willing to concede one important influence: the stock market's changing attitude toward "dotcoms."

The much ballyhoo'ed "new economy" startups of the late 1990s, Internet-based companies, or dotcoms, initially received a positive reception by the stock market. Overvalued by analysts and trading at prices inconsistent with earnings for nearly two years, the dotcoms put fear into the hearts of traditional "brick and mortar" companies. USi and other ASPs offering quick rollouts of complex ERP and CRM products capitalized on the sense of urgency of the traditional firms to compete with the dotcoms or else.

In 2000, the dotcom craze began to ebb. Many of the startups either failed outright or were seriously devalued by market analysts. "The dotcom slowdown," Perry notes, "reduced the urgency of ERP and CRM adoption by brick and mortar companies. This has reduced demands for services from consulting firms specializing in ERP or CRM, demands for ERP and CRM software, and also demands for ASPs offering these products."

Thus, the relationship between ASP adoption trends and the condition of the general economy, though not explicitly causal, does exist. It remains to be seen whether the general economic slowdown predicted by most economists, however short or long lived, will produce incentives or disincentives for ASP use.

CUSTOMER INERTIA . . . .

Another factor that must be considered when evaluating ASP adoption is good, old-fashioned, inertia. In physics as in business, objects tend to remain at rest (or in motion) until acted upon by some irresistible force. In the context of ASPs, the question is whether companies are moved by some compelling reason to change from the technologies that they already use to try something new.

Most vendors agree that education about the value proposition of ASPs is required in order to create momentum that favors the software service model. Large ASPs have left no stone unturned in their efforts to evangelize the value proposition, including seminar programs, email blitzes, direct mail campaigns, telemarketing, purchasing advertorial space in business and technology publications, and participating in conferences and trade shows as speakers and panelists. The belief is that articulating the value of ASP will drive customers to the model of their own accord.

Smaller ASPs, particularly many software companies and ISPs, are often less effective—for reasons of budget limitations or lack of marketing savvy—at getting the word out about services to prospective customers. This is one reason, cited by many large ASPs, that the overall ASP adoption picture appears poor. In the words of one ASP marketeer, "A lot of the smaller ISVs have good products that may be suitable for an ASP deliver model, but they just have no go-to-market strategy." Without one, motivating users to change from current software acquisition and usage models to the new ASP mode can be a Herculean undertaking.

ASPs providing enterprise-class applications have been a focal point of industry growth, according to both market analysts and the vendors themselves, and most of the sign-ups for service have occurred in this segment of the burgeoning ASP market if vendor claims and financial statements are to be believed. Some vendors attribute this trend to their success in getting the value proposition before key corporate decision makers.

According to a reader survey conducted by a technology trade press publication in October 2000, decisions about ASPs are made by information systems managers in 71 percent of the businesses surveyed, with involvement by business executives in only about 48 percent of the cases. The survey suggests that the prospects of ASPs are bright and that adoption is an accomplished or imminent fact in 30 percent of smaller companies (those with less than 1,000 employees) and nearly 70 percent of larger companies (with more than 10,000 employees) surveyed. Industry specialization is not a factor in the decision to adopt ASPs according to the study. Even in more traditionally conservative firms (defined by the publication as government, education, medical services), "interest in ASPs is high . . . with more than 50 percent of respondents in each sector are either using, exploring or planning to use an ASP in the next 13 to 24 months."

The problems with the survey, however, is that it offers no survey sample size, and, more importantly, that it seems to fly in the face of empirical data gathered from news reports of ASP sign-ups, total market size data based on reported vendor revenue, and interviews with vendors themselves—many of whom report that they are scratching their heads wondering how to attract customers.

The stark contrast between vendor-reported and survey-generated data can be clearly seen in the matter of a study conducted by the Oracle Applications Users Group (OAUG) and market analyst, The Aberdeen Group, which was conducted at OAUG's conference in April 2000. Here's what happened.

Oracle Corporation, which offers its applications through its own ASP, Oracle Business On-Line, and also through third-party ASPs, repeatedly reported to analysts and the trade press that "thousands of customers had signed up" to obtain Oracle applications on an ASP basis. The April survey of 1,024 of OAUG's 2,200 member companies revealed a very different picture. In a carefully worded statement, provided to the press in October by OAUG and Aberdeen, it was made clear that plans to use ASPs to implement electronic-business applications were "virtually nonexistent" among Oracle Corporation's enterprise network users. The leading impediment to using ASPs, according to the survey, was that the "large users don't know enough about just how ASPs work to sign on with them." Oracle Business On-Line clarified that it had signed up only about 100 customers to date, but that thousands had expressed interest in the company ASP and its partner ASPs.

It goes almost without saying that, for as long as businesses are confused about what ASPs are, what they offer, and why they may be preferable to traditional application services, inertia will win the day, and ASP vendors will continue to search in vain for customers. In the absence of reliable statistical trends and valid reportage of adoption rates by vendors themselves, it would be extremely helpful to customers to have even reliable anecdotal evidence about the value of ASPs. Attention turns to this issue next.

BUILDING AN EMPIRICAL CASE . . . .

USI's Perry reports that the ASP is now providing on a CD-ROM a solid set of case studies describing successful ASP implementations by USi customers. Given the vendor's undisputed lead in the industry (earnings topped $75 million each quarter in 2000), the company is in a rare position to back its business case with concrete case studies.

By contrast to USi, case studies have not been as forthcoming from other vendors, nor has their been much reportage of ASP customer successes in the trade press. In 2000, from January through October, *Computerworld* offered approximately 150 stories that mentioned ASPs. The preponderance of these articles covered industry news (i.e., which applications were being fielded and by what companies) and analyst prognostications—including a report about one study, offered by Evans Marketing Services in January, that one-third of all large corporations would be using at least one ASP-rented application by the end of that year! About 10 percent of the articles mentioned customer experiences with ASPs, and, of these, only a handful contained any detailed description of the service that the customer was utilizing and the customer's benefits derived from the ASP relationship.

Although a number of other "second-tier" publications (subscriber base of under 100,000 readers) did carry a number of case study–based stories about ASP customers, the limited circulation of these publications, as well as the limited use of Web-based resources (including case studies on the Web pages of vendors) continues to cause an empirical evidence gap.

The lack of case study–based evidence testifying to the benefits of ASP relationships is exacerbated by the case studies that are in circulation which criticize ASPs. In fact, of the customer cases that were offered in *Computerworld* in the timeframe under scrutiny, several related to the dislocation of customers and hardship brought about by the sudden closure of the ASPs Pandesic and ebase One in July. What was overlooked in the reportage, according to one disgruntled ASP vendor, was that both were companies with different names and bad track records before they claimed to be ASPs and failed in that endeavor.

It also does not help the empirical case for ASPs that the Gartner Group, seizing on the Pandesic and ebase One failures, portrayed an uncertain future for nearly all ASPs in the near term. In a report released in August, the analyst made the somewhat confusing claim that the industry was poised for a massive shakeout that would leave only 20 of 480 current ASPs standing. This statement raised more than a few eyebrows because the firm was also projecting an 80 percent per year growth in ASP revenues, growing from $1 or $2 billion in 2000 to over $20 billion by 2004.

Vendors quickly chimed in with their own dismal forecasts. Microsoft placed the number of surviving ASPs at about 60 worldwide within a year or two. A-services, the joint venture between Compaq and Cable & Wireless, placed the number at about 40. And IBM, which has been working with Qwest Communications to provide back-end data center services, estimated that only a dozen or so vendors would remain. Most vendor estimates focused only on large, full-service, big infrastructure ASPs.

In the words of one vendor, the Gartner Group's "sky is falling report" had to happen. With most technologies, said the ASP insider, there is a hype curve: first comes the hype, then the disillusionment, then things settle down somewhere in the middle. The Gartner Group report started the movement toward disillusionment.

TECHNICAL HURDLES ·

Companies do not purchase solutions that they perceive to be ill-suited or unready for business use. Over the past three years, many technical hurdles that were potentially limiting to ASPs have been surmounted, but a few remain.

One technical limiter of ASP adoption has been the technology for delivering application services effectively across a WAN. Costly private leased lines provided the connectivity between past generation outsourcing vendors and their customers' headquarters. Early ASP advocates suggested that the Internet and VPNs enabled across the Internet would eventually provide a cost-effective networking solution for ASPs. In reality, most ASPs were forced by the unreliable performance of the Internet (sometimes disparaged as the World Wide Wait) to settle for private networks to deliver the goods.

The good news is that ASPs are able to capitalize upon the pragmatism that descended on the WAN market, ending the Frame Relay versus Asynchronous Transfer Mode (ATM) wars that had long been the bane of IT managers. Traffic can be exchanged between the two services using protocol conversion devices located on the customer premise or in the carrier networks. And to the user, it looks like one seamless network. The hybrid network is also more affordable and that, combined with telecommunications vendor contract discounts for large ASPs, equals private networks with high-performance, high-bandwidth, and high-reliability characteristics at discount prices. For customers requiring connections for employees on the road, ASPs can generally offer Internet or VPN access as an add-in service. (See Figure 6–2.)

The not-so-good news has been linked to the "last mile"—the wiring from the network point-of-presence (POP) to the customer premise. (See Figure 6–3.) Except in cases where the customer is willing and able to support expensive private connections directly to the company site, obtaining broad bandwidth ("broadband") connectivity across the entire path from the ASP to the customer location has required the purchase and provisioning of broadband services—such as xDSL—from the local exchange carrier (the local telephone company) and the business site.

Obtaining broadband services in the last mile has been a source of significant delay in ASP service roll-out in some cases. Numerous ASPs have responded by entering into special arrangements with competitive local exchange carriers (CLECs) or with interexchange carriers (sometimes called "long distance carriers") to secure desired service commitments. The carriers too have responded with programs targeted at ASP customer broadband provisioning, and infrastructure is slowly being rolled out to major cities.

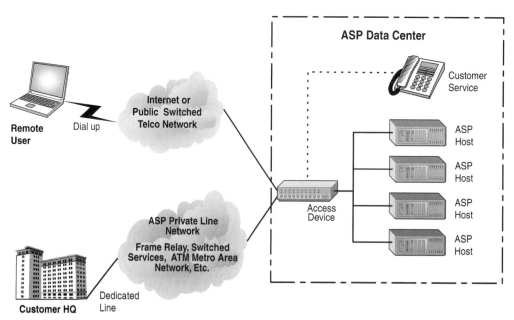

Figure 6–2
Delivering ASP services across a private network.

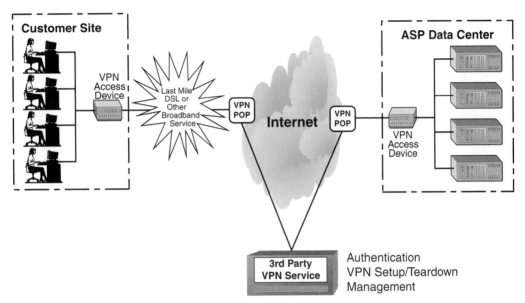

Figure 6–3
Delivering ASP services via an Internet-based virtual private network.

In addition to broadband connectivity, concerns have also been raised about the quality of service available to guarantee adequate bandwidth and low latency for remotely hosted applications. In a conversation with then ASP Industry Consortium Chairman Traver Gruen-Kennedy in fall 1999, he was quite animated in his description of an innovative quality of service protocol that was about to be implemented within the operating system software used by Cisco Systems in its routers and switches, which provide the majority of the networking infrastructure of the Internet, and in corporate enterprise networks. The network-based application recognition (NBAR) protocol, argued Gruen-Kennedy, would enable the specification of application delivery service levels and improved techniques for monitoring SLA compliance.

Cisco Systems added NBAR to its operating system in November 1999 and subsequently made the technology a centerpiece of its CiscoContent Networking architecture. NBAR technology, which is still being applied in many ASPs, is among the first of several strategies for addressing the management and provisioning concerns that are raised by customers considering ASPs.

Finally, as stated in a previous chapter, new applications—and, in some cases, Webified versions of existing applications—are only now coming to the market. Prior to 2000, organizations were forced to deploy traditional, non-ASP-ready applications in conjunction with Web-enabling software such as Citrix Systems WinFrame and MetaFrame, sometimes with unpredictable results.

A March 2000 report from Tolly Research, in which the firm tested different types of applications running on servers with the Citrix Systems Web-enabling technology and communicating with different types of clients (Java, Windows, and ActiveX) concluded that the network and system resource utilization requirements published by vendor "might or might not be accurate." The applications themselves proved to be the variable. This was less a revelation than a well-understood fact among integrators and users of the Citrix product, and a source of jitters for some prospective customers of ASP services.

The researcher recommended that ASPs carefully benchmark each application prior to its use to obtain a more accurate picture of system resource demands and network bandwidth utilization. Said Kevin Flood, Tolly Research's vice president of research, "You have to make sure your applications have enough bandwidth to perform properly. Otherwise, users will experience more and more latency, and there will be glitches in the interface, especially as they continue to scale and add users."

New ASP-ready applications, combined with service level guarantors such as NBAR, should assuage concerns over time about the actual readiness of the ASP value proposition for corporate prime time.

PERFORMANCE MEASUREMENT GAP . . . .

One area of concern about ASPs that has received considerable attention in the trade press is how to measure the performance of applications delivered via this model. There is tremendous concern among end users, evidenced in numerous opinion polls and surveys, that outsourcing applications to an ASP results in a loss of control over how those applications will perform.

Although some of these concerns have been assuaged through the use of private networks and segregated hosting platforms (see previous chapter), this is a short-term solution. As more and more ASPs move toward a shared model for service delivery in order to realize the economies of scale possible through infrastructure and personnel sharing, and as increasing use is made of the Internet and virtual public networks to deliver applications to end users, concerns about control will again emerge.

What would fix the problem in some user minds is a performance monitoring and reporting tool that offers statistical data on ASP application performance "end-to-end"—that is, from the hosting platform, across the network or Internet to the user desktop or other client device. Although top ASPs are able to capture this type of performance data in private networks, Internet-based delivery makes performance monitoring much more elusive. Technologies in development for Internet end-to-end performance monitoring appear promising and are discussed in a later chapter.

A related issue, however, is how the performance information will be provided to the ASP customer. Most of those ASPs who do utilize systems and network management applications to measure how well their hosted applications are performing do not share this information with customers in its "raw form"—though a few will do so if the customer so requests; most provide summary reports only. This may change over time as customers express their desire for a real-time view, accessible via a browser, into the performance of the hosted application.

SECURITY . . . .

A key concern of potential ASP customers is security. This is understandable given that the ASP is being entrusted with data and with applications that support potentially mission-critical business processes.

Although many ASPs go to great pains to educate both their customers and their sales force about the security provisions offered in their application hosting solutions, numerous analysts have gone on the record with criticisms of ASP security provisioning. Less well-capitalized ASPs often have poor physical security in place, protection designed to keep unauthorized persons out of the ASP data center. Others lack application security provisions, designed to detect possible intrusions into hosted applications by unauthorized users, and a number of ASPs have inadequate safeguards against network-based attacks, including denial of service attacks that prevent user access to hosted applications.

A more complete analysis of security technologies is offered in a later chapter. For now, it is important to note that an increasing number of third-party security service providers are popping up to supply ASP security needs on an outsourced basis. This fact, plus improvements in network, system, and application security techniques, and a greater insistence among prospective customers that effective security provisions be implemented before signing over applications to a hosting service, are all contributing to the refinement of security practices within the ASP space.

STANDARDS AND BEST PRACTICES . . . .

Alluded to in the previous chapter, standards and practices are still evolving in the ASP space. At this point, most of the best practice "certifications" available in the industry are fairly meaningless, including ISO 9000 Management Systems standards-based certification. Put simply, an ISO 9000 auditor is not saying anything about the quality of an ASP who is certified, only that the vendor has some procedures in place that appear to control how services are delivered.

For the most part, system vendor-backed certifications still appear to be tied more to how much equipment the ASP purchases from the vendor of the certification than to any measurement of quality of service offered by the ASP itself. For the most part, criteria for obtaining one of the growing number of vendor "certifications"— such as SunTone for Sun Microsystems—is a closely held secret, mitigating its value in determining ASP service quality.

Some "Big Five" audit/accounting firms are developing ASP standards and practices, and the ASP Industry Consortium itself is slowly articulating guidelines for evaluating ASPs that may lead to standards and practices in the field. Until these programs yield fruit, consumers must make their own evaluations based on observations, on-site visits, and so on.

THE RIGHT APPLICATIONS . . . .

USI's Perry likes the expression, "If you don't need transportation, it doesn't matter what kind of car you buy." Perry is alluding to the fact customers are unlikely to purchase applications from an ASP if the applications the ASP offers are not themselves regarded as useful or purposeful to the customer.

To be successful in attracting customers, ASPs must provide the right application functionality and offer best-of-breed solutions. Many smaller software vendors have niche products that answer the needs of a small community of end users, to which they have already marketed. Hanging out an ASP shingle will not expand the sales of the software into untapped markets if the need does not exist.

By contrast, software vendors sometimes create their own requirements for the ASP delivery model, according to Perry and other commentators. She notes that PeopleSoft's Version 8 Enterprise Resource Planning suite is a "jump ahead" of previous releases, "offering very attractive and completely new functionality." She says that it places existing customers of PeopleSoft at a difficult crossroads: "Imagine that you are a PeopleSoft customer who has just spent the past two years implementing their package. Now, you confront a new version that provides a jump ahead in functionality. What will you do?"

Perry notes that the problem would not exist if the software were being obtained from an ASP. ASPs can keep companies on the "bleeding edge" of technology without bleeding their coffers dry. This logic only applies, however, when the application is a product that consumers want and need.

The word to some ASPs who are troubling over slow customer growth: Take a look at the software that is being offered and ask the question, "Is this something that the customer needs?" If it isn't, no amount of borrowing from the hype around ASPs will help to make the software any more attractive.

CONCLUSION . . . .

This discussion constitutes a survey of some of the factors that may be impeding the "ASP revolution" anticipated by vendors and analysts. It is not intended to condemn ASPs or even to raise doubts about the validity of the ASP value proposition. It is, however, a set of observations based on the nearly daily interviews conducted during the researching of this book and reflects the real concerns of IT professionals and business decision makers who comprise the potential future customer base for ASPs.

ASP vendors can feel free to ignore the above concerns or to dismiss them as the idle ruminations of a cynical user community. However, nothing in the field of technology is inevitable, not even ASP adoption. Without answering the concerns of end users with tangible solutions, an ASP vendor must depend on luck rather than rationality as a basis for growing his business.

That isn't exactly a strategy that would earn an "A" from any self-respecting professor at the Harvard Business School.

Part 2

ASP Enabling Technology

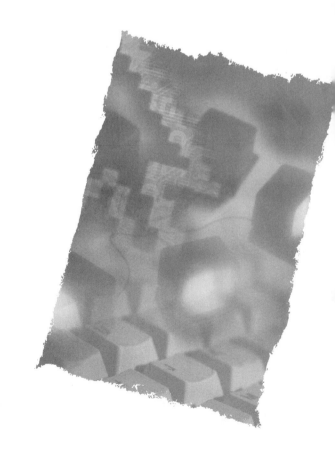

7

Basic Concepts:
Application Software

In this chapter...

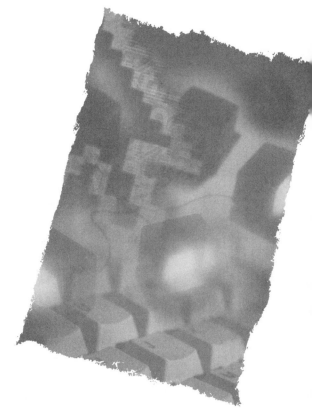

One central organizing concept of ASP is the hosting and delivery of application software using a platform other than the traditional desktop computer or server located at the business premise and maintained by business personnel. The ASP hosts the software, typically at a remote location, and extends the interface to "client devices" at the customer site via a network.

Although there are a few variations on this theme, such as "colocation" ASPs that set up and manage the necessary hosting platform at the customer premise and maintain it using ASP personnel stationed at the customer site, they are the exception, not the rule. For the most part, the term "ASP" implies the remote hosting of software and the delivery of application software as a service across a WAN, as depicted in Figure 7–1.

Given that application software is the heart of the ASP value proposition, it is worthwhile for those considering the ASP option to familiarize themselves at a basic level at least with what applications are, how they are created, and how they work to deliver services in support of business processes. This will aid understanding of how application services are enabled for delivery by ASPs.

WHAT IS APPLICATION SOFTWARE? . . . .

Application software is a broad term that embraces three distinct categories:

- single user applications designed for use on a single desktop computer by one operator
- multiuser applications hosted on a server equipped with a multitasking, multiuser operating system
- multiuser, client/server applications, whose component parts may be spread over multiple host computers that interoperate in accordance with a carefully defined message passing scheme

What all of these types of applications share in common is that they are all programs or sets of programs. Programs comprise variables—likened to the ingredients in a cooking recipe—and statements—instructions that define in a logical and step-by-step way what to do with the ingredients to produce a result.

These variables and instructions are typically written in a high-level programming language, such as COBOL, C, C++, FORTRAN, BASIC, Pascal, or LISP, which is then translated into a low-level programming language using a "compiler" utility. The compiled code is much closer to the machine language used by the hard-

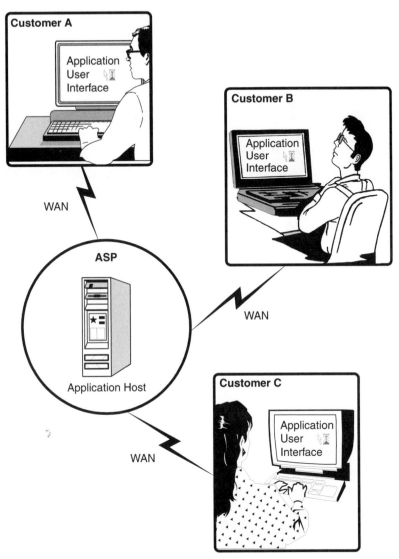

Figure 7–1
Software delivery via the ASP model.

ware of the computer itself to facilitate high-speed execution. It is possible, by the way, to code directly in a low-level language, such as assembler, but this approach requires a skills set that is generally found in only the most expensive programming staff. The greater availability and lower cost of trained personnel with high-level application programming language skills, combined with the proliferation of efficient compiler utilities, has favored the use of high-level languages for application software development.

It should also be noted that some new application "languages" came to the fore as commercial products over the past two decades intended primarily to facilitate rapid code development by nonprogrammers. So-called fourth-generation languages (4GLs) made their debut in the middle 1980s and held out the promise of replacing programmers altogether. Using English-type commands, vendors argued, nonprogrammers could develop programs that would then be converted to high-level language code, compiled and executed.

In many cases, a 4GL was leveraged to create programs designed for use with a specific vendor's database product, runtime environment, or just-in-time compiler. Ultimately, many 4GL environments proved so complex that, instead of removing the expense of programming staff, they merely encouraged the development of a new cadre of 4GL "programmers" that marketed their expertise in the 4GL language rather than (or in addition to) expertise in a high-level, or third generation, language.

An example of a successful 4GL is Sun Microsystem's Java, which was revamped and renamed in 1995 following the poor industry reception offered for its predecessor, OAK. Java is an object-oriented language similar to C++. However, Java is generally viewed as a simpler language to use in application development than C++ because it eliminates the cryptic commands often associated with common programming errors.

Java source code files (files with a .java extension) are compiled into a format called "bytecode" (files with a .class extension). These Java "classes" can then be executed on a broad range of computers, mainly because Java interpreters and runtime environments, known as Java Virtual Machines (VMs), have been developed to support most server operating systems. Bytecode can also be converted directly into machine language instructions by a just-in-time compiler.

Java was reengineered by Sun to provide a number of features that make the language well suited for use on the World Wide Web. Small Java applications, called Java applets, can be downloaded from a Web server and run on any computer featuring a Java-compatible Web browser, such as Netscape Navigator or Microsoft Internet Explorer.

In addition to applets, Java can also be used to create a servlet: essentially, an applet that runs on a server, typically a Web server. Without getting too far ahead of the discussion, there are reasons for preferring the use of servlets to another mechanism commonly used on Web servers, that is, the Common Gateway Interface (CGI). CGI enables an application written in virtually any programming language (including Java) to be executed in response to browser request. However, the CGI-executed program disappears once it has fulfilled a request. By contrast, Java servlets are persistent. Once a servlet has been started, it remains in memory and can fulfill multiple requests. The benefit is that there is no time wasted to set up and tear down a program function. By consequence, servlet-based applications execute more quickly, and users sense a greater degree of interactivity from the Web site.

Recently a new crop of so-called fifth-generation languages has begun to appear that incorporate the concepts of knowledge-based systems, expert systems, inference engines, and natural language processing. Because they are usually tied to a specific vendor's database offering, object-oriented programming model, or other proprietary technique or component, no fifth-generation language has yet established itself as the dominant application development language.

In summary, there are five generations of application programming languages currently, as shown in Figure 7–2. In general, the higher the language is on the chart,

- The more program structure has been built into the language itself
- The greater the ease with which applications can be implemented using the language
- The lower the skills requirement for implementors (the language is more user friendly and requires less formal programming skill)
- The less typing is involved in building applications with the language (owing to visual or preformatted functions or components)

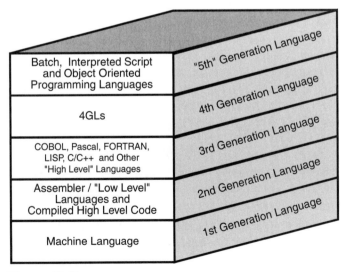

Figure 7–2
Computer languages: a generational view.

- The more limited developers are in designing applications using the language (predefined structures and preformatted functions restrict diversity, though most higher level generation languages allow developers to make calls to "outside" routines written in lower level languages)
- The easier it is to learn the language
- The more graphical the development environment
- The more useful features are available to aid in debugging code, tracking data structures, and preserving data types

By contrast, the lower a generation language is on the chart,

- The more manual coding the developer will need to do
- The less constrained the developer is by language-imposed capability restrictions
- The more complex functionality the developer can engineer into the resulting application
- The lengthier the development life cycle, owing to iterative code testing requirements
- The more work that the designer will need to perform mentally, and potentially the greater the likelihood of programming error

Scripting languages, macrolanguages, and batch languages might be classified collectively as another category of programming language, though the intent of these languages is typically to augment, rather than replace other program languages and development methods. Scripts, macros, and batch files feature English-type commands that make them accessible to nonprogrammers. Rather than being compiled, these programs are "interpreted" by a special command processor when they are executed. In many cases, scripts, macros, or batch files are created to automate certain routine environmental setup functions. For example,

- A script may be written to instruct a modem to dial a particular telephone number whenever a data communications program (a compiled software application) is executed.
- A macro may be programmed within a word processor to minimize the keystrokes required to format a document.
- A batch file may be created to set up certain environmental variables (monitor resolution, audio volume, etc.) prior to launching a computer game or other multimedia application.

Although some of these quasi-application languages may be rich in terms of the commands and functions that they offer, only very rarely will scripts, macros, or batch files be used to create an entire application—mainly due to their slower execution speed when compared with compiled code.

In the final analysis, the determination of which type of application language is best used to create an application has much to do with the nature of the application itself. FORTRAN is generally viewed as well suited to calculation-intensive applications, but is often regarded as ill-suited to lengthier programs. Pascal is viewed as very well structured and readable, but less flexible than C. Most observers agree that too much time has been spent debating the relative merits of one language over another. Other, and possibly more important, keys to language selection are the platform(s) for which the application is being developed, and the skills and preferences of the developers who must do the coding.

APPLICATION DESIGN AND PERFORMANCE . . . . . .

Whether compiled or interpreted, the performance of application software is first and foremost a function of the underlying program code—or, more precisely, the efficient use of hosting platform resources by the code. This is as true today as it was in the early days of computing, when computer processors were slow, and resources, such as memory, were scarce.

From the outset of the computer revolution, it was necessary to pay close attention to machine resource utilization when writing software. A programmer could easily overtax computer processing resources with code that was too convoluted or too large to load into memory (think of memory as a chalkboard that temporarily holds program instructions and variables so they can be referenced by machine components). Violating the environmental parameters imposed by hardware specifications would cause programs to act unpredictably, to "abend" (fail abruptly), or to lock up entire systems.

Despite technology constraints, there always seemed to be a cadre of programmers who produced "elegant code"—that is, efficient programs that used the fewest and most direct instructions, and the smallest possible number of variables. The origin of the term "hacker" is rooted in this period. A hacker was a moniker for someone who manifested a mastery of the application development craft: it had this positive connotation for many years before it was associated with developers of computer viruses and other malicious programs.

Hackers tended to avoid twisted logic and convoluted instruction statements, referred to as "spaghetti code," both because these features tended to make programs more resource intensive and because they made code more difficult to maintain and upgrade over time. Looking back at the constraints imposed by early server operating systems and hardware architectures, the accomplishments of the hackers were little short of miraculous. The programs they produced stand today in stark contrast with much of the "bloatware" sold by commercial vendors.

In the 1980s, there was an effort to define application development methodologies that embodied the techniques of hackers so that they could be leveraged by less masterful programmers to produce elegant code. These methodologies also grew out of a need to enable teams of programmers to work together to create software that would capitalize on improving computer and operating system capabilities and on up-and-coming client/server architectures. These "structured approaches" were further promoted as a means to expedite application development, shortening the extremely lengthy application development life cycle that often accompanied large and complex software development efforts.

The new software development methodologies brought with them new software design philosophies. Instead of designing an application as a monolith—that is, a single block of program instructions and variables—new application development methods sought to create applications as "systems" comprised of many discrete program building blocks sharing a well-defined framework for interaction. The heart of the new application design was initially the relational database, which stored variables, program elements, and preformatted components such as report formats and standard screen definitions. This move to a distributed application architecture was the beginning of a software "deconstruction" trend that continues today.

As noted, a few of the structured application development methodologies were "productized" by database vendors and others in the form of packaged "application development environments." These development environments offered, among other things, support for a specific 4 GL, prefabricated code for utilizing certain common environmental resources (the Windows graphical user interface, for example) and visual development tools that enabled programmers to see how their application module displayed on the screen and connected to or interoperated with other modules before the code was compiled.

Some products were touted as rapid application development (RAD) tools, and offered "code generators"—programs that interpreted diagrams or scripts and generated application code in a low-level application language—that became notorious, in many cases, for generating "inelegant" code. Over time, the best of the RAD product features have been largely integrated into modern application development environments as a matter of course.

The advent of structured methodologies and application development environments should have led to the consistent creation of high-quality, high-performance applications. For a number of reasons, however, the results have been mixed. One reason for the mixed results that are being witnessed today is straightforward enough: the platform to which application software is being written is itself in a more or less constant state of change.

In the past, and in many cases today, application software was developed to operate on a specific host platform comprised of an operating system and a hardware infrastructure. Software developers who were interested in supporting heterogeneous platforms comprised of different hardware and operating system software components were required to write completely different versions of their code to meet the specific requirements of each supported platform. One goal of the developers of later third generation programming languages, such as C++, and of 4 and 5GLs, was to address this issue by making a language that was more or less platform agnostic. Programs written in the platform-agnostic language could then be compiled using a platform-specific compiler and "ported" to the new platform with ease. This remains a holy grail.

In place of this effort, specialization has become the order of the day. According to many observers and analysts, many software developers have abandoned the support of multiple hardware and operating system platforms to focus on specific operating environments that appear to enjoy widespread industry adoption with respect to specific functions.

Market share data from analysts is a poor guide to understanding operating environment preferences according to one study. Of the 5.7 million operating environments shipped in 1999, Microsoft NT dominated with 38 percent, Linux was second with 25 percent, Novell had 18 percent, UNIX vendors 15 percent, and all others accounted for the balance of 4 percent. However, such market share data alone is insufficient to evaluate the purpose to which a particular operating environment deployed within business is being put.

Many industry observers dismiss as incorrect the popular perception that all operating environments are general purpose in nature. Businesses tend to use different operating environments for very different purposes.

The four "uses" most often cited by companies deploying Microsoft NT and Novell Netware operating environments are, in order, file and print services, electronic messaging, communications services, and database support. By contrast, companies fielding UNIX servers rank database support as their number one use for the operating system, followed by electronic messaging and custom application development. Linux, though capable of supporting a broad range of applications, is primarily used to support Web servers; in contrast to UNIX, less than 10 percent of companies use Linux to host databases.

Thus, though operating environments are functionally similar, they tend to fill very different application niches. This has driven software developers to develop applications, first, to work with the platforms that the market prefers to use for applications of a given type, and second, to work with platforms that enjoy the greatest distribution in the market. Although this trend does not promote the noble goal of "platform agnosticism," it puts food on the table for the ISVs.

Of course, this phenomenon is good news for those developers authoring single user software running on a single platform, and even for multiuser software operating in a simple two-tier client/server architecture (see Figure 7–3). In each instance, application software can be tailored, as it has been the case traditionally, to fit the operating environment of a particular hosting platform where the application must execute. With single user/single platform software, the software resides on the system where it is executed, and is operated by the user. With simple, two-tier client/server, application logic is typically contained in a database server, which is accessed by multiple users equipped with client software operated on a PC or workstation. To the extent that the software is designed to operate within a set of parameters defined by the operating system and hardware capabilities of each hosting platform, acceptable application performance should be forthcoming.

The trend to expand client/server computing beyond the realm of simple two-tier configurations complicates this one-to-one relationship between software-host compatibility and application performance. Beginning with the interest in ERP and MRP systems in the early 1990s, then exploding with the advent of the Internet and World Wide Web in the middle of the decade, the move toward three-tier, four-tier, and *n*-tier client/server application architectures increasingly tied application perfor-

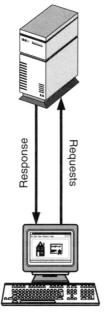

Figure 7–3
Simple two-tier client server.

mance to the efficiency of networks and "middleware" used to tie together application program elements that resided on different platforms. In other words, application performance was increasingly linked to how well the client/server infrastructure performed as a whole, rather to the efficient utilization by an application of a specific host server's resources.

Figure 7–4 provides a simplified diagram of a Web-enabled three-tier client server application, circa 2000. Note that the application utilizes, within the company premise, a tier of database servers to hold data, preformatted reports, and other components used by a second tier of application servers. Application servers contain business logic and code elements designed to receive requests from the client tier (PCs), to process those requests and present them to the database servers, and to respond to the client with the requested results. Middleware is used to ensure that these transac-

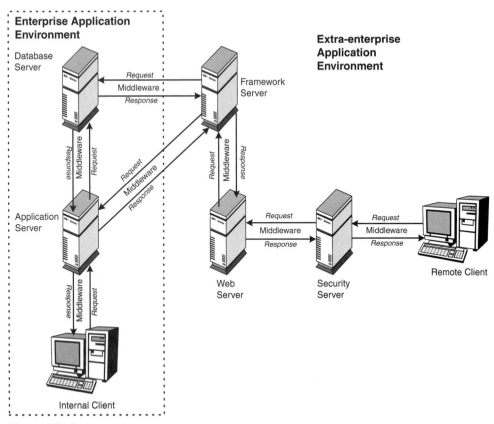

Figure 7–4
A simplified *n*-tier client/server application design.

tions occur per the application designer's plan and that no transaction request or response gets lost within the plumbing of the three-tier client/server infrastructure.

With the "Web-enabling" of this three-tier client/server solution, an additional
set of technologies is brought to bear. Additional Web servers are carted out to facilitate access to the application by browser-equipped Web-based clients. Such a strategy
may also require the introduction of a framework server that provides translation of
the output from the internal application into HTML format or other formats required
by the client devices (wireless personal digital assistants (PDAs), wireless cell
phones, Internet applicances, etc.). Still other servers may be deployed to enhance the
security of the remotely accessed application.

Even in the simplified diagram in Figure 7–4, it quickly becomes evident that the
performance of the overall application is as much a function of the middleware used to
connect the application elements as it is a function of the efficient host resource utilization characteristics of the discrete application components themselves. Middleware has
thus received a tremendous amount of attention from vendors seeking to Web-enable
legacy applications. The next chapter discusses middleware in greater detail.

CONCLUSION . . . .

Application software is the heart of the ASP value proposition. Yet much of the current software offered by ASPs was designed for a pre-ASP reality in which applications owed their reliability, stability, and performance to a carefully designed and
managed relationship with the operating system and hardware platform on which they
were hosted.

In the period just prior to the advent of ASPs, application developers began designing software for use across distributed corporate networks, leveraging client/
server architecture and placing increasing responsibility for application performance
outside of the server host—on the middleware used to connect application components together and on the networks used to provide the necessary connectivity infrastructure. Some would argue that the difficulties that often accompanied n-tier
client/server application deployment are but a small preview of dilemmas that are
bound to mitigate the capability of ASPs to deliver on their value proposition.

ASPs argue otherwise. They point to maturing middleware technology, the advent of new applications designed with ASP deployment in mind, and the rise of Web
technologies designed to support Web delivery of application services to make their
case. Each of these technology-based arguments are explored in greater detail later in
this book.

8 Basic Concepts: The Role of Middleware

In this chapter...

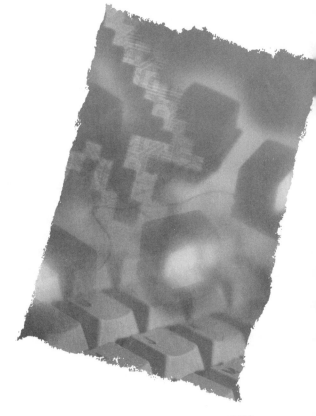

DETERMINANTS OF APPLICATION PERFORMANCE MOVE OUTSIDE THE BOX . . . .

The previous chapter examined application software programming concepts and surveyed the evolution of software architectures. The techniques and designs described in the chapter form the basis for most of the application software offerings of contemporary ASPs.

The chapter ended with a brief discussion of the impact of the client/server revolution on application software, particularly as it relates to the factors determining application performance, stability, and reliability. In the past, the performance of application software—its efficiency in operation, its propensity for abends (that is, in Microsoft NT Server parlance, its likelihood of causing the appearance of the "dreaded blue screen of death")—was tied directly to how well the application programmer had attended to the restrictions (and opportunities) imposed by the host operating environment during code design. With the advent of n-tier (3-tier and beyond) client/server architectures, the factors influencing application performance and stability moved beyond the host operating environment and into the network.

Against this backdrop, middleware—the "glue" binding together distributed application components—has increasingly garnered the attention of vendors, analysts, and developers as a key enabler of network-based computing models. Some vendors have begun implementing proprietary middleware schemes into their product architectures in an effort to deliver distributed application solutions that bear the vendor's own brand-name "end-to-end." Other vendors are endeavoring to grow their solution sets for distributed application environments by purchasing vendors of commercial middleware products—a practice that is seeing ongoing consolidation within the middleware software market.

At the same time, standards efforts are advancing within the Internet Engineering Task Force and elsewhere to define nonproprietary architectures and frameworks for gluing application components together across Web-technology based infrastructures. Despite the existance of standards-based middleware frameworks in the past, none have received broad industry adoption. It remains to be seen whether a standards-based approach will gain support as application software architectures move beyond the enterprise and into the world of ASPs.

As of this writing, middleware remains a key enabler, as well as a potential Achilles' heel, of distributed application architecture generally and of the ASP value proposition, in particular. Middleware efficiency, as much as application/host environment affinity, will determine whether the "application experience" delivered by the ASP to end users can compete with the traditional experience delivered by locally hosted applications.

MIDDLEWARE 101 . . . .

It should be noted that middleware is a much used, yet poorly defined, term describing two distinctly different functions. Generically, the term refers to software used to "glue" together application elements.

A distinction appears when the term is viewed at a somewhat finer resolution. Some middleware is included within client/server applications themselves. These applications are designed as a set of separate elements that may reside on different host systems. A kind of middleware may be included to facilitate transactions between these internally defined elements of single application.

A second type of middleware is offered itself as a software product. This type of middleware takes advantage of APIs or other software features (sometimes called "hooks") that have been designed into various application software packages in order to facilitate interapplication message passing. The purpose of this type of middleware is to enable two or more different applications to interoperate as though they were a single application.

This distinction may seem trivial, but it is important to keep in mind when sifting through vendor marketing literature. For example, Microsoft's Distributed inter-Net Applications (DNA) architecture, introduced concurrently with its Windows 2000 operating system, includes both intra- and interapplication middleware components. DNA is Microsoft's strategy for addressing n-tier client/server computing. Intra-application middleware components include Object Linking and Embedding (OLE) and Open Database Connectivity (ODBC) interfaces which have been developed by the company to facilitate data access among and between Microsoft and some third-party software products. However, the DNA architecture also includes interapplication middleware such as Microsoft's MSMQ message queuing product and DCOM protocol.

This chapter focuses on middleware in the interapplication context. The intra-application meaning of the term is useful to understand, however, because it provides a model that has been "writ large" by some vendors to create products that address some interapplication integration problems.

FLAVORS OF MIDDLEWARE . . . .

Middleware is connectivity software that provides services to enable multiple processes running on one or more machines to interact across a network. Middleware made its first appearance in the late 1980s in response to mounting requirements to enable mainframe-based applications to interoperate with newer distributed computing platforms. However, in the early 1990s, with the rise of n-tier client/server applications such as ERP and MRP, middleware was increasingly used to facilitate interapplication communications across heterogeneous and distributed computing environments.

Figure 8–1 illustrates the functional role of middleware. Middleware provides a set of services that sit between the application software and the operating system and network services of a network-attached host (sometimes called a "node"). Middleware services, which are often "exposed" (made available for use by application programmers and integrators) by means of an API, enhance the typical connectivity services of operating systems and networks to enable a richer and more robust connection between applications on different hosts. Most middleware products provide both an API for interfacing application software to middleware and a platform interface used to connect the underlying host platform to the middleware product. Communication among hosts is accomplished via the network transport that connects hosts together.

Middleware comes in many flavors. Most products are proprietary and feature a mix of structures and services that make the definition of a clear-cut taxonomy difficult. However, analysts tend to use four descriptive categories to group similar products together for purposes of market trend assessment. This taxonomy is about as good as any available. The four categories are as follows:

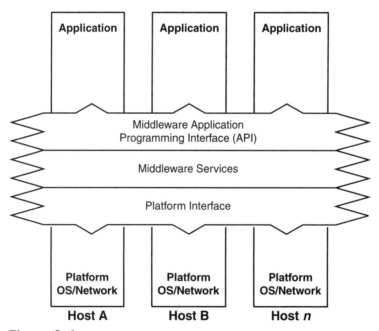

Figure 8–1
Functional view of middleware.

- Remote Procedure Call (RPC) Middleware: Enables the logic of an application to be distributed across a network so that programs on remote hosts can be executed as though they were being called locally.

- Message Oriented Middleware (MOM): Provides a means for program-to-program data exchange through asynchronous messaging between applications.

- Transaction Performance (TP) Monitors: Controls transaction applications and performs business logic computations and database updates.

- Object Request Brokers (ORB): Enable the "objects" that comprise an application to be distributed and shared across heterogeneous networks.

What all of these types of middleware share in common is that they seek to resolve application connectivity and interoperability problems. However, they approach the problems in very different ways.

Many products are blatantly proprietary, which exposes the user to dependency on a single vendor's product. Moreover, the sheer number of products has proven to be a barrier to intelligent selection, standardization, and use.

It is not uncommon to find multitier client/server applications, which have been developed and deployed on a "phased rollout" basis (in a phased rollout, additional application functionality is deployed for use by end users in stages over time). Rollouts may span several years, and development work may be conducted under the auspices of numerous application architects, resulting in the use of multiple types of middleware within the same application. Often this is a reflection of what products were popular at each rollout phase and what preferences each application architect brought to the development process.

The result is often an application "kluge"—defined in an earlier chapter, using the *New Hacker's Dictionary* interpretation, as "a crock that works" (as in the sentence, "I've kluged around the problem for now, and will fix it later"). These *n*-tier client/server application kluges are both very difficult to maintain over time and to recover in the event of a disaster.

To keep their computing environments manageable, developers need to select a small number of middleware services that both meet their functional requirements and fit the platforms they intend to support. Traditionally, this has not been the modus operandi.

Part of the reason is that developers often have difficulty deciding upon and sticking to application design choices. From the outset, many developers change their minds from one application to the next regarding the amount and type of functionality to include on the client and server sides of an application. Whatever they decide for one application will set middleware requirements for that application which may not be the same for the next application.

Of course, the solution to the problem is to adopt a programming standard for all applications and to enforce it consistently across all application development efforts. Until this is done, the numerous middleware products on the market will probably be deployed on a "point solution" basis (solving a specific problem encountered in a specific case), rather than providing a strategic middleware service infrastructure.

When packaged client/server versions of ERP and MRP software suites began to appear in the 1990s from companies such as SAP, PeopleSoft, and others, one of the selling points stressed by vendors was that purchasing these "off the shelf" products would mitigate the problems that plagued homegrown software, which were associated with design philosophy shift and inconsistent middleware usage. In the time that has transpired since, this is widely regarded as a specious argument.

Most package vendors compete with each other on a feature/function/price basis. When one vendor adds a desirable function to its product, its competitor must respond with an equivalent or superior feature in its product. To keep up with the competition, vendors have repeatedly licensed the software of third-party vendors (or purchased the third-party company outright) to add to their own offering. With a comparatively short time in which to get new versions of software to market, the vendors have often strayed from the middleware standards enforced in their core application set and used whatever middleware that could expedite the "integration" of the third-party product.

The result is that some of the leading packaged ERP and MRP products today are no less kludgy than their home-grown counterparts. This accounts in part for the lengthy deployment time requirements and frequent deployment failures associated with ERP and MRP package implementations and represents a set of headaches that have helped to make these applications among the favorites for outsourcing to ASPs.

In any case, middleware remains an important enabler of n-tier client/server architecture and, as such, an important enabling infrastructure component for ASPs offering n-tier client/server applications on a subscription basis. A closer look at each of the flavors of middleware is useful to see the benefits and potential drawbacks that each delivers.

RPC . . . .

RPC is the grandfather of middleware services, tracing its origins to the mid 1970s. RPC was used by programmers to enable a client program on one computer to execute a server program on another computer and return the results to the requesting client. By standardizing RPC calls, designers could shortcut the application development process by eliminating the need to custom-code specific procedures for every cross-server request. From this standardization effort, RPC middleware protocols were born.

Sun Microsystems is credited with the development of the first, widely adopted RPC protocol—part of its Open Network Computing (ONC) architecture in the early 1980s. At last inspection, the IETF was evaluating the specification for possible adoption as a standard.

RPC is also the centerpiece of the Distributed Computing Environment (DCE) intitiative promoted by The Open Group, an international consortium of computer and software manufacturers and users dedicated to advancing the interoperability of technologies from multiple vendors. DCE was an early effort to describe a common set of services, to be included by operating system vendors and server hardware manufacturers (including mainframes and PCs) with their products, which could be leveraged by all application developers to "glue" their products together with other products. The effort ran afoul, however, of application development approaches that rarely considered integration with other, potentially competitive, software products— except as an afterthought. When the requirement presented itself to interoperate with another application, the developer simply turned to one of many middleware point products for a solution rather than designing an application to work with DCE RPCs. When they needed a mechanism for exchanging data or extracting program generated variables from a remote application, software developers were just as likely to turn to an assortment of competing products that included MOM and distributed ORBs.

Despite the mixed reaction to DCE, RPCs continue to enjoy widespread use in situations where synchronous communications are desirable. Synchronous refers to the fact that an RPC, once issued by one application to another, begins a procedure that does not complete until a response is received or a time-out occurs. The client program waits for the response or time-out before proceeding to other tasks.

RPCs are typically embedded within the client portion of a client/server application program. Because they are embedded, RPCs are sometimes considered an intra- rather than an interapplication middleware solution, which may or may not be the case depending on how they are used. When the client program is compiled, the compiler creates a local "stub" for the client portion and another "stub" for the server portion of the application, as shown in Figure 8–2. These stubs are used when the application requires a remote function.

RPCs require greater direct involvement by the software developer in the mechanics of client/server application communications than do other middleware approaches. However, RPCs can deliver flexibility in application architecture not found in other middleware approaches because RPCs do not require knowledge of the location of the remote application.

RPC is considered appropriate for client/server applications in which the client can issue a request and wait for the server's response before continuing its own

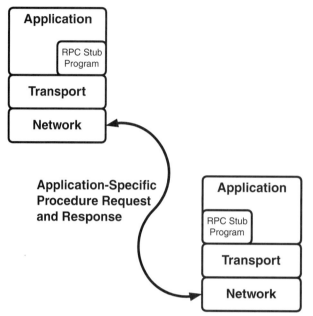

Figure 8–2
Remote procedure calls.

processing. RPCs are generally not preferred for applications involving distributed objects or object-oriented programming.

MOM . . . .

Message-oriented middleware, as depicted in Figure 8–3, is software that resides on both the client and server parts of a client/server architecture and typically supports asynchronous interactions between the client and server applications. MOM is often touted as a flexible architecture because it enables applications to exchange messages without requiring a "hard-coded" address (i.e., the name or identifier of the host system on which the application resides) within the network for either the sending or receiving applications.

MOM messages can contain formatted data, requests for action, or both. MOM systems typically provide a message queue service to hold messages in temporary storage if the destination process is busy or off-line. If the destination process is busy, the message is held in a temporary storage location (the queue) until it can be processed.

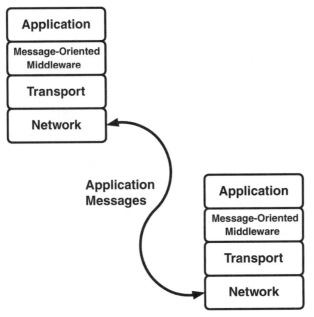

Figure 8–3
MOM messaging.

MOM typically operates in an asynchronous, peer-to-peer mode, but many MOM systems support synchronous message passing, as well. The asynchronous message passing that typifies MOM finds it frequently deployed in connection with event-driven applications—that is, with applications in which one function triggers one or several others. With most MOM products, application programmers are insulated from the complexities of client/server relationships. They leverage middleware APIs and pass messages to the middleware directly, rather than having to code a specialized application stub, as in RPC.

Asynchronous and synchronous messaging schemes have various strengths and weaknesses that are understood only in the context of the application itself. Synchronous messaging binds applications together tightly, ensuring that messages are received and acted upon before application processing continues. However, asynchronous messaging is less network-resource intensive: Messages sent do not wait for a response and are instead queued by the receiving application until they can be processed. The more sophisticated MOM products offer a synchronous messaging mode that "fails over" to asynchronous mode when networks are busy, applications are busy or unavailable, or when other user-specified criteria apply.

MOM has been around since the late 1980s. There are many products in this space offering a variety of proprietary messaging protocols and queuing methods.

Most server platforms and networking protocols are supported, but not by all products. A cost-multiplier of MOM derives from the fact that the middleware software, called the kernel, must run on every platform of a network. This may be offset, however, by the benefits of fast implementation and the reduced programming expense when compared with RPC.

It is also worth noting that, because the MOM kernel resides on all platforms that must communicate, it does consume processor cycles and memory on all client and server platforms. Both platform and network capabilities need to be closely reviewed before selecting a MOM product. Furthermore, heterogeneous platform environments often require different versions of the MOM kernel, which can lead to problems from a software administration and maintenance point of view.

MOM can be used in conjunction with RPC, with the latter providing synchronous communications between applications that require them. MOM can also be used effectively in connection with object-oriented architectures.

ORB ·

Before launching into a discussion of ORB, it may be useful to set the stage by discussing object-oriented programming (OOP) and how it differs from traditional procedure-oriented programming. For most nonprogrammers, OOP remains a mysterious concept which becomes even harder to understand when one asks a programmer for an explanation. One has the nagging feeling that it is something important that we should all know about. This feeling worsens when the words "object-oriented" are used by vendors to suggest an advantage or strength of their product. Yet, what object-oriented means remains elusive.

The simplest way to see the difference between object-oriented and procedure-oriented programming is to use the recipe metaphor advanced in the previous chapter. In procedure-oriented programming, each program contains a "recipe" consisting of data (sometimes called variables or structures), which are the ingredients to be used in the recipe, and functions, which are the procedures for using the ingredients. The program, when executed, performs the prescribed functions in a step-by-step method using the data provided.

In OOP, the same structures and functions exist in code, but the code itself is organized into modules called objects. Objects are then grouped, like individual recipes in a card file, into classes. Just as a recipe card file may be organized by dish type (all recipes for cooking meat or for baking cakes may be grouped together in the recipe box), object modules are organized into classes. An object is said to be an instance of a class, just as a cupcake is an instance of a broader category of baked goods. Objects respond to messages that are appropriate to their class. These messages often contain arguments that produce a certain response: to make 12 cupcakes, OOP calls for a message to be sent to the cupcake object that describes what kind of cupcake to bake and in what quantity. So, this OOP thing is as easy as baking a cake.

Some may wonder why OOP is preferable to good old-fashioned procedure-based programming. The answer is in two parts. For one, many observers of programming trends have noted for some time that applications are not written, they are rewritten. The same procedures are coded and used over and over again, even within the same software, consuming programmer time and energy. In the 1980s, there were several efforts within the IT industry to develop reusable code repositories to enable a building-block approach to software. Most schemes failed to realize their goal—that of creating a reusable code stockpile—owing to minute differences in the way that code handled the differences in operating environments and platforms.

Object-oriented programming grew out of this effort and embraced a philosophy of platform agnosticism. That is, the objects and classes that were created were independent of any particular relationship with any particular execution environment. Code required to fit applications to specific hardware and operating system software environments was simply encapsulated into objects of a class named for that function and environment.

The second value of the object-oriented approach was its preference for a more human-like language for handling the interaction between objects. Languages such as C++ and SmallTalk enabled complex functions to be accomplished using simple, Englishlike commands. One could create a list from the joining of several objects without writing pages of cryptic code defining the structure of such a list and delineating all of the data that needed to be accessed or generated by multiple procedure-oriented programs. These lists, if valuable, could themselves become modules of a class called list.

One final strength of OOP is called inheritance. Inheritance enables subclasses of objects to be created readily that can inherit the properties of parent classes. This saves the programmer time in rewriting an entire class just to add a few objects that have slightly different messages or behaviors.

Inheritance promotes code reuse and should expedite development time, reduce the number of lines of code required by an application, and minimize bugs. This adds up to faster deployment and lower maintenance costs for software. C++, Xerox Corporation's SmallTalk (and its vendor brands such as IBM's VisualAge), and Java are all examples of OOP languages.

Back to ORBs. The discussion of OOP noted that each object communicates with other objects via messages. An ORB is a middleware technology that manages communication and data exchange between objects. ORBs promote interoperability of distributed object systems by enabling developers to build systems by cobbling together objects from different vendors. The ORB acts as something of a gateway be-tween different object systems.

ORBs conceal the complexity of cross-system object interaction from the devel-oper. In effect, the ORB adds a "single-point-of-maintenance" for object interaction. As shown in Figure 8–4, an ORB provides services approximating those of a tele-phone exchange: It provides an interface definition for use by programmers in linking together all objects to the ORB, plus it provides the location and, in some cases, the activitation of remote objects, and handles the communication between clients and objects. Ideally, like the telephone exchange, the ORB enables objects to interact re-gardless of their location—to reach out and touch each other as though they were within close proximity.

The ORB provides a framework for cross-system communication between ob-jects. It also provides the means for objects to interoperate regardless of their environ-mental properties, that is, programming language, host operating system, host hardware and physical network location. In effect, the ORB makes the objects transparent.

There are many ways to deploy the basic ORB concept. ORB functions can be compiled as client software, run as separate processes, or ORBs can be provided as part of an operating system's services. This accounts for the diversity of ORB archi-

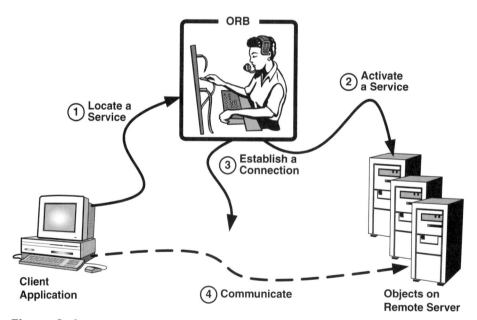

Figure 8–4
Object request brokers.

tectures that are being promoted within the industry today, including the Object Management Group's (OMG) common object request broker architecture (CORBA) specification, Microsoft's COM and DCOM, IBM's system object model (SOM), and Sun Microsystems remote method invocation (RMI), part of its Java specification.

TP MONITORS . . . .

RPCs, MOM and ORBs comprise a common type of middleware that provides services for program-to-program communication. By contrast, TPM provide application enabling services—that is, they provide applications access to the services of RPCs, MOMs, and ORBs, and to the underlying network, in a managed way to ensure optimum performance of the distributed environment.

TP monitors, simply put, are the traffic cops of n-tier client/server. They monitor transactions as they move from one stage of a process to another, ensuring that transactions reach their logical conclusion, or, in the case of a problem, that some appropriate action is taken.

Some TP monitors are combined with load balancing servers, which forward transactions to the least busy of two or more identical servers. As shown in Figure 8–5, TP monitor technology multiplexes client-initiated transaction requests on a fixed number of defined application processing routines. Clients are bound, serviced, and released as their transactions are handled by the back-end database, which only sees a managed, continuous stream of processing routines forwarded by the TP monitor.

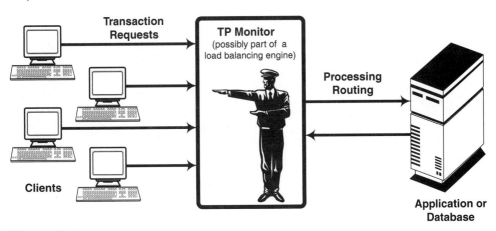

Figure 8–5
A transaction performance monitor in operation.

TP monitors are typically used to map client requests to application processing routines in the most resource efficient manner. An application processing routine may include an RPC-serviced synchronous session, an asynchronous MOM-based process, or some other predefined process and communications method. For more than 25 years, TP monitors have been employed to make applications traversing the client/server platform perform as efficiently as possible. The technology is core to some of the application hosting frameworks used by ASPs today.

BACK TO THE FUTURE . . . .

The popularity of various middleware schemes has shifted over time. In the absence of a dominant middleware architecture, most developers have deployed the middleware *de jour* to solve specific application communication problems. In early two-tier client/server applications, data access middleware ruled the roost, providing convenience in accessing backend databases from PC clients. TP monitors, combined with RPC for server access, came to the fore when three-tier client/server applications began to appear. With the advent of WANs, asynchronous MOM achieved preeminence as the solution of choice for internetworked applications. Today, the popularity of the object model for application design appears to be favoring OOP technology.

However, for all the popularity of middleware, little or no attention has been paid by vendors or developers to ensuring the interoperability of middleware products themselves. There are no compatibility standards that enable the replacement of one middleware product with a newer "best of breed" version, possibly from another vendor. This standards gap—the absence of uniform operational descriptions that can provide plug-and-play interoperability and enhance management and administration over time—shows little sign of being corrected anytime soon.

In the absence of such standards, vendors (Microsoft, IBM, and Sun Microsystems are only three examples) have begun to collect numerous point middleware products into middleware software suites. Over time, these suites are expected to become more integrated and, in the case of some vendors, to be delivered as integral operating system services.

For now, many business IT professionals find themselves taxed with the requirement to administer multiple middleware products, all deployed to support different parts of the same application. This is part of the burden that will be transferred to ASPs as application service responsibility moves outside the traditional enterprise and into the outsourcing world.

9

Basic Concepts:
The Application Server

In this chapter...

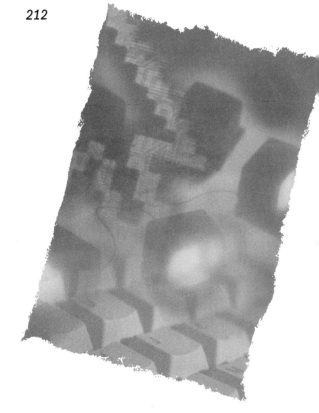

FROM APPLICATION SOFTWARE
TO APPLICATION SERVER · · · · · · · · · · · · · · · · ·

The preceding chapters have looked at application software and enabling middleware services that comprise the heart of the ASP value proposition: application delivery. The term application software covers a lot of territory, including applications that are written for deployment on a single host or PC where they are intended for use by one person, to software deployed on a single host or server but designed for use by many concurrent users, to applications designed to be hosted "on a network"—that is, across a complex arrangement of distributed server systems—for use by many end users at the same time.

Despite this variety, however, the simple fact is that most of the application software that is becoming available for subscription from ASPs today was not originally designed for delivery via the ASP model. That is to say, most software lacks the architectural features required for shared use across a WAN using Web technology.

For example, many desktop applications are designed for deployment and use in a specific environment, such as a single-user desktop PC operating the Microsoft Windows operating system and interface. These applications are designed to take advantage of local processors, local peripheral devices (storage, mouse, keyboard, audio card and speakers, video display, etc.), and local operating system and user interface functions. Although it is possible to "network" a single-user application—that is, to operate it across a LAN—usually the remote system, called a client system, must meet certain specific configuration requirements.

To network a single-user Microsoft Windows application, for example, typically the client system must itself be a Windows-compatible PC. More often than not, substantial quantities of application code elements (for example, dynamic link libraries, or DLLs) need to be installed locally on the client PC in order to facilitate its use with remotely installed elements hosted elsewhere in the network.

At the opposite end of the spectrum from the single-user, PC-based application, complex client/server applications are typically and explicitly designed for network-based use. In normal deployment, software application elements are spread across multiple servers—conceived as "tiers" of servers—and on clients. Middleware is used to support communication between server-side elements and client-side elements and also between elements distributed between servers at different tiers.

This is not to say that, unlike single user applications, client/server applications are automatically "ASP ready." Quite to the contrary, most client/server applications deployed before the Internet became popular as a business medium (and even for a few years after the Internet revolution) were not designed to take advantage of Web technology at all. These applications rarely, if ever, provided a software client that could operate within the environment created by a Web browser (with or without a local Java Virtual Machine.) Instead, special client software needed to be installed (and managed) on each and every workstation interacting with the client/server application—a methodology that is inconsistent with the ideal of a "universal client" represented by a Web browser.

Additionally, with most client/server applications, the middleware that was deployed to handle communications between clients and servers—and between servers on different tiers—within a corporate enterprise was not designed to handle such communications within a Web technology context. Web technology-based networks are characterized by varying latencies (delays) in messaging and by a lack of persistent connections and sessions. Such a network environment is hostile to the operation of many middleware products.

THE RISE OF APPLICATION SERVERS . . . .

It is now easy to see that additional technology is required to make non-Web-ready applications work with Web technology—and, by extension, with the ASP delivery model. The software industry has responded with software products known as application servers.

Application server is an umbrella term for numerous products designed to Web-enable software that may not be designed for use with Web technology. Application servers provide the means for ASPs to host applications and to deliver them to their customers across a Web technology interface.

A Web technology interface typically comprises one or more Web servers that interact with Web browser–equipped clients in accordance with the standard protocols developed for the Internet. The next chapter describes Web technology in greater detail. For now, it can suffice to say that application servers provide the mechanisms to integrate non-Web-ready applications and their computing infrastructure to Web servers in order to leverage the ubiquitous Web browser as a client.

There are many types of products described as application servers by their vendors. Some are sophisticated application interface extension products, similar in many respects to terminal servers once used to connect users to mainframes. These application servers provide the means to share an application by extending its user interface to efficiently network to a Web browser or Java Virtual Machine–equipped client system. They may also provide services that enable the sharing of a hosting server's resources (memory, processor cycles, storage, etc.) efficiently among many "concurrent instances" of the application, created as a result of simultaneous application accesses by multiple end users.

Some application servers of this type also provide logging and security services that aid in tracking hosted software usage for historical and billing purposes and to prevent access to application services by unauthorized persons. The current interest in commercial ASP services has resulted in significant advances in these additional management features.

A second type of application server software consists of Web-enabling middleware products delivered by vendors of database software for exclusive use with their own products. These Web-enablers provide the necessary connections for linking database-centric applications to Web technology.

This is particularly useful if a company already has a significant investment in a particular database product and seeks a comparatively inexpensive and expeditious way for "Webifying" its applications. However, such application servers expose their users to vendor "lock-ins" and may limit their ability to leverage new strategies and technologies which have not been embraced by the database vendor as they become available.

A third type of application server may be called a framework server. Framework servers deliver a strategy, often based on an object oriented programming model such as the CORBA or COM (see the previous chapter), which enables Web-ready systems to be created from a combination of existing and new application components (usually coded using C++ or Java languages).

In other words, these frameworks provide a new kind of middleware functionality that can be used to integrate back-end databases and older application logic with front-end interface technologies to support software use via the Web, across wireless networks, or by virtually any other delivery method desired by the organization.

OUT OF THE BOX WEB-ENABLED SOFTWARE ON THE RISE . . . .

Each of the types of application servers discussed provide mechanisms to facilitate the deployment of non-ASP-ready software in a hosted application setting. At the same time as these products are reaching the market, there is also a trend in certain segments of the software industry to design application software explicitly for ASP-based delivery to users. Examples of this trend include Sun Microsystem's Star-Office™ suite, Great Plains's enterprise resource planning and e-commerce products (recently acquired by Microsoft to facilitate that vendor's move into small and medium business market ASP services), and the latest versions of Oracle's and PeopleSoft's ERP and e-business applications.

Sun's StarOffice consists of a set of applications that offer functionality tradition-ally considered the exclusive domain of single user, desktop-deployed software: word processing, spreadsheet, presentation development tools, and so on. StarOffice develop-ers wrote their software with both shared usage and deployment via Web technology in mind. Used in connection with Sun's forthcoming StarPortal™ software, which adds se-curity and management functions required by ASPs for multiuser support, the software is touted by the vendor as a replacement for the traditional desktop by a "Webtop."

Similarly, software company Great Plains (see Figures 9–1 and 9–2) has created a suite of accounting and e-commerce applications that are designed for use with Microsoft's Windows server operating systems in combination with Microsoft's Web technology products, Internet Information Server and Commerce Server, and its data-base products, SQL Server and database. The result is a robust, ASP-ready configura-tion that has become so successful that Microsoft had already inked agreements to buy Great Plains in 2001, creating Microsoft Great Plains Business Solutions.

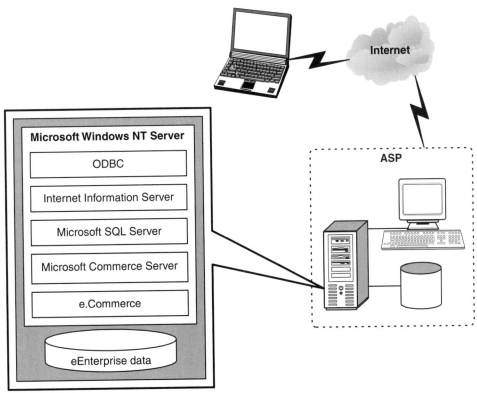

Figure 9–1
Microsoft Great Plains e-commerce application in single server configuration.
Source: Microsoft Great Plains Business Solutions.

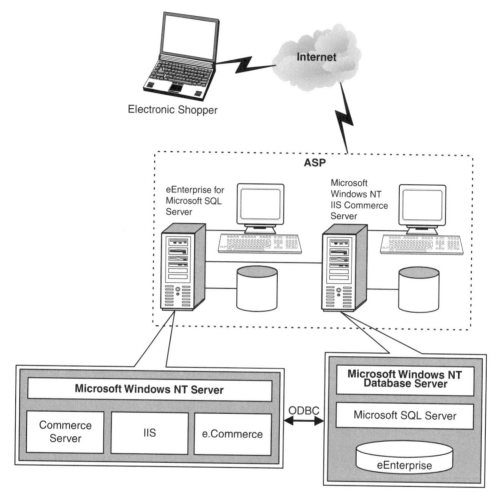

Figure 9–2
Microsoft Great Plains e-commerce application in multiserver configuration.
Source: Microsoft Great Plains Business Solutions.

Not to be surpassed by ASP-ready enterprise resource planning and e-business software products, traditional client/server ERP vendors, such as PeopleSoft and Oracle, are building "integrated application servers" directly into their software suites. PeopleSoft touts its Version 8 product as "pure Internet" and references the fact that no coding is required for client systems, which can access hosted applications through a Web browser.

As depicted in Figure 9–3, the centerpiece of PeopleSoft's Internet architecture is an Internet application server that leverages middleware technology from BEA Systems

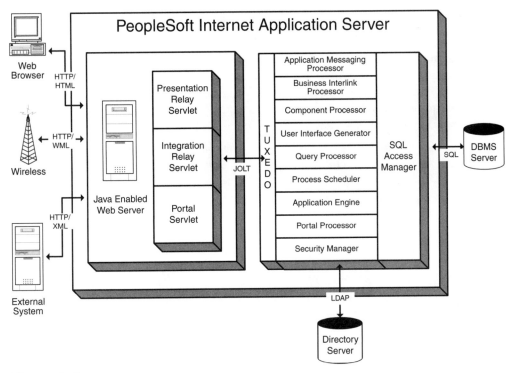

Figure 9–3
PeopleSoft's Internet architecture. *Source:* PeopleSoft, Inc., Pleasanton, CA. www. peoplesoft.com.

(BEA's Tuxedo Transaction Processing Monitor and Jolt, a set of software components to let Java programmers make BEA Tuxedo service requests from the Java language) to facilitate the integration of back-end applications and databases with a Web delivery technology (i.e., technology based on HTML, XML, and HTTP standards).

Similarly, Oracle Corporation has integrated its application server, previously a standalone product, into the 9i version of its relational database management system (RDBMS). Discussed in greater detail later, this software facilitates the rapid deployment of Oracle database–driven applications, including the company's own e-commerce application suite, to the Web technology interface and enables Oracle applications to be delivered by ASPs, including the company's own Oracle On-Line service.

Until all software is designed for ASP delivery, third-party application servers will be needed to facilitate application hosting. This redesign is likely to take several years, bolstering projections by analysts of steadily growing revenues for makers of application server products.

APPLICATION SERVER MARKET GROWING . . . . . .

According to analysts, the market for application server software is demonstrating steady growth as more and more companies Web-enable their internal environments and as ASPs make increasing use of application servers to enable software for subscription-based delivery. Exactly how much growth depends on the analyst—and on how the term "application server" is defined.

One prominent analyst uses a definition that excludes terminal server-style application servers, but includes database Web-enablers and framework products as defined earlier in this chapter. According to the analyst, application server software platforms are deployment and execution environments used for the execution of business logic, data access, and integration—and/or application integration. Application servers provide the minimum set of services required to deploy interoperable components as coherent applications. They provide their functions in a logical middle-tier of a multi-tier environment between clients and back-end applications and data sources. The minimum set of services are support for distributed, component-based solutions, security, transactions, a single and well-defined developer interface, runtime load balancing, and data persistence.

The analyst further states that application servers do not replace client/server middleware—a contention of some vendor marketing materials—but instead supply an integration point for applications and Web technology. Application servers offer ease of interoperation, support for a specific application development paradigm, and a level of abstraction beyond the capabilities of point middleware products.

This definition, by its complexity, demonstrates how even industry analysts are struggling to come to grips with the proliferation of so-called application servers in the market. It makes considerably more sense following a more detailed analysis of several application server products on the market today—many of which are being used by ASPs to Web-enable their software offerings. The balance of this chapter takes a closer look at each type of application server.

APPLICATION SERVERS
FOR SINGLE USER APPLICATIONS . . . .

Application "terminal servers," though not included in above analyst's definition of application servers, have provided a key enabling technology for many ASPs seeking to augment or replace software loaded onto individual desktop systems with comparable products hosted at the ASP. The replacement of expensive distributed desktops with centrally served and managed "Webtops" was an early battle cry of the ASP movement and remains a significant component in the value proposition of many ASPs.

The desire to share desktop applications from a common host system predates the current fascination with Web technology and ASPs. For nearly 20 years, prior to the advent of distributed systems, centralized mainframe systems hosted all application and delivered access to users via dumb terminals.

When distributed computing first appeared, but before LANs became the dominant distributed computing architecture, there was considerable experimentation with an alternative architecture consisting of a centralized minicomputer host serving applications to attached terminal devices. This application hosting architecture mimicked the mainframe model, but within a small office or business unit setting.

As described in a previous chapter, Microsoft's NT Server Terminal Server Edition (TSE) operating system borrowed both its name and philosophy from this historical model. The vendor added "terminal services" to its NT Server product in order to facilitate the use of the platform by ASPs and others in a shared "application hosting" role. This capability is also embodied in the vendor's Windows 2000 server operating system.

Other significant vendors in this space include Citrix Systems (whose core MultiWin technology is used by Microsoft), and Tarantella. An overview of these products will help to identify the common ingredients of this type of application server solution.

Citrix Systems

Citrix Systems Independent Computing Architecture (ICA) traces its origins to the late 1980s. At that time, the company focused on the development of enabling software for remote application access. Originally, the vendor's products targeted users who were on the road, working from home or otherwise separated from their office PCs, and who required access to applications "back at the office." To meet the needs of this market, Citrix developed innovative technology for operating PC-based applications remotely, via low speed dial-up connections.

The key to this solution was technology for moving only the end user interface components of remote applications back and forth across the link. In this way, the remote application's performance was not as badly impacted by the slow connection speeds of the day.

Citrix Systems entered into the world of application hosting as an outgrowth of its efforts to devise an efficient server-centric computing solution, primarily for remote access. According to spokespersons for the company, Citrix designers believed that applications would eventually move off of the desktop and into the network, thereby providing multiuser, hosted application access. They were ahead of their time.

In 1992, as part of a license agreement with Microsoft, Citrix Systems obtained the rights to develop multiuser "extensions" to the NT server operating system. With these extensions, collectively referred to as MultiWin technology, the NT operating system was enabled to host Windows-compliant applications for concurrent use by a broad range of client devices (Windows PCs and other devices) across a variety of dial-up links and network connections. The extensions formed the basis for a product offering: WinFrame.

Initially, WinFrame found only a niche market. However, interest in the technology increased as a by-product of a debate over "fat client" PCs and "thin client" network computers that arose at about the same time (1995) that WinFrame for NT was announced.

A coalition of companies, nicknamed SONIA after members Sun Microsystems, Oracle, Netscape Communications, IBM, and Apple, sought to unseat Microsoft and Intel from their dominance of the corporate desktop. Bolstered by reports from the Gartner Group and other analysts that the cost of ownership for "fat client" (i.e., Microsoft Windows PC-based) computing would eventually bankrupt companies, SONIA sought to substitute a new thin client solution for the desktop. By using thin client network computers (NCs) in place of PCs, and by hosting application software on "fat servers," the coalition argued, Windows PC management costs could be dramatically reduced.

In the end, Microsoft responded to SONIA with effective management solutions that reduced the cost of ownership for PCs. The entire issue became something of a red herring—but not before Microsoft saw the wisdom of licensing the core technology of WinFrame, MultiWin, from Citrix Systems and integrated it directly into its NT operating system product family, creating the NT TSE operating system.

However, the Microsoft's implementation of MultiWin technology in its NT Server 4.0 TSE operating system did not observe all of the particulars of Citrix Systems's ICA. For one thing, Microsoft substituted the remote device protocol (RDP), an International Telecommunications Union (ITU) standard network protocol, for Citrix Systems's proprietary ICA interface protocol.

RDP, while standards-based, supported only TCP-IP networks and was tuned for use with high-bandwidth (large capacity) enterprise networks—two facts that limited its utility in slower, less capable WAN settings and in dial-up remote access scenarios.

Moreover, the Microsoft TSE solution supported only Windows 16- and 32-bit PCs and Windows CE (a compact version of the Windows OS) devices, including

Windows Terminals, as clients. Web browser client support was promised by the vendor in a later edition of the RDP protocol (RDP version 5.0).

Citrix Systems responded in 1998 with the announcement of its MetaFrame application server, a product aimed at already MultiWin-enabled NT and Windows 2000 servers. Understandably, MetaFrame created some confusion among analysts and trade press writers when first announced because it was perceived as redundant—duplicating the functionality to the TSE and Windows 2000 servers. In fact, MetaFrame was an enhancement to the Microsoft multiuser operating system products that restored the Citrix architecture, enabled Web-based application delivery, and repositioned the platform as an application server for ASPs.

Adding MetaFrame to NT TSE servers reenables the use of the Citrix Systems ICA Network Protocol, which delivers more efficient application performance across both high- and low-bandwidth network connections than does RDP or another competitor, the X.11 protocol (see sidebar). The ICA protocol offers a compressed operations mode for use in extending application interfaces to remote devices connected via low bandwidth pipes. It also offers an uncompressed operations mode for use when client devices are connected directly to a link (such as the enterprise network) that offers greater bandwidth capacity. According to the vendor, delivering a Windows application interface using the ICA protocol requires less than 5 kilobits-per-second of network bandwidth, enabling even the most "bloated" Windows application to be operated efficiently across low bandwidth links while delivering performance comparable to local application execution on client systems.

Complementing the efficiencies of the ICA protocol, Citrix Systems has also developed SpeedScreen—a technology for improving application delivery performance by reducing the amount of data that must traverse a communications link. As an end user interacts with a MetaFrame server-based application, SpeedScreen optimizes data transfer by managing the screen "repainting" function of the hosted application.

With many applications, whenever a user presses a key on the keyboard or clicks a mouse button, the entire screen is refreshed "or repainted" with the new information received from the application. SpeedScreen intercepts this process, compares information previously transmitted to the ICA client with information that is about to be transmitted, then transmits only the changed information. In so doing, the amount of bandwidth consumed by application interface communications between server and client may be reduced by as much as 30 percent, according to the vendor, while total packets transmitted may be reduced by 60 percent. The result is less information traveling the network and better application performance, especially across low bandwidth connections.

In addition to link performance, restoring ICA architecture to Microsoft's NT TSE Server had the effect of expanding the client connectivity options available to

X.11: ANOTHER PROTOCOL FOR APPLICATION INTERFACE DELIVERY

At about the same time that designers at Citrix Systems were beginning to look for methods for extending Windows-based application access to remote users, work was also being done in many parts of the UNIX world to create a common, extensible, and user-friendly application interface for applications running under the UNIX operating system. The X Protocol, based on techniques initially developed at the Massachusetts Institute of Technology, was the result.

Today, X is a technology with many commercial sponsors that continues to be developed under the auspices of the X.Org, part of The Open Group. X describes the way that an application's processing and display functions are designed. X can be distinguished from older Microsoft Windows applications at a structural level. Generally speaking, Windows applications and their user interface elements are designed to execute entirely within a local PC environment. That is why a technology like Citrix ICA is required. Citrix MultiWin extensions add functionality to the NT and Windows 2000 operating systems to enable application display components to be split apart from application processing components and delivered to an alternate location. No such requirement exists in the world of X.

The X Protocol establishes a client/server relationship between an application and its display. The X client consists of the application itself, its processing instructions or logic, while the X server consists of the application's display instructions. An X application's logic can execute on one machine, while its interface can be provided on another machine.

This client/server application architecture would appear to make the X application just the thing for ASP delivery. Criticisms of the X networking protocol, however, derive from its dependence on high bandwidth networks to operate efficiently. X.11, the current generation protocol, assumes that a high-capacity connection exists between client and server. It is very slow in operation over low bandwidth "pipes." The same may be said about the RDP protocol used by Microsoft in its TSE operating system products.

Citrix ICA addresses the limitations of RDP and X.11 by delivering a more efficient communications protocol, as well as supporting technologies, such as SpeedScreen, which facilitate acceptable application performance on remote devices over a broad range of connection types, capacities, and speeds.

ASPs and their customers. MetaFrame servers are among the first application servers to deliver functionality required for a "PC free" or "network-based Webtop" environment. The MetaFrame ICA desktop client enables complete access to all local system resources, such as full 16-bit stereo audio, local drives, COM ports, and local printers, if available. The mapping of local resources can be performed automatically or by means of administrative utilities. Specialized client capabilities such as modem dial-up are also supported. Mapped resources can also be shared with the MetaFrame server, if desired.

Of course, not all MetaFrame implementations utilize a full-fledged Webtop model (e.g., one in which there are no applications locally installed on the client). In many MetaFrame implementations, clients are themselves Windows PCs delivering a mixture of locally installed and remotely accessed applications. MetaFrame offers a feature known as "Seamless Windows" to accommodate this scenario.

Seamless Windows is a shorthand expression referring to the capability of Citrix ICA to support the integration of local and remote applications on the local Windows 95, Windows 98, or Windows NT 4.0 desktop. With Seamless Windows, the user can gain access to hosted applications without having to load a remote desktop environment. While connected in a MetaFrame server, the user can gain access to local applications using the Windows Task Bar. Icons for both local and remote applications can be installed on the local Windows desktop, and both local and remote application windows can be cascaded on the local desktop.

The Seamless Windows environment also supports the definition of multiple keyboards to facilitate command entry in local and remote application environments. This prevents specially mapped key combinations used by MetaFrame (such as ALT+TAB) from interfering with similar key combinations used by locally executing apps.

Seamless Windows also supports the use of the Windows clipboard in conjunction with both local and MetaFrame-hosted applications. Users can cut, copy, and paste information between applications running remotely on the server or locally from the desktop.

Building on the concept of a Seamless Windows environment, MetaFrame also delivers an easy-to-use method for accessing remotely hosted applications. Similar in concept to the Microsoft Windows "Network Neighborhood," MetaFrame can present links to "published" (remotely hosted) applications in a client-based "Program Neighborhood" facility.

In operation, Program Neighborhood presents "application sets" to MetaFrame client users—a view of the applications published on a given MetaFrame server or server farm, which that user is authorized to access. A single user authentication operation, usually performed at the time of user sign-on, identifies the user to all MetaFrame servers and populates the Program Neighborhood with icons and links for each hosted application that is available for the specific user based on his or her account or user group. Published applications appear as icons and are preconfigured with such properties as session window size and video and audio settings and supported level of encryption as are appropriate to the user and his or her client device.

The preceding applies when the client device is itself a Windows PC. However, ICA architecture supports a broad range of clients, including older 16-bit Windows PCs, newer 32-bit desktops, UNIX workstations, terminal devices, and a raft of new information appliances.

On the server side, the MetaFrame solution offers scalability, manageability, and security functions that are consistent with the requirements of the ASP delivery model. Load balancing services are available to group multiple MetaFrame servers into server farms. The load balancing service dynamically routes users to the least busy server to deliver the best possible application performance and server resource utilization.

In addition, Citrix Resource Management Services provide MetaFrame application server administrators with a suite of management tools for analyzing and tuning servers, and for performing ongoing system monitoring, capacity planning, application audit tracking, and billing functions. MetaFrame's integral, policy-based user authentication and security features can be augmented with SecureICA™ Services. SecureICA provides a higher, more efficient level of security between the ICA client and the MetaFrame server by encrypting the data stream that is being sent over the network. The service utilizes RSA Security's RC5 block cipher, a powerful encryption algorithm that utilizes key codes of up to 128 bits in length—a standard in current encryption technology. (A more thorough discussion of security is provided in a later chapter.)

Citrix Systems ties much of its value proposition to its ICA architecture and communications protocol, which can be used to serve a wide variety of applications—including Windows, UNIX-based and mainframe-based—to a wide variety of clients over virtually any connection, regardless of bandwidth or speed. ICA architecture combines the application server with the operating system so that the application and application server reside on the same physical system. This distinguishes the Citrix MetaFrame solution from other types of application server solutions and gives the MetaFrame solution, according to the vendor, several advantages over competitors, including:

- Lower cost for extra server equipment
- Centralized and simplified management
- Elimination of processing overhead associated with the need to translate between protocols (RDP, X.11, etc.)
- Less complexity

Other players in the application server space, notably New Moon Systems and Tarantella Inc., have a different point of view.

New Moon Systems

New Moon Systems positions itself as a viable competitor in the application server space dominated by Citrix System with its MetaFrame product. Like MetaFrame, the New Moon offering, called Canaveral iQ™, supplements the functionality of Microsoft Terminal Server Edition operating systems to enable a more robust hosting platform for server-hosted Windows applications. The vendor's application management architecture is depicted in Figure 9–4. The solution is aimed at enterprises and application service providers delivering software products via the Web.

The primary components of this architecture, as identified in the diagram, include support for application delivery technologies such as Microsoft's Terminal Services; the New Moon Canaveral iQ™ Application Management Platform; LDAP-compatible directory services; and, User Provisioning, Application Infrastructure, and System Administration components. Together, these primary components enable organizations to offer software as a service quickly and effectively.

The centerpiece of the solution is the New Moon Canaveral iQ application management platform, which provides the infrastructure required to control delivery of these Windows-based and third-party applications across a Web interface.

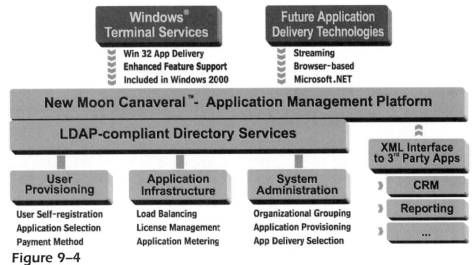

Figure 9–4
New Moon Systems "Application Management Architecture" *Source:* New Moon Systems, Inc., San Jose, Ca. *www.newmoon.com*

Canaveral iQ provides administrators with a graphical user interface for configuring and managing the hosted software environment and an infrastructure for integrating the application management platform with network and data center resources. With the product, administrators can set up applications for delivery, set up servers to host the applications, and set up users and organizations to access third-party Windows-based applications.

The architecture leverages Lightweight Directory Access Protocol (LDAP)-compatible directory services such as Novell Directory Services or Microsoft Active Directory to serve as data repositories for user and application information. The LDAP directory framework utilizes a hierarchically structured database that permits the effective management of extremely large data sets—effectively aggregating and segregating entities. It is used to store user and data center resource elements; to hold user subscription and preference data; and, to control, replicate, update, and synchronize both user information and hardware/software data.

The User Provisioning component allows for self-provisioning and provides the services necessary to support user registration, application selection, and payment for service providers that require this function. It provides an interface to capture the user information, enables the expeditious set up of control variables such as applications available for subscription and payment options, again for a service provider model. Rich data collection capabilities are also available to facilitate demographics information gathering that may be required by an enterprise, the ASP, or its sponsors and advertisers.

The Application Infrastructure component enables administrators to control how applications are delivered. This component permits administrators to establish and tune server loads, to create and manage license policies, and to identify quantifiable resource utilization indicators so the use of resources can be metered effectively. The component also provides the means to associate costs with application use so application delivery expenses can be computed and monitored.

The System Administration component enables administrators to organize user communities into manageable groups. It allows administrators to monitor and control the actions within and the interactions among user organizations, applications, and servers.

Support for application data exchange using XML is provided to support the transfer of hosting service data to Customer Relationship Management, billing and other applications that may be used in connection with ASP operations.

New Moon offers its own application delivery service in Liftoff, but has de-emphasized this feature and instead thrown support behind Microsoft Terminal Services as the primary "terminal server" component. The solution supports application interface delivery across an RDP link to any browser-equipped client, but spokespersons claim that link support is being expanded to support other protocols, including Citrix ICA.

"New Moon Canaveral iQ eliminates security risks and concerns that have slowed the acceptance and growth of outsourcing data management by the enterprise sector," according to Marc Lowe, New Moon's president and CEO. "By utilizing enterprises' already-established data centers, server farms and desktops, New Moon Canaveral iQ immediately provides companies the ability to leverage their investments in existing network environments, and to enjoy the benefits of centrally managed applications. Canaveral iQ's long-term success will underscore the importance of software as a service and will give enterprises the confidence needed to begin outsourcing greater amounts of IT."

Tarantella

Tarantella has long been noted as a developer of enabling technologies for server-based computing solutions. In February 2001, the company announced an upgrade to its flagship product, Tarantella Enterprise 3, incorporating ASP-specific capabilities into an already robust "application router" [a.k.a. application server] solution. These features included the ability to log billing information for export to third party customer billing applications, the capability to aggregate up to 50 servers into a single array and to support up to 10,000 users in a single array. With Tarantella Enterprise 3, user traffic can be intelligently balanced to distribute processing load across geographically dispersed networks.

The following April, a further enhancement to the product was released providing support for such critical ASP features as firewall traversal (so that clients can access the ASP-provided applications without opening additional ports in the client side firewall or installing a VPN) and the ability for a client to use a secure proxy server. The upgrade also delivered local client drive and printer mapping, so that clients could save files locally, as well as print to their local printer.

Unlike the Citrix approach described above, Tarantella bridges the gap between Windows application terminal server solutions and more complicated server framework products offered by companies such as IBM and Hewlett-Packard Bluestone. Tarantella resides on a web server host, separate from servers hosting the application software itself. From this vantage point, Tarantella can broker access to resources of a wide range of applications—including Web, UNIX, Linux, Microsoft Windows NT (Windows 2000), IBM AS/400, and mainframe applications.

The location of the Tarantella application server—separate from the application software that it Web-enables—provides a load balanced, scalable and manageable infrastructure for application hosting. Since Tarantella itself is responsible for ensuring the performance and allocation of application sessions to all end users, it provides a single point of management for all application services enabled in its infrastructure.

The Tarantella server itself can be replicated, creating Tarantella arrays, to support scalable and fault tolerant deployment. In an array configuration, one Tarantella server is designated as the primary and all others are designated as secondary servers. The difference: administrative changes are made via the primary, while secondary servers run user sessions.

Tarantella, like New Moon Canaveral iQ, utilizes a third party directory server to store an up-to-date database of network resources (host names, etc.) The vendor is flexible about how this information is maintained and Tarantella is compatible with any of a number of popular directory servers, including Novell s Network Directory Server, Microsoft Active Directory, or Netscape Directory Server. Tarantella provides the interfaces to these directory server products that are necessary to support its operations. It can also store the directory information locally, on the Tarantella server.

A key enabler of the Tarantella solution is the federated naming scheme, which it uses to simplify resource allocation in a potentially complex and heterogeneous application hosting environment. Here s how it works.

The need for a uniform naming scheme becomes pronounced in a heterogeneous host environment—one that is comprised of different application software servers, each running a different operating systems and a different hardware configuration. In such an environment, each server may have its own resource naming methodology, complicating the management of application and server resources in response to demand. As environments become more heterogeneous, some sort of naming system resolution method is required. Tarantella developers chose a quasi-standard naming scheme, originally developed by X/Open Company LTD (now the Open Group), called X/Open Federated Naming (XFN). XFN has been implemented to simplify the job of managing server resources and improving the consistency of application services across the entire ASP platform.

Tarantella's core product comprises a suite of server engines managed by means of unique, Java-based, graphical user interfaces called Object Manager and Array Manager. These management tools provide the necessary functionality to publish applications and documents for use by remote clients; to invoke, monitor and control user application sessions; to view applications in operation and stop them as needed; and to manage security and arrays. The server engines themselves, as depicted in Figure 9–5, include the following:

- Jserver: The Jserver is a Java technology application. It is the decision-making process that maintains the configuration and database, and interfaces to JNDI, an application programming interface to the naming system used by Tarantella software. The Jserver process handles Webtop construction, application launch and resumption, load balancing, session

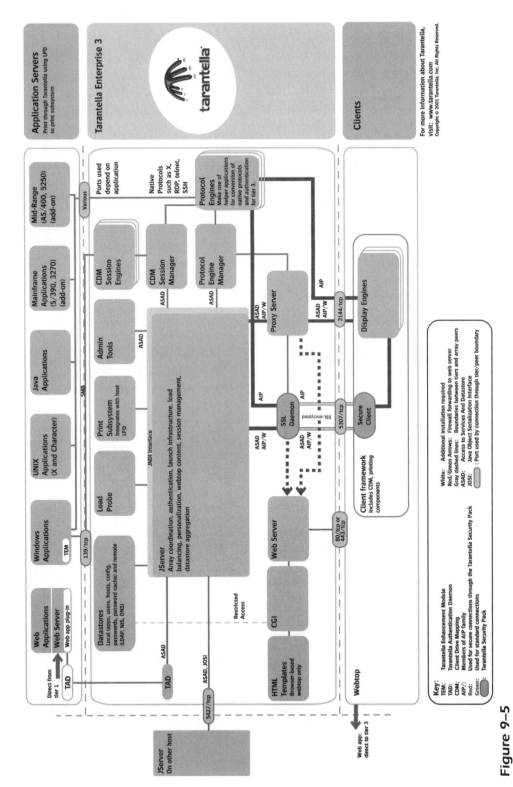

Figure 9–5
Tarantella Enterprise 3 Asp Edition, Under The Hood, *Source: Tarantella, Inc., Santa Cruz, Ca. www.tarantella.com.*

management, array replication and authentication. It connects to the Protocol Engine Manager to launch applications and verify UNIX passwords.

- Tarantella Proxy Server: The Tarantella Proxy Server oversees and controls the Jserver and Protocol Engine Manager, restarting them if they stop unexpectedly.
- Protocol Engine Manager: The Protocol Engine Manager hands off connections to Protocol Engines and executes UNIX logins.
- Protocol Engines and Display Engines: Borrowing from the client/server architecture of X Windows, Tarantella uses Protocol and Display Engines to provide the means for users to view and interact with hosted applications.

Protocol engines run on the Tarantella server where they emulate a client interacting with the application running in the ASP network. According to the vendor, the Protocol Engine understands the standard protocols that the application uses. It translates these into an Adaptive Internet Protocol (AIP) message that the Display Engine, located on the client, understands. Using this method, existing applications continue to run on servers they are running on today, untouched and without any re-engineering or rewrites needed. Protocol engines themselves are implemented as native binaries to ensure optimal performance on the server.

In the Tarantella scheme, Display Engines are Java applets that are downloaded on demand. They are small programs—around 200Kb—and provide just enough functionality to render the application and allow input/output to the user. As a result they are quick to download, even over low-bandwidth networks.

Many aspects of Protocol Engine and Display Engine design, according to the vendor, have been driven by the constraints imposed by current Java technology and by the browser environment in which users are expected to operate. Application functions and operations that are not supported by native Java have been accommodated in custom-developed server-based Protocol Engine code instead. These operations are fixed by the Protocol Engine and sent down to the Display Engine as a supported operation.

Similarly, the vendor has developed workarounds for the vicissitudes of operating applications within a browser-based interface. Typically, users navigate through browsers by going forward and backward through pages. In the process, traditional Java applets may find themselves buried under several pages, and may actually be deleted from the browser cache file over time. Tarantella engineers developed a workaround for this problem by providing the means to reconnect automatically without first shutting down the application.

Other innovations by the vendor address the network environment in which Tarantella must operate to deliver application interfaces to end users. Tarantella embraces the concept of a Webtop—the web equivalent of a desktop computing environment—in its design. Tarantella gathers all objects (applications, documents, etc.) associated with a user and dynamically creates a web page to represent this information. This web page contains a smart Java applets that present information as icons. When the user clicks on these icons, requests are issued to invoke applications or view documents.

If desired, Tarantella provides the functionality to add locally installed applications to the Webtop in order to provide a consistent point of entry to all business applications that the end user requires.

The Tarantella Webtop itself is built of standard HTML and Java components, and is fully customizable. Tarantella provides HTML templates, or 'themes' for the layout and presentation of the Webtop. These themes can be applied to users or organizational units, and make it easy to create Webtops with the consistent corporate or departmental styling. The vendor maintains a website filled with customization examples, and provides instructional code for use in developing a customized user interface to replace Tarantella defaults.

Working with such a variety of Java classes (programs in Java-speak) requires significant intelligence in class management and caching. Tarantella optimizes solution performance by caching (storing) standard applets such as the Display Engine and authentication applet on the user machine so they do not need to be downloaded every time the user connects to the ASP. Login and application parameters are also stored locally once they have been adjusted to the speed and bandwidth of the typical client connection. These cached applets are self-updating: whenever classes are modified by the ASP, they are automatically re-deployed and cached the next time the user logs in.

Though originally designed for use with client systems running the Java Virtual Machine, Tarantella has taken advantage of a Native Client for Windows, Unix and Linux, to ensure compatibility with client platforms that do not have the JVM installed or just prefer using a native client. According to the vendor, the operation of the application service is identical whether a JVM or Native Client approach is used.

In addition to server and client capabilities, a comprehensive architecture for application services must also provide a mechanism for communications. For Tarantella, this is the Adaptive Internet Protocol.

In the vendors view, an adaptive protocol is necessary to be able to deliver access to multiple types of client devices over a variety of network connections. The Tarantella Adaptive Internet Protocol does this by providing heuristic mechanisms that optimize the responsiveness of applications by monitoring, measuring and adapting the ways in which data is transferred between applications and the client systems. To adapt to changing network conditions, the Tarantella Adaptive Internet Protocol measures a variety of performance parameters including available bandwidth and latency. It adjusts the operation of the overall system in response to its findings, saving bandwidth by using Java drawing capabilities for some graphics functions, color management, data compression, queue management for graphics operations and metering adjustments for busy networks.

The Adaptive Internet Protocol begins its functions following the successful login and bootstrapping of the client system to the Tarantella application server. The user logs on to the ASP site, is authenticated, and a Webtop is downloaded. When the user asks for an application on the Webtop, a session is initiated by the Session Manager by invoking the correct Protocol Engine, which in turn invokes the application. (The relationships between Protocol Engines and applications is maintained in the datastore.)

The Display Engine, located on the user's machine, then connects and authenticates itself. The Status Manager receives this authentication and passes it onto the Session Manager, which then connects the Display Engine to the right Protocol Engine.

This is when the Adaptive Internet Protocol link begins. First, a set of parameters identifying the characteristics of the client device and network connection are passed to the AIP. In response, the AIP tunes itself for optimal performance. Finally, the interface of the application is displayed on the user client system and work may proceed. AIP remains vigilant and monitors any changes in the network characteristics.

It should be noted that Tarantella has a special interpretation of the meaning of the term, sessions. A session is associated with each application the user invokes.

Administrators can configure an application session to be resumable. That is, users can disconnect themselves from the Tarantella server but leave resumable applications running. When the user reconnects to the session, the application is presented in the same state as it was left. Typical reasons for doing this are to reduce startup time for applications and to provide client resilience. The latter may be of particular importance. In a network-centric environment, the connection from client to server is critical. If a connection is interrupted, the server must be able to recreate the state associated with the client when it reconnects. Tarantella's suspend/resume facility allows this.

Tarantella administrators can choose to disallow the resume facility, on a per-application basis, to save server resources. For example, a simple calculator application is unlikely to need resuming. Administrators also have the ability to terminate application sessions while they are running.

The vendor claims to be able to support Web applications, Windows applications, UNIX-based X Windows applications (including OpenGL), UNIX system character applications, Linux applications, AS/400 applications with 5250 emulation and mainframe-based applications with 3270 Terminal Emulation. The Tarantella Server can be installed on a wide range of UNIX and Linux OS server platforms given 120MB free disk space, plus another 100MB at install time, 128MB RAM, and a minimum 100MHz processor. Of course, server resource requirements increase with each user and application served. Approximately 4 MB of memory and 3MHz (for RISC systems)-5MHz (for Intel systems) of system CPU cycles are required per user. Additional memory is required for each application that is intended for delivery via the Tarantella Application Server - ranging from less than a megabyte for text applications to 2.5 megabytes for some X Windows applications.

Tarantella has been deployed by a Who s Who of ASPs and enterprise customers. Case studies and testimonials are available on the company s web site at www.tarantella.com.

ON TO FRAMEWORKS . . . .

Tarantella, New Moon and Citrix Systems products, though quite different in their design and implementation, comprise a class of application servers that are based on a common design philosophy: application interface extension or emulation. The value proposition offered by the vendors for their solutions is that they can be used to ASP-enable existing applications—whether Windows or X Windows or text based—with minimal or no application redesign.

The performance of these solutions is contingent upon the proper implementation of server-side components, the efficiency of network connections, and the support provided for target client devices. Another determinant of the ultimate success of this solution has to do with how "well-behaved" the application software is when deployed in its traditional, non-Web-enabled setting.

For example, if an application makes unusual or nonstandard use of system resources when operated in its intended environment, it will almost always create problems in a Web-enabled, server-hosted setting. One reason for Citrix System's lead in the emulation-based application server market is that Citrix engineers have had many years of experience in coping with application misbehavior. Similarly, the reason that Tarantella places so much emphasis on protocol and display engine development in its marketing materials is because these engines represent, collectively, the successful surmounting of "undocumented application features" (i.e., code bugs and nonstandard system calls) and testify to the integrity of the Tarantella solution overall.

Emulation-based application serving, though technically complex, is still regarded by some analysts as a lesser form of the application server art. These "screen scrapers," as some critics—borrowing from earlier systems integration vocabulary—refer to emulation-based application servers, are not, in their view, "true" application servers at all. From the analyst commentary cited earlier, "true" application servers are deployment and execution environments used for the execution of business logic, data access and integration, and/or application integration. By this definition, emulation-based application servers are mere Tinker Toys: real men use frameworks.

Ultimately, the need for a more framework-based application server product has more to do with the nature and architecture of the application being served than it does with any presumed deficit of emulation-based application servers. The two respond to very different requirements.

Application architectures range from the comparatively straightforward to very complex. Figure 9–6 illustrates three simplified application architectures.

The top illustration in Figure 9–6 describes applications that are well known to most desktop PC users: the application provides an interface to the end user, accepts input, and delivers output. A word processor or spreadsheet might fit into this category.

The middle illustration describes a somewhat more complex architecture in which the user leverages a standard interface to interact with application logic, which,

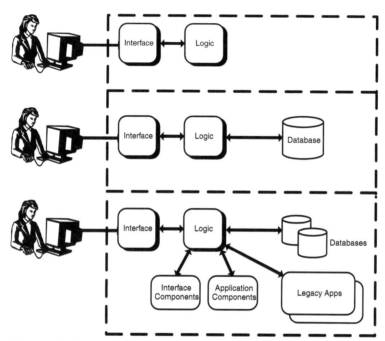

Figure 9–6
Three simplified application architectures.

in turn, draws upon a back-end database to respond to the user's input. Numerous database-driven applications, from the most simple recipe file to the most complex inventory control system, follow this general architecture.

The drawing at the bottom of Figure 9–6 depicts what might be described as a complex enterprise application, in which multiple components are cobbled together to build a user interface, which is then operated by the user to input information or requests. The interface itself may be constructed "on the fly"—based on parameters such as the type of user seeking access (language, interface preferences, etc.), security policies (policies that govern what data and functionality the user is permitted to access), and the type and capabilities of the client device being used to make the access (i.e., wireless phone, PC, browser, PDA, etc.).

With the user interface in place, the application receives and processes user input within the context of application or business rules. The application logic works through a complex process of determining what application components are required to handle the user request and what data sources must be included in request processing. Further complexity is added by the myriad information sources, ranging from databases to legacy applications, with which interaction may need to be coordinated in order to respond to the input. Furthermore, the input may drive additional processes for updating many back-end data stores and processes.

ERP or MRP systems are illustrations of such applications. Over one million business rules may be programmed for a medium-sized ERP installation in order to support a broad range of business tasks. Such applications typically make extensive use of client/server platforms in nonASP deployment settings to distribute processes among many machines.

Strictly speaking, the architectural complexity of an application does not mandate the use either of an emulation-based or framework-based application server. The dynamic client interface of a complex application can be extended via an emulator just as readily as the comparatively straightforward interface of a desktop application. Nonetheless, the decision to use a framework-based application server is generally associated with more complex applications because of its potential to serve as a central point of application management and integration.

To illustrate this point, Figure 9–7 depicts two deployments of the same application. At the top of the illustration, a complex application creates a dynamic user interface and an emulation-based application server is used to forward the interface through a Web server to an external client. The ASP offering this solution would need to dedicate at least one such platform for each customer.

In the lower part of the drawing in Figure 9–7, a framework-based application server, with its capability to integrate application components databases, legacy applications, and even interface components, provides a potentially more robust solution.

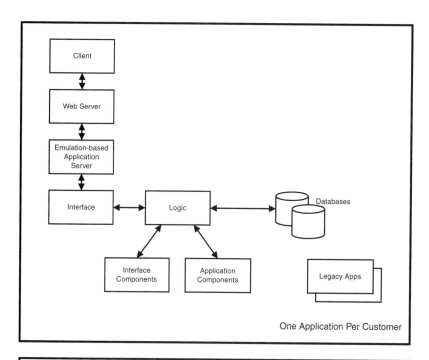

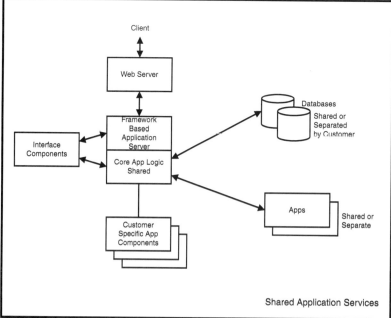

Figure 9–7
Dedicated and shared applications.

Depending on the nature of the application software involved, the ASP might be able to consolidate several customers of the same software service into one platform.

Such a scenario would enable ASPs to derive economies of scale by leveraging the framework-based application server to integrate a single instance of an application's logic together with the multiple application components, back-end databases, and other components that have tailored for each customer individually. Simply put, a well-designed framework-based application server can simplify ASP solution delivery for multiple customers while providing a central point for application integration, customization, and management.

The key to understanding the value of framework-based application servers is to keep in mind the manner in which most complex enterprise applications are being designed today. Most enterprise software vendors have begun to adhere to architectural models that are themselves "componentized." Object oriented programming techniques, as discussed in a previous chapter, result in applications that are themselves a compilation of Java classes, C++ objects, or other functional packages. The user interface is maintained as one set of objects, the business logic as another. These objects take data from a database(s), and, in some cases, from the output of legacy applications. They are assembled together in accordance to business rules or some other logical scheme to deliver the appropriate output in the right format as dictated by user input.

The framework-based application server can leverage this componentization to enable the sharing of some components while providing an efficient mechanism for the management and integration of customized components. This foundation provides not only platform sharing capabilities, but also enhanced scalability and manageability. Combined with other techniques for platform consolidation, such as storage sharing, ASPs can potentially derive significant cost efficiencies from the use of these "application brokers."

ORACLE iAS

Some database vendors have consolidated their application development models around framework-based application servers to deliver "seamless, end-to-end platforms for application development, integration and service delivery." Their intention may have less to do with support for ASPs than with their desire to capture the market share in application servers that they enjoy in their core software products—a top-selling database, in Oracle's case. However, ASPs are also the beneficiaries of such efforts, which are being seen not only from Oracle, but from other database vendors—from Microsoft to IBM to Sybase—as well.

In the case of Oracle, the company offers a core database engine and a suite of enterprise applications that take advantage of its relational database management

system. In June 2000, the company supplemented these products with the announcement of an Internet platform architecture consisting of its existing products, plus a
new Internet application server (iAS) and suite of Internet application development
tools. iAS product complemented the company's version 8i database and provided a
Java-based solution for porting traditional client/server applications to the Web
browser.

The vendor submitted that the solution was less expensive to use and more functional than generic framework-based application server products from other vendors.
According to announcement materials, iAS incorporated into one complete and seamlessly integrated product a wide range of middleware functionality previously available only from multiple products from multiple vendors.

A key component of iAS was its caching functionality, which was targeted at
speeding up the delivery of dynamic data for custom applications such as Web catalogs. Oracle8i Cache stored the most-frequently accessed data "in the middletier"—a
name more and more frequently associated with a tier of application servers in modern Web technology parlance. The result of caching frequently accessed data is that
users receive accurate information more quickly, while improving database performance in other processing-intensive activity.

Oracle iAS helped to differentiate the vendor's product line from competitors,
capitalized on the current trend among business to embrace e-commerce, and extended Oracle enterprise application architecture to Web technology. With iAS, the
vendor also delivered a "native" Web-based application serving solution for its own
line of enterprise applications, the Oracle E-Business Suite. Later in 2000, when the
vendor released its 9i version database, iAS was delivered as part of the package and
no longer needed to be purchased as an add-on. Key elements of the application
server, now termed "Oracle9i AS," are shown in Figure 9–8.

As depicted in Figure 9–8, Oracle conceives of its application server as a set of
services and utilities that provide the basis for scalability and reliability. The six services include the following:

- Communication: Oracle9i AS Communication Services are responsible
  for handling requests from the numerous supported clients, including
  Web-based, wireless, and wired. The Web-enabling portion of the solution
  is closely tied to the Apache Web Server, a leading Web server platform.
- Presentation: Oracle9i AS facilitates the delivery of application output in a
  variety of ways, including browser-readable HTML documents, PERL
  scripts, Java Servlets and JavaServer pages, and through a forms capability that can be adapted to support the display restrictions of wireless devices such as Web-enabled cell phones and PDAs. The application server

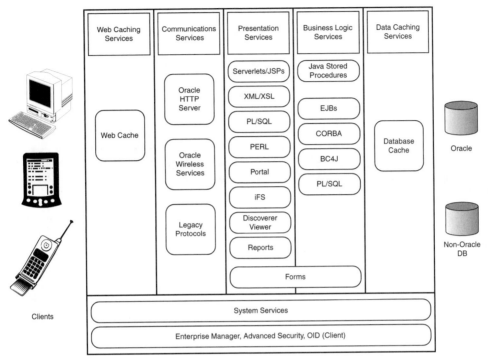

Figure 9-8
Oracle9i application server elements. *Source:* Oracle Corporation.

can also be used in conjunction with other Oracle tools to create information portals that display information and provide application access to end users on a continuous basis. A high-level language, PL/SQL can be used to create dynamic HTML-based PL/SQL Server pages which combine static pages with dynamic content. Other proprietary technologies, such as Discoverer Workbooks and Oracle's Internet File System (iFS), are also supported, as are powerful reporting utilities.

- Business Logic: Oracle9i AS is conceived by the vendor as an important part in its "grand design" to control all enterprise applications within the customer site. The application server is delivered with a robust JVM for executing business logic and with tools to support several ways for developing business logic itself. To serve as a central integration point for all application development and execution, the AS is designed to support both Java development approaches (Java Stored procedures and Enterprise JavaBeans) and high-level, model-driven techniques such as the CORBA.

Business logic services also include Oracle Business Components for Java (BC4J) a 100%-Java, XML-powered framework that enables productive development, portable deployment, and flexible customization of multi-tier, database-enabled applications from reusable business components. BC4J can be used to create and test business logic in components that automatically integrate with databases, reuse business logic to support different application tasks, and access and update Java-based application data and other functionality without modifying applications themselves. Not to be ignored is the vendor's own PL/SQL scripting language or its forms processor, which can integrate outputs from multiple database queries and other processes together into content-rich output.

- Web and Data Caching: Oracle9i AS Data Management Services delivers both Web page and data caching capabilities. The Web cache component improves the performance and scalability of Web servers, enabling frequently accessed content to be provided without the need for processing by Web servers themselves. The database cache component provides a mechanism for off-loading application-specific data from the general database to specialized application data stores within the application server itself, expediting data access and application performance.

The vendor supplements this package of services with a single management console, Oracle Enterprise Manager, which can provide access to all data and applications running on its Internet platform. The overall solution was touted in announcement materials as a replacement for the kludging together of numerous individually developed software components at a great financial and competitive cost.

The "one-stop-shop" approach inherent in the Oracle Internet platform architecture appeals to ASPs (and corporate enterprises) seeking a "one throat to choke" solution for application serving. Needless to say, the solution plays well to service providers who offer Oracle e-business suite applications to customers.

Some concerns continue to be raised, however, about the potential constraints that may arise from using an application server solution so closely aligned with a single vendor's technologies. For this reason, a raft of "generic" framework-based application servers (see Table 9–1) exist in the market from a variety of software and server companies. Most provide the minimum set of services required to deploy interoperable components as coherent applications. They are viewed as providers of a "logical middle tier" of a distributed multitiered environment—situated between clients and back-end applications and data sources—where they typically offer support for distributed, component-based solutions, security, transactions, a single and well-defined developer interface, runtime load balancing, and data persistence.

Table 9–1   Framework-Based Application Server Vendors

Company Name	Product Name	Web Site	Interface Method
Allaire	*ColdFusion*	www.allaire.com/products/coldfusion/40/	ActiveX, C++, Java
Apple	*Web Objects*	www.apple.com/webobjects/	ANSI C, C++, Java
Art Technology Group	Dynamo Personalization software	www.atg.com/products/highlights/highlights_main.html	Java
BEA Web Logic	Tengah	www.weblogic.com/products/tengah/tengahabout.html	Java
Bullet Proof Corporation	JDesigner Pro	www.bulletproof.com/	Java
Elemental SoftWare	Drumbeat 2000	www.drumbeat.com/	ActiveX
GemStone Software	GemStone/J	www.gemstone.com/products/j/main.html	Java
HAHT	*HAHT Site Application Server*	www.haht.com/Go.html?Page=HS_Pr_HSOverview	ANSI C, C++, ActiveX
Halcyon Software	I-ASP	www.halcyonsoft.com/asp/whitepaper.html	Java
HP BlueStone	Total-e-Server	www.hp.com/	C, C++, Java
IBM	*WebSphere*	www.software.ibm.com/webservers/appserv/	Java
Inprise	Inprise Application Server	www.inprise.com/appserver/	Java
Internova	Colibri Engine	www.internova.com/colibri/main.asp	Java, ActiveX
Intersolv	NetExpress	www.microfocus.com/products/enterapp.htm	C++

(continued)

Table 9–1   *Continued*

Company Name	Product Name	Web Site	Interface Method
Lona Technologies	Orbix OTM	www.iona.com/products/transactions/ orbixotm/index.html	Java
Lotus	*Domino*	www.lotus.com/home.nsf/tabs/ domino	ActiveX
Microsoft	*MTS/IIS*	www.microsoft.com	ActiveX
Netscape	*Application Server*	www.netscape.com/appserver/v2.1/ index.html	Java
New Atlanta	Servlet Exec 2.0	www.newatlanta.com/products.html	Java
Novera	J Business	www.novera.com/jbusiness.html	Java
Open Connect System	WebConnect	www.openconnect.com/pressrel/ 120898.html	Java
Oracle	*Oracle WAS*	www.oracle.com/products/asd/oas/ oas.html	Java
Pervasive Software	*Tango*	tango.pervasive.com/products/tango/ webjump/	Java, ActiveX
Pramati technologies	Proton	www.pramati.com/products.htm	Java
Progress Software	Aptivity	Softwarew.progress.com/java/ apptivity/apptivity.htm	Java
Prosyst	Enterprise Beans Server	www.prosyst.com/prosyst/champion. htm	Java
Seagate Software	Seagate Info APS	www.seagatesoftware.com/crystalinfo/	ANSI C, C++
Secant Technologies	Secant Extreme Server	www.secant.com/secant/extreme_ enterprise_server_ejb.htm	Java
SilverStream	*SilverStream*	www.silverstream.com/information/ press/v2press_f.htm	Java
Sun	*NetDynamics*	www.netdynamics.com/	Java
Sybase	*Enterprise Application Server*	www.sybase.com/products/ application_servers/	ActiveX, ANSI C, C++, Java

Table 9–1   *Continued*

Company Name	Product Name	Web Site	Interface Method
Tempest	Tempest Software	www.tempest.com/products.html	ANSI C, C++, Java
Unify	Vision App Server	www.unify.com/Products/vision.htm	ANSI C, ActiveX
Unify	Ewave Engine	www.unify.com/Products/ewave/index.htm	Java
Visient	Arabica EJB Server	www.visient.com/Arabica_server_main.htm	Java
Vision	Jade	www.vision-soft.com/products/products.htm	Java
Visisoft Inc.	Com Studio	www.visisoft.com/cando.htm	C++

In the final analysis, application servers deliver the necessary technology to Web-enable applications otherwise not developed for deployment via Web technology. Although an increasing number of applications are being developed with hosted deployment in mind, application servers remain the ASP's key enabler for delivering on their value proposition.

10 Basic Concepts: Web Technology

In this chapter...

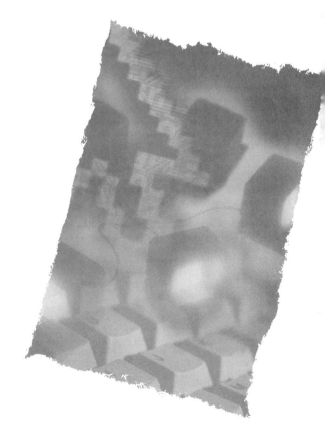

ONTO THE WEB ....

Any functional description of an ASP typically includes the phrase "application de-livery via Web technology." This is not the same as saying that ASPs use the public Internet and World Wide Web to connect customers to their services. Most, in fact, do not.

The reliability and performance, not to mention the security characteristics, of the public Internet have many firms concerned about entrusting mission critical appli-cation services to this network infrastructure. Instead, most ASPs (but not all) utilize either private network connections—or VPN connections created through the public network—to extend application access to their customers.

Having said this, it must also be said that Web technology is the primary mecha-nism for application delivery, whether delivery is accomplished via public or private networks. Web technology refers to a collection of protocols and their implementa-tions on supporting hardware and software that have evolved over time to facilitate the use of the public Internet. These technologies provide a powerful model for infor-mation and application distribution that has been embraced by virtually all ASPs.

The term Web technology is a handy catchall for a number of elements. Most people are familiar with some of these, including Web browsers, the software used to access and "surf" the Internet. The "Web pages" that you visit on the Web are also software of a sort, written in a Web technology protocol called the HTML and stored on computer platforms called Web servers. Web pages are accessed on the Internet using HTTP.

Added to this list are a number of standards-based and nonstandardized ele-ments such as the JVM, which is used to execute Javascript and Java Applets and Servlets embedded on Web pages or served from remote host systems, and a growing number of specialized protocols that are being developed to improve the speed of Web content distribution, to protect against information misuse and corruption, and to deliver services designed to improve the manageability of both networks and the ap-plication payloads that traverse them. This chapter provides an overview of Web tech-nology and looks specifically at those elements that are leveraged by ASPs to deliver their application services.

CONTEXT FOR WEB TECHNOLOGY ....

The origins of Web technology are linked to the development of the Internet itself. The Internet that we know today began as an experimental host-to-host interconnect implemented by the U.S. government in 1969. The effort bore the inauspicious moniker "ARPAnet"—named for the Advanced Research Projects Agency (ARPA) of the Department of Defense.

ARPA perceived the advantages that might accrue to interconnecting computer resources at different research and development centers and to developing mechanisms that would facilitate interactive communications (via TELNET) and file exchange (via the File Transfer Protocol, or FTP). The rudimentary capabilities of ARPAnet evolved into a set of networking protocols (called the TCP/IP suite for its two most-recognized components) for host-to-host communications and modern networking generally.

Also important was a methodology developed during the implementation of the original network that relied upon Requests for Comment (RFCs) as a mechanism for suggesting new or improved protocols and for soliciting feedback from scientists, experts, and other interested parties. This remains the methodology by which the IETF evaluates and adopts new protocols for use across the Internet.

The ARPAnet was extended over time to major supercomputing sites and to educational and research institutions worldwide. The National Science Foundation greatly enlarged the reach of this backbone network with its own NFSNet and, soon thereafter, many additional public and private networks—based both within the United States and abroad—linked up.

Stories vary regarding who first coined the term "Internet" to describe this infrastructure. Regardless of the author, the name is apropos. By the 1990s, so many networks had joined up that the the percentage of traffic traversing the Internet shifted from primarily education- and research-focused to commercial in nature.

In 1995, the operation of the public Internet was turned over to large commercial Internet Service Providers (ISPs), such as MCI, Sprint, and UUNET, who took responsibility for the "backbones" or core network and continue to enhance their capabilities and capacities. Regional ISPs link into these backbone networks and, in turn, provide lines for corporate subscribers, including smaller ISPs that deliver "on-ramp" sevices to private consumers.

Although TCP/IP provides the primary networking protocol used to interconnect the more than 20 million host systems (from mainframes, to minicomputers, to PCs, and appliances) interconnected via the Internet, gateways are also provided to enable non-IP networks to participate in the network utility. So great is the current traffic on the net that the original innovators, colleges and research centers, are working to build new Internets dedicated to their traffic exclusively.

One initiative, called Internet2, is being driven by a consortium led by over 180 universities working in partnership with industry and government to develop and deploy advanced network applications and technologies and to accelerate the creation of a next-generation Internet capable of supporting a set of revolutionary Internet applications. According to the consortium Web site at www.internet2.org, Internet2 re-creates "the partnership among academia, industry and government that fostered today's Internet [while it was] in its infancy." Working groups are developing protocols required to support such "science fictionlike" applications as a real-time multimedia exchange that would allow doctors to operate—via sophisticated visual and robotic interfaces—on remotely located patients.

Similarly, government entities originally involved in the Internet have begun work on a next-generation network. The Department of Defense, National Aeronautics and Space Administration, National Institutes of Health, National Institute of Science and Technology, and the National Science Foundation joined together in October 1997 to launch an initiative to create an advanced, all-optical Internet that could support such applications as basic science research, crisis management, education, environmental monitoring, federal information services, health care, and manufacturing. The initiative received funding of more than $80 million in 2000 and, as of this writing, seeks another $71 million to develop a network 1,000 times more capable than the current public Internet.

Another direction of Internet diversification is represented by MBONE, a specialized subnetwork of the current Internet. What distinguishes MBONE from the rest of the Internet is the support of connected servers for a specialized multicasting network protocol. This protocol enables the successful "broadcasting" of audio/video information over the MBONE network, enabling distance learning, video conferencing and telephony, and a wide range of other multimedia applications.

All these variations on the core Internet idea suggest a future set of network-based service supports that will take the Internet to an entirely new level as a medium for information exchange and interaction. However, here and now, the primary application for the Internet is the Web page.

The "Web" in Web page is a culmination of an idea first advanced by Tim Berners-Lee, who is widely credited with having invented the World Wide Web in 1989. From Berners-Lee's concept of a hypermedia-based mechanism for global information sharing, and his groundbreaking "Web browser" application aimed at making the sum of human knowledge available to anyone with access to the Internet, the seeds of the present-day World Wide Web were planted. In 1994, Berners-Lee founded the World Wide Web Consortium (W3C) at Massachussets Institute of Technology in conjunction with the European Organization for Nuclear Research (CERN), DARPA, and the European Commission. The goals of the organization continue to be:

- To make the Web universally accessible by promoting technologies that take into account the vast differences in culture, education, ability, material resources, and physical limitations of users on all continents

- To develop a software environment that permits each user to make the best use of the resources available on the Web
- To guide the Web's development with careful consideration for the new legal, commercial, and social issues raised by this technology

To advance these goals, the W3C concentrates its efforts on the promotion of its vision through the establishment of a community of engineers working in concert to identify the technical requirements for a truly universal information space, the development and design of Web technologies to realize this vision, and standardization of Web technologies through the production of specifications (called "recommendations") that describe the building blocks of the Web. W3C makes these recommendations freely available to all.

In the view of the W3C, the Web itself is an application built on top of the Internet. The "design principles" guiding this application include:

- Interoperability: W3C works to ensure that specifications for new Web technology languages and protocols are compatible with one another and allow any hardware and software used to access the Web to work together.
- Evolution: W3C pays special attention to the evolution of other technologies that may use the Web in an effort to future-proof the Web itself against technological obsolescence. W3C engineers embrace principles such as simplicity, modularity, and extensibility to enhance the likelihood of successful integration of the current Web with emerging technologies such as mobile Web devices and digital television.
- Decentralization: Decentralization is the newest principle embraced by the W3C and generally considered the most difficult to apply. The organization seeks to limit or eliminate dependencies on centralized registries or other mechanisms that might impede the "scaling" of the Web. At the same time, the organization is struggling to identify and implement strategies for security and availability that generally depend on such centralized mechanisms.

These principles guide the work carried out by working groups within the organization. In general, activities are guided by a "mandate" from the users of the W3C membership. Suggestions are formulated as "activity proposals," which are reviewed by the members. A consensus on a technical proposal results in its assignment to a working group, of which there are approximately 30 at the present time.

Working groups are comprised of representatives from member organizations, invited experts, and others, and produce results ranging from technical reports and open source software, to services, such as validation services. As of this writing, some technologies under development at W3C include:

- Remote Description Framework (RDF)—RDF integrates a number of W3C activities related to Web-based "metadata" standards. Metadata is data about data and is used for a number of purposes, but primarily to facilitate the identification and exchange of data across a Web infrastructure. Various RDF efforts target the standardization of site maps, content ratings, stream channel definitions, search engine data collection ("Web crawling"), digital library collections, and distributed authoring using XML as an interchange syntax. RDF is also being explored as a mechanism for enabling "device-independent Web delivery." Using an RDF standard approach, called Composite Capabilities/Preferences Profiles or CC/PP, for managing and communicating "device profiles," W3C hopes to ensure the compatibility of the Web with a growing list of client or server devices, including PCs, Web appliances and Web-enabled wireless phones. RDF also plays a role in W3C's efforts to develop a mechanism for assuring the privacy of Web surfers.

- Additional Standards associated with XML—XML is an important technology for formatting "structured data" intended for exchange between applications running on different systems. A specification (based on SGML, a 1986 ISO language standard for use with large technical documentation projects) was set forth by W3C in 1998, but additional work is being done to expand the breadth of the technology and to define standard schemas or vocabularies for interapplication exchanges, query facilities for extracting data from Web pages and improving interaction between databases and the Web, linking languages that enable cross-links between XML documents to be embedded in the documents themselves, support for mathematical data exchange, and so forth.

- Extensible Stylesheet Language (XSL)—a language for expressing stylesheets that enable the rapid formatting of text into predefined formats. XSL consists of (1) XSL Transformations (XSLT), which provides a language for transforming XML documents, and (2) an XML vocabulary for specifying formatting semantics (XSL formatting objects).

- New Graphics Formats—including WebCGM (computer graphics metafile), a bit-mapped graphic format, and scalable vector graphics (SVG), a vector graphic format, are in development. Bit maps are comprised of dots, as opposed to lines or vectors. The W3C is also involved in the development of a synchronized multimedia integration language (SMIL), which is intended to enable the simple development of TV-like multimedia presentations using any text editor.

- TV/Web, Voice Browsers—technologies for enabling Web surfers to access television programs broadcast to the Web, to interact with the Web with voice commands.

In addition to concerning itself with the protocols and standards used to format and exchange data, the W3C has also, as noted earlier, inserted itself into the ongoing debate over privacy and the Web. In June 2000, the consortium announced the Platform for Privacy Preferences Project (P3P), which seeks to form a standard approach "for users to gain more control over the use of personal information on Web sites they visit."

Basically, P3P provides a standardized set of multiple-choice questions to Web site operators, covering all the major aspects of their site's privacy policies. The responses provide a snapshot of how a site handles personal information about its users which is stored in a standard, machine-readable format. P3P enabled browsers can "read" this snapshot automatically and compare it with the user's privacy preferences. The user will have a ready means to determine what a site's privacy policies are so he or she can decide whether to load the site HTML.

Adding to the activities of the IETF on matters pertaining to Internet connectivity, and to those of the W3C on matters pertaining to the World Wide Web, Web technology is also developed (some would argue, mostly developed) in the commercial sector. Java and ActiveX technologies, originated by Sun Microsystems and Microsoft Corporation, respectively, have added entirely new levels of interactivity to the HTML-based Web page and play a significant role in Web-enabling applications. Similarly, many of the efforts to provide security for Web-based data interchange originated not within IETF or W3C, but within the business community.

As noted in an earlier chapter, when proprietary protocols, languages, and methods achieve dominance in the industry, they become de facto standards. In the case of some technologies, such as Netscape's Secure Socket Layer (SSL), submission by their creators to a standards body has occurred only after the technology achieved widespread industry adoption. When this occurs, the formalization of the technology as an approved standard is often handled expeditiously.

HOW IT WORKS . . . .

Simply stated, the technologies that have been developed to support interserver communications across the Internet, as well as that remarkable "application" called the World Wide Web, are extensive, complex, and evolving. At root, however, is a Web technology-based transaction, a relatively straightforward operation, as summarized in Figure 10–1.

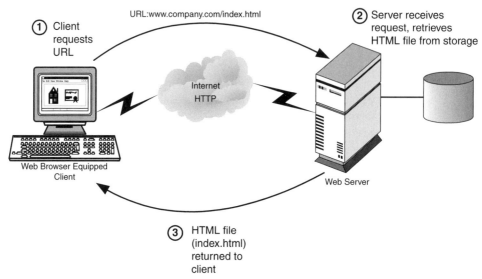

Figure 10–1
Requesting a HTML file with HTTP.

In Figure 10–1, access to a Web site (that is to say, access to a specific HTML-encoded page) is requested by a Web browser–equipped client. The client locates the Web server that hosts the Web site by using the server's uniform resource locator (URL), a unique address assigned to the server (and to its files) within the Internet. The HTTP mediates the process of requesting the HTML file from the server and returning it to the requesting client. It is literally as simple as one, two, three.

This is the basic method by which Web technology serves "static content" to browser-based clients. However, the evolution of the Web favors its use as a dynamic medium, rather than as a simple utility for displaying text and graphics. To obtain dynamism, technologies have evolved that enable browser-equipped users to interact with the Web site. The oldest of these is the CGI, a Web server extension that specifies how the Web server should execute a local application and how it should pass the output to the browser-based client requestor. Figure 10–2 depicts this process.

It is worth noting that the increased desire for interactivity was closely linked with the desire to exploit the potential market represented by Internet surfers. It should come as no surprise that among the earliest Web-based applications were the early CGI-based "shopping carts" that ushered in the e-commerce era of the late 1990s.

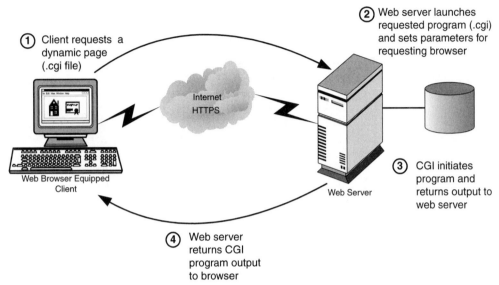

Figure 10–2
Calling a Web server–based program through CGI.

SECURITY: A MISSION-CRITICAL COMPONENT OF WEB TECHNOLOGY . . . .

E-commerce also imposed another requirement on Web communications: security. Troubled that surfers would not place credit card orders (or expose personal information about themselves) in an unsecure environment, an advancement was offered in the form of HTTP Secure (HTTPS), based on SSL from Netscape Communications Corporation.

In the vendor's description of the technology in its marketing materials, "SSL is a set of rules followed by computers connected to the Internet . . . [that] include encryption, which guards against eavesdropping; data integrity, which assures that your communications aren't tampered with during transmission; and authentication, which verifies that the party actually receiving your communication is who it claims to be." SSL security is in effect when the URL displayed in a browser is preceded by the protocol acronym "https" rather than "http."

Technically speaking, SSL uses a program "layer" located between the HTTP and TCP layers of the Internet (recall that the Internet is a large TCP/IP network). As its name implies, the SSL protocol leverages "sockets" (special program interfaces) that are built into the software of both the browser and the Web server to enable the exchange of digital IDs between them. The exchange of digital IDs, which include "public encryption keys" for use in encrypting data sent by one application to the other, establishes a mechanism for authenticating the identities of the communicating machines, safeguarding the data that is exchanged from eavesdropping while traversing the network, and ensuring that the data sent is the data received.

SSL uses the public-and-private encryption key methodology combined with a cryptographic encoding system devised by RSA Security, a leader in data encryption. This system merits a bit of closer attention before proceeding.

Public key encryption is basically a system in which two encryption keys are used to scramble and descramble messages. One key, the private key, is held by the owner and can be used to descramble messages that have been scrambled with the owner's second key, the public key. The public key is shared with those who want to communicate with the owner. They use it to encode traffic that is being directed to the key owner.

Public/private keys are issued by a certification authority, a trusted third party who can attest that the owners of keys are who they says they are. In the U.S. system, a copy of the private key is held by the trusted third party for use by the government if the owner is suspected of nefarious wrongdoings and a court ordered surveillance is authorized.

Taken to the level of a Web exchange in Figure 10–3, owners (licensees, actually) of Web server and Web browser software are provided with keys as part of their software. Web server owners typically register their keys to obtain certification, which in turn enables them to offer secure services in connection with their Web sites. Browser owners may elect whether to certify and to obtain a special digital ID for themselves. Whether they request formal certification or not, their browsers will support SSL sessions—signified by HTTPS—with an SSL-enabled host.

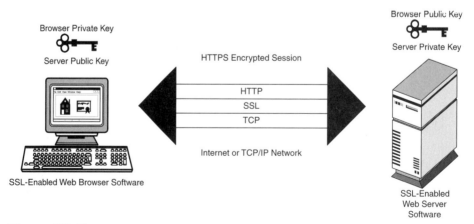

Figure 10–3
Key exchange in a Secure Socket Layer session.

In a nutshell, this is how SSL security works. SSL technology is now an integral part of approximately 98 percent of all Web server and Web browser software products. In 1999, SSL became the foundation of a transport layer security (TLS) protocol, which awaits ratification as a formal IETF standard.

Despite its widespread availability, SSL is not the only security protocol available for use with the Web, however. A contender, in the form of the Secure HyperText Transfer Protocol (S-HTTP), was developed by a consortium of companies led by Enterprise Integration Technologies (EIT) in the mid-1990s. (EIT itself was purchased by Verifone in 1995. Verifone was, in turn, acquired by Hewlett Packard Company, where it provides point-of-sale payment solutions.)

SSL and S-HTTP have very different designs and goals, leading some commentators to suggest that it is possible to use the two protocols together. Although SSL is designed to establish a secure connection between two computers, S-HTTP targets the secure sending of individual messages. This is in line with the point-of-sale perspective (think automatic debit cards and smart token-based payment systems at some automobile fuel pumps) of the protocol's originators. However, the use of the technology within the industry has dropped off substantially. Even though most browsers continue to support S-HTTP, few Web servers utilize the protocol.

In addition to the security provided through SSL and TLS, there are many other aspects to security that are dealt with in a later chapter. One point worth mentioning here is that the Web server also provides an important security role by authenticating the source of traffic and controlling the access that is provided to visitors. Most Web servers use authorization routines to evaluate the "header information" contained in data packets that are directed to it from external devices (browser-based clients or other servers). By comparing this information with a list of machine or domain identifiers that are authorized for access, the Web server can restrict access to certain information or deny access entirely.

Although Web server access controls are no substitute for securing information while it is in transit, they are an important component of a secure Web technology infrastructure that must be provided if ASPs are to garner consumer confidence and enjoy economic success.

EXPANDING INTERACTIVITY . . . .

As stated earlier, CGI provided a basic level of interactivity for Web sites and a richer set of functionality for Web servers. In many people's minds, CGI is associated with PERL, a programming language frequently used to create the "scripts" processed by CGI. However, CGI is a protocol for enabling Web servers to communicate with programs; it is not a programming language, nor is it language specific. CGI can be implemented in virtually any language, including C, Python, and TCL.

Despite this language agnosticism, however, CGI has its disadvantages. CGI processes tend to be slow because each request made by the visitor interacting with the page launches a new program. Moreover, as the number of individuals accessing a Web site increases, and the number of processes they launch increases, the performance of the Web server platform declines.

Web servers are software and run on hardware platforms, though it is not uncommon to witness an administrator point to a server (the hardware kind) and exclaim that it is one of his or her Web servers. As a software program operating on hardware, Web servers perform well when they utilize their host hardware environments efficiently. Starting too many CGI processes concurrently can overtax server memory and input/output subsystems. The result of this overhead may be a general slowdown in server performance (one cause of the notorious "world wide wait") or, worse yet, a server crash.

It should come as no surprise that soon after CGI was introduced and came into widespread use, developers turned their attention to more efficient "interaction processors" and "content delivery architectures."

For Microsoft, one solution to the CGI performance problem was Microsoft Active Server Pages (that other ASP). The vendor leverages its own Visual Basic script interpreter (VBScript) and embeds it into its flagship Web server, the Microsoft Internet Information Server (IIS).

In the UNIX world, Sun Microsystems and others have leveraged Java to create servlets (applets written in the Java language and executed in the Web server environment) and Java Server Pages (JSP) that are connected to a JVM. The distinction between Web server software and the operation of a separate JVM has led some to the conclusion that this architecture represents the first application server (as discussed in an earlier chapter).

An important distinction exists between the Windows and UNIX offerings. Microsoft VBScript pages, like CGI processes, do not persist. Each time a program is activated by a Web page user, it performs its function and evaporates. Servlets, on the other hand, are cached by the JVM once they have been accessed. Some commentators argue that this is an advantage of Java implementations from a performance standpoint.

A relative newcomer from the Open Source community is PHP. PHP was originally an acronym for personal home page tools, but is now understood as a HyperText Preprocessor.

PHP is similar in many respects to JSP and ASP technology in that it makes use of specialized code tags inserted within an existing HTML document. However, it is one of the few interactivity solutions to date that does not rely on an external programming or scripting language used in conjunction with an execution engine. No VBScript processor or JVM is required; PHP is designed solely to serve Web pages and is used on over 3.3 million Web sites at last count.

As Microsoft, Sun, the Open Source community, and many others endeavor to push the limits of what a Web server can do, Perl itself has been steadily improving. Most Web servers ship today with Perl script accelerators, such as mod_perl, from Apache, overseers of a very popular Web server product of the same name. Apache's solution integrates the Perl interpreter within the Web server software itself and provides mechanisms for caching executed Perl scripts in order to expedite their reuse.

In the final analysis, there is no one Web server product that is inherently superior to any other. Chances are that the Web server selected by an ASP will be based on criteria ranging from budget, to supportability with available staff skills, to support for the specific application set that the vendor plans to offer on a subscription basis.

Table 10–1 provides a summary of many popular Web server products.

Table 10–1 Popular Web Servers

Web Server	Operating System(s) Supported
AOLserver	Digital UNIX, SCO, HPUX, Windows NT, Linux, Windows 95, FreeBSD, Windows 98, IRIX, Solaris
Allegro RomPager	NetBSD, Digital UNIX, BSDI, AIX, OS/2, Windows 3.x, SCO, HPUX, Novell NetWare, Macintosh, Be OS, Embedded, Windows NT, Linux, Windows CE, MS-DOS, VM/CMS, MVS, VMS, QNX, AS/400, Windows 95, FreeBSD, Windows 98, IRIX, Solaris, Amiga
AnalogX SimpleServer:WWW	Windows NT, Windows 95, Windows 98
Baikonur Web App Server	Windows NT, Windows 95
Commerce Server/400	AS/400
EMWAC HTTP Server	Windows NT
ESAWEB	VM/CMS
EmWeb Embedded Web Server	HPUX, Embedded, Windows NT, Linux, Windows 95, Windows 98, Solaris
Enterprise Server	Novell NetWare
GoAhead WebServer	HPUX, Embedded, Windows NT, Linux, Windows CE, QNX, Windows 95, Windows 98, IRIX
Hawkeye	Linux
Internet Information Server	Windows NT

(*continued*)

Table 10–1 *Continued*

Web Server	Operating System(s) Supported
Java Server	OS/2, HPUX, Windows NT, Linux, Windows 95, IRIX, Solaris
Jigsaw	Java_VM
Lotus Domino Go Webserver	Digital UNIX, AIX, OS/2, HPUX, Windows NT, Windows 95, IRIX, Solaris
Netscape Enterprise Server	Digital UNIX, AIX, HPUX, Windows NT, IRIX
Oracle Web Application Server	HPUX, Windows NT, Windows 95, Solaris
RapidControl for Web(tm)	NetBSD, Digital UNIX, BSDI, Windows 3.x, SCO, HPUX, Windows NT, Linux, MS-DOS, Windows 95, FreeBSD, IRIX, Solaris
Roxen WebServer	Digital UNIX, AIX, HPUX, Windows NT, Linux, Windows 95, FreeBSD, Windows 98, IRIX, Solaris
Savant	Windows NT, Windows 95, Windows 98
Servertec Internet Server	NetBSD, Digital UNIX, AIX, OS/2, Java_VM, SCO, HPUX, Novell NetWare, Macintosh, Embedded, Windows NT, Linux, AS/400, Windows 95, FreeBSD, Windows 98, IRIX, Solaris
Shadow VM Web Server	VM/CMS
Spinnaker	Windows NT, Windows 95
Spyglass MicroServer	Embedded, Windows NT, Linux, Solaris
Stronghold Secure Web Server	NetBSD, Digital UNIX, BSDI, AIX, SCO, HPUX, Linux, FreeBSD, IRIX, Solaris
VM Webgateway	VM/CMS
Viking	Windows NT, Windows 95, Windows 98
WebSite Professional	Windows NT, Windows 95, Windows 98
Xitami	NetBSD, Digital UNIX, BSDI, AIX, OS/2, Windows 3.x, SCO, HPUX, Windows NT, Linux, VMS, QNX, Windows 95, FreeBSD, IRIX, Solaris
Zeus Web Application Server	NetBSD, Digital UNIX, BSDI, AIX, SCO, HPUX, Linux, FreeBSD, IRIX, Solaris
vqServer	NetBSD, Digital UNIX, BSDI, AIX, OS/2, Java_VM, SCO, HPUX, Macintosh, Be OS, Windows NT, Linux, Windows 95, FreeBSD, Windows 98, IRIX, Solaris

CONCLUSION ·

This whirlwind tour of Web technology has only scratched the surface. Clearly, Web technology–based platforms and protocols are being harnessed by ASP to extend their services across a broad range of network interconnects, ranging from the Internet to private networks. It is important, therefore, to understand what Web technology is and what role Web servers play in the delivery of the ASP value proposition.

Another way to think about the primacy of Web technology within the ASP model is to look at the topology of a typical ASP infrastructure. Web server platforms stand between application servers and the networks that interconnect the provider to the consumer. Clearly the efficiency of this infrastructure component will go a long way toward determining the performance—and the security—of applications delivered across the wire.

11 Putting It All Together: The Hosting Environment

In this chapter...

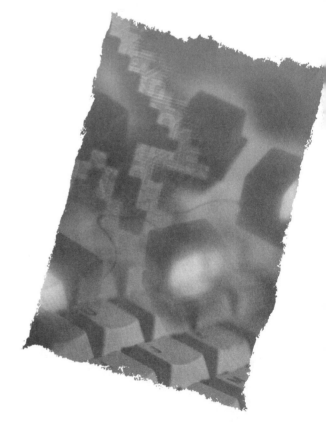

THE APPLICATION HOSTING ENVIRONMENT . . . . .

The preceding chapters in this section have examined some of the software building blocks required for ASPs to deliver their value proposition. In this chapter, the building blocks will be put together to facilitate a greater understanding of the application hosting environment—the infrastructure used by ASPs to deliver application services to customers.

It should be noted that different vendors have different architectural preferences for application hosting. The recurrent themes found in the vendor descriptions of their hosting platform architecture, however, are threefold: performance, security, and scalability. The emphasis placed by vendors on these three infrastructure characteristics makes a great deal of sense from a marketing standpoint.

Performance is a key requirement for the success of the ASP value proposition. Much of the "secret sauce" that one ASP uses to discriminate its service solution from those offered by competitors comes down to performance enhancing hosting configurations devised and implemented by the vendor. These enhancements, usually a combination of hardware- and software-based data caching and load balancing technologies, speed the performance of the hosted application from the end user's perspective. These performance enhancements are what the ASP vendors depend on to make application delivery via private or public basis compete—in terms of the end user's experience, at least—with locally executing application software.

Security is the another characteristic emphasized by ASPs when describing their infrastructure, and for good reason. Numerous surveys have assessed "consumer confidence" about ASPs over the past few years. As the concept of subscribing to an application service has garnered mindshare, so has concern about the security threats inherent in network-based applications. Security concerns continue to top the list of reasons given by IT and business decision makers to explain their reluctance to embrace the ASP concept.

Security has many meanings. The security-related concerns of potential ASP subscribers can be further detailed to include:

- The accessibility of private corporate information stored on ASP storage platforms by unauthorized persons generally, by hackers, and, in some cases, by ASP personnel themselves
- The security of information that is being transmitted or exchanged across a network during a remote application session
- The vulnerability of hosting platforms, especially those connected to the Internet, to viruses and other malicious programs
- The integrity of data stored in a shared hosting environment, particularly when the data storage infrastructure is shared

- The longevity of the ASP itself and the potential that a company's key applications will be left without a host if the ASP experiences a business failure

Many of these security concerns are underscored by the almost daily reports of security "holes" discovered in application code, hacker break-ins, email viruses, and encryption "cracks" by 12-year-old "script kiddies" that try to hack into home PCs tied into cable systems and occasionally seek bigger prizes in corporate Web sites. They are lent even more credence by the results of an annual survey conducted by the Computer Security Institute (CSI) and Federal Bureau of Investigation (FBI) which shows that the costs of computer crime are on the rise.

As shown in Table 11–1, total annual losses reported by survey respondents in CSI/FBI studies had increased from $100,119,555 in 1997 to $265,586,240 in 2000. Most security analysts attribute this increase to several factors, including the increased access being provided to nefarious wrongdoers by the increasing use of networking technology by companies, the increased sophistication of hackers themselves, and the widespread availability of software tools that make "experts" out of "novices" more quickly in the hacker community, and, of course, the standardization of application software, Web hosting software, application server software, and other software "layers" that enables a single "hack" to be exploited widely and very rapidly.

Security concerns participate in a broader context of reliability concerns held by prospective ASP users. Given the recent abrupt closures of several ASP shops, and the widely publicized burden placed upon user organizations to "find a replacement host and fast" when their provider has a business failure, a shadow of doubt persists in many potential customer minds regarding not only the technical solvency, but also the business solvency, of the ASP approach.

In part to address this concern about long-term stability, vendors are also emphasing platform scalability in their market messages. They stress the architectural elements of their hosting platforms that enable it to grow in capacity as customer needs grow. Diagrammic representations of solutions are beginning to include elements such as load balancing and caching—and, in some cases, specific references to application servers with "proven scalability features" (such as IBM WebSphere or BEA Systems WebLogic or HP Bluestone Total E-Business Server)—to communicate both that the ASP's solution will scale over time and, implicitly, that the ASP will remain a valued partner over the long haul.

All in all, to address performance, security, and scalability concerns, ASPs are pulling out all the stops to demonstrate that the customer's trust in their service is well founded—especially at a technical level. A few, including USi, EDS, and Corio, have begun to provide increasingly detailed architectural views of their hosting platforms for scrutiny by prospective customers—and by competitors. While these descriptions, as illustrated in Figures 11–1 through 11–5, offer little detail about the "special

Table 11–1   Cost of Computer Crime on the Rise

How Money Was Lost	Total Annual Loss			
	1997	**1998**	**1999**	**2000**
Theft of proprietary info	$20,048,000	$33,545,000	$42,496,000	$66,708,000
Sabotage of data or networks	$4,285,850	$2,142,000	$4,421,000	$27,148,000
Telecom eavesdropping and wiretapping	$1,181,000	$807,000	$785,000	$5,991,200
System penetration by outsider	$2,911,700	$1,637,000	$2,885,000	$7,104,000
Denial of service	N/A	$2,787,000	$3,255,000	$8,247,500
Spoofing	$512,000	N/A	N/A	N/A
Virus	$12,498,150	$7,874,000	$5,274,000	$29,171,800
Unauthorized insider access	$3,991,605	$50,565,000	$3,567,000	$22,554,500
Telecom fraud	$22,660,300	$17,256,000	$773,000	$4,028,000
Laptop theft	$6,132,200	$5,250,000	$13,038,000	$10,404,300
Financial fraud	$24,892,000	$11,239,000	$39,706,000	$55,996,000
Insider abuse of net access	$2,911,700	$1,637,000	$2,885,000	$7,104,000
TOTAL	$100,119,555	$136,822,000	$123,779,000	$265,586,240

Source: 2000 CSI/FBI Crime and Security Survey, Computer Security Institute, San Francisco, CA.

sauce" innovations that vendors use to distinguish their hosting solutions from those of competing vendors, nearly all diagrams are accompanied by narrative that goes to great lengths to describe the hosting infrastructure as "state of the art," "high performance," "integrating best of breed software and hardware technologies," and "rock solid"—terminology designed to reassure the prospect that their data and business processes could not be in better hands.

In point of fact, there is nothing inherently more or less reliable about application hosting at an ASP than hosting applications within a corporate-owned and operated facility provided that appropriate attention is paid to infrastructure design requirements for high-availability, high performance, and security.

(*text continues on page 264*)

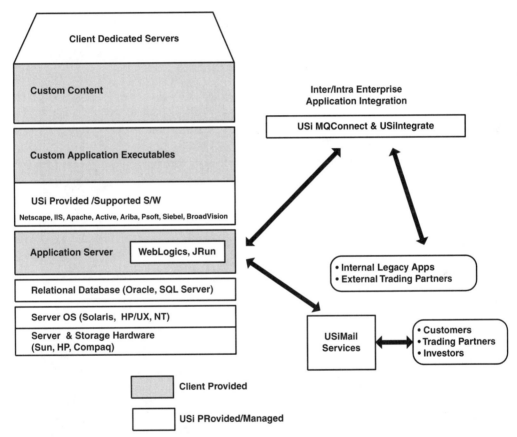

Figure 11-1
USinternetworking ASP technology stack. *Source:* USinetworking, Annapolis, MD.

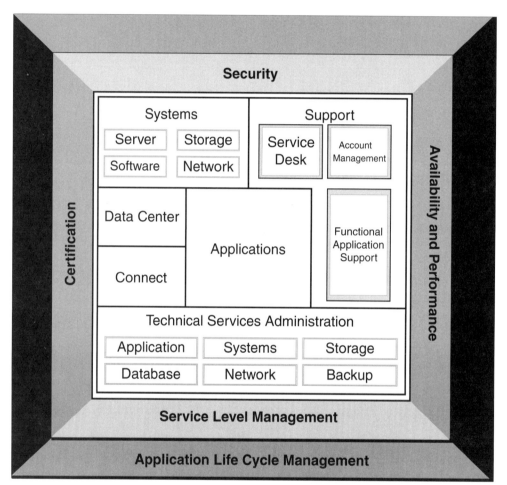

Figure 11–2
Corio's intelligent infrastructure. *Source:* Corio, Inc., San Carlos, CA.

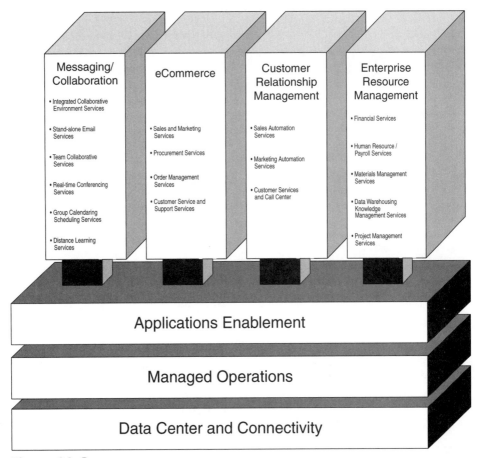

Figure 11–3
Electronic Data Systems (EDS) Applications Hosting Infrastructure Model.
Source: Electronic Data Systems (EDS), Plano, TX.

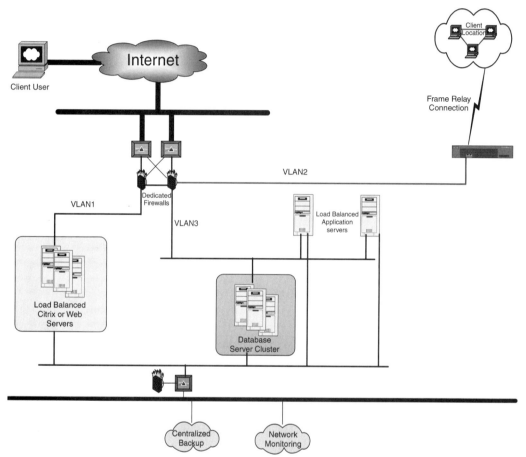

Figure 11–4
EDS Enterprise resource planning platform architecture. *Source:* Electronic Data
Systems (EDS), Plano, TX.

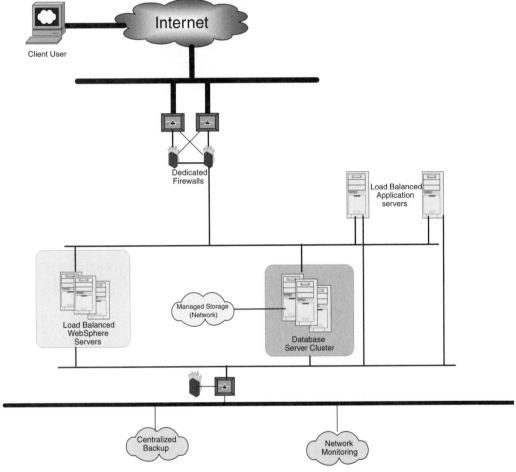

Figure 11–5
EDS e-commerce platform architecture. *Source:* Electronic Data Systems (EDS), Plano, TX.

THE BASIC APPLICATION
HOSTING INFRASTRUCTURE . . . .

The basic application hosting infrastructure combines components discussed in the previous chapters. Putting them together produces the simple configuration diagram depicted in Figure 11–6.

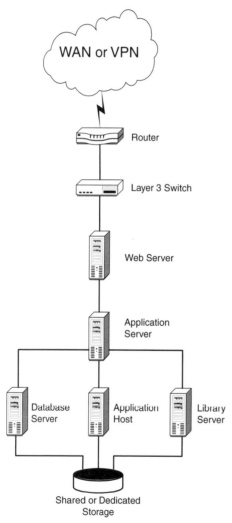

Figure 11–6
The basic application hosting configuration.

As shown in the figure, the components of this configuration are a router or another data communications device that connects the internal LAN of the hosting platform provider to the WAN used to connect the ASP to its customer. (We'll look more at this network interface in the next chapter.) In this diagram, a router is used to make the LAN/WAN connection and the router is, in turn, connected to a switch that enables traffic to be directed to other devices installed in the network.

Because virtually all application hosting solutions depend on Web technology, the next device layer consists of a Web server. The Web server provides numerous services, including the receipt of requests from the end user and the forwarding of application responses back to the end user.

Below the Web server is an application server. Recall from an earlier chapter that the application server delivers functionality required to present the application software interface to the Web server for delivery to the end user. These servers may also provide numerous other integration and session management functions, as well.

To fulfill its primary mission, however, of extending the application interface to the Web server, the application server communicates with the application host or database server (depending on the nature of the application itself) to pass requests and to receive responses. Remember that some applications have extremely complex, multitier, client/server designs. This complexity will be reflected in the actual configuration of the application server-application host-database server nexus.

Finally, the application hosts and database servers need to access data storage devices that store information that is being processed by the application. These storage devices may be dedicated to the individual application service solution offered by the ASP to each customer, or they may be configured as a common storage platform shared among multiple customers.

To summarize, Figure 11–6 comprises a simplified application hosting configuration that is the foundation of the infrastructure used by virtually every ASP today. It is termed "simplified" because this configuration omits any features designed to deliver availability, performance, scalability, or security capabilities that are required if ASPs are to deliver their value proposition and meet end user concerns.

To aid in understanding the complexities of a business-ready application hosting architecture, the following sections build on this basic configuration by adding high-availability features, performance enhancements, and security capabilities.*

*The author wishes to acknowledge the assistance of Michael Linett, president of Zerowait, a Newark, Delaware-based systems engineering company, for his contributions to the architectural description provided in this chapter. Zerowait is widely acknowledged as a leader in the engineering of high performance, high availability, and secure architectures for Web technology–based infrastructure. The company's clients are a "who's who" both of successful dotcoms and well-known "brick and mortar" companies that are beginning to leverage Web technology to enhance their business models.

ADDING HIGH-AVAILABILITY FEATURES . . . .

High-availability is an industry buzz phrase that encompasses numerous technologies for ensuring the continous availability of applications and data. A fundamental requirement of ASPs is that they ensure the availability of their service on a 24 hour, seven day per week, 365 days per year basis for their customers. Although it is understood that 100 percent availability is a holy grail, even within closely managed, non-ASP, IT environments, ASPs need to deliver realistic service levels that have been established with the customers, often described in terms of maximum downtime per month.

Readers may hear the term "uptime" (the opposite of downtime) used as a synonym for availability. High-availability is also sometimes described in terms of "nines": two nines (99 percent) means that downtime or inaccessibility of ASP services will not exceed 87.6 hours per year or 7.3 hours per month; three 9s of availability (99.9 percent) translates to a maximum allowable downtime of about nine hours per year or 45 minutes per month; four 9s (99.99 percent) of uptime translates to less than one hour of downtime per year or about five minutes per month, and five 9s (99.999 percent) uptime translates to just over five minutes of downtime for the entire year.

Usually, the closer that a customer's solution comes to "five 9s," the more the ASP charges the customer for the solution. The availability cost curve can be almost exponential in nature, discouraging most companies from seeking five 9s from their vendors (or from their internal IT operations). However, some enhancements to the basic hosting configuration depicted in Figure 11–7 can meet most availability requirements at an acceptable price.

At first glance, the configuration shown in Figure 11–7 may suggest a case of double vision on the part of the illustrator. Nearly every device in the basic configuration shown in Figure 11–6 has been replicated. There are two routers connecting the switch LAN to the WAN, and also two LAN switches. Moreover the number of Web servers, application servers, and application host/database server platforms have also been doubled. Storage itself is also duplicated or mirrored. This replication, called redundancy, is at the heart of high-availability.

High-availability architecture seeks to replicate all necessary devices and services that are required to deliver the objective of the configuration. It should be noted that the network connections, indicated by the lines connecting devices together in the diagram, have also been replicated. In such a "fully meshed" network, there are many physical and logical paths provided from Point A to Point B in order to enable data and commands to bypass a failed device or network interruption and still access critical resources.

High-availability is a pervasive concept with implications for hosting platforms from the application level down to the device and component level. Data, for exam-

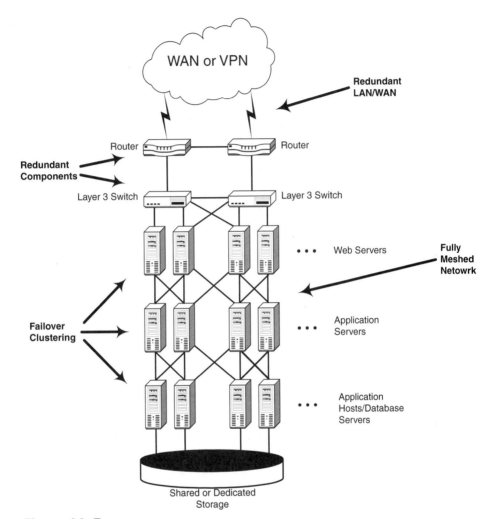

Figure 11–7
Application hosting platform optimized for high availability. *Source:* Based, in part, on insights offered by Michael Linett, president of Zerowait, Inc., Newark, DE.

ple, can be replicated both within a storage array (using RAID technology) and also between two (or more) storage arrays that have been configured to "mirror" one another across a storage or network interconnect. The arrays themselves can be equipped with other high-availability features such as redundant power supplies and "hot spare" disk drives that can be used if a primary device fails. Even the interconnects between "mirrored" arrays and/or between arrays and servers can be duplicated and configured for automatic "fail over" if one interconnect becomes unusable for some reason.

Moving up the diagram, application hosts and database servers can be deployed that both have high-availability redundancies built into their chassis, and also "clustered fail over" relationships between two or more machines. Server clustering technology has a lengthy and rich history, but did not find a "killer application" to drive its adoption by business until the advent of the World Wide Web. The $24 \times 7 \times 365$ environment of the World Wide Web helped to drive high-availability cluster architectures to the forefront. Solutions range from "true application clusters," in which application processing is shared among multiple processing nodes, to "fail over clusters" in which one machine idles until the primary machine fails, then assumes the load while the primary is off-line and being repaired.

High-availability configurations have also been applied to network cabling infrastructures and to networking devices such as routers, switches, and hubs. Considerable work has been done in the world of routing algorithms and network protocols by companies such as Cisco Systems, and by the IETF, to standardize techniques for ensuring that network device failures or connectivity breaks are identified swiftly, and alternative paths for traffic are implemented rapidly. Such self-healing networks are increasingly engineered into the network infrastructure of most ASPs.

The WAN/LAN interface—the connection point between the ASP and the outside network—is also replicated in a high-availability configuration. Vendors should obtain network services from at least two different carriers or network service providers. Ideally, these redundant services should not be located on the same physical cables or "trunks." Obtaining redundant services through separate trunks will help prevent an outage resulting from a single line cut, whether accidental or deliberate.

High-availability architecture also extends to the facility in which the hosting platform is housed. Most ASPs, for example, equip their hosting facilities with a redundant power source such as an uninterruptible power supply and generator that can be brought on-line to replace commercial power in the case of a power outage.

FROM HIGH-AVAILABILITY TO PERFORMANCE AND SCALABILITY . . . .

High-availability features aid in ensuring the accessibility of mission critical applications entrusted to an ASP. However, the value of these provisions is moot if the application being accessed does not deliver an acceptable "user experience" to the customer.

Welcome to the world of performance engineering! In Figure 11–8, our diagram of a high-availability configuration has been further complicated through the deployment of caching and load balancing equipment.

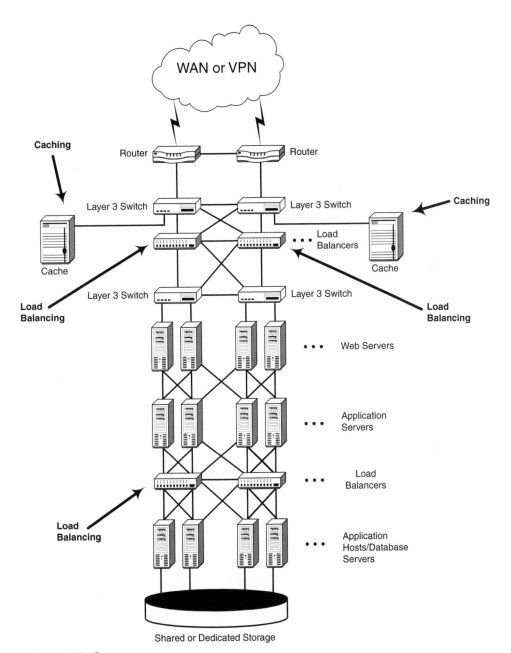

Figure 11–8
A high-performance configuration. *Source:* Based, in part, on insights offered by Michael Linett, president of Zerowait, Inc., Newark, DE.

The concept of caching is relatively straightforward. Traditionally, a cache is a temporary storage location for information that is frequently accessed. Caches are typically used to expedite access to frequently accessed data or, alternatively, to reduce the load placed on system components when performing the same operations over and over again.

Caching is used in many ways at many levels of the ASP delivery model. Hosted applications themselves are often designed to create and use memory caches to hold data that is frequently accessed by various application functions. Similarly, the microprocessors and motherboards found in servers often provide caching areas to speed their operation.

Moving outside of the server hardware platform itself, Web caching is a relatively new technique for improving the performance and reducing the latency involved in delivering Web content. In Figure 11–8, Web caching devices have been placed strategically around Web servers to facilitate a reduction in the load on the overall system, while expediting the responsiveness of the system to the end user.

In normal use, a Web cache is typically placed between Web servers and a client, where it monitors requests for objects such as HTML pages, images, and files, and saves copies of these objects to its own disk storage. When a request is monitored for an object that already exists in the cache storage, the Web cache responds to the request directly, from its own cache, rather than sending the request down the line to be processed by the Web server.

The benefits of Web caching are simple. First, the Web cache reduces latency by reducing the number of requests and processes that need to be forwarded to the Web server and to the application servers and application hosts. This generally translates to a perceived improvement in the response time of the Web technology–based application at the browser client.

Second, Web caching reduces the amount of traffic that must traverse the backbone LAN of the ASP. This reduces the potential for data collisions and packet discards on overtaxed network components and, in some cases, makes the overall network more manageable.

The preponderence of Web caches used by ASPs are proxy caches. These are shared caching solutions that are similar in principle to the cache used on a common Web browser (browsers cache the Web pages that a Web surfer visits then reads back the locally stored cache to quickly refresh information on the screen whenever the BACK key is actuated), but on a much grander scale and in a much more configurable way.

These caches operate in accordance with a set of rules that determine what objects to serve from cache, and under what circumstances. Some of these rules are set in the HyperText Transport Protocol, and others are set by the administrator of the cache. Generally speaking, objects that are to be cached are identified by their headers and by validation routines that verify that the object is worthy of caching. Secure objects are not routinely cached, but objects such as unchanging visual components (pretty borders around application interfaces, etc.) typically are. In addition to deciding what and what not to cache, the rules generally describe how often and in what way to check the freshness of the data stored in the cache, and when to perform a refresh operation.

The efficacy of Web caching is usually described in terms of its hit rate. The higher the hit rate (requests that are served by the cache rather than being passed to the Web server), the more efficient the cache is said to be. An efficient shared Web cache will generally evidence a hit rate of 50 percent or more. The efficiency of a Web cache used in connection with an ASP may be greater or less than 50 percent based on the nature of the user interface and the specific applications that are being hosted.

Another performance-oriented improvement that has been made to the illustration in Figure 11–8 is the addition of load balancing functionality. Load balancing has been mentioned earlier in this book to describe the efficient distribution of application sessions across application servers or hosts. Often this type of load balancing functionality is already part of the application server software that is used by the ASP.

For example, Citrix Systems offers technology for creating "MetaFrame Server Farms" from application hosts enabled with Citrix software. In such an arrangement, one server is configured as the Master ICA Browser and can be used to balance the load of user sessions across the other servers in the farm. With the addition of Citrix Load Balancing Services (an additional software product), load balancing is performed automatically.

In addition to application-level load balancing, load balancing may also be provided as an integral function of server or storage clustering configurations. With Microsoft's Wolfpack NT clustering solution, for example, load balancing is accomplished by means of the Windows Load Balancing Service (WLBS). WLBS installs as a standard Windows NT networking driver, using the LAN as the cluster interconnect. Once installed, it is transparent to both server applications and to connected TCP/IP clients. WLBS enables the cluster of two or more NT servers to be accessed as though they are a single server. In operation, WLBS automatically balances the networking traffic between the servers in the cluster, scaling the performance of one server to the level required. When a server in the cluster fails or goes off-line, WLBS automatically reconfigures the cluster to direct the client connections to the remaining computers. The off-line computer can transparently rejoin the cluster and regain its share of the workload.

With the introduction of Windows 2000, Microsoft expanded on WLBS (recast as the Windows 2000 Cluster Service) and added a networking load balancing capability. Network load balancing servers (also called hosts) configured in a cluster communicate among themselves to provide scalability and high-availability, according to the vendor. Network load balancing scales the performance of a server-based program, such as a Web server, by distributing its client requests across multiple servers within the cluster. As traffic increases, additional servers can be added to the cluster, with up to 32 servers possible in any one cluster. The solution also provides high-availability by automatically detecting the failure of a server and repartitioning client traffic among the remaining servers within 10 seconds, while providing users with continuous service.

Sun Microsystems has also developed a server clustering technology, its Sun Cluster 3 architecture, which leverages its Solaris Operating System and "private cluster communications interconnect" to deliver, among other things, load balancing functionality across cluster member servers. According to the vendor, the solution does more than to provide fail over services, it also enables (as does Windows 2000) scalability beyond a single node, while maintaining the view of a single system for clients.

Beyond cluster load balancing is another variant of the technology aimed at using network infrastructure efficiently, particularly within the context of Web-based content delivery. The earliest manifestations of this technology are load balancing appliances and switches such as those offered by ArrowPoint Communications (acquired by Cisco Systems in June 2000). ArrowPoint's "Content Smart" Web switching architecture originated as an innovation on existing network load balancing approaches.

Traditional network load balancing was accomplished by evaluating the TCP header information in packets traversing a TCP/IP network then directing the traffic on the best route to an appropriate destination. Such schemes did not pay any attention to the content of the traffic, only to its destination address. Such a scheme required all content to be replicated on all load balanced servers. The vendor asked why load balancers could not more explicitly direct traffic based on the type of content that was being requested (the content of the request being indicated by a URL, file type indication, cookie, or by some other means).

This simple question drove a great deal of development effort at ArrowPoint and elsewhere in the industry to develop content aware load balancing mechanisms, facilitated by content aware protocols and sophisticated load balancing algorithms. The effort is continuing today and shows considerable promise in terms of refining the architecture for efficient, load balanced information and application hosting and delivery. Through the acquisition of ArrowPoint, Cisco Systems is at the forefront of defining a "distributed services layer with a content routing layer," as well as the technology for leveraging this layer to deliver content routing products that will enable ASPs and others to set policies for effective content routing that will respond dynamically to network changes.

Not to be excluded from this brief overview of content aware load balancing is Nortel Networks. Nortel acquired another content networking pioneer, Alteon Web-Systems, in October 2000. Prior to the acquisition, Alteon was setting speed records for Web server load balancing and cache utilization efficiency by routing traffic based on URLs. Implemented on its own Gigabit Ethernet switch platform, the vendor's "WebOS" provided a way to expedite traffic across TCP/IP networks based on Web addressing which made the technology ideal for adoption by ASPs like Interliant, which announced in November 2000 that it was deploying Alteon 180e and 184 Gigabit Ethernet Web switches in five of its data centers—four in the United States and one in the United Kingdom—to provide high-speed connectivity, high-performance load balancing, and nonstop availability for servers and firewalls. In addition, Interliant announced plans to enable Nortel Networks global server load balancing and content-intelligent switching functions in the same Web switches for intersite resilience and optimized content retrieval.

Although load balancers are shown in Figure 11–8 as devices, they may be just as readily provided as switch-based software. However the functionality is delivered, the purpose remains the same: to improve overall network performance and to deliver to the end user a satisfying experience with the hosted application.

The performance enhancing features described may also provide the linchpin of the ASP's strategy for facilitating scalability of the hosting platform in response to customer needs over time. Simply put, one can view the ability to add one or more load-balanced application hosts as a rough indication of overall platform scalability—provided, that is, that the other elements of the infrastructure, including Web servers, application servers, storage, and the application software itself, can support the increased load overall. This is an important point to explore when considering the ASP offerings of different vendors.

SECURING THE INFRASTRUCTURE · · · · · · · · · · · ·

Perhaps the most frequently cited concern of prospective users of ASP services is the security of the ASP service. Some of the concerns raised by prospective customers are familiar to all outsourcing arrangements and reflect a perception of vulnerability derived less from technical exposure than from a sense of a loss of control.

For example, users sometimes voice concerns that anonymous ASP workers may have access to their data or that their dependence on an ASP to support a mission critical service exposes them to high dollar losses should the ASP itself close up shop. Both of these observations, though valid, are not unique to ASP arrangements. They need to be addressed by referring to employee screening practices and access safeguards deployed by the vendor (in the case of the ASP personnel issue) and by SLA and contract arrangements established between the customer and the vendor (in the case of the longevity issue).

However, there are other, more technical, security considerations that the ASP vendor needs to address in its application hosting infrastructure. Figure 11–9 depicts the infrastructure that has been discussed up to this point, and adds security functionality.

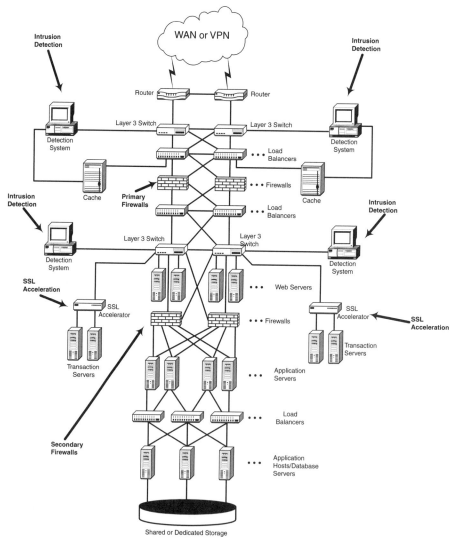

Figure 11–9

The hosting infrastructure with security enhancements. *Source:* Based, in part, on insights offered by Michael Linett, president of Zerowait, Inc., Newark, DE.

Specifically, the diagram introduces the concept of a "firewall sandwich" combined with intrusion detection systems and SSL accelerators. Explanations for these enhancements first require that the reader gain familiarity with some of the basic concepts of security.

SECURITY 101 . . . .

Security is a broad concept with many components. Typical definitions typically include references to:

- authentication—methods for proving the identity of a user—as a prelude to opening a session, providing access, or otherwise allocating resources
- data integrity—methods for ensuring that unauthorized parties cannot intercept and/or tamper with communications or data
- nonrepudiation—methods to ensure data cannot be changed without appropriate permissions

Considerable work has been done in the industry in all three of these areas. Extensive authentication schemes have been developed, for example, that depend on everything from "tokens," such as physical card keys, public/private key certificates, or embedded machine indentifiers (sometimes called "what you have" authenticators); to password and ID systems (so-called "what you know" authenticators); to biometric systems that authenticate identity based on thumb prints, hand geometry, retinal patterns, handwriting analysis, or voice print analysis (so-called "what you are" authenticators).

Similarly, encryption schemes, such as the public/private key encryption methodology embedded in the SSL security methodology discussed in a previous chapter, continue to advance to deliver data integrity. Computer and network encryption technologies have been driven as much by improvements in ciphers themselves as by advances in the capabilities of cipher breakers.

Finally, nonrepudiation methods have advanced, including digital signatures and digital watermarks, which are intended to prevent an unauthorized person from altering a message, data set, or communication belonging to another without the originator's permission. This type of technology has become more important with the advent of e-commerce on the World Wide Web, where consumers are concerned that an electronic order for 50 widgets might be increased to 500 widgets by an unscrupulous vendor. Nonrepudiation protects both the vendor and the user against claims that the terms of an order have been altered.

One of the first efforts to define a comprehensive security system for Web-based transactions was undertaken in 1997 by Visa International and Mastercard

International, who together defined and adopted the Secure Electronic Transactions (SET) protocol to enable bank-issued credit card transactions over the Internet. The protocol addressed primarily the authentication of the card holder and provided mechanisms for nonrepudiation so that cardholders could not deny that they had made purchases.

Today, however, there are a broad range of systemic security solutions—some proprietary and others standards-based—that are managing to keep ahead of the growing capabilities of cyberthieves. Protocols such as the Remote Address Dial-In Service (RADIUS), developed by Livingston Enterprises and now a specification with the Internet Engineering Task Force; Kerberos, developed by the Massachusetts Institute of Technology and now overseen by the Open Software Foundation as part of its Distributed Computing Environment (DCE) functional specifications; and, FORTEZZA, part of the National Security Agency's Multilevel Information System Security Initiative (MISSI), all endeavor to provide frameworks for developing interoperable security products that will work with networked systems. None of these efforts has garnered universal support from the vendor community, however, resulting in the situation today: a mix-and-match, best-of-breed approach to securing various aspects of the enterprise.

MICROSOFT EMBRACES KERBEROS

While none of the systemic protocols for platform security have obtained universal adoption within industry, Microsoft has given one protocol, Kerberos, a boost by adopting it as the "primary authentication mechanism" within the Microsoft Windows 2000 environment. The vendor has implemented extensions to the protocol that permit its implementation in connection with smart cards, which may be used during network login to authenticate users seeking access. The vendor touts this capability as a means for providing seamless access that leverages Kerberos authentication and Microsoft's variant of public key technology (keys are stored in the smart card).

Kerberos is an industry-standard authentication protocol that provides high security together with good scalability. Figure 11–10 depicts the basic operation of Kerberos.

Central to the operation of Kerberos is a trusted server called a key distribution center (KDC). When the user logs onto the network, the KDC verifies the user's identity and provides credentials called "tickets," one for each network service that the user wants to use. Each ticket introduces the user to the appropriate service, and optionally carries information that indicates the user's privileges for the service.

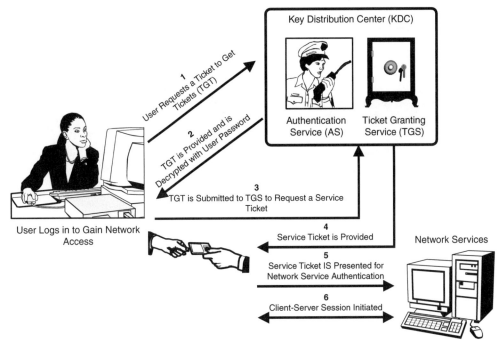

Figure 11-10
Kerberos in operation.

The keys to the effective selection and deployment of security technologies are striking a balance between the desired level of security and confidentiality and achieving the performance desired of the production application that is being secured. This is just as true for corporate IT security as it is for ASPs.

LAYERS OF SECURITY . . . .

A convenient way to think about security in an ASP environment is to relate security provisions to the layered model of networks advanced by the International Standards Organization, the open systems interconnection (OSI) model. The OSI model defines seven distinct functional layers associated with most networks. For TCP/IP, the relevant layers are the application layer (where communications applications such as FTP, email, and HTTP operate), transport layer (where TCP operates), the network layer (where IP operates), and the link layer (the domain of device drivers, network interface cards and cabling). Table 11-2 depicts this model.

Table 11–2   *Layers of Network Protection*

Open Systems Interconnect (OSI) Layer	Primary Focus	Examples of Security Provisions	Comments
Application layer	Applications running on networks, including FTP, email, HTTP hosted applications	S-HTTP in Web technology networks, various proprietary and standards-based protocols for application security	Application security provisions are largely judgment calls on the part of ASPs and leverage "best of breed" technologies and single sign-on (SSO) solutions.
Transport layer	TCP	SSL, TLS, secure shell (SSH), socket security (SOCKS)	Message encryption schemes, SSL is most popular and a foundation of IETF's TLS standard
Network layer	IP	IPsec	Establishes secure tunnels for encrypted data communications
Link layer	Drivers, network interface cards, cabling	No specific protocols	Enablers of security schemes implemented at higher layers

Application level security consists of whatever provisions have been made for authentication, authorization, and access within the application environment itself. These may include a system of secure passwords and IDs, specialized tokens such as smart cards, or biometric identifiers, which provide identity checks and validations. The identifier is validated and access to the desired application resource in accordance with some internal function of the application or through a proprietary or standards-based security framework like RADIUS, Kerberos, or FORTEZZA is granted.

Note that in the absence of a universally adopted security framework for application security, numerous products have appeared on the market to aggregate the authentication, authorization, and access control processes of numerous applications into one management platform. Often referred to as Single Sign-On Systems (SSO), these products are intended to simplify both the end user's sign-on process and provide a point of consolidation for security managers.

Most of the work in securing network or Web-based communications has not targeted the application layer of the OSI stack. The exception is S-HTTP, which was described in a previous chapter. S-HTTP was designed to secure HTTP messaging by enabling request and reply messages to be signed, authenticated, encrypted, and so forth. However, the protocol is not widely used and was largely eclipsed by SSL security, which is more widely available and more readily deployed.

Moving down the OSI stack, transport layer security is the main focus of most current network security initiatives. SSL is one protocol that works at the Transport layer to provide privacy and reliability between two communicating applications. SSL encompasses three primary processes or protocols.

- Handshaking: This protocol negotiates the parameters to be used in encrypting communications between the client and server session. When the client and server begin communicating, they agree on a protocol version, select cryptographic algorithms and optionally authenticate one another, and use public key encryption techniques to generate shared secret messages.
- Recording: This protocol is used to apply a message authentication code (MAC) to each block of application data that is created for transmission over the wire and to encrypt it for transmission. The receiver receives the message, decrypts it, verifies the MAC, and delivers it to the relevant application-level protocol (e.g., HTTP).
- Alert: This protocol signals if errors have occurred or when the session is being terminated.

SSL, as previously observed, is supported by most Web server and Web browser software and supports various modes of operation that make it relatively easy to deploy and widely adopted. SSL became one of the foundations for the IETF's work to develop a standard protocol called transport layer security (TLS).

Two other transport layer protocols worth mentioning are Secure Shell (SSH), a protocol for secure remote login, secure file transfer, and secure forwarding of TCP/IP and X Windows system traffic, and Socket Security (SOCKS), envisioned as a framework to enable client/server applications to use firewalls conveniently. SSH is widely implemented in UNIX, Windows, and Macintosh systems, but is entirely host-focused, providing no user authentication function. SOCKS has labored under the burden of requiring the replacement of standard network system calls within an application with special SOCKS calls (a process endearingly termed SOCKS-ification). Vendors are only now beginning to do so in their application software.

Network layer security focuses on the IP layer of the TCP/IP protocol stack. Over the years, the IETF has labored to develop a set of portable security protocols that could travel with IP regardless of its implementation (e.g., regardless of what kind of link level protocol was being used with IP as the network protocol). The IP security protocol suite (IPsec) is the result. The key ingredients of IPsec are shown in Figure 11–11.

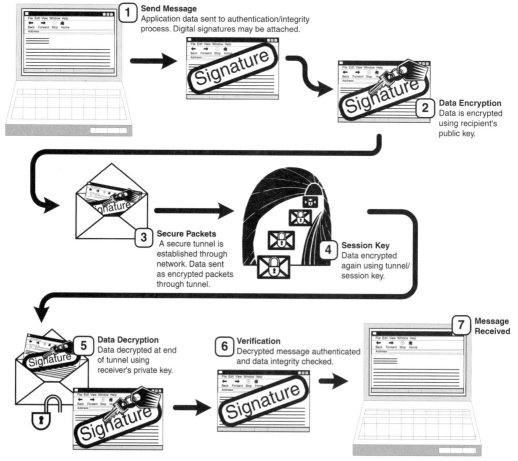

1 Send Message
Application data sent to authentication/integrity process. Digital signatures may be attached.

2 Data Encryption
Data is encrypted using recipient's public key.

3 Secure Packets
A secure tunnel is established through network. Data sent as encrypted packets through tunnel.

4 Session Key
Data encrypted again using tunnel/session key.

5 Data Decryption
Data decrypted at end of tunnel using receiver's private key.

6 Verification
Decrypted message authenticated and data integrity checked.

7 Message Received

Figure 11–11
IPsec in action.

IPsec comprises a standards-based platform to develop secure networks and tunnels between two or more machines. Secure tunneling via the protocol suite creates circuitlike connections through which data moves. IPsec also encapsulates each data packet into a new packet that contains the information required to set up and tear down the tunnel as required. Packets are encrypted using the Internet key exchange (IKE), an application layer protocol that uses digital certificates to authenticate communicating machines.

Given its standards-rich base and its ability to "tailor" security services based on a combination of IP address, transport protocol, and application, IPsec is garnering substantial interest in the vendor community. However, the implementation of the protocol suite currently awaits the development of component technologies that can leverage the benefits without reducing the efficiency of protected networks. Most analysts agree that there is usually a requirement to field a combination of security protocols, and most environments will eventually use some combination of transport-level protection in combination with IPsec.

At the lowest level of the OSI model is the link layer. Security controls at this layer are usually enablers of grander network, transport, or application layer security strategies. For example, a machine identifier, stored on a network interface card, may be used to identify that machine and to authorize it for the use of certain network or application assets.

PHYSICAL AND LOGICAL DESIGN . . . .

The benefit of the OSI model as a framework for understanding the diversity of network security protocols and where they fit in the security infrastructure cannot be understated. However, the practical matter of how and where to implement security controls is not fully illuminated by such an analysis. Instead, it is beneficial to look at the technologies that are currently being fielded which leverage the security protocols and provide, in some cases, ways to implement security that will not impair the efficiency of the network or the applications that use it.

In Figure 11–9, the illustration of a model ASP infrastructure included a "firewall sandwich." Such a topology delivers numerous advantages from both a security and a performance standpoint that need to be clearly understood.

First, it is useful to review what a firewall is. Simply stated, firewalls are a commonly deployed technology, either software or hardware based, used to control the flow of traffic from one network to another. Firewalls generally use programmed rules to determine whether the ingress to the network it is protecting should be permitted or denied to a requestor. It does this in a variety of ways including:

- Packet filtering—the firewall evaluates the headers of individual packets for their source and destination and compares this information with rules in order to determine whether to permit or deny ingress.
- Circuit filtering—the firewall determines whether to pass data traffic based on rules about new and established circuits.
- Application gateways—firewalls that process messages specific to a particular IP applications.

Although commonplace, firewalls are not a panacea for security. They are best thought of as perimeter defenses that may be effective in stopping certain types of unauthorized access. Moreover, certain firewalls impose a latency penalty on network performance by stopping and interrogating each and every packet before allowing it to traverse the firewall into the protected network. New, specialized firewall appliances and switch-based firewalls are generally thought to be less latency prone than are software firewalls deployed on Web servers themselves.

One approach to obtain peak performance from firewalls is to replicate the firewall devices themselves and to use a load balancer to direct traffic in a managed way to each device. Moreover, it may be useful to deploy two levels of load balanced firewall protection—one between the WAN and the Web servers on the internal network, the second between the Web servers and the application servers—to protect the back-end application hosts, application hosts, database servers, and data storage infrastructure.

One reason for this sandwich is to further protect the core infrastructure from attack. Hackers have developed considerable expertise at breaking the integrity of firewalls. Often such attacks take the form of a "spoof." Spoofing refers to the misrepresentation of the source network address in a message packet header to make the packet appear to be from a valid and approved source. Firewalls cannot, as a rule, distinguish spoofed packets from the genuine article. Setting up another line of firewalls—in effect, sandwiching the Web servers between firewalls—affords an additional capability to verify and validate inbound traffic, while providing a location to mask the valid IP addresses of hosts that forward outbound traffic to the Web server using network address translations.

Firewalling needs to be backed up by active intrusion monitoring and detection capabilities. Figure 11–9 provides two locations for detection systems that operate on a continuous basis to monitor for tell-tales of intrusions. Audit trails and logs of traffic patterns provide a useful mechanism for identifying deviations from normal operations that may signify the activities of an intruder. Monitoring products are available

PROXY SERVERS AS FIREWALLS AND CACHES

Even though firewalls can be implemented on proxy servers, the two terms are often—and mistakenly—used synonymously. In fact, proxy servers act as "middlemen" between a Web technology–based network and users. There, they may serve as gateways or caches.

In their gateway role, proxy servers serve as a local point of connection for company servers and users that share a high-speed connection onto the external network. Requests from an end user browser, for example, are placed to the proxy server, which, in turn, forwards the request to the remote network host. The proxy server then receives the response and forwards it back to the requesting user. Adding firewalling technology to this process may help to isolate users and servers connected to the proxy from unsolicited responses, viruses, and certain types of attempted intrusions.

Proxy servers are also sometimes used to improve Internet or Web technology–based network performance by caching some accessed content locally for reuse by many requesters. This only works if the content that is cached is more or less static in nature. For data that changes frequently, caching is generally inappropriate.

Like firewalls, proxy servers have the potential to become choke-points in a network. If proxy server use is recommended by an ASP vendor—whether it is within the vendor's shop or at the customer's end—be sure to evaluate the consequences of the approach carefully with an eye toward ensuring the scalability of the solution over time.

Another key point to consider about proxy servers is that they sometimes obfuscate efforts to derive accurate information about network and application performance because of their caching functions. They can also introduce a layer of complication into efforts to troubleshoot performance problems. On the other hand, however, properly deployed proxy services can improve application performance and facilitate the sharing of expensive, high-speed network access facilities.

both commercially and from government-funded security services that can be deployed to assist in intrusion detection and monitoring.

Figure 11–9 also provides a reference to an SSL accelerator. Such devices, which are specialized appliances that offload SSL protocol handling from Web servers, can help to expedite SSL processing, reducing the latency that is imposed on

Web server operations by handshaking, recording, and alerting functions. SSL accler-ators are increasingly used by e-commerce Web sites to expedite the performance of shopping cart applications, but may be harnessed effectively to enhance the perfor-mance of subscription-based ASPs as well.

CONCLUSION . . . .

This chapter provided a quick survey of some of the high-availability, performance, and security techniques available to ASPs in delivering applications across networks. When all is said and done, an assessment of these technical capabilities needs to be wedded to an audit of ASP business processes to assure that the ASP offering meets with customer requirements.

A final word about security: No security implementation is foolproof. The best way to secure information is not to place it on a network in the first place. Business demands, however, necessitate that information be shared among decision makers, creating the need for networks. In the final analysis, the type and pervasiveness of se-curity technology deployed by a company (or an ASP) must always be weighed against its impact on the performance and usefulness of the system itself. Through proper design and engineering, some of the performance penalties imposed by secu-rity technology can be offset. Businesses that are evaluating ASPs must keep these points in mind and be sure to ascertain whether the ASP has done enough to provide a secure service, rather than to dismiss the ASP option simply because networks are inherently insecure.

12 Networked Services

In this chapter...

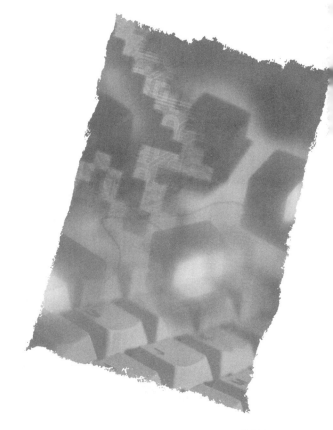

DELIVERING SERVICES ACROSS A NETWORK . . . . .

Although it isn't explicitly stated in the acronym, all ASPs depend on WANs to deliver their services. From the user standpoint, this dependency is straightforward. To use a remotely hosted application, the user needs to "log in"—to make a connection to the application—across a WAN, usually via a Web browser.

Of course, the network connection that supports an "application session" is largely transparent to the user. That is to say, the user is not aware of the type of network service that is being used, who is providing it, or what path data exchanges between the local client and remote host are actually taking. The user also does not know how the bandwidth of the connection is allocated and or how network latency and availability are being managed.

Moreover, the user is typically unaware of how other network-based services might be impacting the application. For example, the proper operation of an ASP-hosted application may itself depend on the services of a storage service provider (SSP) another type of Service Provider (sometimes collectively referred to as xSPs) that provides the storage resources used by the application across a network interconnect located either within the ASP hosting facility or outside of it.

One thing is certain. The efficiency (or inefficiency) of the network interconnect between the user and the ASP service, and in some cases between the ASP and other service providers, goes a long way toward determining the performance and security—as well as the user's perception—of the service itself. When the network is poorly managed and congested, applications may perform slowly. When the network fails, the hosted application is just as unavailable as a locally installed application would be on a failed PC.

It is important to understand how the network services that are required in order to deliver application services are provisioned and managed by the ASP before inking an application services contract with the vendor. This chapter provides an overview of the network technologies that are available to ASPs in order to facilitate evaluation of this technical aspect of ASP operations.

PRIVATE AND PUBLIC NETWORKS . . . .

The point has been made several times in this book that, though most ASPs harness Web technology to deliver application services, few ASPs actually deliver services using the public Internet. The vicissitudes of the Internet, in terms of extremely limited quality of service (QoS) guarantees and poor security, cast a long shadow of

....

What is QoS?

Quality of service or QoS is a buzz phrase in the networking industry. It refers to four basic characteristics of networks that affect network performance and to provisions that are made to optimize them. These characteristics generally include network-imposed delay, jitter, bandwidth, and reliability.

- Delay refers to the elapsed time for a packet to be passed from the sender, through the network, to the receiver. The longer the delay, the more stress is placed on the transport protocol to operate efficiently. In the case of TCP, longer delays translate to larger quantities of data being held "in transit" in the network pipe. This places stress on the counters and timers in the protocol itself. Because TCP is a "self-clocking" protocol—that is, the sender's transmission rate is dynamically adjusted to the flow of signal information coming back from the receiver, via the reverse direction acknowledgments (intended to tell the sender that packets are being successfully received)—the longer the delay between sender and receiver, the less sensitive this clock becomes. This is the long way of saying that TCP becomes less sensitive to short-term dynamic changes in network load when delays increase. For delay-sensitive applications such as voice, video, and network-based storage applications, delay makes the system seem unresponsive and degrades the perceived, if not the actual, performance of the impaired application.

- Jitter is another form of end-to-end transit delay. High levels of jitter cause the TCP protocol to estimate round trip time across the network incorrectly. When this happens, TCP reverts to timeouts to reestablish a data flow, often causing serious protocol inefficiency and forcing applications to resend their data packets repeatedly. This type of delay is called jitter because of the noticeable impact it has on multimedia video sent across the Web, which actually jitters with the frequent resends.

- Bandwidth refers to the maximum data transfer rate that can be sustained between two endpoints in the network. Bandwidth is determined not only by the physical infrastructure (the signaling used across a wire or fiber-optic cable), but also by the number of other traffic flows which share common components of this selected end-to-end path.

(continued)

- Reliability is often viewed in network-speak as as the average error rate of the medium (packet collisions and dropouts). Unreliable or error-prone network paths can introduce delay by requiring the frequent retransmission of lost packets. Additionally, reliability is determined by the efficiency of switches in delivering packets in the proper order to receivers. Out of order receipt of packets necessitates the use of special packet reordering processes that can introduce inefficiency into latency sensitive applications.

All networks have delay, jitter, bandwidth, and reliability characteristics. QoS refers to the ways that these characteristics are managed or "shaped" to deliver varying degrees of service quality. Usually a vendor establishes a "menu" of QoS offerings that combines network engineering, bandwidth management techniques, and other services, which promise to deliver a certain service quality level. In general, the best QoS levels also carry the highest price tag.

It should be noted, however, that most QoS agreements contain "best effort" clauses (that is, the vendor is only obligated to do its best to deliver the promised service level) owing to the fact that some service level degradation may be beyond the ability of the service provider to control.

doubt on the "network of networks" as a reliable or predictable platform for mission-critical services.

This is not to say that the Internet will never be a platform for application delivery. Some of the initiatives to expand and enhance the Internet infrastructure in order to deliver greater speed, security, and QoS offer hope that the ubiquitous public network will one day deliver all of the necessary support for mission-critical business processes.

Today, however, only limited use of the public network is made by ASPs. Some smaller ISPs, for example, who have seized on the ASP model to develop new sources for revenue in a business with notoriously razor-thin margins, have begun to offer "Web top" applications such as StarOffice Suite from Sun Microsystems or the latest Microsoft Office applications (retooled for delivery via the ASP model) to their local clientele. The local and personalized support offered by an ISP for these applications, which were formerly delivered as locally installed PC software, as well as the less-than-mission-critical nature of the software itself, helps to justify the Internet an acceptable mode for service delivery.

The public Internet is also often used in connection with ASP software offerings in the e-commerce space. As depicted in Figure 12–1, many businesses have found it

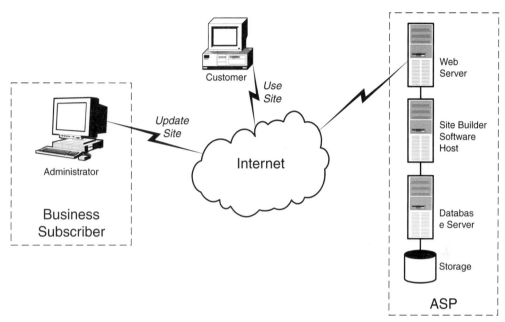

Figure 12–1
E-commerce site builder software hosted at an ASP and accessed via the Internet.

preferable to subscribe to an e-commerce site builder software package hosted by an ASP rather than to field the software locally—especially when the ASP will also serve as the Web host for the site that is ultimately built. Using the ASP-hosted site building software eliminates the need to replicate hosting platforms used by the business to create the site and the Web host to host the site.

Once the ASP-hosted site building software is on-line, site administrators (business personnel) use it remotely to create the HTML Web pages and their supporting databases. After the site "goes live" (e.g., is made available for access and use by Web-based consumers), administrators access the site builder software only periodically to make changes and updates to site content.

Such an application is a "natural" for ASP delivery, because it spares the business the cost of fielding software whose main feature (site creation) may only be used once. Given the nature of subseqent administration activity, as well as the desire that access to the site be provided via the Internet and World Wide Web, the Internet-based network interconnect may also be sufficiently robust for use with the service.

But what happens when the e-commerce site must exchange data with mission-critical order processing, inventory control, or manufacturing and distribution systems located at the subscriber's facility (or hosted at another ASP)? These "back-end" systems may be extremely sensitive to the delays of the Internet. They may require con-

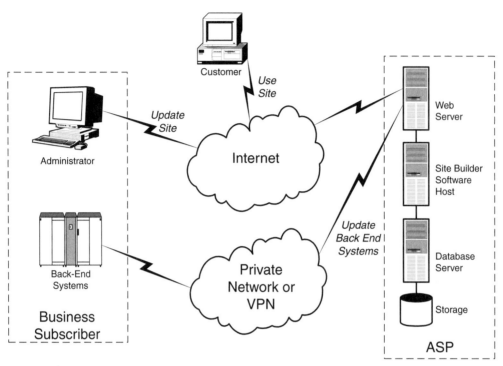

Figure 12–2
Back-end system connections may require private networks or virtual private networks.

nections that deliver enhanced security against hackers. They may require fault tolerant characteristics that ensure their availability on a $24 \times 7 \times 365$ basis. In short, as depicted in Figure 12–2, the connections may need to be serviced using private networks or managed public services such as VPNs.

In fact, most enterprise applications hosted by ASPs depend on dedicated private or virtual private networks, rather than the Internet, to provide the subscriber-to-ASP connection. Even though Web technology is often used in connection with the service arrangement, the public Internet may not be used at all.

WHAT IS A PRIVATE NETWORK? . . . .

Private network is a confusing term to many business people. To purists, the term is something of an oxymoron, because the only way to guarantee the privacy of anything is to keep it to oneself! However, in common parlance, a private network is any of several networking arrangements in which the access to and use of the networking interconnect is limited to a designated group of communicators.

Few purely private networks exist today. Even within the business premise, corporate networks are typically engineered to facilitate some communication with public networks, including the Internet, if only to pass email traffic to customers, shareholders, or employees on the road.

In point of fact, external networks are inherently nonprivate in the sense that they utilize the shared physical infrastructure (lines, trunks, switches, etc.) comprising that modern telecommunications behemoth, the Public Switched Telephone Network (PSTN). Although communications technology has progressed beyond the point (in most U.S. locales, at least) in which a human operator is required to make and break connections between two or more communicating parties (a scenario that provided a springboard for many mystery stories in the past), the shared nature of local, metropolitan, and WANs defies their categorization as purely private in nature.

What telecommunications providers do offer are a broad array of "dedicated" communications facilities, as well as a number of shared service offerings that afford a certain "guaranteed" bandwidth or throughput capabilities and/or special management services. An example of dedicated communications facilities are digital cross-connect services used by many companies to interconnect headquarters with outlying branch office sites. Examples of the shared services offerings include frame relay and ATM networks and the shared dual-ring SONET networks that appear to be springing up daily around major metropolitan areas.

Digital cross-connect services are provisioned by the telecommunications carrier using a switch platform of the same name (i.e., digital cross connect switch or DCCS). In a common implementation, a company will lease a T-1 circuit from the telco that provides 1.544 megabits per second of bandwidth organized into 24 voice or data channels (64 kilobits per second per channel). The facility runs from the business headquarters site to the telephone company central office and terminates at the DCCS switch. As shown in Figure 12–3, outlying offices will also be provisioned with dedicated circuits operating at either full or fractional T-1 capacities (fractional refers to provisioning of a subset of the number of circuits offered in a full T1). Fractional lines are used where appropriate to provide the best mix of capacity and cost. The DCCS switch provides a connection between the facilities.

The actual facilities (T-1, fractional T-1, etc.) used in a dedicated cross-connect solution may vary from implementation to implementation, especially in light of newer digital circuit offerings from carriers, including T-3 (the equivalent of 28 T-1s) and others. However, the root value proposition remains the same. In these arrangements, the allocated circuits are dedicated to the subscriber and not shared with other businesses served by the telco. The solution is not, however, completely dedicated, because the DCCS switch platform may be handling many customers concurrently.

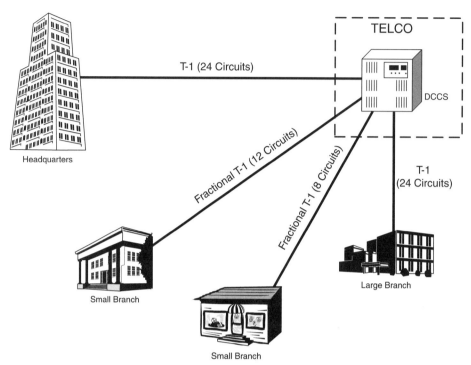

Figure 12–3
Example of a T-1 digital cross-connect solution.

Another way to provision a "private" network is to subscribe to a specialized network service, such as Frame relay, ATM, or SONET-based optical networking services which are increasingly becoming available from traditional carriers and value-added network (VAN) providers.

Industry insiders often refer to these services using the term "cloud." For example, it is not unusual to hear someone remark that they have a "connection to the frame relay cloud," or that data traffic "passes through the ATM cloud." This is basically industry vernacular used as shorthand to avoid describing in detail the particulars of the technology supporting each service.

As shown in Figure 12–4, the service cloud may be shared among many companies and their sites. So, how can these services be properly described as private? The answer has much to do with the protocols themselves.

In the case of both frame relay and ATM, customers who subscribe to the network services are provisioned with "virtual circuits"—analogous to physical circuits in a strategy such as digital cross-connection. In the frame relay world, these virtual circuits come in two "flavors": permanent virtual circuits (PVCs) that are used to con-

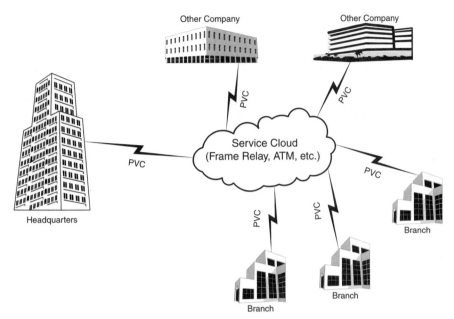

Figure 12–4
Private networking through a service cloud.

nect two identified endpoints and are billed at a fixed fee, and switched virtual circuits (SVCs) used to connect two endpoints on an ad hoc basis, which are usually billed on the basis of usage.

In frame relay, a PVC is usually associated with a dedicated port on the vendor's frame relay switch. Moreover, companies subscribing to PVCs can often choose from a schedule of port "throughput rate" commitments from vendors (called committed information rates or CIRs). This service performance option is typically selected by the business based on the requirements of the application they will be using across the link and the budget available to support the application.

In addition to frame relay, vendors have been rolling out since the mid-1990s ATM network services to those customers that need special provisioning for their data traffic, as well as higher data transfer speeds. ATM offers two types of PVCs between endpoints: virtual channel connections (VCCs) and virtual path connections (VPCs).

VCCs are individual paths through the ATM service cloud. Understanding how these paths are distinguished from one another, thereby making the network connection a "private" one, requires a bit of explanation about ATM itself.

In an ATM network, data is moved in a series of envelopes called "cells." ATM cells are fixed-size, 53-byte containers that are roughly analogous to frames in a frame relay network. Each cell has five bytes of "header" information—information placed at the beginning of the cell or ahead of the bits of application data that are being moved. Cell header bits identify the subscriber, the quality of service that is to be afforded to the cell, and many other important pieces of information describing the data transfer. Because they are unique to each service subscriber, these cell header bits effectively distinguish one subscriber's data from another's. They enable a VCC for each subscriber that is separate from the VCCs of all other subscribers.

VPCs are aggregations of VCCs. That is to say, VPCs have multiple virtual channels running through them—like wires through a cable—that may be allocated among a subscriber's voice, video, and data applications. Each channel within the VPC can have its own QoS settings.

Some companies make use of both frame relay and ATM services at different locations within their private networks. Internet working standards have been implemented into multiplatform switches from Cisco Systems, Lucent Technologies, Nortel Networks, and other networking equipment vendors to facilitate frame-to-cell exchanges.

Cloud-based network services offer several features that dedicated cross-connect circuits do not. Most important among these is the capability of off-loading management requirements to the provider of the service. The term managed network service provider has appeared fairly recently to better describe the management component of many connectivity service solutions.

ONTO THE RING . . . .

This is not meant to suggest that the telecommunications industry has moved away entirely from private circuit-based solutions and into the world of cloud-based data services (though there are many who argue that such a change will occur in time with the rollout of converged, Next Generation Networks). In fact, just when businesses were getting used to the notion of purchasing networks as a service, the major telcos—together with newcomers like Qwest Telecommunications, Level Three, and Metromedia Fiber Network—refocused attention back on the link layer.

In the late 1990s, both the traditional telcos and the newer carriers began spreading the word about the availability of a networking infrastructure for use by companies seeking "carrier-grade" voice and data networking capabilities at a acceptable cost. Since that time, the vendors have been seeking to extend and retask for business users the SONET-based fiber-optic network infrastructure originally deployed to meet the needs of the telco providers themselves in many metropolitan areas of the United States and Europe.

In the United States, SONET networks trace their origins to the core interexchange carrier switch network (the core network of switches providing long distance or exchange-to-exchange connections), which, under the aupices of AT&T, began to roll out SONET technology in 1984. The SONET network was originally conceived as a high-speed, high-bandwidth, fiber-optic network that utilized a standardized multiplexing scheme, SONET, to promote switch interoperability. The technology was rolled out as a number of interconnected dual-ring topology networks to provide redundancy, self-healing, and fault tolerance.

Although primarily a core IXE switch network infrastructure, the physical reach of SONET deployments extended into the turf of the regional bell operating companies (RBOCs)—especially into the central offices of large local exchange carriers serving densely populated metropolitan areas such as New York, Boston, Chicago, and many of the other "NFL cities." With the break-up of AT&T, and the subsequent deregulation of local and long distance telephone services, a number of telecommunications vendors and competitive local exchange carriers (CLECs) seized on the prospect of leveraging SONET infrastructure where available (and building it out when practicable) for resale to business consumers.

The value proposition of the SONET ring network is simple. Its tremendous speed and capacity provides companies with a high-speed, multipurpose link between sites connected directly to the network.

The speed of SONET is expressed in terms of Optical Carrier levels, as stated in Table 12–1. These OC levels, which were defined to accommodate the circuit switching of high-speed facilities and services including T-1, T-3, and ATM, place SONET networks ahead of most other digital networking interconnects in terms of bandwidth and speed.

As depicted in Figure 12–5, the attachment of corporate voice, video, and data networks to a SONET ring provides a company with a MAN infrastructure par excellence. Using this infrastructure, businesses can realize significant performance improvements over other interconnects, as well as cost advantages.

Metromedia Fiber Network (MFN), one of a growing list of alternative SONET ring providers that has been building out its own offering around the original carrier rings in major metropolitan areas, lists the advantages of using private SONET rings on its Web site at www.mmfn.com:

- Virtually unlimited bandwidth at a fixed cost. Even as your capacity requirements increase—up to OC-192—your costs will remain the same through the life of your contract.
- Unparalleled security. When you lease fiber from MFN, it is for your exclusive use. No other customer traffic will utilize your fiber.

Table 12–1   SONET Optical Carrier Levels

OC Level	Megabits	Number of 64-kbps Channels
OC-1	52	672
OC-3	155	2,016
OC-9	466	6,048
OC-12	622	8,064
OC-18	933	12,096
OC-24	1,244	16,128
OC-36	1,866	24,192
OC-48	2,488	32,256
OC-96	4,976	64,512
OC-192	10,000	129,024

- Unmatched survivability. We use the highest grade of fiber-optic cabling making our network virtually error free. Our network topology is designed to provide maximum diversity while essentially eliminating any single point of failure.

- Customized network management. The MFN network is built to meet your business requirements. With virtually no capacity limitations, MFN gives you built-in growth and complete control over your own network expansion.

- The fastest transmission speeds available. Metromedia Fiber Network uses only the highest grade fiber-optic facilities; our fiber has the capacity to transmit up to two terabits of data per second.

Source: Metromedia Fiber Network Home Page, www.mmfn.com.

Metromedia distinguishes its network from those of competitors on the basis of price and privacy. Unlike traditional telco offerings, the carrier charges for its service on a flat fee basis (traditional carriers charge on a metered basis). Also, a Metromedia Fiber Network is not shared among companies, but reserved to the subscriber exclusively.

Billing methodologies aside, all carriers offering SONET-based ring services can make a legitimate claim regarding the privacy of their network offerings. SONET was conceived as a scheme for keeping circuits separate from one another in the IXC switch environment. If it errs, it is on the basis of too much, rather than too little, provisioning for privacy. In fact, SONET's tremendous capacity for customization and configuration makes it more complicated to deploy and difficult to manage than other networks.

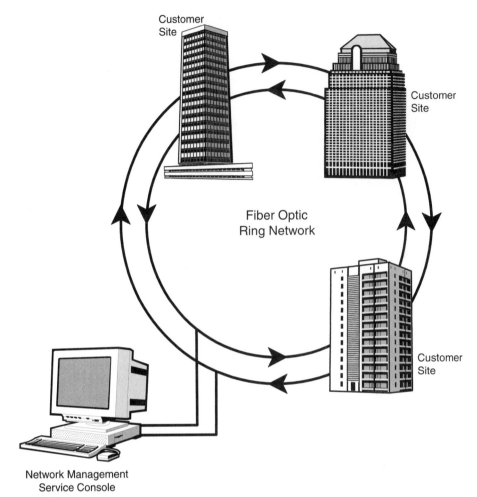

Customer
Site

Customer
Site

Fiber Optic
Ring Network

Customer
Site

Network Management
Service Console

Figure 12–5
A fiber-optic SONET ring network.

That is the claim of companies such as Yipes Communications, headquartered in San Francisco, California, which delivers fiber-optic networks to companies based on Gigabit Ethernet (a 1,000 MB per second component of the familiar Ethernet standard) and IP, rather than pure SONET.

Leveraging long-term provisioning relationships with fiber-optic network backbone providers, such as Level Three and UUNET, Yipes serves customers in metropolitan areas with a direct-to-the-company-doorstep, bandwidth-on-demand service that facilitates the interconnection of corporate IP networks located in offices in and around a metro area. (See Sidebar.) The company also offers a WAN solution between company sites located in Yipes-served areas.

Yipes embraces an IP-for-everything mentality, noting that the current trend in the convergence of voice, video, and data networking is not to squeeze all traffic into separate virtual circuits running on a high-bandwidth, multiplexed facility, but rather to treat voice, video, and data as data simply. Utilizing IP protocols such as Voice over IP, Video over IP, and TCP/IP networking, companies can use IP itself as the point of convergence for these different data streams and move all data using a single network protocol.

The merits of this argument aside, Yipes does deliver a relatively easily deployed solution for extending networks at high-speed over geographically dispersed locations. Through strategic relationships with partners such as switch-maker Extreme Networks and optical hub manufacturer Colo.com, Yipes is able to connect customer sites to its network offering efficiently.

Yipes assures the privacy of its MAN solution through a combination of dedicated ports and bundled traffic management services. When data is passed to the Yipes WAN, a VPN tunnel is established to provide a privacy guarantee.

The Yipes solution has already garnered the attention of numerous ASPs. In December 2000, the company announced that its services had been tapped for use by eonBusiness (Denver, Colorado), NxTier Technologies (Worcester, Massachusetts), and M4Internet (Palo Alto, California) to provide high-speed, low-latency interconnects between the ASPs and their customers. B2B e-commerce provider VerticalNet selected Yipes to provide connectivity for its hosting data centers in Horsham and Philadelphia, Pennsylvania, in February 2001, and Web- and ASP-hosting service provider, Exodus Communications, announced in March 2001 that it was rolling out Yipes to serve its "Internet data centers" in Boston, Chicago, and Silicon Valley.

The success of Yipes and other managed service providers has stimulated increased competition in the high-speed network provisioning space. In January 2001, AT&T announced an Ultravailable Broadband Network—a fully managed metropolitan-area service that lets businesses connect sites that are up to 25 miles apart via fiber-optic rings that use Dense Wave Division Multiplexing (DWDM) rather than SONET. The service allows customers to select the amount of bandwidth they require—up to 2.4G bit/sec—and promises network uptime guarantees of "five 9s" (less than five minutes of downtime per year). Pricing for the service, however, is an order of magnitude greater than what customers must pay for optical networking provisioning from Yipes Communications or similar services from other newcomers such as GiantLoop Networks (Waltham, Massachusetts) and XO Communications (Reston, Viginia), but the telecommunications giant hopes to legitimate the pricing based on increased availability.

THE YIPES PRIVATE NETWORK SOLUTION

Yipes Network Architecture

The Yipes network is based upon a three-tiered ring architecture. A high-level diagram of the architecture is presented in Figure 1.

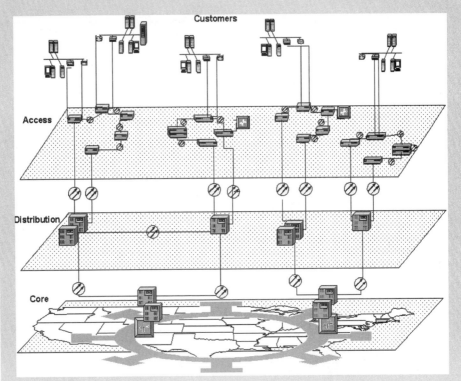

1: Three-tiered regional IP-over-fiber MAN architecture.

Access

At the top tier of Figure 1 is the customer access level. Local fiber-optic rings which span city streets are used to connect customer premise equipment (CPE) at customer distribution points. The distribution points consist of Gigabit Ethernet switches located in multitenant buildings to which customers connect with 10 or 100BaseT Category 5 cable, or

100BaseFX /1000BaseSX multimode fiber. The access level is connected with fiber rings operating at 1 Gbps full duplex using layer two switching or wire-speed layer three OSPF [5, 6] routing protocol. This provides redundancy in the event of ring failure. This top tier of the architecture is diagrammed in more detail in Figure 2.

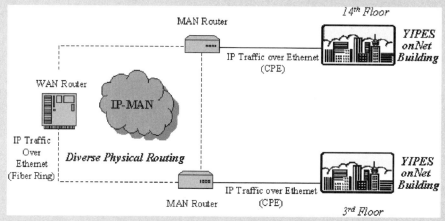

2: Access tier of IP-over-fiber MAN architecture.

Distribution

At the middle level of the architecture of Figure 2 is the metropolitan distribution tier. This level ties multiple fiber rings to a common Yipes point of presence (PoP) at which is located an aggregating gigabit router—the "Giga-PoP." Also at this level, multiple Giga-PoPs are linked around adjacent metropolitan regions forming a regional optical Internetworking infrastructure. For example, all Giga-PoPs in the San Francisco Bay area are linked by a ring of fiber constituting a Yipes regional backbone (Figure 3). Because switches at a customer's location

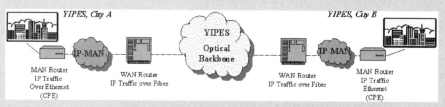

3: Regional IP-over-fiber network at the distribution level.

and the Giga-PoPs are all nonblocking gigabit devices, all network connections on a regional level will see latency times on the order of a few milliseconds or less.

The level of the architecture in Sidebar Figure 3 forms the core for managed IP-over-fiber network services. The fiber backbone between Giga-PoPs consists of one or more gigabit links as determined by traffic demands. And again, a logical ring topology is used to ensure redundancy.

This extends the effective area of MAN services throughout an expanded metropolitan geographic region, creating a regional managed network services infrastructure. Multiple buildings in a city or buildings dispersed throughout a region can be interconnected on a customer-specific basis to create virtual private links between customer locations, or to link business partners in extranets. All this is achieved simply by entering switching or routing configurations that link specific ports on the Premise Ethernet switches. Because interconnection latencies across regional areas are on the order of a few milliseconds, excellent QoS can be provided for delay-sensitive traffic.

Core

The third tier of Yipes's architecture connects regional areas across the nation, and potentially around the world. This is referred to as the "core."

This level is implemented through multiple IP backbone carriers to transport traffic between Yipes regions. Connections are made from the Yipes metropolitan gigabit backbones to tier one backbone carriers using gigabit wire-speed WAN routers (Figure 4). These routers are

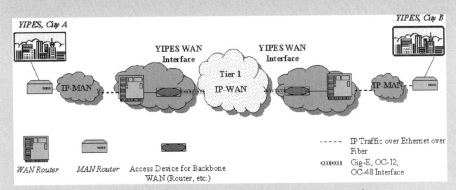

4: Yipes regions intereconnected by IP backbone carriers.

connected via Gigabit Ethernet, OC-12, or OC-48 links at multiple peering points. At this level routers are running BGP4 protocol to route traffic over the most efficient path. In the case of traffic traveling between Yipes private regions, it is carried via tier one IP backbones with specific SLAs in place. This ensures that the Yipes SLAs provided to customers are also met when Yipes's interregional traffic is carried by a partner network.

Internet bound traffic (Figure 5) is routed to the nearest or most efficient backbone carrier at a given application session. In order to

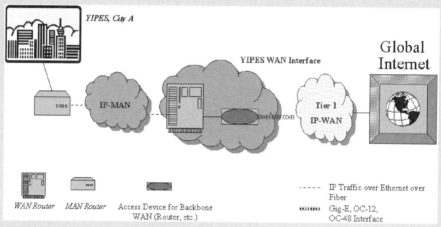

5: Connectivity to the public Internet.

ensure multiple paths and complete redundancy throughout a metropolitan region, multiple colocation and peering arrangements are established. For example, in the Bay Area region, Yipes has colocation facilities in San Francisco, Palo Alto, and Santa Clara. Both public and private peering and transit agreements provide Yipes with capabilities to pass traffic directly to tier one IP backbones such as Level Three, Qwest, or UUNet via Gigabit Ethernet, OC-3, and OC-12 links.

Yipes is replicating this model throughout the United States in all major cities. The result is a scalable, redundant, multipath architecture that offers the maximum flexibility in traffic management, QoS, and provisioning-on-demand.

The design of an IP-based physical architecture to execute this model must give careful consideration to the dynamic, rapidly changing market of fiber and network hardware providers. Yipes has positioned itself to be the arbiter of the best-available technologies.

As new IP hardware comes to market, Yipes is able to either upgrade or migrate on a device-by-device or on a PoP-basis. For example, when 1 Gbps router interfaces are superceded by 10 or 100 Gbps interfaces, Yipes will be able to deploy such improvements in step with the growth of Yipes's network. This ensures that the services Yipes offers its customers will always be congruent with the best-of-class networking hardware available.

This applies likewise with interregional links and peering arrangements. As the services of IP backbone network service providers (NSPs) evolve with respect to bandwidth, QoS, latency, and price, Yipes will move rapidly to leverage these improvements into the Yipes network and hence to our customers. Because Yipes will have the fiber and PoP infrastructure already in place, future leaps in network technology can be rapidly deployed with minimal physical involvement or capital outlay.

The Yipes solution has already garnered the attention of numerous ASPs. In December 2000, the company announced that its services had been tapped for use by eonBusiness (Denver, Colorado), NxTier Technologies (Worcester, Massachusetts), and M4Internet (Palo Alto, California) to provide high-speed, low-latency interconnects between the ASPs and their customers. B2B e-commerce provider VerticalNet selected Yipes to provide connectivity for its hosting data centers in Horsham and Philadelphia, Pennsylvania, in February 2001, and Web- and ASP-hosting service provider, Exodus Communications, announced in March 2001 that it was rolling out Yipes to serve its "Internet data centers" in Boston, Chicago, and Silicon Valley.

The success of Yipes and other managed service providers has stimulated increased competition in the high-speed network provisioning space. In January 2001, AT&T announced an Ultravailable Broadband Network— a fully managed metropolitan-area service that lets businesses connect sites that are up to 25 miles apart via fiber-optic rings that use Dense Wave Division Multiplexing (DWDM) rather than SONET. The service allows customers to select the amount of bandwidth they require—up to 2.4G bit/sec—and promises network uptime guarantees of "five 9s" (less than five minutes of downtime per year). Pricing for the service, however, is an order of magnitude greater than what customers must pay for optical networking provisioning from Yipes Communications or similar services from other newcomers such as GiantLoop Networks (Waltham, Massachusetts) and XO Communications (Reston, Viginia), but the telecommunications giant hopes to legitimate the pricing based on increased availability.

Source: "Managed IP Optical Internetworking: A Regional IP-over-Fiber Network Service Architecture." A White Paper from Yipes Communications, Inc. Reprinted with the permission of Yipes Communications, Inc. ©2000.

LAST MILE ISSUES . . . .

Most of the MAN/WAN services that serve as alternatives to the public Internet for delivering ASP services to customer desktops confront a single, all-important limitation known in telco jargon as the last mile.

"Last mile" is telco vernacular for the telecommunications facility that connects the customer premise to the local exchange carrier (or in some cases, directly to the POP, of a network carrier). It is an imprecise term because the actual distance between the consumer and the ASP's network may be many tens of miles or just a few hundred feet. Whatever the actual distance, the last mile may seem like an insurmountable distance for would-be consumers of ASP services who are not located in metro areas already served by fiber rings.

Most major telecommunications carriers are seeking to address the problem, and to capitalize on the potentially huge revenues from Internet and data networking traffic, with digital subscriber line (DSL) technology. Sprint, MCI/WorldCom, and others are aggressively deploying DSL access multiplexers (DSLAMs) into their POP sites nationwide to provide high-speed data network "on-ramps."

DSL delivers high-speed connectivity through a unique digital signaling algorithm over existing telephone wires. It is considered particularly well suited for the bandwidth demands of small- to medium-sized businesses and small office/home office markets because of its coverage area, which includes most business and residential districts. Constant improvements in the technology are expected to yield steadily improving speeds from the DSL, with 40 to 50 Mbps over telephone wires foreseeable within five years.

More than a few observers have pointed out that DSL's capability to use existing copper telephone lines is both the greatest strength and the greatest drawback of the technology. Lines are owned by the ILECs, the incumbent telephone companies, who have jealously guarded their turf against new competitors, including CLECs and old guard interexchange carriers. Delays and expense associated with DSLs have generally derived from the labor- and systems-intensive effort involved in working with ILECs to provision the service across incumbent local exchange carrier (ILEC) facilities and to obtain the information needed for billing services.

High-speed alternatives to DSL include dial-up networking, satellite microwave, and fiber-optics. Speeds for dial-up connections are limited to 56 Kbps per circuit by the vicissitudes of analog signaling technology. Satellite-based broadband services are still difficult and costly to deploy. Fiber-optic connectivity is constrained by jurisdictional right-of-way issues and high cost.

Some industry observers look to cable modem technology, or broadband wireless communications, to compete with DSL. Cable modem vendors indicate that the capacity of the technology rivals that of a T-1, but at a fraction of the cost. However, delivering the service requires an infrastructure upgrade within the cable service provider's distribution network (from coaxial cable to mixed coax/fiber-optic cable), the implementation of multiple "nodes" to alleviate the speed degradation that accrues from too many users on a shared network, and the extension of the cable television network itself from primarily residential to commercial areas.

Broadband wireless is another promising technology for last mile connectivity. Current wireless technology, called 2nd generation or 2G, delivering data transfer speeds of between 10 to 19 kilobits per second (Kbps), is no speed demon. However, wireless advocates are holding out hopes that 3G wireless, which is being rolled out in Europe and Japan, will deliver on promised speeds of between 384 Kbps to 2 Gbps. The technology has caught on in areas around the world where high-speed digital services are in short supply, but confronts significant challenges in the United States, where carriers have seen lackadaisical interest in broadband wireless and poor profit margins on services already deployed.

By March 2001, most carriers had only grudgingly supported the implementation of an interim step in the technology, referred to as "2.5G," capable of bumping speeds to about 400 Kbps. This upgrade enables vendors to keep current switching equipment in place while they struggle to cultivate demand for wireless data services in the United States. Some hope that a 2.5G upgrade will whet consumer appetites for wireless data networks, a market with few "killer applications" thus far to drive consumer demand.

If internal wireless LANs are any indication, the security of broadband wireless communications will require hefty security provisioning if the technology is to succeed. In February 2001, the Internet Security, Applications, Authentication and Cryptography (ISAAC) Research Group at the University of California in Berkeley published a report identifying many security flaws in the wireless Ethernet standard from American National Standards Institute (ANSI), 802.11b. The vulnerability of wireless networks to eavesdropping made the application of encryption technology and VPN tunneling technology critical to wireless security, the research group determined.

A second challenge for broadband wireless is the delivery of service assurances. To keep pace with demand, wireless network providers commonly seek to increase the capacity of cells used to handle calls. This strategy forestalls the need (and the cost) of deploying additional cell towers, but it is a trade-off. Because wireless services reuse radio frequencies to realize greater capacities, the potential for interference due to overlapping frequencies increases with the density and proximity of one cell to another. Optimizing these factors has been the traditional focus of wireless network management.

The problem, however, is that a dearth of tools exist to identify conflicts so they can be resolved proactively. Blocked or dropped calls, reported by customers, are often the first sign of a frequency overlap problem in the wireless voice services of today. When customer inconvenience mounts, they change service providers.

Wireless data networking is a different story. Entrusting a wireless network with mission-critical data mandates a higher standard for service monitoring, proactive service management, and service guarantees. Many believe that the technology of wireless, at the present time, isn't able to deliver on these requirements.

For now, the last mile is a wired mile. ASPs are at the mercy of the speed at which private lines or services can be rolled out to their prospective customers. In the best of circumstances, business customers will already have high-speed frame relay, ATM, or fiber-optic connections that can be retasked to connect up with the networks carrying ASP traffic. At worst, the company may need to wait the 60 to 120 days reported in many areas, and incur the expense, for facilities to be extended to its location. This cost may be, for many companies, an inhibitor of ASP adoption.

VIRTUAL PRIVATE NETWORKS AND PROXIES . . . . .

With many of these identified network options, there is a need to provide security for data communications that goes beyond Web technology–based protection mechanisms such as SSL or TLS. This reflects the fact that networks, though touted by their vendors as private, do in fact have shared and publically accessible components. Even in circuit-based connectivity methods, vulnerability exists. Telephone switches have been successfully "hacked" to enable intruders to eavesdrop on communications or make unauthorized use of the service.

The industry's response to the need for privacy in a public infrastructure is a VPN. VPNs are established by creating a "tunnel" through the network cloud whose two endpoints are secure from access by anyone other than the authorized communicators. Encrypting data that passes through the tunnel provides an additional measure of protection.

There are three relatively popular VPN schemes at present. The first of these is part of a suite of security protocols developed by the IETF to deliver security services to the IP network protocol, IPsec. A second is the point to point tunneling protocol (PPTP), which is endorsed and advocated by Microsoft Corporation. The third is a hybrid of PPTP and Cisco Systems's proprietary layer 2 forwarding protocol, known as the layer 2 tunneling protocol (L2TP). All are either approved standards or proposed standards called (Requests for Comment or RFCs) under evaluation by the IETF.

Although three standards may seem to some like two standards too many, it is important to understand that VPNs developed from two different sets of needs. As shown in Figure 12–6, some companies utilized VPNs like remote-access servers, enabling road warriors with laptops, or other authorized individuals, to dial into their protected corporate network either directly or across an Internet connection. In such

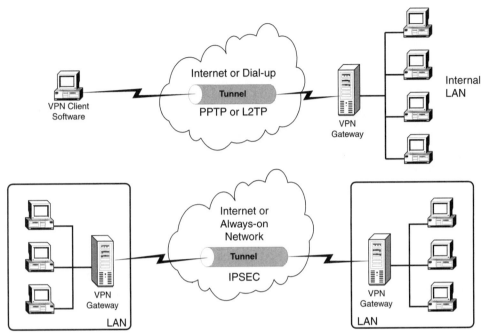

Figure 12–6
Virtual private network tunneling.

settings, the remote user, called the client, initiates the creation of the tunnel in order to begin communicating with the corporate network. Usually this is done by running a special client software on the local machine that communicates with the gateway protecting the destination LAN to authenticate the client, set up the tunnel, and begin work. PPTP and L2TP were developed largely to address the security requirements of such connections.

At other companies, the need for VPNs was to protect and secure connections between LANs located at geographically separated sites. These connections, which were "always on," required a different kind of protection, and provided drivers for the development of IPsec. In the case of LAN-to-LAN tunneling, a security gateway at each endpoint serves as the interface between the tunnel and the private LAN. Users on either LAN can use the tunnel transparently to communicate with each other.

PPTP, supported in most Microsoft operating systems, is an extension of the point to point protocol (PPP), which is commonly used to support dial-up access to the Internet. PPTP encapsulates PPP packets using a modified version of the generic routing encapsulation (GRE) protocol, which enables PPTP to handle packets not only from IP networks, but also from Internet Packet Exchange (IPX) and network basic input/output system extended user interface (NetBEUI) nets.

PPTP uses PPP's authentication mechanism, password authentication protocol (PAP), modified by Microsoft to leverage the vendor's own security domain scheme. The vendor has also introduced its own version of PPP's native encryption protocol, enabling PPTP with the Microsoft Point-to-Point Encryption (MPPE) protocol. Although the protocol offers the network agnostic advantage alluded to earlier, it suffers from a lack of strong encryption capability and a lack of support for token-based authentication methods.

Similarly, L2TP derives from the work of a particular vendor, Cisco Systems, to establish methods for supporting tunnels through the Internet and through other network clouds such as frame relay, prior to the advent of IPsec. L2TP was originally L2F—layer 2 forwarding, a method devised by Cisco to identify and forward packets securely at the transport layer (layer 2 of the open systems interconnect model of the ISO) to their intended destination.

Like PPTP, L2F tunneling is not dependent on IP, and can work with alternative transports, such as frame relay or ATM. L2F also uses PPP for authentication of the remote user, as does the Microsoft offering. Key differences between the two, however, include the capability of L2F to support external authentication systems such as terminal access controller access control system (TACACS+) and RADIUS for password or token-based authentication. L2F also allows tunnels to support multiple, simultaneous connections.

L2TP is an effort within IETF to combine the best features of L2F and PPTP in order to create a protocol for the IPsec suite that will support the dial-up tunneling scenario and the integration of external authentication systems, such as RADIUS. IPsec will augment these provisions with its protocols for data encryption via cryptographic keys.

IPSec itself is well on the way to becoming the most widely implemented VPN standard for LAN-to-LAN tunneling and encryption. The three key building blocks of the IPsec VPN scheme are the authentication header (AH) protocol, the encapsulating security payload (ESP) protocol, and the IKE protocol.

As discussed in the previous chapter, IPSec provides the mechanism for a sender (or a security gateway) to authenticate and/or encrypt each IP packet being sent across a link. By separating the authentication and encryption steps into two protocols (AH and ESP), the protocol provides for two operational modes: transport and tunnel.

In transport mode, only the transport-layer segment (which contains addressing information) of an IP packet is authenticated or encrypted. This mode of authentication/encryption may be valuable in relatively secure MANs and WANs. However, much more security is thought to be necessary for secure Internet communications. Hence, IPsec offers tunnel mode.

In the tunnel mode, the entire IP packet is authenticated and encrypted. Tunnel-mode IPSec offers a much more robust protection against hostile forces lurking in the Internet. By encrypting the entire packet with a strong encryption algorithm, IPsec tunnels effectively foil eavesdroppers.

IPSec makes use of many standardized cryptographic technologies to provide confidentiality, data integrity, and authentication and provides two ways to handle key exchange and management within IPSec's architecture: manual keying and IKE for automated key management. Manual key exchange might be practicable for a VPN supporting a handful of communicators, but automated key management is a must for an arrangement involving multiple endpoints.

Numerous products have appeared in the market that offer the security gateway functionality required for a VPN. Most solutions cluster around four discrete platforms: routers, firewalls, integrated VPN hardware, and VPN software residing on client or server systems themselves. Industry preference is for implementations of VPN protocols in hardware rather than software in order to prevent latency. Many VPN-enabled routers, firewalls, and integrated products feature specialized embedded accelerators for fast encryption and decryption of packets. An industry group, the Virtual Private Network Consortium (VPNC), has been formed to test the conformance of VPN products with standards and to ensure their interoperability. To find out the ongoing results of product testing, visit the VPNC Web site at www.vpnc.org. Additionally, tests are routinely performed by trade press publication test labs and are reported in both print and on-line versions of the publications.

SPAWNING YET ANOTHER "SP" . . . .

The existance of standards for secure tunneling does not mean that setting up a VPN—or managing it over time—is easy. This is especially true if the organization is an ASP that is constantly adding customers (in the best case scenario) and occasionally losing customers. As with networks themselves, ASPs often enlist the services of a new breed of network security service providers or network security management providers to provide the necessary skills and resources.

In some cases, VPN gateways are implemented at the ASP hosting center and at the customer's premise. In other cases, VPN provisioning is performed at the POP of the network service provider. The former solution has the advantage of securing the last mile, as well as the MAN or WAN interconnecting the ASP to its customers, but may be troublesome from the standpoint of deployment and maintenance. The latter solution enables the expeditious connection of customers and their business partners to secure hosted applications.

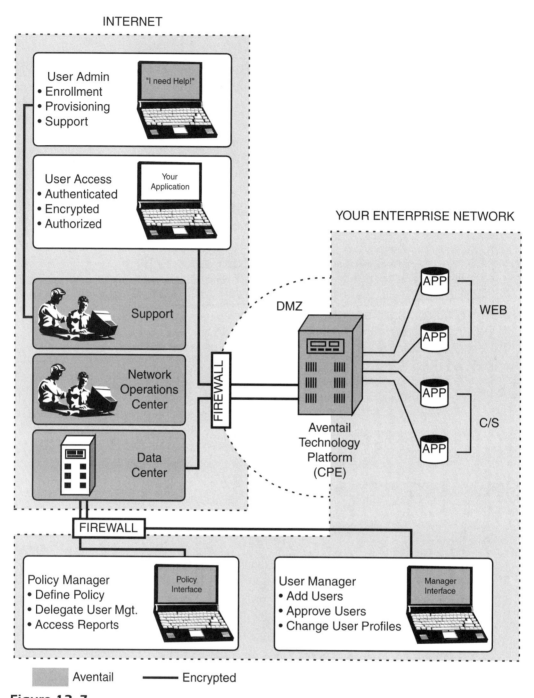

Figure 12–7

Aventail.net's proxy service offering. *Source:* Aventail, Seattle, WA. www.aventail.net.
Copyright © 2001 Aventail Corporation. All rights reserved.

Another approach, offered to ASPs by Aventail.Net and others, is to use a proxy server (see Figure 12–7). In this approach, the proxy server handles all authentication and encryption services and provides a repository for the ASP-hosted application and data during the user session. This effectively insulates all ASP infrastructure against direct access by end users.

The Aventail.net proxy may be physically remote from the ASP, located at the vendor's own data center, reducing the requirement for the ASP to provide connections to all customers directly. Instead, in the Aventail.net approach all accesses to the ASP are made via secure tunnels through the Internet to the vendor's own extranet portal.

This configuration places the burden for availability and service level adherence in the hands of a third party—an attractive proposition for many ASPs. However, the responsibility for SLA compliance remains with the ASP, creating potential risks as well.

This concludes the second section of this *Essential Guide.* It should be apparent by now that delivering the ASP value proposition requires a considerable amount of expertise in several areas. These include:

- Selecting and enabling applications for network-based use
- Configuring the hosting platform infrastructure with the proper Web server, application server, application hosting, and storage capabilities for high performance, high availability, and security
- Obtaining and managing a secure network infrastructure to deliver the application over a MAN or WAN—and across the last mile—with sufficient speed, reliability, and security to encourage customer confidence in, and satisfaction with, the resulting user experience.

Few ASPs have all of the prerequisite skills, knowledge, and capabilities to meet all of these requirements. Most depend on third-party service providers to deliver some part of the infrastructure that enables them to deliver promised value at agreed-upon service levels—24 hours per day, 7 days per week, 365 days per year.

In the final section of this book, attention will turn to the business side of the ASP solution. We look at sources of information about ASPs; criteria that should be considered when evaluating providers, contractual, and SLA characteristics; and what can be expected in an ASP service relationship.

Part 3

Business Relationship

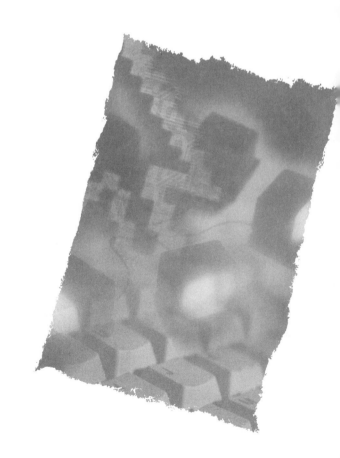

13 Building an ASP Solution

In this chapter...

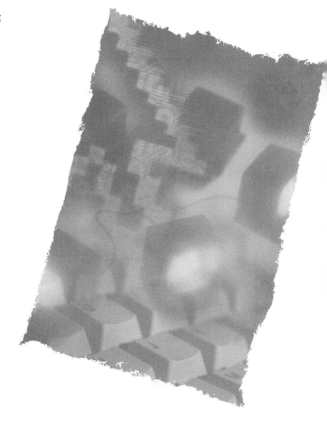

To this point, this *Essential Guide* has looked at the ASP value proposition and at the technologies used to enable application delivery as a service. Equipped with a better understanding of what ASPs are and the many ways that they can "deliver the goods"—support application delivery across a network—it is time to turn to the practical matter of identifying and implementing an ASP solution to meet company needs.

"Company needs" is the key phrase. ASPs actually serve two distinctly different customer groups with two different, though sometimes overlapping, sets of services. An ASP's customer base may comprise organizations that are themselves in the software development business. That is, ISVs may seek an ASP to provide a platform for the Web technology–based delivery of their software products to their customers.

Some analysts segregate ASPs offering such services into a separate camp. Application infrastructure provider, or AIP, is a term that has been coined to distinguish ASPs providing hosting services for an ISV's application software from those offering software as a subscription service to business.

It follows from this distinction that the other customer base for ASPs comprises all types of corporate organizations—large and small—who are seeking to rent, rather than *buy,* application software. (The word "buy" is italicized because commercial software users do not technically buy software. They license the software for deployment and use on local hardware.)

This simple distinction gets fuzzy, however, when a business that is not an ISV turns to an ASP vendor with a request that the vendor host an application that has actually been developed by the business itself. Some would respond that this is still a "mainstream" business use of an ASP: it is still a case of the ASP delivering the application service back to the customer only. This is different from an AIP arrangement in which the ISV wants the ASP to host its application so that other businesses can subscribe to it.

The problem with this fine distinction is that, in a growing number of instances, it may be completely false. Consider the case of a large automobile manufacturer engaged in what the pundits call the "deconstruction of internal business processes." This automobile company has decided to take business processes associated with the design and manufacture of a particular model of car and push them out into the company's supply chain. That is to say, suppliers will henceforth be responsible for designing and building the components that go into the car and will have their own personnel report to the assembly line to perform the actual installation. (This sort of thing has already happened at Volkswagen and is a hot topic of discussion in just about every American automobile manufacturer as of this writing.)

The problem that the automotive manufacturer in this example confronts is that not all of its suppliers are equipped with technologies that allow them to share information with the systems that the manufacturer uses to coordinate production schedules and other logistical matters among suppliers. The chief information officer finds herself on the horns of a dilemma. Does she:

1. Find new supply chain partners who have the necessary software capabilities? (A difficult and undesirable task.)
2. Equip the supply chain partner with systems to interface with home office applications? (An expensive option prone to backfire if the supplier decides to do work for a competitor.)
3. Host the necessary applications at an ASP and provide access to the supply chain partners on a subscription basis?

The third solution has the advantage of avoiding an expensive and risky technology transfer to the supplier and obviates the need to ditch loyal suppliers simply on the basis of their level of IT. Number three is a winner.

If we assume that all of the application software required to facilitate this scenario is readily available in the form of commercial, off-the-shelf, best-of-breed packages that can be, or are already, hosted at an ASP, the resulting arrangement is a traditional, mainstream ASP play. The distinction between hosted application service and application infrastructure provisioning is preserved.

If, however, a "home grown" application must also be hosted by the ASP for access by supply chain partners, the distinction made between ISV and business consumer models of ASP use falls apart. The ASP is, in effect, hosting an application that has been developed by the customer for subscription by users in other companies (the supply chain partners). This is what is meant by the overlap that sometimes occurs between the ISV services and the general business solutions offered by ASPs.

Whatever services the ASP is called upon to provide, they are driven by the requirements of the organization requesting the ASP service itself. One way that ASPs differ from each other is in the extent to which they can customize their offerings to meet the specific needs of prospective customers.

The good news for prospective ASP customers is that the current highly competitive state of the market is fostering a willingness among vendors to facilitate just about any service scenario that might be sought from them. This is good news in the sense that many companies will likely be able to find solutions from among the current cadre of ASPs at an acceptable price. It is also good news in the sense that ASPs themselves will gain experience from the diversity of solutions they deliver that will, in turn, provide the basis both for the ongoing refinement and specialization of ASP solution offerings, and also for the development of best practices and standards that will benefit both consumers and vendors.

What is not so good about this situation is that supporting a diversity of solution scenarios impairs the ability of ASPs to fully exploit economies of scale derived from the sharing and reuse of expensive infrastructure, technology, and personnel expertise within their own shops. Many ASPs survive on razor-thin margins today, and the coming "shake out" in the ASP industry anticipated by some analysts will reflect in

THE ASP AS A B2B MARKETPLACE BUILDER

The current B2B market is in a state of disarray. The futures of many pioneering vendors of e-marketplace services appear to be in doubt as a result of the general economic slowdown that has affected the technology sector overall. Moreover, the progress of efforts such as Rosetta.Net and BizTalk.org to develop industry-specific standards for B2B inter-application messaging has also slowed significantly.

In the absence of industry-wide standards for B2B integration via Web technology, "rolling your own" e-marketplace solution can be an expensive and failure-prone undertaking. By contrast, using a managed application hosting model or ASP can provide an excellent strategy for companies interested in B2B today. By making the ASP hosted application the centerpiece of the B2B strategy, companies can insulate themselves from standards shifts and, potentially, from costly e-marketplace failures.

That's the position of Dennis Law, Vice President of Hosting Services for Electronic Data Systems (EDS) in Plano, TX. EDS already offers a B2B hosting service based around established, mainframe-based, Electronic Data Interchange (EDI) standard, platforms, as well as other dedicated solutions. According to Law, the vendor is working to advance the model for Web technology hosted marketplaces that enable "the immediate exchange of information across enterprise boundaries in a many-to-many, hosted, trading house environment."

Key to success, he says, will be the resolution of a number of issues, including:

- Simplification of integrating applications from multiple marketplace members with the hosted application;
- Reengineering of business processes and "sub-net" practices to better align them with an e-business approach; and,
- Engineering of a platform that delivers zero latency and high availability at an acceptable price.

"We are trying to refine the delivery framework for net markets in a way that ensures that transactions are properly recorded and monitored, but without the expense currently associated with zero latency and high availability environments," Law explains. "Until now, people have been trying to develop e-marketplaces in silos: putting up hardware, then trying to integrate applications to it. We have test environments and are developing specific solutions tailored to vertical markets such as airlines, financial institutions and others, as well as solutions for regional markets and horizontals."

The bottom line on hosted e-market services, according to Law, will be increased business efficiency through improved communications and collaboration across enterprises. EDS is combining a number of its assets, including its global industry group strategic planning and consulting services, XML development shops, and managed Web hosting operations to realize the goal of taking B2B "to a new level with a better ROI."

part the success of ASPs in optimizing the large capital expenditures they have made as they have built out their hosting capabilities.

By extension, this situation translates to risk. Vesting an ASP with responsibility for the operation and management of important business applications exposes the business to potentially costly downtime in the event of an ASP business failure. As some companies learned from the closure of two ASPs in the summer of 2000, the sudden loss of necessary information processing can have a jarring effect on operations.

This risk should be considered seperately from the risks associated with technology dependency itself, however. Systems, networks, and data become unavailable from time to time, owing to a variety of man-made and natural events, whether applications are locally deployed or hosted at an ASP. The argument could be made that selecting the right ASP—one that provides high-availability solutions with key resources replicated across multiple data centers—actually reduces the company's exposure to technology disasters, and usually at a much lower cost than would accrue to a strategy of full data center replication and mirroring using company-owned facilities.

Still, there is risk associated with any outsourcing arrangement. This risk must be offset by the cost advantages and other benefits that will accrue to using an ASP to deliver important business application services.

OVERVIEW OF THE ASP REVIEW PROCESS . . . .

Figure 13–1 depicts the ASP review process that is underway within a growing number of businesses today. This review process begins with a careful evaluation of requirements and the weighing and estimation of both anticipated benefits and risks. With this analysis in hand, objectives can be formulated and criteria established to identify and evaluate potential service providers.

The next step of the process, as depicted in Figure 13–1, consists of "ASP shopping." Decision makers need to obtain information about ASPs who are delivering solutions of the type that the company seeks. This will require research into the ASP

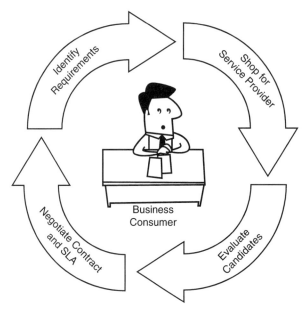

Business
Consumer

Figure 13–1
The ASP review process.

marketplace and may include the engagement of a consultant specialized in ASP "so-lutioneering" (believe it or not, there are more and more of these folks around).

Initial information about prospective ASPs will be used to create a short list of candidates, which must be subjected to more detailed scrutiny to identify the vendor who provides the best fit. This may entail the creation of a formal request for proposal issued to the candidates and will generally entail additional research into the financial solvency of each candidate, interviews with current customers, evaluations of facili-ties and technology, and other investigative activities.

Finally, the business decision maker will develop a contractual relationship with the "winner" and formulate an SLA that can be monitored over time both to evaluate the QoS received from the vendor and to tune the relationship so that it remains con-sistent with changing business requirements over time. With tongue-in-cheek, that's all there is to it.

Figure 13–2 depicts the process as it applies to ISVs seeking a ASP hosting so-lution for their software. The same basic steps apply: identification of requirements and objectives, identification of potentially suitable ASPs, candidate selection, and contract and SLA creation. However, each of these processes have a slightly different flavor in the case of an ISV that are explored in greater detail over the balance of the chapters in this book.

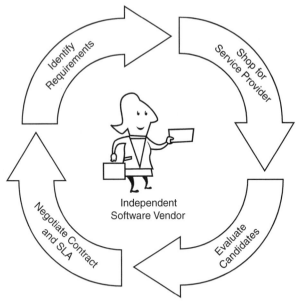

Independent
Software Vendor

Figure 13–2
The ASP review process for ISVs.

PRELIMINARY STEPS . . . .

Before launching into a discussion of the requirements definition component of the ASP review process, some preliminary issues need to be addressed. One is the question of who will lead the ASP evaluation process. The answer, as unsatisfying as it may seem, is—it varies from company to company.

Application software is conceived as a technology support for a business process. Often the decision about who will lead the ASP review process is based on the perceived importance of the business process associated with the application that is being considered for remote hosting. The more important the business process is, the higher up the corporate ladder the decision-making process may climb.

In many cases, the chief information officer, as the bridge between business management and technology management within many organizations, is often directly involved with the decision to acquire ASP services and guides the review process. However, in some organizations, the decision to use an ASP (or to outsource generally) comes from the business side of the house—in some cases, the chief operating officer, chief financial officer, or chief executive officer. It is not surprising, therefore, that the bulk of the marketing materials of many ASPs cater to the business reader, rather than the technical reader.

IT management does need to become involved in the evaluation process, however. The IT department represents the business decision maker's most trusted technology advisor in most organizations. Only the corporate IT department has a vested stake in ensuring that the technology that is fielded by the organization contributes to the company's profitability and goal achievement. It is their raison d'être.

The problem is that, in some cases, IT organizations tend to be hostile to any form of outsourcing. This sometimes results from threat perception: If an external organization can provide the same or better service than the internal IT group and at a lesser expense, why have a corporate IT group at all? Historically, some outsourcing debacles have been traced to outright sabotage by IT personnel who fear for their jobs.

ASPs have gone out of their way in many cases to reassure IT personnel that they exist to augment, rather than to replace, their function. Some speak about the usefulness of ASPs as a means to out-task mundane application deployment and management tasks so as to free up IT staff to pursue more interesting and challenging projects.

Whatever the purpose of leveraging an ASP, it represents a loss of control to most IT organizations. This fundamental concern makes IT management and staff often the toughest critics of ASPs and, by extension, potentially best suited to evaluate the technical solvency of the ASP's proposed solution.

In short, a team approach should be taken when evaluating ASP services. Business and technology managers within an organization need to be involved in the evaluation and decision-making process. This has several advantages including:

- A multifaceted team brings different perspectives to requirements analysis and yields a more comprehensive definition of solution requirements—both technical and business oriented.

- A team approach delivers a more comprehensive and critical review of the suitability of proposed solutions.

- A team approach generates a broader base of understanding within the corporate organization of the advantages, capabilities, constraints, and trade-offs associated with the solution that is ultimately implemented.

- A team approach often encourages a greater sense of "ownership" of the solution that is deployed.

A team effort does require leadership, however. Tasks need to be assigned, schedules made, debates managed and ultimately ended, and decisions reached—all with diplomatic skill. No significant technology adventure can be undertaken without a leader. Ultimate decision-making authority should be vested in the senior manager (or suitable designate) responsible for the business process that will be directly affected by the ASP.

THE REQUIREMENTS AND OBJECTIVE SETTING PROCESS . . . .

Remote application hosting is an alternative approach to internal software deployment and management. Some organizations may wish, therefore, to begin their requirements analysis process by having the internal IT group create a proposal or plan for how it would (or is) provide the application service in question. This exercise, which is essentially a competitive bid for the service being considered for outsourcing to an ASP, can yield important baseline information, including:

- Business case for application: cost savings, risk reduction, and/or business process enablement, and return on investment expectations based on the business case
- Identification of, and costs for, necessary application software and application host hardware components
- Collateral costs for network upgrades, storage upgrades, WAN upgrades, and/or desktop client upgrades required to support the application and to facilitate its use
- Deployment costs and time frames
- System vulnerabilities and costs to provide high availability and application recovery capabilities
- Staffing requirements and costs for application deployment
- Staffing requirements and costs for application management
- Performance capabilities of the application once deployed and metrics for performance measurement
- Average downtime per year for application infrastructure (historical or projected)
- Definition of user community for the application, including populations not served within existing network infrastructure
- Definition of application availability requirements based on anticipated usage
- IT and user population training requirements, strategy, time frame, and costs

The components of the internal IT "application deployment plan" address the same issues that will need to be researched and documented prior to seeking an ASP solution. Whether the data is gathered by means of an IT competitive bid exercise, or researched as a preliminary step in an ASP provisioning effort, the data must be collected.

Basically, the data addresses three sets of issues:

1. Deployment Issues and Costs: What application is being rolled out, how soon will it be available for use, and how much will it cost if deployed locally in a way that ensures its availability to the end users who need it?

2. Infrastructure Issues and Costs: What is the impact of the new application and its usage requirements on existing technical and personnel resources, and what costs will accrue adjusting or adapting resources (i.e., obtaining more bandwidth for networks, obtaining staff skills training, etc.) to support the application?

3. Business Benefits and Risks: What risks accrue to the application, and how much will it cost to manage risks? Are the risks offset by the expected benefits from the application? What is the return on investment, when will it be realized, and how will it be measured?

Some of this data collected can be used to articulate tasks and standards in an RFP issued to ASPs. The more detailed the breakdown of requirements in the RFP, the easier it will be to evaluate the solution offered by the ASP and to compare it with other proposals on an "apples to apples" basis.

Approaching ASP service provisioning from a structured, requirements-focused perspective stands in stark contrast to the approach often portrayed in the trade press and in some analyst reports. Often one reads descriptions of ASP engagements premised on an innovative idea offered by the service provider, then adopted by the customer. For example, an ASP has built an application service that enables companies to enable employees to access, view, and manage their own 401K retirement plans. The vendor touts the advantages accrued to this strategy in an interview in the trade press. The article is read by a corporate executive who thinks to herself, "This is a neat idea." She contacts the ASP, makes a contract, then advises her human resources department of the new capability they will soon be enjoying.

Many ASPs are awakening to the fact that this *Field of Dreams* scenario ("if you build it, they will come") is generally inconsistent with reality. Rarely does an ASP solution roll out in such a manner. Except in the case of very rarified and vertically focused applications, the preponderance of ASP contracts are for horizontal or general purpose applications and are signed only after a careful evaluation of requirements; an exhaustive comparison of costs, benefits, and risks of internal versus out-tasked approaches to accomplishing the same goal; and, some sort of vendor "comparison shopping" effort.

SETTING OBJECTIVES . . . .

The objectives guiding an ASP service acquisition may go well beyond the deployment of the application itself. It is not, after all, the practice of most companies to deploy applications for their own sake, but to enable other business goals. Thus, the first level objective in seeking the service of an ASP should be a business objective: *Deploying application X will enable the business to take orders, speed shipments, or realize some other business advantage better, faster, more cost-efficiently, or with less risk.*

Ideally, the objective can be stated in performance terms using the format "condition-task-standard." Conditional statements identify requirements/prerequisites for performing the task. This is followed in a performance objective by a statement of the task itself. Then, the objective is concluded with reference to a standard that will be used to measure or evaluate the completion of the task. For example, *given a need to support supply chain partners with application technology to enable their integration with corporate ERP in order to achieve manufacturing line-cost reduction objectives of 30 percent by 2005 (CRITERIA), an ASP will be engaged to deploy the corporate ERP system in a hosted environment and to provide highly available, subscription based access to suppliers via the Internet (TASK) within six months and at a cost not to exceed $X (STANDARD).*

Stating an objective using performance-based language can seem a bit stilted at first, but the benefits are several. For one, writing an objective using the condition-task-standard format forces the planner to review and specify the prerequisites and requirements that are driving the task, thereby providing the context for the task itself. In this way, objectives can be reviewed at a later time by someone other than the planner and can be more clearly understood with respect to their intent.

The same can be said of the task statement: Properly written, a task statement will provide a concise encapsulation of the effort to be undertaken. Tasks can be taken, often word for word, to create a detailed statement of work for a project or contract.

Standard statements provide a convenient way to record authoritative criteria (formal technology standards, for example) and to specify measurable results that are expected to be manifested by a properly executed task. These statements form the basis for testing and quality assurance, and also create the opportunity to establish a feedback loop that can be used to evaluate and refine the objectives statements themselves.

Ideally, an application project (whether it involves the services of an ASP) will be guided by a set of general objectives supported by a list of detailed "enabling objectives" covering specific subtasks that will realize or bring about the general objective. Enabling objectives, too, can be stated using the condition-task-standard format to facilitate the development of a better understanding of task dependencies, to provide a more detailed statement of work, and to generate a thorough set of criteria for testing and acceptance.

Planners vary in terms of how they state their objectives, of course. Performance language is just one approach that offers value.

WHERE TO FIND INFORMATION ABOUT ASPS . . . .

Armed with a clear set of requirements, the planner is ready to begin a search for potential candidates to serve as the company's ASP. (Actually, some companies secure different application services from different ASPs or use an intermediary to serve as an integration point for several services.)

A common question is where a planner can go to obtain timely information about ASPs and their current offerings. Although there is no one comprehensive source for information about all ASPs, a good start for research efforts is the ASP Industry Consortium. The Consortium has a large and growing membership of ASP vendors, though not all ASPs belong; it is actively working to advance and promote the ASP model through the development of standards and best practices.

There are also many sites dedicated to ASPs on the World Wide Web. These vary in terms of content and currency. Table 13–1 provides a table of sites that were available at the time of this writing.

Another potential source of information and assistance may be found among the growing list of IT and business consultants who are developing specialized practices in ASP solutioneering. All of the "Big Four" accounting/IT consulting firms have dedicated practice areas in outsourcing and some have adopted (co-opted) the ASP phenomenon, as well.

USE OF CONSULTANTS . . . .

This raises an interesting point regarding the use of consultants in developing ASP solutions. Consultants have long served in an IT advisory capacity within many business organizations. Their services are often used when:

- Knowledge/skills requirements for a task are unavailable within a corporate organization.
- Senior management wants to control a planning effort or project but lacks the time to participate directly.

Table 13-1   ASP Information Sources

Resource	Access
ASP Industry Consortium	401 Edgewater Place, Suite 500 Wakefield, MA 01880 phone: 781-246-9321 fax: 781-876-8805 or via the Web at www.aspindustry.com
a-com	Via the Web at www.a-cominteractive.com
AMR Research	Via the Web at www.amrresearch.com
Application Rental Guide	Via the Web at www.findapps.com
ASP Advisor	Via the Web at www.idc.com/aspadvisor/default.htm
ASP Connection	Via the Web at www.aspconnection.com
ASP Directory	Via the Web at www.asp-directory.com
ASP Insights	Via the Web at www.aspinsights.com
ASP Planet	Via the Web at www.aspplanet.com
ASP Street	Via the Web at www.aspstreet.com
ASPnews.com	Via the Web at www.aspnews.com
ASPOutsourcingCenter.com	Via the Web at www.aspoutsourcingcenter.com
International Data Corporation	Via the Web at www.idc.com
SearchASP.com	Via the Web at searchasp.techtarget.com
The ASP Exchange	Via the Web at www.theaspexchange.com
The List	Via the Web at asp.thelist.com
Web Harbor	Via the Web at www.webharbor.com
xSP Registry	Via the Web at www.aspregistry.com

- Politics or expedience dictates the use of a neutral third party with "no axe to grind" or "turf to defend."

There is nothing particularly mysterious or hypertechnical, however, about ASP arrangements that would tax the existing technical or business knowledge and skills sets of most modern companies. Certainly, there is nothing about these arrangements that mandates the use of external knowledge experts. Thus, the use of consultants will probably be predicated on one of the other listed rationales.

A consultant can, based on his or her identification with senior management (and typically high cost in terms of fees), actually manage the ASP review process for an organization in some situations. Recalcitrant team members within the organization may be more inclined to cooperate with the planning process if it is helmed by a neutral consultant who reports directly to management.

However, as in many other areas of corporate endeavor, consultants represent a cost over and above the cost for engineering a company's plans and strategies internally, without the assistance of an outside advisor. Thus, the actual value of consultant participation or leadership in ASP acquisition efforts needs to be weighed against this expense.

Planners should also keep in mind that many consultants, though "position neutral" with respect to internal decisions about outsourcing, are not necessarily vendor neutral. They may have relationships with ASPs that should be fully disclosed prior to their involvement in a vendor evaluation process.

Also, business managers considering the use of a consultant should be clear about the fact that consultants are never a suitable replacement for internal staff effort. Consultants may be used productively to augment staff resources, but it is erroneous to believe that using consultants obviates the need to allocate internal staff to ASP planning. As a rule, when a consultant is hired, his or her work needs to be overseen by a business manager. Additionally, the knowledge gained by the consultant in the review process needs to be transferred effectively to internal staff. Both these facts support the conclusion that, though consultants can play the role of a coach effectively, they do not eliminate the need for a team.

Used judiciously, consultants can greatly assist the ASP solution finding effort. They can bring to the planning effort practical insights gained from ongoing research and experience with ASP solutions deployed for other clients. They can also help in the structuring of RFPs, policing up the details of vendor responses, evaluating and comparing bids, and even negotiating SLAs and contracts (or advising those within the company who directly perform vendor procurement and contract negotiations).

ISV NOTES . . . .

The ISV seeking an infrastructure provider to help take its software product to the ASP delivery model follows the same basic project initiation steps as has been outlined for companies. However, the preliminary "competitive bid" step takes a different form.

The ISV should focus on modeling what the costs, benefits, and risks would be to host its application product using internal resources. This internal hosting plan can then be used to define the objectives and parameters that will need to be met by an ASP or AIP service.

The good news for ISVs is that, in most cases, no one has a vested interest in internal hosting. The objective is not to serve software to internal personnel, but to the community of consumers. Thus, there is no inherent conflict between company IT control or turf and functions that are to be outsourced to the ASP.

The same information sources cited earlier can be referenced by ISVs to identify potentially suitable service providers. Also, consulting assistance is available as needed in the area of competitive service evaluation.

CONCLUSION . . . .

As depicted in Figure 13–3, this chapter has covered the preliminary steps in the ASP planning process. It offers one method (and not necessarily the only one) for identifying the requirements that will be sought from an ASP solution and emphasizes the use

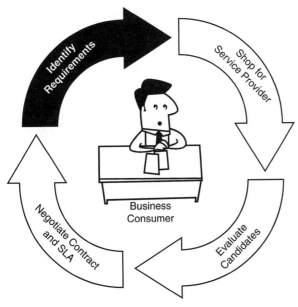

Figure 13–3
The requirements phase is complete.

of objectives stated in performance language to help to crystallize business goals, their technology requirements, and measurement criteria.

In the next chapter, we turn our attention to the details of the process involved in screening potential ASPs to winnow down the list to a few qualified vendors. Along the way, we continue to identify important considerations for that other community of customers for ASPs—ISVs.

14 Setting ASP Selection Criteria

In this chapter...

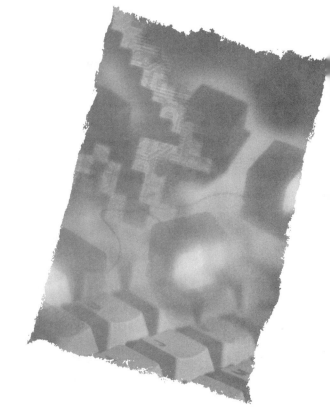

The ASP review process requires due diligence on the part of the consumer—whether that consumer is an ISV seeking an application service infrastructure for use in offering its product to prospective customers, or a mainstream company seeking to secure an application service from a vendor for use by its own personnel. In this context, due diligence includes the formulation of a detailed requirements analysis, as well as the careful scrutiny of prospective service providers. Both are prerequisites for developing a productive and beneficial relationship between the ASP and the customer.

In the last chapter, we looked at some steps that companies can take to define their requirements and formulate objectives to guide ASP selection. We also identified sources of information pertaining to the ASP market to aid in identifying potential vendors and at the potential contributions that consultants can offer to the ASP review process.

This chapter covers the second part of due diligence: identifying ASPs that are potentially qualified to meet business requirements and evaluating them in accordance with formal criteria drawn from both business and technical requirements and current best practices and standards surrounding services of this type. Ideally, such evaluations are conducted as part of a formal RFP process.

THE RFP PROCESS . . . .

As depicted in Figure 14–1, an RFP process begins with the creation of a requirements specification. The requirements specification covers technical requirements for the solution and spells out the deployment time frame and service levels that are being sought. The RFP also has a business information section that typically includes a discussion of protocol that must be followed by ASPs wishing to bid for the company's business, a request for financial information from the prospective vendor, and a request for a formal bid price from the vendor.

Once this package is prepared, it needs to be directed to the list of ASPs that have been identified as prospective candidates for the service provisioning role. On the deadline date, responses (bids) received from the vendors are opened and checked for completeness and compliance with the RFP instructions. Those that conform with instructions are submitted to the ASP project team for review. The first review determines whether the ASP's proposal offers a solution that meets all specified technical requirements. Those that do not meet technical requirements are discarded. Bids that pass this test proceed to a second review, which examines the financial information and business practices information presented by the vendor.

Vendors who pass both the technical and business review may be asked for presentations of their solution. These may be conducted on-site or, preferably, as part of

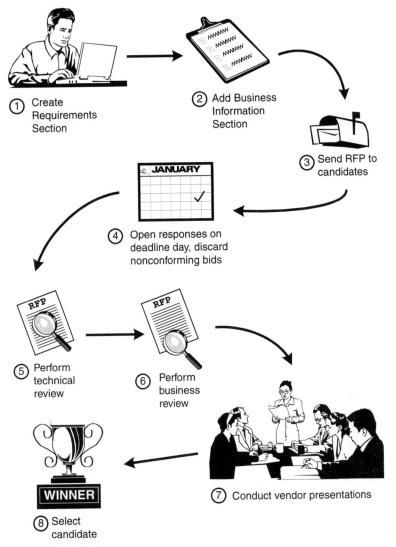

① Create
Requirements
Section

② Add Business
Information
Section

③ Send RFP to
candidates

④ Open responses on
deadline day, discard
nonconforming bids

⑤ Perform
technical
review

⑥ Perform
business
review

⑦ Conduct vendor presentations

WINNER

⑧ Select
candidate

Figure 14–1
The RFP process.

a visit to the vendor facility. Based on what is learned from these visits, and the results of criteria-based scoring, and, of course, price, a vendor is selected.

A process of this type is commonly undertaken by companies when considering the proposals of service vendors for projects involving long-term commitments or price tags with many zeros. How formally the process is handled in connection with

ASP service selection will likely be determined by the criticality of the applications being sought and its expense to the organization.

Straightforward as the process may seem, there are "devils in the details." The first is the issue of how to identify prospective candidates in the first place.

In the preceding chapter, a table of references was provided to enable you to find out more information about specific ASP software services and the vendors who are providing them. Critics might say that this resource, while useful, does not go far enough to help you to identify the subset of ASPs from among the pool of more than 1,700 self-described vendors who might be able to meet your service objectives.

In point of fact, there is no simple solution to this issue. One approach is to contact the vendor of the software that is being sought as a service. Ask them about the ASPs with whom they have established partnerships or other business relationships and who they recommend for consideration as solution providers. This strategy may run afoul of the software vendor's proprietary interests, however—especially in those cases where the software company has its own ASP offering that competes with the offerings of third-party ASPs. It is worth knowing about the vendor's own ASP in any case, so that it can be included in the list of prospective providers.

Another strategy is to search on-line resources for press releases or case studies involving ASP delivery of the software that is being sought. In addition to discovering providers, planners can also learn about the experiences of other companies who have used the service. It should be kept in mind, however, that releases older than about a year from the publication of this book may reflect the first instances of service relationships established by the ASP. Many of these early relationships were "sweetheart deals"—involving special pricing and SLAs designed to attract initial customers and to garner an early market share lead for the ASP—and may not reflect the customer experience with the ASP today. Whether the customers in the case studies enjoyed any special considerations, chances are probably good that the customer in question was referred to the trade press writer or included on the press release because it is one of the vendor's "star accounts," and the experience of the customer reflects the best possible implementation of the vendor's service.

THE REQUIREMENTS SPECIFICATION . . . .

While the search for candidate ASPs proceeds, attention can be turned to the development of a requirements specification. As previously stated, an ASP-focused requirements specification identifies exactly what is being sought from the ASP. It is part checklist and part survey, and it is a key component of the process by which the technical suitability of an ASP is evaluated. Typical components of the requirements specification include the following.

Introduction and Identification of Goals

This section describes the vision of the requirements specification. It includes:

- A description of the software solution that is being sought
- A delineation the time frame by which the solution is needed
- A "usage description" that includes the number of users, the access methods that will be used to operate the hosted application, and a high-level description of availability, performance, and security requirements

Short and succinct, this is a high-level overview of exactly what solution is being sought.

Detailed Specifications Section

This part of the specification sets forth a series of detailed requirements for the ASP solution. Ideally, these requirements can be drawn from the general and enabling objectives formulated in the first stage of the ASP review process (see the previous chapter). If a formal objectives-setting has not been undertaken, writing detailed specifications will require a somewhat more laborious process than what is described here.

For ease of understanding, detailed specifications are usually grouped together in some logical way. (This logical grouping presents itself readily if performance-based general and enabling objectives were previously defined.) Alternatively, one way to group specifications may be the following:

- Application Specifications: This set of specifications will provide the prospective ASP with a better idea of the application capabilities that are being sought. The detailed specifications should describe all end user and application inputs that must be supported by the application, all outputs that must be supported, measurable performance expectations, and QoS requirements.
    - Application Identification: Specify what application is being sought and whether the organization is open to substituting best-of-breed alternatives for the application.

- Use of Templated Versions: Indicate whether templated (noncustomized) versions of applications are acceptable or if customization may be required.

- Support for Application Inputs: Identify what input methods need to be supported for the application. Must the application provide not only a user interface, but also support batch updating? Are any real-time connections between the hosted application and back-end applications required?

- Support for Application Outputs: Identify what output capabilities are required. Explain what reports and report formats (printed and/or displayed) are needed.

- Support for Interapplication Messaging: Indicate whether the application needs to make automated updates to back-end systems or databases and how this transfer is expected to occur?

- Support for Middleware-Enabled Transactions: Indicate what middleware technologies, if any, must be supported to facilitate application integration with back-end systems.

- Application Performance Requirements: Indicate the performance (specified in transactions per second or by some other metric) expected of the application.

- Application Response Time Requirements: Indicate the response time expected of the application.

- Application Concurrent User Support: Indicate the number of concurrent user sessions expected. Identify how users will access the application?

- Application Access Parameters: Indicate whether application access is to be shared between different user communities (e.g., internal company personnel, business partners, suppliers, etc.) and indicate (1) how access will be made to the application and (2) any access restrictions that must be enforced with respect to each community.

- Application Management and Administration: Indicate the application management and administration features that need to be made available to company personnel.

- Application Management Reporting Requirements: Identify the application-specific management reporting expected from the ASP. The planner will want to receive reports on-line regarding the health, status, utilization, and performance/response time of the application hosted by the ASP.

- Platform Specifications: ASPs vary widely in the hosting platforms they deploy. The application requirements—especially the performance specification—will determine much about the configuration of the ASP hosting solution overall, including the application server that is used, the middleware that is supported, and the use of performance enhancing technologies such as caches and load balancers. This section, therefore, advises the vendor about the requirements sought from the ASP hosting platform, but it does not dictate how the platform is to be configured.

- Availability Requirements: Identify the availability requirements associated with the application. Are special provisions required, such as mirroring to ensure application availability? If so, these requirements should be stated.

- Security Requirements: Specify the security requirements for the application. Are any special systems or methods employed to control user authentication and access with respect to existing applications that must be expanded to the ASP hosted app (for example, Single Sign On systems)? Are there any special equipment requirements?

- Storage Requirements: What are the data storage requirements for the application? Specify the initial capacity and rate of growth for storage, and indicate any preferences (positive or negative) regarding the use of a storage infrastructure shared with other customers.

- Disaster Recovery Requirements: Specify the requirements for recovery of the application in the event of an ASP or company facility disaster. Describe what capabilities need to be delivered by the ASP to facilitate the use of hosted applications from alternative company facilities (in the event of a company disaster) and specify expectations that need to be met by the ASP in providing expeditious recovery of the hosted application at an alternative site in the event of an ASP facility disaster.

- Platform Metrics Reporting: Identify the platform-specific management reporting expected from the ASP. Customers may want to receive reports on-line regarding the health, status, utilization, and capacity of the platform supporting their application.

- Network Specifications: Like the ASP hosting platform, the network services that the ASP deploys to support a hosted application are often determined by the ASP itself. However, the planner needs to specify the characteristics and capabilities required of the network interconnect in order to ensure that the ASP can deliver an acceptable solution.

  - Locations of communicators/users: Identify where application end users will be physically located (company facility address, branch office address, addresses of business partners or suppliers who will use the application). Identify how many users who will be accessing the application are mobile to determine access requirements via the Internet or dial-up.

- Use of Existing WANs and MANs: Identify current WAN or MAN facilities in use by the company if it is desired to leverage these facilities for ASP hosted application access.

- Network Security Requirements: Identify network security preferences (encryption, tunneling, etc.).

- Network Disaster Recovery Requirements: Identify disaster recovery requirements for networks at the company premise(s) and at the ASP facility (redundancy of network carriers, alternate facility pathing, fail over of primary network facility to secondary or backup facility, etc.).

- Performance/Quality of Service Requirements: Describe the performance and quality of service characteristics expected of the vendor-provisioned network.

- Network Management Reporting Requirements: Identify the network-specific management reporting expected from the ASP. Customers may want to receive reports on-line regarding the health, status, utilization, and capacity of the networks supporting their application.

● Hosting Facility Requirements: The planner may wish to identify characteristics of the facility used by the ASP to host an application. Suggested criteria include the following.

- Construction Requirements: ASP facilities should comply with (or exceed) industry standard construction, electrical wiring, plumbing, heating ventilation and air-conditioning, and fire protection codes that are appropriate for data centers. Standards are available from state and local government building offices and from the National Fire Protection Association (NFPA).

- Power Backup Requirements: ASP facilities should be equipped with alternative electrical power sources to protect against outages in utility power.

- Security of Dedicated Platform Areas: The ASP should provide secure facilities for the dedicated platforms of its customers. With respect to shared infrastructure, the ASP should implement appropriate measures to restrict access to approved technical support personnel only. ASP facilities should also have appropriate access controls.

- Location of Hosting Facilities: ASP facilities should be located in geographic locations that are not prone to natural disasters. They should probably be sufficiently distant from the customer location to ensure that regional disasters do not affect both customer and ASP facilities.

- ASP Personnel and Support: ASPs employ a cadre of personnel that parallels the IT staff of a large corporation. The requirements specification should be sure to address the following issues.

  - Personnel Security Issues: Personnel employed by the ASP should be subjected to background checks and provided special orientation and training germane to the delivery of customer-sensitive and company-confidential application services.

  - Support Personnel: A cadre of support personnel should be dedicated to the customer application, hosting platform, and network. If personnel are shared among multiple customers, hours of effort associated with the planner's application should be identified.

  - Single Point of Technical Contact: The vendor should provide contact information for a qualified technical support person (and backup) possessing a high degree of familiarity with the specific application service that is being provided to the customer. Methods should be established for contacting appropriate technical support to address problems in an expeditious way.

  - Application End User Support: The vendor should provide a 24-hour-user support service to address the problems that users may have in accessing the hosted application. Methods should be established for routing end user requests to the appropriate organization (to resources within the customer's organization or the ASP's).

- Service Level Specifications: Although a formal SLA will be worked out with the vendor in connection with the contract made with the ASP, the technical specification may be an appropriate location for setting service level requirements that must be addressed by the ASP in its RFP response. Some service levels, those pertaining to application availability and platform/network performance, have already been articulated. Others that may be specified include the following:

  - Recovery of Service Following a Disaster: The planner should state the expectation of the company with respect to the timely recovery of application access following an unexpected interruption of service resulting from natural or man-made events. This postdisaster restoral time frame should be accompanied by a provision for testing the viability of the ASP strategy or auditing of tests performed by the ASP itself.

  - Response to Application Change Requests: Planners should indicate the time frame in which they expect application change requests to be facilitated by the ASP. A change management process should be defined and documented.

- Uptime: Planners should specify a minimally acceptable amount of up-time for the application and its enabling infrastructure. Normal down-time for system or application maintenance and unplanned downtime from unexpected interruptions should be distinguished from one an-other. Normal downtime should be specified using industry average measurements unless high-availability provisions are being obtained from the vendor.

The list is by no means comprehensive or sufficiently detailed to address all of the requirements that may need to be specified. The ASP Industry Consortium pro-vides a useful document, *A Guide to the ASP Delivery Model,* available for download from their Web site at www.aspindustry.com, which may provide additional issues that need to be addressed in the requirements specification. The best guides, however, are the objectives that have been developed based on the internal implementation alternative generated by the company's own IT organization.

An important thing to keep in mind is that ASP-based services are not inher-ently more capable, available, secure, or downtime free than internally deployed ap-plications. They can generally usually be made more available, less prone to downtime, and more capable if the customer is willing to spend more money. The same is true for applications deployed by the company itself. It is somewhat unfair to compare the cost for a locally deployed application engineered to one set of availabil-ity and performance standards with an ASP solution that is being held to higher stan-dards of performance and availability. High availability and performance engineering features cost money. This apples-to-oranges comparison is a common trap in which planners often find themselves when considering the ASP alternative.

Time Line for Implementation

Another section of the technical specification is the articulation of the time frame tar-geted for implementing a solution. Depending on the work that needs to be done within the customer organization that is requesting the service (i.e., architecting a database, normalizing data from existing applications that will be used to populate the hosted application database, training end users, etc.), specification of the service im-plementation time frame may be as simple as stating a "due by" or "live" date, or it may entail the preparation of a complex schedule and a full-blown project implemen-tation plan that carefully breaks out tasks, resources, and milestones, and the depen-dencies between them.

In internally controlled and managed system deployment projects, often com-plex applications do not roll out "all at once." Often the functionality is broken down into a series of phased deliverables, and target dates are assigned based on a subset of functions that will be available for use by a defined date. Similarly, network provisioning to multiple sites may need to roll out over a period of time dictated by the type of network being used and the need to wait for "last mile" telco provisioning in some cases. These constraints often apply to the implementation of complex applications provided by an ASP, as well—though the implementation curve for an ASP may be dramatically shorter than that of a corporate IT organization based on many factors including:

- The ASP's experience gained from repeated deployment of the same software to different customers
- Predefined hosting platforms at the ASP and rapid access to necessary hardware
- Standing agreements with network provisioning agents that enable faster core and "last mile" facility implementation
- Knowledgeable personnel
- Close relationships with application software companies and better access to technical support resources to aid in problem resolution

The point is that although ASPs may be able to make good on their claim to deploy more rapidly, the deployment of complex applications will still require an interval of time to be completed. Most applications offered by ASPs are not simply utility services that can be "turned on" with a phone call. Thus, the deployment time frame required by the company may separate some vendors from the pack of candidates.

It should also be kept in mind that, like successful internal application deployment projects, ASP deployments need to have a dedicated project manager who champions and oversees the project. This project manager will coordinate activities and resources with the vendor.

Vendor Response Q&A

Having specified what is sought from the ASP and provided a date by which the service needs to be in place and available, the next part of the requirements specification consists of a set of questions to the vendor asking how the ASP will set about meeting all requirements within the time provided. The approach to designing this questionnaire will vary from company to company (which is another way of saying that there is no right way to design the questionnaire itself).

Often the requirements enumerated are summarized into numbered questions. Each question asks the vendor to explain how its proposed solution will meet the specified requirement. If the vendor wishes to propose an alternative, and the planner is open to suggestions about alternative applications or approaches, the option may be provided for the vendor to propose a different approach.

It is useful, by the way, to use some sort of consistent numbering scheme when articulating specifications so that the specifications can be referenced by number in the vendor's response. This practice simplifies the verification of the vendor response as comprehensive.

In addition to questioning the vendor with respect to specifications and requirements, the Q&A portion of the specification is also where the vendor can be queried about other important matters. These may include:

- The number of customers that currently utilize the ASP: In a shared infrastructure setting, the number of customers sharing a network or hosting platform may have an impact on the performance of the network or platform overall. If this is the case, ask the vendor for an explanation of how overall performance is managed and how the possibility of "oversubscription" is handled. The number of customers served by the vendor also provides insights into the amount of experience the vendor brings to the implementation of the application on behalf of the planner's company.

- The number of data centers or hosting environments offered by the ASP: Because of their location on high-speed core carrier networks, many ASPs with multiple data centers are able to replicate entire hosting platforms at geographically distant locations. This is good news for companies considering the use of ASPs to support mission-critical applications, those concerned about potential network interruptions or congestion and their impact on application availability and performance, and those whose user communities are far flung. Be aware that host replication may be an expensive option, however.

- Certifications: As previously discussed, certification programs in the ASP industry are often less a reflection of any real capability than an indication of what equipment or software vendor "clubs" the ASP has elected to join. Membership may have some meaningful benefits, of course. Certification may suggest that the vendor's personnel may have received specialized training or that the ASP enjoys expedited delivery and/or discount pricing on vendor products. Obtain a list of the certifications touted by the vendor and ask for an explanation of how they benefit customers by adding value to services. Be wary of vendors who indicate that they are ISO 9001 certified. For the reasons discussed in a previous chapter, this "certification" does not have any meaning other than that the vendor has documented procedures for accomplishing certain tasks and that those procedures have been certified by someone (virtually anyone) to reflect the actual way that the vendor performs those tasks. Also, be wary of claims about the ASP's adherence to "best practices" as what comprises "ASP best practices" is only now being defined within such groups as the ASP Industry Consortium.

- Check for staff professional credentials: The ASP infrastructure may leverage software, hosting platform, and network products from a particular set of vendors (likely the same vendors who have "certified" the ASP). If this is the case, find out how many staff members have completed training and development courses or obtained professional certifications in the vendors' technologies.

- External Audit Reports: Ask for information about security and business continuity audits and tests that may have been performed by external auditors to verify representations made about these attributes of the ASP's hosting environment(s).

- Reference Accounts: Ask for a minimum of three reference accounts, preferably companies that utilize application services similar to those that are being requested from the ASP.

Risks

A separate section of the specification should address the subject of risks. Ask the vendor to identify any risk potentials that might mitigate successful deployment of the service within the specified time frame.

THE BUSINESS INFORMATION SECTION . . . .

With the technical specifications section of the RFP completed, attention turns to the business information section. This section has three basic components: response instructions, a financial information request, and a bid price request.

RFP Response Instructions

First, the document requires a set of instructions indicating what is contained in the RFP and what the ASP should do with it. The instructions should indicate the format for the ASP's response in terms of the number of copies, conventions to be followed (using numbered specifications in written responses), what documentation needs to be provided to supplement the vendor's response, and so on.

The introduction should also provide an overview of the protocol that will be observed for evaluating responses. Planners may wish to use the "50/50" method in which 50 percent of the ASP's "score" will derive from the completeness and appropriateness of the technical response to stated requirements, and the other 50 percent will derive from the financials and pricing provided by the ASP. Some companies have their own strategies, which may be applicable to acquiring an ASP service.

The due date for responses should also be specified, as should the contact information for a knowledgeable person tasked with handling inquiries or requests for clarification relating to the RFP. Some mention should also be made of the consequences for submitting an incomplete or late bid. The date of bid acceptance should also be stated.

Financial Information Request and Bid Price

In addition to response instructions, the business information section also seeks to collect some information of its own for evaluating which includes some critical information gathering of its own. Two information items that need to be collected from the ASP are company financials and bid price.

Given the rate at which the ASP industry is expected to "consolidate" over the next few years, some analysts place the likelihood at about 60 percent that most current ASPs will not exist in their current form (i.e., will be out of business or acquired) within a year or two. This underscored the necessity of assessing the business solvency of an ASP before entrusting it with a mission-critical application.

The traditional approach to assessing the solvency of a service provider is to look at its financial statements for the current year and however many previous years as are required to spot financial trends. Gathering financial statements is extremely important in the case of ASPs as well, but it may not be as useful a guide as one might hope.

One typical attribute of most current ASPs is their short tenure. Some vendors may not have several years of corporate credentials to offer to customer prospects. This may not be a cause for concern in and of itself, because the vendor may be able to show significant backing from software vendors and excellent credit, earnings, and financial references.

Some may have dismal financials that reflect both the impact of the "bursting of the dotcom bubble" in the summer and fall of 2000 and the "sweetheart deals" made with customers early on to garner market share quickly. In the first matter, ASPs almost uniformly assert that the dotcom debacle—the failure of Web-based companies that were first warmly embraced, then utterly rejected by investors—did not directly affect them from a revenues standpoint. In many cases, ASPs had very few customers who were properly classed as dotcoms; most did not even utilize the Internet and World Wide Web to distribute application services. However, the huge sucking sound made by the many dotcoms that simultaneously went down the drain between June and December 2000 did quell much of the exuberance around innovative technology solutions, including ASPs.

Those few ASPs that were publicly traded found their stocks devalued significantly—virtually overnight. Many more that had not made an initial public offering saw creditors and private investors fleeing to more stable sectors.

There is considerable truth to this hard luck story told by many ASPs, but it does not change the fact that the vendors must be able to make a convincing argument, based on solid business case, that they will remain a viable as providers of an important business service. They must be able to justify the company's confidence in their claims that they will provide an acceptable service at least over the term of the contract and without a reduction in service quality.

The final component of the business information section is a request for a bid price. It is understood that some adjustment of this price may be required when the ASP performs its own analysis of business requirements and how best to meet them, but the quote provided by the vendor should include pricing for known costs such as software licenses and typical hosting platform costs. To the extent that the company has done an effective job of capturing all requirements in its specification, the bid price should be very close to the contract price.

It should be noted that many ASPs have discovered that the early ASP billing model—that of delivering the service and its enabling infrastructure *first*, then endeavoring to recoup the investment through a monthly subscription fee—took a tremendous toll on their early venture capital-funded budgets. Huge infrastructure costs, compounded by the tendency to custom configure hosting platforms and networks on a customer-by-customer basis, probably accounted for most of the failures of first-generation vendors.

Planners should look for vendor bids to require an up-front investment by the customer, especially when dedicated hardware platforms are specified, followed by a monthly subscription fee adequate to cover the vendor's ongoing application licensing, network provisioning, systems and network management, and other labor costs.

Some vendors may provide option-based pricing covering different availability and support levels. Additional line item fees may be indicated for special security provisions, high-availability configurations, remote mirroring, and other fault tolerance capabilities, and for dedicated data storage. Custom features, such as connections between the ASP and back-end systems, or special networking to enable diverse end user communities to access the hosted application, and of course special modifications to the applications themselves, generally always accrue special costs.

RFP RESPONSE REVIEW AND VENDOR SELECTION

Not every ASP contacted with a formal RFP will respond. Sometimes this is due to the lack of an appropriate solution that will meet specified requirements. In other cases, it may be an indication of just how strapped the ASP has become in terms of time and resources that it simply cannot dedicate the effort required to make a formal response.

Indeed, some would argue that the quality of the RFP response—its completeness and timeliness—are harbingers of the service quality that a customer can expect from the vendor if selected. Failure to complete RFP questions or to deliver responses on time may be an indicator that the vendor lacks formal response procedures and tends to negotiate agreements on an informal, case-by-case basis. This point may have little weight in acquiring less important applications from an ASP, but it is certainly significant to a company that is about to entrust the ASP with a mission critical application and/or sensitive corporate data.

In any case, some RFP responses may not observe the specified format. Planners will need to decide whether to turn them away or consider them anyway.

However, for an RFP covering a complex implementation (which translates to big dollars for the vendor), the planner is likely to receive at least a few qualified responses. These need to be reviewed carefully to identify two or three "best of finals" candidates.

Invitations should be extended to the finalists to present their offerings to the company in person. Ideally, presentations should be made at the company premise to the ASP review team and any senior management officials who need to be involved. A second step should involve a visit to the facility where the vendor will be deploying the hosting platform. Both of these steps provide opportunities for the prospective partners to learn about each other. The ASP site visit also provides an opportunity for the review team to see more clearly the characteristics of the staff and infrastructure to which they are about to entrust their business process.

Selection of the ASP that will be engaged to service the company should be based upon the scoring of the RFP response, the oral presentation and field review, and, of course, the price for the service.

CONCLUSION . . . .

As depicted in Figure 14–2, the ASP review process is nearly complete. Requirements have been identified, formalized, and submitted to prospective service providers who have responded with their best solution and bid price. From these bids,

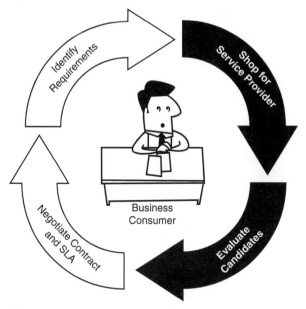

Figure 14–2
An ASP is selected.

best of finals providers have been identified, visited, and one has been selected to provide the required service to the company.

It goes without saying that not every ASP procurement will follow this path exactly. In some cases, an ASP will be selected simply upon the recommendation of a trusted advisor. In other cases, the application being sought will be of such a rarified and vertical nature, only one ASP can provide the necessary service. However, when there is more than one provider available that can meet company needs for a complex application deployment, the more formal the requirements definition process is, the greater the likelihood that solution purchased will meet the need.

The next chapter discusses the components of an ASP contract and an SLA—two documents that will formalize the relationship between the customer and service provider.

15 ASP SLAs and Contracts

In this chapter...

Т he preceding chapter provided an overview of a "due dilligence" process that may be used to identify an ASP that meets a company's requirements. Due dilligence is necessary both to ensure that a candidate ASP's solution is technically sound, and to increase confidence that the ASP itself is financially solvent.

On the latter point, planners need to keep clearly in mind that there are no guarantees about the future financial health of most ASPs. Dunn and Bradstreet reports may give an indication of the recent financial activity of the firm, particularly with respect to its credit record. Audited financials reflect the vendor's performance in previous years. However, these are not in and of themselves meaningful predictors of future financial performance.

ASPs that are publicly traded claim they have an edge in the selection process. Their operations, after all, are subject to the scrutiny of governmental agencies and financial analysts on an ongoing basis. In other words, because more information is available about these firms than may be forthcoming about privately held companies, the handful of NASDAQ-traded firms argue that they are the "safer" play.

The merits of this argument aside, it is often the case that a publicly traded ASP simply does not offer the application that is being sought by the customer. This is particularly true for companies seeking ASP-delivered software that is specialized to a particular business process or unique to a particular industry niche.

There are many more smaller ASPs offering specialized, vertically oriented software than there are large, publicly traded ASPs offering commercial, off-the-shelf (or horizontally oriented) application packages. The reason for this is straightforward: the ASP model potentially offers greater advantage to vendors of niche application software than to large and diversified ISVs as a matter of proportional cost of doing business.

Most independent software vendors-turned-ASPs note that they have embraced this delivery mode for their vertical applications because it provides a less costly approach for marketing and licensing software to customers. ASP-based delivery, for example, alleviates the need for the vendor to field a costly direct sales force to cultivate the comparatively small number of prospective customers that would find the software to be of interest. Establishing the software as a service, then advertising its availability to customers via trade press publications or Web sites that are popular with prospective clientele, is a go-to-market strategy with a powerful lower cost/ higher return appeal. As previously stated, AIPs such as Liverpool, UK-based "7" exist to facilitate ISVs with this scenario.

For planners seeking reassurance that a smaller player can provide stable service over the long term, some solace may be taken from two facts. First, it should be kept in mind that specialized software from small ISVs has always been adopted at some risk. Generally, however, the perceived benefits have provided an offset. For example, using a smaller vendor often affords customers greater influence over product

ARE PUBLICALLY TRADED FIRMS REALLY THE SAFER CHOICE?

It would be an exercise in oversimplification to agree with publically traded vendors of ASP services that they are a safer choice based on requirements to disclose financial information and earnings projections on a quarterly basis. Requiring of to deliver financial results quarterly often presses them into "reseller" relationships with software or infrastructure technology vendors, and limits their ability to innovate to meet customer needs. For many public ASP companies, profitability is a reflection of how well they manage reseller relationships rather than an indicator of the appropriateness of their business model or solution set.

An interesting perspective on ASP solvency may be provided by examining the rate of turnover that has occurred within the executive ranks of the company. How many CEOs the company has had over the past three years (or since its inception) is often an indication of the stability of the organization as a whole.

The bottom line is that the criterion for selecting an ASP must go beyond the simple evaluation of financials at Edgar's Online. The right vendor will be one with a record of both service stability and steady execution of business-leading solutions.

development, a greater "affinity" with support personnel, and the availability of enhanced "exit strategies" such as source code escrow, which enable the customer to deploy an application internally and to continue its development using internal resources should the vendor fail. These same risks and benefits continue to present themselves in relationships with small ISVs-turned-ASPs.

Another important trend in the small ASP market is the aggregation of niche players into vertical portals. Some ISVs that share the same vertical market focus have banded together to provide a suite of services to customers while sharing the costs and infrastructure of their ASP operations. In some cases, this is being done with the assistance of third-party intermediaries such as B2B portal service providers. In other cases, the aggregation is part of an initiative sponsored by large hardware and software vendors and their large industry clients.

B2B portal service providers recruit smaller vertically focused ASPs in order to create B2B communities that will serve specific "niche markets" (manufacturing, health care, scientific research, human resources, etc.). Usually these companies, which include Ann Arbor, Michigan-based Fullscope, Inc.; Syndey, Australia-based

A PARABLE FOR OUR TIMES

> One ASP marketing person interviewed for this book communicated the following story that may be useful to keep in mind.
>
>> I just got off the phone today with a Global 2500 company that went with a small ASP for order management applications because the team from the ASP vendor came in and dove into the thorniest business issues to get a grounding on what their applications would be expected to solve. They cared about how their software would make a difference. The result? This Global 2500 CIO is now a pitch person for an ASP vendor the size of his company's travel budget.

Vertical Markets, Inc.; Fairfax, Virginia-based WebMethods; Exchange.com in Cambridge, Massachusetts; and many others, endeavor to supplement a comprehensive set of industry-specific application services with their own complement of integration and customization tools which enable clients to personalize a "Webtop" for use by their employees and business partners/suppliers.

Fullscope's November 2000 deal with Komatsu Limited, the American subsidiary of the Japanese manufacturer of electronics, manufacturing, and mining equipment, illustrates the utility of this model, which the vendor refers to as "dynamic hosting." Komatsu was seeking a combination of horizontal and vertical applications for use across its diverse and geographically separated business units and turned to Fullscope to provide a "collaborative environment." From press releases and trade press accounts, the arrangement enables the customer to centrally manage, implement, and view projects, while sharing proprietary group ideas, issues, and associated files throughout all of its locations worldwide.

Fullscope, which announced an additional $10 million in venture capital funding one day after inking the deal with Komatsu, claims that its "proprietary Service Delivery Architecture (SDA) and integration platform" provide advantages over other approaches to ASP aggregation, which they segregate into three categories:

- Rehosting—Fullscope regards this as the traditional model in which ASPs rehost and/or remotely operate standard applications for their customers. The vendor asserts that the offerings of ASPs adopting this model are mostly horizontal and limited to such generic solutions as ERP, human resources, financial, and sales force automation software packages.

- Link Hosting—According to the vendor, traditional ASPs seeking to customize their fit to a particular client or industry segment endeavor to "round out their core offering with links to affiliate partners, directing their users to a broader range of services." Missing from these solutions is a central point of integration that creates a true collaborative environment tailored to customer needs, the vendor notes.

- Dynamic Hosting—Fullscope calls this the "latest variant" on the ASP model—offering a destination site where the offerings of multiple partners are aggregated into a single solution that integrates applications, content, and e-commerce services. The company quotes financial analyst projections that such aggregated application service portals—integrated in Fullscope's case via a proprietary, XML, and Java-based platform which enables partner ASPs to "plug in" using exposed application programming interfaces—will reach $6.6 billion by 2003.

The advent of intermediaries and service aggregators such as Fullscope, which deliver value-added repackaging ("integration") of the ASP offerings from smaller service providers, has important ramifications for ASP service acquisition. Planners may derive some reassurance from the fact that they are purchasing service from a more financially solvent vendor, such as Fullscope (the aggregator), than they might if they were working with the ASP directly. In some cases, they may believe that working through an aggregator mitigates the risk of ASP failure and service discontinuation—or, at least, that these risks have been off-loaded to the aggregator.

This view, however, is illusory. In fact, aggregators and portal providers introduce another layer of complexity into the service acquisition process. In subscribing to a small ASP service via a portal provider, you run the same risk of supplier insolvency, but it is further compounded by the risk of potential aggregator insolvency. In some cases, the arrangement may cost you exactly those collateral benefits (access to program developers, affinity with vendor personnel, and convenient exit strategies) that may have accrued to the sourcing of applications from small ASPs directly.

The bottom line, however unsatisfying, is that ASP service acquisition entails a certain amount of risk. This is a truism that applies to all services purchased by a company ranging from janitorial to information system functions. About the only way to mitigate the risk is through the careful selection of suppliers, the verification of their performance record and capabilities, and the effective negotiation of contracts and SLAs.

CONTRACTING FOR SERVICE . . . .

A "chicken or egg" debate surrounds many discussions of contracts and SLAs. Some argue that the SLA is the primary mechanism for controlling the behavior of a service provider. The SLA defines what service is to be provided and how it is to be measured. The SLA is referenced by the contract and is therefore the primary definition of the relationship between the customer and provider. On the other hand, the contract provides the means to enforce the terms of the SLA. The service contract specifies the remedies that are available to the customer for vendor noncompliance with agreed-upon SLA provisions. It is where the proverbial "rubber meets the road" in outsourcing. SLAs are negotiated after the contract is established and become just another exhibit attached to the master document.

For the purposes of this book, it may be useful to think of SLAs and contracts in the following way. SLAs describe the expectations of the customer with respect to the service that the vendor will provide and, in the best cases, define a set of metrics for quantatively measuring the difference between expectations and the services that are actually received. Or, put another way, the SLA is the promise of performance in case expectations and reality are two separate things. (The best ASPs are excellent at managing expectations from the very beginning.)

A contract is the formalization of a compensated relationship between the vendor and the customer that includes:

- The acknowledgment and acceptance by the vendor of the SLA provisions
- A schedule of fees and payments that are to be provided by the customer in compensation for the work performed by the vendor
- A statement of the term or period of time that the contractural relationship will exist
- The specification of remedies available to the customer for the failure of the vendor to deliver the services that have been promised at the service levels that have been specified and agreed to by both parties
- The specification of remedies available to the vendor if contract terms are abrogated by the customer without justification

ASP contracts are often simple "boilerplate" documents containing standardized codicils that reflect a vendor's typical service offering and terms. This boilerplate approach reflects the fact that many ASP vendors are striving to make their service offering a "canned," customization-free, or "productized" application subscription enabled either by a shared hosting infrastructure or a readily deployed, prearchitected, dedicated hosting platform.

Also implicit in this type of contract is the assumption that the relationship being established is fundamentally one of outsourcing in the legal sense of the term. Outsourcing is different from other service relationships between businesses and their vendors in that the customer releases all control over the process that is being delegated to the service provider. In other words, the customer cannot tell the service provider how to deliver the service. It is agreed by the parties that the service provider will control the means by which the service is delivered. The customer can only seek redress if the vendor fails, through whatever means it uses, to realize the service levels agreed to in the SLA.

The opposite of this type of contract is a contractural relationship in which the customer buys a product or service from a vendor based on an exacting description of the characteristics of that product or service and a customer-defined process for developing or delivering the product or service. In such an arrangement, the customer retains full ownership of the product or service and responsibility for the way in which it is delivered. The vendor serves as a proxy hired to execute the customer-controlled process.

Boilerplate contracts work well in situations where the application service that is being provided is grounded on a solid foundation of experience, best practices, and standard infrastructure. Some applications avail themselves readily of delivery via this type of contract. The customer only needs to specify when and where application service is required, and the vendor can enable the software for delivery, make the necessary network accessibility provisions, and—*voila!*—service delivery via the ASP model commences.

When applications themselves are more complex, and/or substantial customization is required, and/or special availability, security, or performance requirements exist, and/or different access methods must be enabled to serve different user communities, and/or complicated interconnections between the hosted application and back-end systems at the customer's data center must be accommodated, and/or any number of other variables need to be taken into account that obviate the efficacy of a "one size fits all" service delivery approach, boilerplate contracts are no longer adequate. To be clear, these factors do not necessarily eliminate the suitability of the ASP option, but they inevitably reduce the usefulness of a standard contract to describe the terms of service that will be provided. ASPs that offer such customized services encroach on the turf of the traditional, full-service IT outsourcer. Those that do not support highly customized solutions tend to be compared with the traditional service bureau provider.

Confusing as it may sound, the more that an ASP behaves like a traditional, full-service, IT outsourcing company, the less its contract can be structured with the assumption of an outsourcing relationship between customer and provider. By specifying the characteristics of a customized solution, the customer may well be taking ownership of the business process involved in service delivery. The ASP becomes more of a hired proxy than a provider of an outsourced service. Figure 15–1 illustrates this situation.

The point here is not to add fuel to the ongoing debate over what kind of vendor is a "true" ASP. Rather, it is intended to set the stage for a discussion of the elements that may be part of a negotiated ASP contract.

Negotiated contracts, as opposed to boilerplate agreements, offer significantly greater flexibility to the contracting parties and, in so doing, also open the doors for

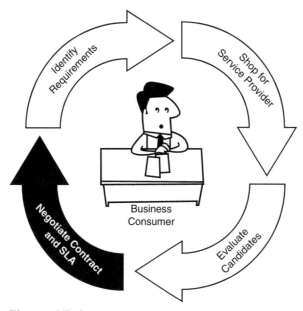

Figure 15–1
Spectrum of ASP services and contracts.

reducing—and increasing—potential risk. A few overarching points that the planner should consider when negotiating ASP contracts include the following:

- Contracts are legal documents and require a careful legal review. Most companies have attorneys to handle contract reviews. Whether the contract is a boilerplate agreement or a voluminous legal manifesto, always have it reviewed by a qualified legal expert before signing.

- Contracts are created under the jurisdiction of a particular legal entity. In the United States, most contracts reference the law of a particular state as the authority governing the construction and enforcement of the contract. Although the Uniform Commercial Code is technically the "great leveler" of commercial contract law enforcement from state to state, the fact remains that some jurisdictions have a reputation for strict enforcement of the letter of a contract whereas others have a reputation for using more "creativity" in the review and interpretation of contract stipulations. Planners may need to obtain a legal opinion about enforceability of contract provisions given the state law under whose aegis the contract is constructed.

- This is doubly important with respect to ASP arrangements negotiated with SPs located in a country other than the customer's home country. The globalization of business enabled by the Internet is causing an uptick in the number of multinational service contracts. If vendors are located in a different country, planners will require a careful review of contracts with an eye toward defining the enforceability of contract provisions given the often significantly different legal jurisdictions involved.

- For ISVs establishing relationships with third parties and intermediaries to host and/or deliver their software on an ASP basis, close attention must be paid, in addition to contractual matters involving hosting services, to the preservation of intellectual property rights with respect to the software itself. Global legal standards for intellectual property rights preservation is a still evolving area of international law. Although significant achievements have been made in Western Europe, North America, and in some countries within the Pacific Rim, significant hurdles remain. ISVs need to pay close attention to this developing legal regime in order to assure the preservation of their rights. They may also need to consider the risk of costs accrued to battling out a contract or intellectual property rights dispute in another country before they agree to foreign jurisdiction over such matters.

To these general considerations can be added a number of specific contractual elements that planners might encounter when negotiating an ASP arrangement. These include the following:

- Definition of Terms—It may be useful to specify in the contract an agreed-upon definition of terms and language. The confusing use of terms like "outsourcing" or "integration," for example, underscores the importance of assigning specific meanings to any important terms used to describe the agreement, the services being provided, and the calculations used to create metrics for evaluating service levels.

- Length of Agreement—The contract should spell out the length of time that the contract will be in effect. Length of contract is a hot issue throughout the outsourcing industry. Experts agree that it is in the best interests of both the SP and the customer to provide for flexible contract duration terms when this can be done fairly in the view of both parties. The problem is that few organizations can agree on what is fair. At first glance, a long service contract seems to benefit both the SP (in the form of predictable revenue and less client churn) and the customer (in terms of solution stability). However, long lock-in periods can actually lead to problems for both parties. If the experience of traditional outsourcing is any indication, issues begin to arise within two years of most outsourcing contracts owing to a variety of both psychological and technical reasons. The appearance of problems tends to coincide with the end of the "honeymoon period"—the six-month to one-year period in which both parties are getting to know each other and are generally willing to forgive-and-adjust to each other's styles, occasional glitches, and so forth. After a year, forgiveness gives way to annoyance as the conflict between shifting business priorities and established service guarantees escalates. Most observers, citing this "two-year itch," argue that contracts should be no longer than three years in duration and that provisions for contract adjustments should be written into the agreement for execution in the last year. That way, both parties can assess whether the agreement has yielded the desired result and whether it can be modified productively to meet changing needs for an additional three year term. If the contract relationship cannot be modified to meet the changing requirements of both parties, each will have six months to one year to transition out of the agreement. If a common basis exists for continuing the relationship, but with some modifications to services, a period of six months to one year will provide adequate time to transition the service to its newly defined state.

- Exit Strategies—The contract should spell out the exit strategies that are available to the customer and the vendor in the event of contract termination, whether at the end of the specified term or as a result of early termination for cause. To protect the vendor against early termination by the customer (owing to customer nonpayment of fees, customer company failure, or customer strategy change), terms should be specified for the collection of notification of termination and the recovery of subscription fee obligations. To protect the customer against a termination of services resulting from vendor nonperformance or vendor failure, provisions may include a combination of financial remedies and vendor-facilitated transition services.

- Litigation—Many negotiated contracts contain litigation clauses that establish venues for litigating or abritrating disputes and that establish liability criteria used to assess or limit damage awards.

- SLAs and Other Attachments—Last but not least, contracts may contain the particulars of the SLA established between the contracting parties, describing the details of the relationship, the expectation of results, and the method used to measure results. The SLA may be embedded in the contract (and frequently is in the case of boilerplate agreements) or attached as an exhibit referenced by the contract.

The above are common features of any service contract, but present several interesting conundrums to planners seeking an ASP solution. One is the desire to fashion a relationship with an ASP that serves the business, while endeavoring to prevent the business from becoming totally dependent upon the provider. Transitioning from an ASP relationship-gone-wrong either to another ASP or to an internally hosted solution can be a tedious and costly experience. A balance needs to be struck between the benefit of the solution and the risk associated with its failure.

A second conundrum is the desire of the planner to ensure that the company receives consistent QoS from a stable and solvent provider, while endeavoring to assure that the provider does not become so successful that it spreads resources too thinly among too many customers. Planners need to discover what, if any, benchmarking the vendor has performed to determine the actual "load-bearing capacity" of its infrastructure and personnel resources. They may also seek contractual provisions requiring vendor disclosure at periodic intervals of the number of customers sharing vendor resources and modifications and upgrades to infrastructure (and staff) that facilitate increased load handling capability. (This kind of disclosure may also provide insights into the business condition of the ASP, especially if a noticeable slowdown in contracts occurs over a given period.)

Finally, the planner may confront the conundrum of wanting to manage the performance of an ASP with a strict and exacting SLA, while endeavoring to foster innovation and improved performance on the part of the vendor. Clearly, the tenuous state of many vendors in the ASP space and the comparative novelty of the ASP model itself provides incentive for company planners to seek protection from risk. By articulating stringent service level requirements, and tying them to punitive contract remedies, some planners feel that they create a "stick" that they can wield over vendor heads.

However, assuming that the company's incentive in seeking an ASP in the first place is to solve a business "problem" by harnessing an ASP to reduce costs, limit risk, and/or enable new or improved business processes, the planner also needs to develop mechanisms for rewarding vendors that deliver consistent services that meet or even exceed requirements. This may be done through a set of performance-based incentives—usually financial in character—that are spelled out in the contract.

Before including any "carot clauses" in the contract, however, it is important to ensure that the added vendor effort is contributing to the return on investment anticipated from the the ASP arrangement at the outset. Bringing an application on-line sooner before deadline, or provisioning outlying user communities with network connections to the application ahead of schedule, may be accomplishments worthy of reward—but not always. What constitutes performance that merits a carot is a decision that needs to be reached within the context of a specific deployment.

In the world of conventional outsourcing, incentive clauses are often used to trade a portion of scheduled fees for a stake in the financial results of the solution. For example, a vendor will knock 20 percent off its platform deployment cost in exchange for 5 percent of the cost savings accrued to the company by the solution. If similar performance-based incentives are included in the contract with an ASP, planners also need to ensure that provisions are made for an independent audit and sign-off of the process leading to payment. This can avoid disagreements over the question of whether the conditions were actually met for making the incentive payment.

TO THE SERVICE LEVEL AGREEMENT . . . .

SLAs, like contracts, are often treated as boilerplate by ASPs. Indeed, some ASP assignments may be well supported by an SLA that specifies simply that (1) application uptime will be 99.94 percent, (2) telephone-based technical support will be available 24 hours per day, (3) all data communications will be encrypted to 128 bits and tunneled via an IPsec standard-compliant VPN, and (4) that end-user response time will be not exceed 10 seconds from the moment that the user presses a key or clicks a mouse button to the time that the system responds and the screen is repainted. SLA provisions of this type go to the availability, support, security, and performance requirements sought from a hosted application.

The issues that remain unaddressed in such a simple SLA, however, are many. First, and perhaps most important, is the question of how SLA compliance will be monitored. Often, the ASP supporting such a simplified SLA offers a monthly management report, supplemented by an "on-line, real-time" SLA monitoring tool, which purport to measure the ASP's compliance with its promised service levels. Failure to meet monthly SLA standards is usually linked to a remedy such as a discount on a following month's service fee. Repeated failures trigger the activation of a termination clause in the contract.

Depending on the criticality and complexity of the application, this arrangement may seem adequate. However, for complex ASP implementations, such a simple approach leaves too many performance measures unaddressed.

In a formal SLA, service level requirements have three components: a specification of the requirement itself, a standard approach for measuring and reporting its fulfillment, and a statement of the consequences of the vendor's failure to meet the requirement. Depending on the nature of the service arrangement, sample ASP SLA requirements might include the following.

Application Deployment Tasks

The tasks associated with provisioning the customer's hosted application will be enumerated and tied to a completion schedule that can be monitored and approved as complete by the customer or a neutral third party. These tasks may include some or all of the following, depending on application complexity.

- The designing of a hosting platform
- The deployment and testing of application hosting hardware and software
- Provisioning of storage infrastructure
- Integration of the application host with an application server
- Integration of the application server with Web server
- Deployment of load balancing and caching technologies
- Provisioning of network interconnects between applications and end users
- Provisioning of network interconnects between the hosted application and any back-end platforms
- Hosting platform stress testing
- Network stress testing (both at the ASP facility and across the ASP provisioned network, and at the customer facility)
- Database loading and testing
- Implementation of SSO systems
- Provisioning of disaster recovery backup solution
- Implementation of active intrusion monitoring and firewalling, and so on

Application Service Monitoring Tasks

These tasks are aimed at measuring the performance and availability of the hosted application, its hosting platform, and the network that is used to connect the ASP with the customer's user communities. Typically, performance expectations are stated in terms of a metric—a quantifiable measurement of some aspect of the application hosting infrastructure that reveals certain insights into the performance of the solution overall.

Some of the key metrics may include the following:

- Client Response Time (Average Time to Screen Repaint)—As previously discussed, this is a measure of the time that elapses between the submission of a request by an end user client system and the receipt of a response from the application hosting environment. Screen refresh or repaint at the client device can provide a practical indication of overall application hosting infrastructure performance.
- System Uptime—This metric is used to gauge vendor compliance with hosting platform availability guarantees.
- Network Uptime—This metric is used to gauge vendor compliance with network availability guarantees. If the vendor outsources its network in-

frastructure to a third-party service provider, this information may be obtained by the vendor, then passed through to the customer.

- Network Hop Count—This metric, obtained using a Traceroute command in TCP/IP networks, may be used to measure the efficiency of the ASP's network solution. For maximum efficiency, the number of "hops" that application traffic must take between routers in the network should be kept to a minimum. A significant increase in the application traffic hop count may suggest that the network is experiencing significant problems (equipment outages or significant congestion), and traffic is being rerouted to compensate for overtaxed or offline equipment. Trace routes can be conducted by the vendor and the results returned to the customer.

These are just a small sampling of the measurements that may be made and reviewed to ensure that vendor hosting platforms are delivering the user experience that customers have been led to expect from hosted application delivery. This data needs to be augmented from time to time by audits of the vendor infrastructure to ensure that promised redundancy features and security provisions remain in place to ensure the security and recoverability of the application hosting environment.

One last note on this subject: as previously stated, many vendors prefer to serve as the broker of performance measurement data for their customers. In other words, the ASP seeks to deploy and use its own tools to obtain data on about the hosting platform, which it then packages in the form of reports for delivery or on-line reference by customers. Some observers argue that this approach exposes the customer to the possibility of "creative accounting" on the part of the vendor. An option worth investigating is for the customer to deploy its own monitoring and benchmarking tools to cross-check the results in vendor-supplied reports.

Customer Service/Operations Tasks

As part of the ASP service level agreement, vendors typically agree to respond to customer service requests within a specified time frame. Most offer telephone lines, which are staffed on a 24-hour basis, for use by customer personnel in reporting issues and problems. Procedures should be specified for handling the requests in an expeditious manner, and the performance of the entire problem management/change management system should be monitored on an ongoing basis to ensure that services are being delivered.

It might be a good idea to perform "spot checks" of customer service lines to verify vendor representations. A recent trade press publication recently ran an article reporting that only a handful of the 24-hour "hot lines" contacted by its staff in the wee hours produced a human response. Most calls were answered by recorded messages testifying to the fact that no one was available to receive the call—but the call was very important to the vendor.

FREQUENCIES, WEIGHTING, AND OTHER MATTERS . . . .

It should be clear from the overview that SLAs are used to translate customer expectations into metrics that can be used, in turn, to evaluate solution performance. The purpose of this evaluation is twofold.

First, measurements are taken to facilitate the identification and analysis of trends that may be developing which threaten to impair the service itself. This is why vendors (and IT departments) measure the performance of their systems and networks internally: to identify issues before they manifest themselves as problems so that some corrective action can be taken.

Measurement enables vendors and customers involved in an ASP relationship to be proactive in their management of the overall solution. Proactive management is superior to reactive management because it enables system and network managers to avoid disaster potentials that can be avoided and mitigate the impact of disaster potentials that cannot be eliminated.

However, measurement—and SLAs—are typically discussed in a different context entirely: as instrumentation for policing the compliance of vendors with contractual obligations. This is an unfortunate interpretation, but a necessary one given the "Wild West" aura that surrounds much of the present day ASP industry. Pragmatism dictates, and due diligence requires, that service contracts be monitored closely to ensure that they deliver the expected value to the customer.

This begs the question of how much monitoring is enough? Can an ASP customer achieve a desired level of comfort about a vendor's contractual compliance by reviewing once-per-month reports of monitored metrics, or is more frequent reporting—or even real-time access to platform performance data—required? The answer to this question varies from one company to the next based on factors ranging from the criticality of the application and the business process that it supports to the personality of the customer manager who is doing the monitoring. In most cases, the need for daily (or hourly) information diminishes as the ASP solution proves itself over time.

A corollary to this question is the issue of what to do with the measured performance data once it is in hand. Some planners endeavor to create "scorecards" to track solution performance. They assign weights to performance measures and reference them to translate vendor performance vis-à-vis SLA-specified metrics into percentage-based scores. When the vendor delivers a certain percentage of promised performance levels, yielding a score that is less than 100, it receives an advisory note that the shortcomings have been identified and should be rectified. If performance levels fall below a certain score, remedies are exercised per the contract—usually in the form of some credit against the following month's invoice.

The scorecard method has the advantage of providing a measured response (pardon the pun) to performance shortcomings. The slightest deviation from promised service levels does not automatically trigger the termination of the contract or a hefty loss of monthly revenue for the vendor. Instead, less than optimal scores (but not failing ones) can stimulate productive discussions between the vendor and customer of ways to realize service improvement.

This is key to making a success out of any outsourcing venture. In a real sense, it is an acknowledgment of the reality that virtually every aspect of the environment in which the application service is being delivered is in a state of flux. For the application service solution to remain useful and relevant to the customer, it will need to be updated and modified on an ongoing basis.

CONCLUSION ·

As illustrated in Figure 15–2, contract and SLA negotiation completes the ASP review process. Once the deal is made, the customer will need to establish "feedback loops" with the vendor to facilitate ongoing adaptation of the solution to changing business requirements, changing technology, and changing realities within the vendor's organization.

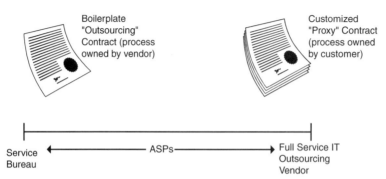

Figure 15–2
The contract and SLA negotiation phase.

A final word about contracts and SLAs: They are, at best, imperfect descriptions of the ASP service arrangement. Although these documents provide an all-important foundation for such practical matters of housekeeping and fees, they are no substitute for the judgment, common sense, and cooperation of both ASP and customer representatives. For the ASP relationship to work at all, it will require advocates *on both sides* who are willing to work together to overcome the technical hurdles that invariably present themselves.

16 Managing the ASP Relationship

In this chapter...

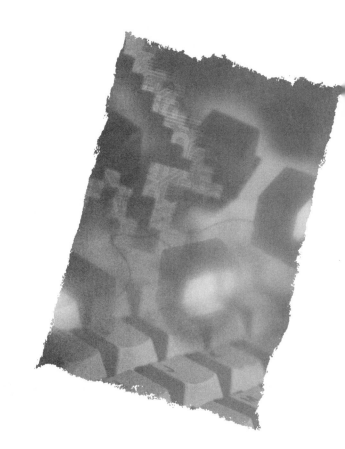

The ASP phenomenon has produced many success stories—and more than a few "war" stories. The trade press has dutifully covered both, but emphasizes the latter, if only because tales of ASP failures and stranded customers are more dramatic or "newsworthy."

Some critics point to negative media coverage of ASPs to explain why the model has been slower than expected in garnering widespread industry adoption. The media's extensive coverage of ASP failures, beginning with the sudden closure of Pandesic in summer 2000, and their assignment of "cover story status" to pundit prognostications about the coming ASP industry purge that will see 60 to 70 percent of first-generation ASPs in bankruptcy courts by 2002, are viewed by critics as having a chilling effect on the ASP market as a whole.

Yet, within the same time frame, the trade press has also covered extensively the entry of new players into the ASP space. So-called "second-generation" ASPs—ranging from brand name outsourcing service companies such as Electronic Data Services (EDS), Computer Sciences Corporation (CSC), and IBM, and well known technology vendors including Microsoft and Oracle, to a new crop of aggregators and AIPs—have largely managed to sidestep the hype surrounding the ASP delivery model and have proceeded to create a growing set of robust hosted business solutions. Trade press coverage of these developments has also been accorded front-page status.

The bottom line is that—despite trade press coverage, the occasional reversals of vendor fortunes, and the whims of Wall Street regarding the valuation of ASP stocks—the idea of network-based application hosting is garnering mind share as a fundamentally sound alternative to self-hosting. Moreover, the ASP model continues to gather momentum, not as the "next big thing" in a string of next big things, but as an increasingly practical alternative—another arrow in the quiver of the chief information officer or IT manager for use in solving certain kinds of business problems. In the not-too-distant future, ASPs will probably lose their distinguishing acronym altogether and become simply another application delivery approach well suited to some business objectives and less well suited to others.

Current trends favoring ASP adoption appear to be, at first glance, opposing forces. One is the budgetary belt-tightening that typically accompanies economic hard times. In its brief 40-year history, corporate IT has weathered numerous "lean economic periods." Inevitably, during these periods, business managers looked inward at their organizations, fixed their attention on IT, and decided that the "core competencies" of their companies did not include technology—but, rather, floor wax manufacturing or dress designing or overnight parcel delivery. They turned to outsourcing as a way to obtain the same service provided by internal IT departments, but at a lower cost.

As of this writing, a burgeoning economic slowdown, following nearly a decade of economic boom, is beginning to produce a renewed interest in outsourcing. That

ASPs will be the likely beneficiaries of this trend is evidenced by the movement of traditional outsourcing players into the ASP space.

Another trend favoring ASPs is the opposite of the cost-cutting mind-set. Within a growing cadre of major companies, bigger IT budgets are favored over smaller ones as the means to realize the revenue opportunities of the Information Age. To reduce costs over the long haul, these companies are embracing business-to-business models that "deconstruct" internally controlled business processes. They are pushing the responsibility and the costs for performing these processes into their supply chain. ASPs enable this deconstruction by providing a ready way for supply chain partners to interface with and participate in the planning and logistics management systems employed by the primary business organization.

In some sectors, such as automobile manufacturing, deconstruction is already well underway. On a Brazilian assembly line of one German automotive manufacturer, the company's own personnel never see a car. They take orders from consumers via the Web and provide logistical coordination across a multinational supply chain. The building of components of the vehicle is outsourced to a number of smaller just-in-time manufacturers, who, in turn, manufacture and deliver the parts to the assembly line—together with the necessary labor to install them. Cars roll off the line, win consumer awards, create happy and loyal customers, and deliver revenues for the German manufacturer that continue to grow "high and to the right."

Ask companies like the German automobile manufacturer that have invested—rather than "divested"—in technology whether they believe in the ASP model. They will likely respond that it is not a matter of belief, but one of economic life or death. Without ASP-hosted applications, supply chain manufacturing shops are the information equivalent of "black holes." The ASP model enables suppliers to interface with headquarters manufacturing resource planning systems and enables the German management team to predict, control, and manage the multinational automobile assembly process that sees thousands of new cars each month roll off the assembly line and into the driveways of consumers.

These two very different perspectives on ASPs—one that views the model as a cost-saving offload of a noncore task and the other that sees ASPs as an integral part of a supply chain process optimization strategy—demonstrate the potential suitability of the underlying application model to a variety of business objectives. The success or failure of the relationship established between the ASP and the customer, however, is not based on the theoretical suitability of an application service delivery model, but upon a constellation of technical and human factors.

From a strictly technical perspective, there is no question about the feasibility of network-hosted applications. To be sure, some nontrivial hurdles still remain to be resolved, including an effective way to load balance and synchronize database transactions across multiple, geographically dispersed, hosting centers. However, technical issues have not proven to be a significant impediment to ASP success.

As evidenced both in the handful of case studies that have appeared in the press regarding the details of ASP engagements (typically, the failed ones) and in the numerous surveys conducted of business managers considering the ASP option, ASP solutions owe their ultimate success to the ability of vendors to meet customer expectations, while addressing customer fears. Some, but not all, of the outcomes of ASP engagements can be traced to the original contracts and SLAs that formalized the legal relationship between the entities involved. In nearly every case, however, the ultimate determinant of the outcome is the careful management of the relationship by both over time.

VIGILANT OVERSIGHT . . . .

What aspects of the ASP relationship must be managed over time? Clearly, technical attributes of the solution, particularly those relating to the performance and availability of the application, need to be monitored. This is usually done in accordance with the SLA negotiated with the ASP vendor and may take several forms:

- Monitoring of CPU utilization, disk utilization, and other platform load and response time metrics via vendor- and/or customer-based monitoring software consoles
- Use of "listeners"—specialized application—or application server-executed functions that provide insights regarding the efficiency of client-server or intraobject communications and response times—reporting through management screens at the customer side
- Use of network level monitoring tools and consoles, including the collection of data via periodic "multi-Router Traffic Grabs" (MRTGs) which can provide detailed information about the traffic in and out of a site on a monthly, daily, or hourly basis

In addition to policing up the performance and availability aspects of the ASP operation, such tools can also be of tremendous use in collecting information that will enable planning—both for capacity and load handling growth and for platform optimization. However, the use of such tools does assume that the customer has a cadre of skilled IT personnel who can be tasked with monitoring consoles and evaluating reports on an ongoing basis. For ASP-hosted applications requiring 24 × 7 availability, the use of monitoring tools requires that customer IT personnel be at the helm of the monitoring console at all times—or, at least, that they be available to respond to email, pager, or other notifications of alerts issued by the monitoring systems. Even if such vigilant monitoring is possible, it may not be of much use in resolving disagreements between the vendor and the customer.

One integrator with significant experience in developing Web hosting solutions for client applications notes that past experience with hosting service providers has exposed gaps in the efficacy of customer-based monitoring. Specifically, it opens the door for disputes. In one case, reported the integrator, discrepancies arose between the reports provided by vendor-monitored and maintained consoles (to which the vendor refused the customer direct access) and monitoring tools engineered by the integrator into the application itself (without the knowledge of the SP). Because no contractual method had been defined for resolving such disputes, the issue became a sore point that resolved itself only when the customer renegotiated the contract with the SP at the next contract review period.

A method preferred by some companies is to use a third-party service to perform availability monitoring and/or performance data collection. A recent proliferation has occurred in the Web site monitoring and measurement service area, led by companies such as NetMechanic (Huntsville, Alabama), Keynote Systems (San Mateo, California), InternetSeer (Thornton, Pennsylvania), Mercury Interactive (San Jose, California), and BB4 Technologies, creators of the widely deployed "Big Brother" management system (Beaconsfield, Quebec, Canada). Services offered by these vendors range from simple server "pinging" and the issuance of HTTP "get" requests on an hourly basis—which can be used both to verify that ASP Web servers are up and running and to make quick measurements of response times—to the deployment of complicated agents that can collect data on remote devices, then return the data to the user, usually via the Web, in the form of real-time event alarms or historical reports.

If an external SP will be used for monitoring and management, whether exclusively or to provide a sanity check on vendor-provided monitoring information, this should be specified at the outset of negotiations with the ASP vendor. Chances are the vendor will not be happy with the arrangement, but they will need to accommodate it if it is portrayed as a potential deal breaker for the overall arrangement.

Planners may also wish to consult with the Management Service Provider (MSP) Industry Association (www.mspassociation.org), formed in June 2000, and headquartered in Wakefield, Massachusetts, for more information about SPs who can augment the operational metrics received from ASPs directly with their own management and measurement capabilities. The organization has a fairly broad membership, including vendors offering a range of management services.

The organization, loosely patterned on the ASP Industry Consortium, defines an MSP vendor as one that delivers IT infrastructure management services to multiple customers over a network on a subscription basis. MSPs, according to the organization, operate similarly to ASPs in that they deliver services via a network that are billed to their clients, but MSPs differ from ASPs, which deliver business applications to end users, by virtue of the target audience for their services: IT departments and other customers who manage their own technology assets. The organization boasted 100 members by March 2001, including a core group of vendors of network and systems management software products.

Whether performed by an MSP or other third-party service, or handled by internal IT personnel, ASP performance and availability monitoring is an absolute prerequisite given the current "Wild West" milieu in which ASPs operate. Over time, as hosting platforms and network services, as well as applications themselves, become more normalized, the need for what might be considered to be extreme vigilance may go by the boards. For now, however, in the absence of industry standards and best practices, monitoring is a must.

Simple (or complex) hosting platform operations management may be extended to include security monitoring. ASPs may be able to provide proxy servers, firewall sandwiches, and single sign-on servers that establish formidable security controls in keeping with contractural obligations. However, the question remains whether passive controls are sufficient to assuage concerns of customers about hackers and unauthorized access to confidential corporate data.

Planners may wish to consider the deployment of (or contracting for) active security measures, such as intrusion monitoring systems. These systems can be remotely administered by the customer to detect unauthorized attempts to access networks, hosts, or data by detecting telltale signatures of such attempts. In response, measures can be taken to identify perpetrators and/or to close security holes.

Extensive information about active security is available on the Web. An excellent place to start is by visiting *www.first.org,* the Web site of the Forum of Incident Response and Security Teams (FIRST).

FIRST was founded in 1990 by a coalition of 11 computer security incident response teams from government, commercial, and academic organizations. By the middle of 1997, FIRST member organizations had grown to number more than 60 from all areas of the world. Today, the organization is a broker of timely information about security threats and about the techniques for dealing with them.

The technologies for monitoring for intrusion range from the simple to the very complex. Sometimes an intruder can be identified by a file that is left behind to enable expeditious reentry onto a site at a later time (a trap door or backdoor attack). In other cases, the intruder may leave behind a program or process (sometimes called a sniffer) that is designed to capture login IDs, passwords, credit card account numbers, or other important data that may be useful in accessing more highly protected information or that can be misused for the financial benefit of the intruder. These and other telltales can be picked up by many intrusion detection software systems.

A major security threat is posed by code errors within application software, application server software, Web hosting software, and the microcode of firewalls and other security products themselves. Hackers who discover such errors and who are able to exploit them have a tendency to document their methods and to share them generously with their peers (a process known as "script sharing") via underground electronic bulletin board systems, or hacker Web sites, or through specialized Internet newsgroups and chat rooms.

With such coordination and communication in the community of hackers and wannabes, the need for a community serving the interests of those involved in protecting systems and networks from intruders is also needed. FIRST is among the leaders in this space and can provide useful references to the best-of-breed technologies for active security at any given time.

ASPs and customers need to view security as a partnership and share the burden for ensuring that hosted applications are safe from unauthorized access and misuse. Unlike performance monitoring, there is nothing implicit in this shared security approach that should raise the hackles of the service provider. Given the level of skill and organization that the wrongdoers are bringing to the situation, ASPs should welcome all of the help they can get.

BEYOND APPLICATION MEASUREMENT . . . .

Application hosting platforms, once instrumented for monitoring and measurement, provide a foundation for an ASP service that can evolve to meet changing business requirements. Proper management establishes feedback loops that can be harnessed to predict changing needs. New data caches and load balanced servers—or even additional network bandwidth—can be allocated in response to trends and patterns that emerge from daily use, enabling the platform to adapt to change instead of being overwhelmed by it.

Traffic patterns and trends may also be used to set and/or reset scheduled maintenance windows. Except in the case of high-availability configurations, SLAs typically set forth preliminary scheduled maintenance periods, during which routine system upgrades and repair are to be conducted. In response to traffic patterns measured over time, it may be necessary to adjust this schedule in accordance with changing application use. It may even be necessary to modify the architecture of platforms (add new high-availability features, for example), so that redundant components can handle off-peak load while work is being performed on primary systems.

All of these methods are productive—and proactive—uses of system and network monitoring data. In addition to platform management, however, performance data can also provide indications of other, nonmachine-related, developments within the ASP organization.

For example, an increase in the frequency of severe problems, such as "disk full" errors, certain application error messages, or blocked access attempts, may be an indication that the hosted application and/or its platform are not receiving the attention and maintenance that they require from ASP staff. This may signal the need to re-think maintenance schedules, or it may suggest staffing problems at the ASP, or an overburdening of ASP infrastructure brought about by assigning too many customers to the same resources.

Managing the ASP relationship has a great deal to do with managing its human element. Like most relationships, ASPs generally put their "best foot forward" at the beginning. They seek to ratify the customer's confidence in them by being highly responsive to requests and treating the new platform with extra care and attention. In so doing, they set customer expectations very high.

It is possible, over time, for this level of support to erode. New customer contracts can divide the attention of support staff. Dedicated resources can become shared.

Within ASPs, as within internal IT organizations, staffing problems can and do develop. Staff turnover is as much the bane of ASP operations as IT operations generally. Finding and training new staff takes time. Experienced hands may be working long hours to compensate for labor shortages and workloads may require task prioritization that favors new installation and deployment tasks over maintenance tasks. Before anyone is aware of the ramifications, service levels may fall below SLA levels.

Confronted by such a situation, the customer needs to vocalize concerns energetically, but diplomatically. Although it is true that the ASP can be—and usually is—held to a higher standard of accountability as a function of the negotiated contract and SLA, customers need to keep in mind that organizational inefficiencies can and do arise. How they are handled—whether through threats or enticements—can determine the efficacy of the relationship over time.

You may also want to encourage the ASP to form a customer advisory council (or participate in such a council if one already exists) to serve as a forum for airing hard-to-quantify service shortcomings and for working together with the vendor to develop solutions. Depending on the vendor, this approach may be seen as having the additional value of good press relations because it demonstrates customer commitment.

Occasional inefficiencies may be easier for the ASP customer to abide in cases where the customer has exercised its options to modify the hosting platform in response to changing business requirements. The ASP's proficiency in responding to change requests may provide a balance for periodic operational inefficiencies that are the inevitable by-product of ASP growth and development.

In cases where the customer's requirements are largely static in nature, ASP inefficiencies may be less readily forgiven. Of course, if the application that is being delivered by the ASP to its customers is of such a static nature that platform adjustments are rarely required, the chances are good that promised maintenance and support service levels will be upheld on fairly consistent basis. If they are not, the contract should provide enforceable remedies to compensate the customer for any losses that may accrue. This provides a reasonably good incentive to the provider to ensure that SLAs are met.

The fact is that the more complex the application hosting solution that is being delivered by the ASP, the more difficult it is for the customer to find suitable service replacements quickly. Similarly, the more complex the service solution, the greater the amount of revenue that is probably being realized by the vendor that is providing it—and the greater the potential economic loss should the customer elect to discontinue the relationship. An ASP relationship is a synonym for interdependency.

Both the vendor and the customer understand the points above, and both have enormous incentives to make the relationship work. If the customer has determined, after careful evaluation of alternatives, that the ASP model provides the best strategy for realizing business objectives, chances are probably better than average that occasional service level shortfalls can be met with a measure of understanding and forebearance. However, if the ASP option has been chosen over the objections of corporate IT or other politically powerful opponents who continue to chafe at the loss of control represented by the outsourcing agreement, chances are better than average that any vendor SLA shortfall will quickly be characterized as a breach of contract. There is considerable truth in the maxim that the seeds of a failed relationship are planted at the time that the relationship itself is formed. This maxim is especially apropro to ASPs.

Almost to a one, press accounts of failed ASP relationships are packed with what is known in literary circles as foreshadowing. That is to say, the method used to arrive at an ASP strategy, of the process used to evaluate and select an ASP vendor, or the contract and SLA created to formalize the relationship, or sometimes all three, contained significant errors. The cause of the failed relationship was not, as frequently asserted by one party or the other, a matter of the failure to abide by contractual terms. Rather, it was the result of a hastily made decision to embrace the ASP model for a particular business application, or a poor assessment of the strength of a particular vendor's service offering, or a failure to address a necessary requirement in the contract. Even in cases where the ASP closed its doors, stranding customers with a sudden loss of service, the customer's failure to provide a transition support requirement in the contract can usually be cited as the cause of much of the difficulty and disgruntlement that ensued.

CONCLUSION . . . .

ASPs are not perfect arrangements, despite the hype and "marketecture" that often portrays the hosted application delivery model as a panacea. Once a company has determined that the model can be leveraged to meet specific and well-defined business cost and business process objectives, a careful evaluation of the service offerings of vendors—accompanied by the exercise of due diligence in vendor selection and the formulation of flexible-but-firm contract and SLA—can deliver a durable arrangement that can withstand the test of time and meet the changing requirements and expectations of customers.

ASPs are a continuation of the service bureau and outsourcing strategies of the past. They build on the latest object oriented technologies for application design, the robust client-server architectures of the Internet and World Wide Web, and the increasingly ubiquitous availability of data networks, to provide an alternative approach for delivering application services.

ASP services are intrinsically no more and no less advantageous than internal application hosting without the context provided by business objectives and processes. It is not enough to simply host an application that could be deployed internally: some meaningful and measurable advantage must be gleaned by the company through its use of the ASP option for the ASP delivery to have any concrete value.

Indications are that the ASP model is realizing its value proposition. For all intents and purposes, ASPs have moved beyond the early adopter phase—characterized by lofty promises and marketing hype. Day by day, more and more companies are seeing the practical value—and inherent limitations—of the strategy.

In the final analysis, ASPs will succeed based on the balance they are able to strike between the benefits of hosted application delivery and the management of the interdependencies they create. For their part, prospective ASP customers need to keep clearly in mind that behind all of the technology is a human organization and a human relationship not easily captured within a contractual framework. To make the relationship work requires that ASP staff be regarded as an adjunct to internal staff. They are not an automated entity devoid of human foibles.

For its part, the vendor needs to keep in mind that the considerable attention paid by customers to such matters as SLA definition, platform monitoring console access, security management, and other factors is a reflection of the youthful status of the industry. Customers are exercising prudence, and not questioning the validity of vendor assertions. The best way to calm prospective customer concerns is not to set expectations unrealistically high, but to be honest and straightforward about the advantages and the risks of the arrangement. This attitude should be present in all phases of the marketing and sales cycle, and it should permeate dealings with the customer over the lifetime of the arrangement.

As of this writing, the consolidation and shake-out of the ASP industry is well underway. In the 18 months that this manuscript has been under development, many changes have already occurred. Many more are likely over the next year. Together with the closure of many "first-generation" ASPs, we have seen the advent of a new "second generation" provider. ASP^2 appears to have taken valuable lessons from the experience of its predecessors. ASP^2 brings a greater business savvy to its capital investments and service pricing and is implementing new architectures to facilitate infrastructure sharing, greater security, high availability, and performance enhancement.

The future will tell how quickly customers will move to embrace the ASP concept. The good news is, now that most of the mystique has been burned away, what remains of the original ASP value proposition is a reasonable and practical strategy for meeting business computing requirements.

Afterword

by Traver Gruen-Kennedy

Former Chairman, The ASP Industry Consortium

Business success, as in life, is often about timing. ASP is a concept whose time has come. Ask an information technology manager what his or her greatest challenge is today and the answer will probably be "time." As business operations become increasingly more complex, there simply isn't enough time in the day to address all the issues that are inherent to keeping critical applications on-line and updated.

Widening that view, time consumption translates into more than just an overworked IT department; misspent time results in inattention to customer needs, distraction from broader technology goals, and a negative impact on the bottom line.

ASPs provide the answer to the problem by offering a flexible model that can suit many purposes because its architecture provides platforms for new types of IT application outsourcing. The ASP model represents true innovation in its architecture for computing while it addresses the primary concerns of any customer who relies on communications tools and mission-critical applications.

A recent survey commissioned by the ASP Industry Consortium shows that businesses are drawn to the ASP model primarily because of the cost savings and the freedom it gives them to focus on core business issues. Another reason most frequently cited was the ability to access applications their organizations would not otherwise be able to afford. Yet ASPs represent much more than a quick fix for business users. The momentum surrounding the

ASP industry—after you cut through the media hype—is poised to transform our economy, bringing our society into a new way of life.

According to Wall Street analyst Bill Dering of C. E. Unterberg, Towbin in New York, "Application service providers will be key to the growth of our global economy over the next decade. Both economic growth and improving productivity have been driven by the effective use of technology and an increasing trend toward outsourcing. ASPs are the culmination of the effective uses of both. Thus, as ASPs flourish, they should help drive economic growth throughout this decade."

The timing of ASP's evolution on the heels of an extended period of U.S. economic prosperity is playing a positive role in market preconditioning for ASP deployment success. The combination of "top line" user benefit and the "bottom line" cost benefit makes ASP so compelling that it simply cannot be ignored. The connection between economic boom times in which technology innovation combined with business specialization via outsourcing business processes is undeniable. The market timing is good, yet during both times of prosperity and recession, ASPs can deliver sustainable value by enabling users to streamline and cut costs even as they improve their systems and infrastructure. As a result, any society or nation wishing to move its population to the "new economy" should embrace the ASP model because it yields affordable access to advanced technology and productivity tools as never before. ASPs simplify the use of technology, and speed its implementation and benefit while lowering or eliminating the cost barrier. All of this is happening at a time when leaders and individuals alike are beginning to voice concerns about the danger and inequity in societies that foster technology "haves" and "have-nots" through their investments, public policies, or ignorance of technology options.

The debate over a growing "digital divide" should and will include ASP technology and business models. ASPs provide an effective means to fill the "digital divide" by making access to applications easy for everyone at a price point that they can afford. By delivering the choice, convenience, and control that end users seek, ASPs will do for applications what the Internet and www have done for information—make them simple to access, easy to use, and very affordable. In fact the timing of ASP development in a post-Web world is logical to most people even if it means abandoning the traditional PC for a simpler, more portable device.

As in the wireless telephone industry, ASPs will bundle application services with user terminals and handheld devices, making it easy to transition from legacy systems to the new ASP reality and methods. As users shift from managing their technology to managing SLAs, the time has come to develop global contract mechanisms and standards for "best practice" with third-party auditors. For business users this means "auditing" the ASP contract and SP implementation of security, transaction, and data management in much the same way as one audits the accounting methods and accuracy of company books today. The result will be a mitigation of risk and an enhancement of reward for ASP users and organizations. An additional way to lower risk while underscoring reward is to make contract enforcement simple, fair, and within the economic grasp of users both large and small. Time is an essential element here, as well. If contract disputes linger then, the ASP industry will suffer. Mediation and arbitration work well at swiftly resolving contractual disputes. The inclusion of a global ASP specific dispute resolution mechanism, as part of the contractual bundle, will enhance the value of the ASP contract by making outcomes more predictable.

The World Intellectual Property Organization, a department of the United Nations, based in Geneva, Switzerland, is working in cooperation with the ASP Industry Consortium to create just such a contract dispute resolution mechanism. Already some 175 countries have agreed to honor and uphold outcomes of this "ASP court" in that judgment outcomes resulting from ASP arbiters will be honored. Now ASPs can write a single contract for an application service user that is binding worldwide. The *one customer, one contract, one world* mantra will be a rallying cry not just for the individual user and the ASP serving him or her, but for entire societies trying to map their citizens to the borderless e-world in which one acts locally and globally simultaneously. Times are changing.

As the ASP industry emerges from its origins converging the legacy IT and telecommunications industries, it will, through fits and starts, take its rightful place in history as the means by which people empower themselves to participate in the global e-conomy. Time will tell.

Traver Gruen-Kennedy is considered by many to be the "Father of the ASP industry." A global technology leader, he is ranked by NetworkWorld *magazine (along with Michael Dell and Bill Gates) as one of the "25 Most Powerful People in Networking." His vision of the convergence of IT and telecommunications with a new global legal and audit infrastructure is widely accepted around the world as the future of software technology, e-business, and the www. Gruen-Kennedy is the former chairman of the ASP Industry Consortium and a key executive at Citrix Systems, Inc., an S&P 500 and Nasdaq 100 software company.*

Glossary

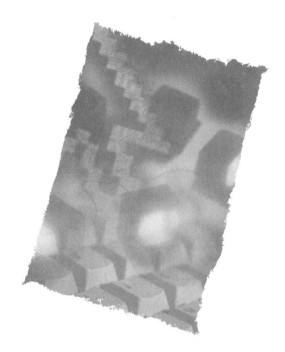

802.11   A family of specifications developed by the IEEE for wireless LAN technology. 802.11 specifies an over-the-air interface between a wireless client and a base station or between two wireless clients. The IEEE accepted the specification in 1997. There are several specifications in the 802.11 family:

- 802.11—applies to wireless LANs and provides 1 or 2 Mbps transmission in the 2.4 GHz band using either frequency hopping spread spectrum (FHSS) or direct sequence spread spectrum (DSSS).
- 802.11a—an extension to 802.11 that applies to wireless LANs and provides up to 54 Mbps in the 5GHz band. 802.11a uses an orthogonal frequency division multiplexing encoding scheme.
- 802.11b (also referred to as 802.11 High Rate or Wi-Fi)—an extension to 802.11 that applies to wireless LANS and provides 11 Mbps transmission (with a fallback to 5.5, 2 and 1 Mbps) in the 2.4 GHz band.
- 802.11g—applies to wireless LANs and provides 20+ Mbps in the 2.4 GHz band.

ANSI   American National Standards Institute. Founded in 1918, ANSI is a voluntary organization composed of over 1,300 members (including all the large computer companies) that creates standards for the computer industry. For example, ANSI C is a version of the C language that has been approved by the ANSI committee. To a large degree, all ANSI C compilers, regardless of which company produces them, should behave similarly. In addition to programming languages, ANSI sets standards for a wide range of technical areas, from electrical specifications to communications protocols.

APPLICATION   A program or group of programs designed for end users. Software can be divided into two general classes: systems software and applications software. Systems software consists of low-level programs that interact with the computer at a very basic level. This includes operating systems, compilers, and utilities for managing computer resources. In contrast, applications software (also called end-user programs) includes database programs, word processors, and spreadsheets. Figuratively speaking, applications software sits on top of systems software because it is unable to run without the operating system and system utilities.

APPLICATION INFRASTRUCTURE PROVIDER (AIP)

A company that provides the necessary infrastructure for hosting applications that are to be delivered as a service.

APPLICATION SERVER   A program that handles all application operations between users and an organization's backend business applications or databases. Application servers are typically used for complex transaction-based applications, but are increasingly used in strategies for Web-enabling applications for delivery via the ASP model. To support high-end requirements, an application server has to have built-in redundancy, monitors for high-availability, high-performance distributed application services and support for complex database access.

APPLICATION SERVICE PROVIDER (ASP)   An agency or company that delivers application software as a service, usually on a subscription or fee basis, using a network.

APPLICATION SERVICE PROVISIONING Another definition of ASP, the act of providing application software as a service.

ASP AGGREGATOR A company that combines and offers for distribution a number of ASP services or suite of products, usually from a variety of partners.

ASYNCHRONOUS TRANSFER MODE (ATM) A network technology based on transferring data in cells or packets of a fixed size. The cell used with ATM is relatively small compared to units used with older technologies. The small, constant cell size allows ATM equipment to transmit video, audio, and computer data over the same network, and assure that no single type of data consumes all of the bandwidth of the line.

B2B Short for business-to-business, B2B is the exchange of products, services, or information between businesses rather than between businesses and consumers.

B2C Short for business-to-consumer, B2C is the retailing part of e-commerce on the Internet. It is often contrasted to B2B or business-to-business.

BACKBONE PROVIDER A backbone provider supplies access to high-speed transmission lines that connect users to the Internet. These lines comprise the backbone of the Internet. Different from an ISP, which provides users access to the Internet, a backbone provider supplies the ISPs with access to the lines, such as T1 or T3 lines, that connect ISPs to each other, allowing the ISPs to offer their customers Internet access at high speeds. Some major backbone providers include MCI, Sprint, UUNET, AGIS and BBN.

BANDWIDTH The amount of data that can be transmitted in a fixed amount of time. For digital devices, the bandwidth is usually expressed in bits per second (bps) or bytes per second. For analog devices, the bandwidth is expressed in cycles per second, or Hertz (Hz).

BOTTLENECK A bottleneck refers to the delay in transmission of data through the circuits of a computer's microprocessor or over a TCP/IP network. The delay typically occurs when a system's bandwidth cannot support the amount of information being relayed at the speed it is being processed.

BRIDGE A device that connects two local-area networks (LANs), or two segments of the same LAN. Unlike routers, bridges are protocol-independent. They simply forward packets without analyzing and re-routing messages. Consequently, they're faster than routers, but also less versatile.

BROADBAND A type of data transmission in which a single medium (wire) can carry several channels at once. Cable TV, for example, uses broadband transmission. In contrast, baseband transmission allows only one signal at a time.

BROWSER An application that make it easy to access the World Wide Web. Two of the most popular browsers are Netscape Navigator and Microsoft Internet Explorer.

BUSINESS SERVICES PROVIDER (BSP) An ASP that focuses on providing and hosting applications related exclusively to business functions.

CACHE A special high-speed storage mechanism. Two common types of caching are memory caching and disk caching. A memory cache, sometimes called a cache store or RAM cache, is a portion of memory made of high-speed static RAM (SRAM) instead of the slower and cheaper dynamic RAM (DRAM) used for main memory. Memory caching is effective because most programs access the same data or instructions over and over. By keeping as much of this information as possible in SRAM, the computer avoids accessing the slower DRAM. Disk caching works under the same principle as memory caching, but instead of using high-speed SRAM, a disk cache uses conventional main memory. The most recently accessed data from the disk (as well as adjacent sectors) is stored in a memory buffer. When a program needs to access data from the disk, it first checks the disk cache to see if the data is there. Disk caching can dramatically improve the performance of applications, because accessing a byte of data in RAM can be thousands of times faster than accessing a byte on a hard disk. When data is found in the cache, it is called a cache hit, and the effectiveness of a cache is judged by its hit rate. Many cache systems use a technique known as smart caching, in which the system can recognize certain types of frequently used data. The strategies for determining which information should be kept in the cache constitute some of the more interesting problems in computer science. Caching concepts are currently being applied to Web-accessible content distribution.

CIRCUIT SWITCHING A type of communications in which a dedicated channel (or circuit) is established for the duration of a transmission. The most familiar circuit-switching network is the telephone system, which links together wire segments to create a single unbroken line for each telephone call. Circuit-switching systems are ideal for communications that require data to be transmitted in real-time. Packet-switching networks are more efficient if some amount of delay is acceptable. Circuit-switching networks are sometimes called connection-oriented networks.

CLIENT/SERVER A network architecture in which each computer or process on the network is either a client or a server. Servers are powerful computers or processes dedicated to managing disk drives (file servers), printers (print servers), or network traffic (network servers). Clients are PCs or workstations on which users run applications. Clients rely on servers for resources, such as files, devices, and even processing power.

CLIENT   The client part of client/server architecture. Typically, a client is an application that runs on a personal computer or workstation and relies on a server to perform some operations. For example, an e-mail client is an application that enables you to send and receive e-mail.

COLLOCATION SERVICE   A Web hosting service in which customers are responsible for the management of their own applications and Web sites.

COMMON GATEWAY INTERFACE (CGI)   A specification for transferring information between a World Wide Web server and a CGI program. A CGI program is any program designed to accept and return data that conforms to the CGI specification. The program could be written in any programming language, including C, Perl, Java, or Visual Basic. CGI programs are the most common way for Web servers to interact dynamically with users. Many HTML pages that contain forms, for example, use a CGI program to process the form's data once it's submitted. Another increasingly common way to provide dynamic feedback for Web users is to include scripts or programs that run on the user's machine rather than the Web server. These programs can be Java applets, Java scripts, or ActiveX controls. These technologies are known collectively as client-side solutions, while the use of CGI is a server-side solution because the processing occurs on the Web server. One problem with CGI is that each time a CGI script is executed, a new process is started. For busy Web sites, this can slow down the server noticeably. An increasingly popular alternative is to use Java servlets.

COMMUNICATIONS PROTOCOL   All communications between devices require that the devices agree on the format of the data. The set of rules defining a format is called a protocol. At the very least, a communications protocol must define the rate of transmission (in baud or bps); whether transmission is to be synchronous or asynchronous; and, whether data is to be transmitted in half-duplex or full-duplex mode. In addition, protocols can include sophisticated techniques for detecting and recovering from transmission errors and for encoding and decoding data.

COMPETITIVE LOCAL EXCHANGE CARRIER (CLEC)   A telephone company that competes with an Incumbent Local Exchange Carrier (ILEC) such as a Regional Bell Operating Company (RBOC).

COMPONENT OBJECT MODEL (COM)   A model for binary code developed by Microsoft. The Component Object Model (COM) enables programmers to develop objects that can be accessed by any COM-compliant application. Both Object Linking and Embedding (OLE) and ActiveX are based on COM.

CORBA   Short for Common Object Request Broker Architecture, an architecture that enables pieces of programs, called objects, to communicate with one another regardless of what programming language they were written in or what operating system they're running on. CORBA was developed by an industry consortium known as the Object Management Group (OMG). There are several implementations of CORBA, the most widely used being IBM's SOM and DSOM architectures. CORBA has also been embraced by Netscape as part of its Netscape ONE (Open Network Environment) platform. Two competing models are Microsoft's COM and DCOM and Sun Microsystems' RMI.

CUSTOMER RELATIONSHIP MANAGEMENT (CRM)   An integrated information system that is used to plan, schedule and control the pre-sales and post-sales activities in an organization. A full-spectrum CRM application architecture consists of the integrated automation of business processes encompassing customer touch points, including sales (contact management, product configuration), marketing (campaign management, telemarketing, data mining) and customer service (call center, field service).

DARPANET   DARPANet originated in 1969 when the Defense Advanced Research Projects Agency, a part of the U.S. Defense Department, recognized a need for an efficient way to exchange military information between scientists and researchers based in different geographic locations. DARPANet originally consisted of a four-computer network. By 1972, it had grown to a network of 37 computers and was renamed ARPANet. ARPANet led to today's Internet.

DATABASE   A database is a collection of data that is organized so that its contents can easily be accessed, managed, and updated. The most prevalent type of database is the relational database, a tabular database in which data is defined so that it can be reorganized and accessed in a number of different ways. A distributed database is one that can be dispersed or replicated among different points in a network. An object-oriented programming database is one that is congruent with the data defined in object classes and subclasses.

DATA CENTER   A centralized location where computing and networking equipment is located. In ASP parlance, the term also refers to a centralized storage facility used by an ASP to retain database information related to the decision-making processes of an organization.

DATA MART   A data mart is a data warehouse that is restricted to dealing with a single subject or topic. The operational data that feeds a data mart generally comes from a single set or source of operational data.

DATA WAREHOUSE   A data warehouse is a repository for data organized in a format that is suitable for ad hoc query processing, data mining, OLAP and/or other analytical applications. Data warehouses are built from operational databases. The operational data is "cleaned" and transformed so that it can be quickly retrieved and efficiently analyzed. A single-purpose data warehouse is sometimes referred to as a "data mart."

DCOM Short for Distributed Component Object Model, an extension of Microsoft's Component Object Model (COM) to support objects distributed across a network.

DE FACTO STANDARD A format, language, or protocol that has become a standard not because it has been approved by a standards organization but because it is widely used and recognized by the industry as being standard.

DESKTOP Shorthand for the operating environment in which a user interfaces with one or more application programs, usually on a PC.

DIAL-UP ACCESS Connecting a device to a network via a modem and a public telephone network. Dial-up access is like a phone connection, except that the parties at the two ends are computer devices rather than people. Because dial-up access uses normal telephone lines, the quality of the connection is not always good and data rates are limited. In the past, the maximum data rate with dial-up access was 56 Kbps (56,000 bits per second), but new technologies such as ISDN are providing faster rates. An alternative way to connect two computers is through a leased line, which is a permanent connection between two devices. Leased lines provide faster throughput and better quality connections, but they are also more expensive.

DIGITAL CERTIFICATES An attachment to an electronic message used for security purposes. The most common use of a digital certificate is to verify that a user sending a message is who he or she claims to be, and to provide the receiver with the means to encode a reply. The most widely used standard for digital certificates is X.509.

DIGITAL SUBSCRIBER LINE (DSL) A family of circuit technologies designed to provide high bandwidth connectivity across twisted pair copper wire. The entire family of technologies is typically referred to using the catch-all xDSL. Specific standards within the family are called by their acronyms. For example, Asymmetric Digital Subscriber Line (ADSL) supports data rates of from 1.5 to 9 Mbps when receiving data (known as the downstream rate) and from 16 to 640 Kbps when sending data (known as the upstream rate.) Very High Speed Digital Subscriber Line (VDSL) handles data transmissions at up to 55 Mbps over short distances, usually between 1000 and 4500 feet (300 - 1500 meters).

DIGITAL SUBSCRIBER LINE ACCESS MULTIPLEXER (DSLAM) A mechanism at a phone company's central location that links many customer DSL connections to a single high-speed ATM line. When the phone company receives a DSL signal, an ADSL modem with a POTS splitter detects voice calls and data. Voice calls are sent to the PSTN, and data are sent to the DSLAM, where it passes through the ATM to the Internet, then back through the DSLAM and ADSL modem before returning to the customer's PC. More DSLAMs a phone company has, the more customers it can support.

DIRECTORY SERVICE A network service that identifies all resources on a network and makes them accessible to users and applications. Resources include e-mail addresses, computers, and peripheral devices such as printers. Ideally, the directory service should make the physical network topology and protocols transparent so that a user on a network can access any resource without knowing where or how it is physically connected. There are a number of directory services that are used widely. Two of the most important ones are LDAP, which is used primarily for e-mail addresses, and Netware Directory Service (NDS), which is used on Novell Netware networks. Virtually all directory services are based on the X.500 ITU standard, although the standard is so large and complex than no vendor complies with it fully.

DISTRIBUTED COMPUTING ENVIRONMENT (DCE) a suite of technology services developed by The Open Group for creating distributed applications that run on different platforms. DCE services include Remote Procedure Calls (RPC), Security Service, Directory Service, Time Service, Threads Service, and Distributed File Service. DCE is said to provide robust security and fault tolerance.

DNA Short for Windows Distributed interNet Applications Architecture, a marketing name for a collection of Microsoft technologies. Windows DNA is Microsoft's extensible platform for developing interoperable Web applications that get to market quickly. It is based on what Microsoft learned while developing server-side technologies such as Internet Information Services (IIS) and COM+ component services, as well as the company's involvement in developing Internet standards and building successful sites such as Expedia.com. Most of all, Windows DNA is the result of the company's work on reinventing itself in order to meet the challenges of tomorrow's Internet-enabled business environment. Windows DNA is a complete, interoperable solution that represents every aspect of Internet application development, including messaging, data management, warehousing, integration with other enterprise applications, information exchange via XML, presentation through all types of clients, including Web browsers, WAP-enabled cell phones, and set-top boxes.

E-BUSINESS Electronic business is any process that a business organization (for-profit, governmental, or nonprofit entity) conducts over a computer-mediated network.

E-COMMERCE   Electronic commerce is any transaction completed over a computer-mediated network that involves the transfer of ownership or rights to use goods or services.

E-MAIL   E-mail (electronic mail) is the exchange of computer-stored messages by telecommunication. E-mail messages are usually encoded in ASCII text. However, you can also send non-text files, such as graphic images and sound files, as attachments sent in binary streams. E-mail was one of the first uses of the Internet and is still the most popular use. A large percentage of the total traffic over the Internet is e-mail. E-mail can also be exchanged between online service provider users and in networks other than the Internet, both public and private. E-mail can be distributed to lists of people as well as to individuals. A shared distribution list can be managed by using an e-mail reflector. Some mailing lists allow you to subscribe by sending a request to the mailing list administrator. A mailing list that is administered automatically is called a list server. E-mail is one of the protocols included with the Transport Control Protocol/Internet Protocol (TCP/IP) suite of protocols. A popular protocol for sending e-mail is Simple Mail Transfer Protocol and a popular protocol for receiving it is POP3. Both Netscape and Microsoft include an e-mail utility with their Web browsers.

ELECTRONIC DATA INTERCHANGE (EDI)   A form of electronic communication that allows trading partners to exchange business transaction data in structured formats that can be processed by applications software.

EMULATION   The ability of a program or device to imitate another program or device. Communications software packages often include terminal emulation drivers. This enables your PC to emulate a particular type of terminal so that you can log on to a mainframe or other type of server.

ENCRYPTION   The translation of data into a secret code. Arguably, it is the most effective way to achieve data security.

ENTERPRISE RESOURCE PLANNING (ERP)   Packages that enable the creation of a single corporate image from disparate, decentralized divisions, enabling users to visualize underlying business processes, reshape these processes, and renovate their businesses. ERP modules may be able to interface with an organization's own software with varying degrees of effort, and, depending on the software, ERP modules may be alterable via the vendor's proprietary tools as well as proprietary or standard programming languages. An ERP system can include software for manufacturing, order entry, accounts receivable and payable, general ledger, purchasing, warehousing, transportation, and human resources. The major ERP vendors are SAP, PeopleSoft, Oracle, Baan, and J.D. Edwards.

Lawson Software specializes in back-end processing that integrates with another vendor's manufacturing system.

EXTENSIBLE MARKUP LANGUAGE (XML)   A meta-language approved as a World Wide Web Coalition (W3C) Recommendation in February 1998. It is a simplified version of Standard Generalized Markup Language (SGM) that captures the key SGML advantages (e.g., extensibility) without its more obscure features. Because it is a meta-language (a language to define languages), it offers Hypertext Markup Language (HTML) capabilities. HTML is just one instance of an SGML document while Extensible Markup Language (XML), like its "parent" SGML, is a language that can be used to create HTML. Today's mature SGML-aware tools (e.g., content-creation applications, composition engines, document component managers) are converted for XML compliance.

FAILOVER   A backup operation that automatically switches to a standby database, server or network if the primary system fails or is temporarily shut down for servicing. Failover is an important fault tolerance function of mission-critical systems that rely on constant accessibility. Failover automatically and transparently to the user redirects requests from the failed or down system to the backup system that mimics the operations of the primary system.

FAULT TOLERANCE   The ability of a system to respond gracefully to an unexpected hardware or software failure. There are many levels of fault tolerance, the lowest being the ability to continue operation in the event of a power failure. Many fault-tolerant computer systems mirror all operations—that is, every operation is performed on two or more duplicate systems, so if one fails the other can take over.

FILE TRANSFER PROTOCOL (FTP)   The Internet protocol and program used to transfer files between network nodes.

FIREWALL   A system designed to prevent unauthorized access to or from a private network. Firewalls can be implemented in both hardware and software, or a combination of both. Firewalls are frequently used to prevent unauthorized Internet users from accessing private networks connected to the Internet, especially intranets. All messages entering or leaving the intranet pass through the firewall, which examines each message and blocks those that do not meet the specified security criteria.

FRACTIONAL T-1   One or more channels of a T-1 service. A complete T-1 carrier contains 24 channels, each of which provides 64 Kbps. Most phone companies, however, also sell fractional T-1 lines, which provide less bandwidth but are also less expensive. Typically, fractional T-1 lines are sold in increments of 56 Kbps (the extra 8 Kbps per channel is used for data management).

FRAME RELAY   A packet-switching protocol for connecting devices on a Wide Area Network (WAN). Frame Relay networks in the U.S. support data transfer rates at T-1 (1.544 Mbps) and T-3 (45 Mbps) speeds.

GOPHER   Internet search and retrieve protocol. A protocol designed to allow clients to search for, retrieve, and display documents over the Internet.

HIGH AVAILABILITY (HA)   Architectural provisions that contribute resiliency and fault tolerance to computers and networks.

HORIZONTAL APPLICATION   Software that may be used across many or all vertical market segments.

HOST   (n) A computer system operating application software or managing access to data storage that may be accessed by another system or end user workstation located at a different physical locale. The term is often used when there are two computer systems connected by modems and telephone lines or when the systems are connected to a TCP/IP network, including the Internet. In the latter setting, each host has a unique IP address. (v) To provide the infrastructure for a computer service. For example, there are many companies that host Web servers. This means that they provide the hardware, software, and communications lines required by the server. Applications and other content that are hosted on the server may be controlled by someone other than the hosting service provider.

HOSTING SERVICE PROVIDER (HSP)   A company dedicated to providing Web hosting services. Typically operates a Web server farm, either at a data center or collocation facility.

HUB   A common connection point for devices in a network. Hubs are commonly used to connect segments of a LAN. A hub contains multiple ports. When a packet arrives at one port, it is copied to the other ports so that all segments of the LAN can see all packets. A passive hub serves simply as a conduit for the data, enabling it to go from one device (or segment) to another. So-called intelligent hubs include additional features that enable an administrator to monitor the traffic passing through the hub and to configure each port in the hub. Intelligent hubs are also called manageable hubs. A third type of hub, called a switching hub, actually reads the destination address of each packet and then forwards the packet to the correct port.

HYPERTEXT MARKUP LANGUAGE (HTML)   The authoring language used to create documents on the World Wide Web.

HYPERTEXT TRANSFER PROTOCOL (HTTP)   A protocol running over IP and designed for the World Wide Web. Provides packaging of information that can contain instruction headers and other data about the content.

HYPERTEXT TRANSFER PROTOCOL SECURE (HTTPS)   The secure version of HTTP using certificates that can uniquely identify the server and client, and encrypt all communication between them.

IEEE   Institute of Electrical and Electronic Engineers. Founded in 1884 as the AIEE, the IEEE was formed in 1963 when AIEE merged with IRE. IEEE is an organization composed of engineers, scientists, and students. The IEEE is best known for developing standards for the computer and electronics industry. In particular, the IEEE 802 standards for local-area networks are widely followed.

INTERNET ENGINEERING TASK FORCE (IETF)   The main standards organization for the Internet. The IETF is a large open international community of network designers, operators, vendors, and researchers concerned with the evolution of the Internet architecture and the smooth operation of the Internet. It is open to any interested individual.

INCUMBENT LOCAL EXCHANGE CARRIER (ILEC)   A telephone company that was providing local service when the Telecommunications Act of 1996 was enacted, opening local telco services to competition.

INDEPENDENT COMPUTING ARCHITECTURE (ICA)   Citrix Systems application hosting technology and the name given to its protocol for application interface delivery across a network or dial-up connection.

INDEPENDENT SOFTWARE VENDOR (ISV)   A company that creates and/or sells original computer software.

INTEGRATED SWITCHED DIGITAL NETWORK (ISDN)   A technology offered by many telephone companies across the world. ISDN combines voice and digital network services in a single medium, making it possible to offer customers digital data services as well as voice connections over digital telephone lines or normal telephone wires.

INTEREXCHANGE CARRIER (IXC)   A telephone company that provides connections between local exchanges in different geographic areas.

INTERNET   A global TCP/IP network connecting millions of computers. As of 2001, the Internet has more than 400 million users worldwide, and that number is growing rapidly.

INTERNET PROTOCOL   IP specifies the format of packets, also called datagrams, and the addressing scheme. Most networks combine IP with a higher-level protocol called Transport Control Protocol (TCP), which establishes a virtual connection between a destination and a source. IP by itself is analogous to the postal system. It allows a user to address a package and drop it in the system, but there's no direct link between sender and the recipient. TCP/IP, on the other hand, establishes a connection between two hosts so that they can send messages back and forth for a period of time.

INTERNET DATA CENTER A term coined by Exodus Communications to describe its data centers designed especially for service delivery via the Internet and World Wide Web.

INTERNET INFORMATION SERVER (IIS) IIS Web server developed by Microsoft that runs on Windows NT/ Windows 2000 platforms. Server is bundled and tightly integrated with Windows NT/2000 operating system.

INTERNET SERVICE PROVIDER (ISP) An agency or company that provides a connection to the Internet, usually as a leased line or a dial-up link.

IPSEC Short for IP Security, a set of protocols developed by the IETF to support secure exchange of packets at the IP layer. IPsec has been deployed widely to implement Virtual Private Networks (VPNs). IPsec supports two encryption modes: Transport and Tunnel. Transport mode encrypts only the data portion (payload) of each packet, but leaves the header untouched. The more secure Tunnel mode encrypts both the header and the payload. On the receiving side, an IPSec-compliant device decrypts each packet. For IPsec to work, the sending and receiving devices must share a public key. This is accomplished through a protocol known as Internet Security Association and Key Management Protocol/Oakley (ISAKMP/Oakley), which allows the receiver to obtain a public key and authenticate the sender using digital certificates.

INTERNATIONAL STANDARDS ORGANIZATION (ISO) Founded in 1946, ISO is an international organization composed of national standards bodies from over 75 countries.

INTERNATIONAL TELECOMMUNICATION UNION (ITU) An intergovernmental organization through which public and private organizations develop telecommunications. The ITU was founded in 1865 and became a United Nations agency in 1947. It is responsible for adopting international treaties, regulations and standards governing telecommunications.

JAVA An object-oriented language developed by Sun Microsystems that is similar to C++, but simplified to eliminate language features that cause common programming errors. Java source code files (files with a .java extension) are compiled into a format called bytecode (files with a .class extension), which can then be executed by a Java interpreter. Compiled Java code can run on most computers because Java interpreters and runtime environments, known as Java Virtual Machines (VMs), exist for most operating systems, including UNIX, the Macintosh OS, and Windows. Bytecode can also be converted directly into machine language instructions by a just-in-time compiler (JIT). Java is a general purpose programming language with a number of features that make the language well suited for use on the World Wide Web. Small Java applications are called Java applets and can be downloaded from a Web server and run on your computer by a Java-compatible Web browser, such as Netscape Navigator or Microsoft Internet Explorer.

JAVA 2 PLATFORM ENTERPRISE EDITION (J2EE) J2EE is a platform-independent, Java-centric environment from Sun for developing, building and deploying Web-based enterprise applications online. The J2EE platform consists of a set of services, APIs, and protocols that provide the functionality for developing multi-tiered, Web-based applications.

JAVABEANS A specification developed by Sun Microsystems that defines how Java objects interact. An object that conforms to this specification is called a JavaBean, and is similar to a Microsoft ActiveX control. It can be used by any application that understands the JavaBeans format. The main difference between ActiveX controls and JavaBeans are that ActiveX controls can be developed in any programming language but executed only on a Windows platform, whereas JavaBeans can be developed only in Java, but can run on any platform.

JAVA SERVLETS A Java applet that runs in a Web server environment rather than a Web browser environment. Java servlets are an increasingly popular as an alternative to CGI programs. The biggest difference between the two is that a Java applet is persistent. This means that once it is started, it stays in memory and can fulfill multiple requests. In contrast, a CGI program disappears once it has fulfilled a request. The persistence of Java applets makes them faster because there's no wasted time in setting up and tearing down the process.

JAVA VIRTUAL MACHINE (JVM) An abstract computing machine, or virtual machine, JVM is a platform-independent programming language that converts Java bytecode into machine language and executes it. Most programming languages compile source code directly into machine code that is designed to run on a specific microprocessor architecture or operating system, such as Windows or UNIX. A JVM—a machine within a machine—mimics a real Java processor, enabling Java bytecode to be executed as actions or operating system calls on any processor regardless of the operating system. For example, establishing a socket connection from a workstation to a remote machine involves an operating system call. Since different operating systems handle sockets in different ways, the JVM translates the programming code so that the two machines that may be on different platforms are able to connect.

KERBEROS An authentication system developed at the Massachusetts Institute of Technology (MIT). Kerberos is designed to enable two parties to exchange private information across an otherwise open network. It works by assigning a unique key, called a ticket, to each user that logs on to the network. The ticket is then embedded in messages to identify the sender of the message.

LATENCY In general, the period of time that one component in a system waits for another component: essentially, latency is wasted time. For example, in accessing data on a disk, latency is defined as the time it takes to position the proper sector under the read/write head. In networking, the amount of time it takes a packet to travel from source to destination. Together, latency and bandwidth define the speed and capacity of a network.

LAYER 2 SWITCHING Link Layer, or Layer 2, switching—commonly called LAN (local-area network) switching—is the wire speed connection of at least two LAN segments transparently to form a single, logical LAN. In this type of switching, application-specific integrated circuits (ASICs) or switching integrated circuits (ICs) provide wire speed performance to link LANs together. Local traffic stays on each segment; only traffic intended for delivery off the segment will be transmitted by the switch.

LAYER 2 TUNNELING PROTOCOL (L2TP) An extension to the PPP protocol that enables ISPs to operate Virtual Private Networks (VPNs). L2TP merges the best features of two other tunneling protocols: PPTP from Microsoft and L2F from Cisco Systems. Like PPTP, L2TP requires that the ISP's routers support the protocol.

LAYER 3 SWITCHING Network Layer, or Layer 3, switching is a bit of market-speak that refers to at least three different kinds of network switching implementations:

1. Application-specific integrated circuit (ASIC) or hardware-based routing: Routing technology has been modified for performance, with the support of many routing functions being done in the hardware. This provides network-layer routing of such protocols as Internet Protocol (IP) and Internetwork Packet Exchange (IPX) at wire speed performance of more than one gigabit per second full duplex per port.
2. Route once, switch many: This is a tactical technology that was implemented by local-area network (LAN) vendors to use switches to offset performance and latency problems with older routers. With the switch "front ending" a router, the packets go through the switch and the switch allows the first packet to go to the router, which performs address resolution and frame regeneration, and then forwards the packet back to the switch toward the destination. Subsequent packets in a flow are handled by the switch with no help from the router by using the information that was learned by the switch from the first routed packet.
3. Fully proprietary implementations: These implementations are numerous, but are falling by the wayside in

campus LANs due to their complexity, their need for constant management and their divergence from industry direction. Examples of such implementations include switching between virtual local-area networks (VLANs) at layer 2 and desktop software for shortcuts between VLANs or subnets.

LEASED LINE A permanent telephone connection between two points set up by a telecommunications common carrier. Typically, leased lines are used by businesses to connect geographically distant offices. Unlike normal dial-up connections, a leased line is always active. The fee for the connection is a fixed monthly rate. The primary factors affecting the monthly fee are distance between end points and the speed of the circuit. Because the connection doesn't carry anybody else's communications, the carrier can assure a given level of quality.

LEGACY APPLICATION In information technology, legacy applications and data are those that have been inherited from languages, platforms, and techniques earlier than current technology. Most enterprises that use computers have legacy applications and databases that serve critical business needs. Typically, the challenge is to keep the legacy application running while converting it to newer, more efficient code that makes use of new technology and programmer skills. In the past, much programming has been written for specific manufacturers' operating systems. Currently, many companies are migrating their legacy applications to new programming languages and operating systems that follow open or standard programming interfaces. Theoretically, this will make it easier in the future to update applications without having to rewrite them entirely and will allow a company to use its applications on any manufacturer's operating system. In addition to moving to new languages, enterprises are redistributing the locations of applications and data. In general, legacy applications have to continue to run on the platforms they were developed for. Typically, new development environments account for the need to continue to support legacy applications and data. With many new tools, legacy databases can be accessed by newer programs.

LIGHTWEIGHT DIRECTORY ACCESS PROTOCOL (LDAP) A set of protocols for accessing information directories. LDAP is based on the standards contained within the X.500 standard, but is significantly simpler. And unlike X.500, LDAP supports TCP/IP, which is necessary for any type of Internet access. Because it's a simpler version of X.500, LDAP is sometimes called X.500-lite. Although not yet widely implemented, LDAP should eventually make it possible for almost any application running on virtually any computer platform to obtain directory information, such as email addresses and public keys. Because LDAP is an open protocol, applications need not worry about the type of server hosting the directory.

LINUX   A freely distributable open source implementation of UNIX that runs on a number of hardware platforms, including Intel and Motorola microprocessors.

LOAD BALANCING   Distributing processing and communications activity evenly across a computer network so that no single device is overwhelmed. Load balancing is especially important for networks where it's difficult to predict the number of requests that will be issued to a server. Busy Web sites typically employ two or more Web servers in a load balancing scheme. If one server starts to get swamped, requests are forwarded to another server with more capacity. Load balancing can also refer to the communications channels themselves.

LOCAL AREA NETWORK (LAN)   A computer network that spans a relatively small area. Most LANs are confined to a single building or group of buildings. However, one LAN can be connected to other LANs over any distance via telephone lines and radio waves. A system of LANs connected in this way is called a wide-area network (WAN). Most LANs connect workstations and personal computers. Each node (individual computer) in a LAN has its own CPU with which it executes programs, but it is also able to access data and devices anywhere on the LAN. This means that many users can share expensive devices and data. Users can also use the LAN to communicate with each other, by sending e-mail or engaging in chat sessions.

LOCAL EXCHANGE CARRIER (LEC)   A telephone company that provides local area voice and data services.

MANAGED SERVICE PROVIDER (MSP)   A company that manages information technology services for other companies via the Web. An MSP client may use internally hosted applications or an ASP to run its business functions.

MANUFACTURING RESOURCE PLANNING (MRP)

Systems that enable users to manage the processes that make up a supply chain, including deploying inventory, forecasting, and shipping. Sequentially, analysis of demands leads to creation of a master production schedule (MPS). The next step is the development of a material requirements plan (which generally assumes infinite material availability). This in turn generates a capacity requirement plan (CRP), in which capacity constraints are first uncovered.

MEMORY   Internal storage areas in the computer. The term memory identifies data storage that comes in the form of chips, and the word storage is used for memory that exists on tapes or disks. Moreover, the term memory is often used as shorthand for physical memory, which refers to the actual chips capable of holding data. Some computers also use virtual memory, which expands physical memory onto a hard disk.

MESSAGE APPLICATION PROGRAMMING INTERFACE (MAPI)   The Microsoft standard application programming interface for email software. Allows programs to read, create, send and manipulate stored messages.

MESSAGE-ORIENTED MIDDLEWARE (MOM)
Message-oriented middleware is software that resides in both portions of a client/server architecture and typically supports asynchronous calls between the client and server applications. Message queues provide temporary storage when the destination program is busy or not connected. MOM reduces the involvement of application developers with the complexity of the master-slave nature of the client/server mechanism.

METROPOLITAN AREA NETWORK (MAN)   A data network designed for a town or city. In terms of geographic breadth, MANs are larger than local-area networks (LANs), but smaller than wide-area networks (WANs). MANs are usually characterized by very high-speed connections using fiber optical cable or other digital media.

MIDDLEWARE   Software that connects two otherwise separate applications. For example, there are a number of middleware products that link a database system to a Web server. This allows users to request data from the database using forms displayed on a Web browser, and it enables the Web server to return dynamic Web pages based on the user's requests and profile. The term middleware is used to describe separate products that serve as the glue between two applications. It is, therefore, distinct from import and export features that may be built into one of the applications. Middleware is sometimes called plumbing because it connects two sides of an application and passes data between them.

N-TIER   An n-tier application program is one that is distributed among three or more separate computers in a distributed network. The most common form of n-tier (meaning 'some number of tiers') is the 3-tier application, in which user interface programming is in the user's computer, business logic is in a more centralized computer, and needed data is in a computer that manages a database. N-tier application structure implies the client/server program model. Where there are more than three distribution levels or tiers involved, the additional tiers in the application are usually associated with the business logic tier. In addition to the advantages of distributing programming and data throughout a network, n-tier applications have the advantages that any one tier can run on an appropriate processor or operating system platform and can be updated independently of the other tiers. Communication between the program tiers uses special program interfaces such as those provided by the Common Object Request Broker Architecture (COBRA).

NAMING SERVICE   A program that provides mapping between logical names and physical addresses of network-based hardware and software resources. It can be extended by a directory service.

NETWORK ADDRESS TRANSLATION   NAT (Network Address Translation) is the translation of an Internet Protocol address (IP address) used within one network to a different IP address known within another network. One network is designated the inside network and the other is the outside. Typically, a company maps its local inside network addresses to one or more global outside IP addresses and un-maps the global IP addresses on incoming packets back into local IP addresses. This helps ensure security since each outgoing or incoming request must go through a translation process that also offers the opportunity to qualify or authenticate the request or match it to a previous request. NAT also conserves on the number of global IP addresses that a company needs and it lets the company use a single IP address in its communication with the world. NAT is included as part of a router and is often part of a corporate firewall. Network administrators create a NAT table that does the global-to-local and local-to-global IP address mapping. NAT can also be used in conjunction with policy routing. NAT can be statically defined or it can be set up to dynamically translate from and to a pool of IP addresses.

NETWORK-ATTACHED STORAGE (NAS)   A network-attached storage (NAS) device is a server that is dedicated to nothing more than file sharing. NAS does not provide any of the activities that a server in a server-centric system typically provides, such as e-mail, authentication or file management. NAS allows more hard disk storage space to be added to a network that already utilizes servers without shutting them down for maintenance and upgrades. With a NAS device, storage is not an integral part of the server. Instead, in this storage-centric design, the server still handles all of the processing of data but a NAS device delivers the data to the user. A NAS device does not need to be located within the server but can exist anywhere in a LAN and can be made up of multiple networked NAS devices.

NETWORK FILE SYSTEM (NFS)   The Network File System (NFS) is a distributed file system that allows users to access files and directories located on remote computers and treat those files and directories as if they were local. For example, users can use operating system commands to create, remove, read, write, and set file attributes for remote files and directories.

NETWORK SERVICE PROVIDER (NSP)   A company that provides access to ISPs. Sometimes NSPs also

are called backbone providers due to the fact that they provide access to the Internet backbone.

OBJECT   In object-oriented programming, an object is a self-contained entity that consists of both data and procedures to manipulate the data.

OBJECT-ORIENTED PROGRAMMING (OOP)   A special type of programming that combines data structures with functions to create re-usable objects.

OBJECT REQUEST BROKER (ORB)   A component in the CORBA programming model that acts as the middleware between clients and servers. In the CORBA model, a client can request a service without knowing anything about what servers are attached to the network. The various ORBs receive the requests, forward them to the appropriate servers, and then hand the results back to the client.

ONLINE ANALYTICAL PROCESSING (OLAP)   A category of software tools that provides analysis of data stored in a database. OLAP tools enable users to analyze different dimensions of multidimensional data. For example, it provides time series and trend analysis views. The chief component of OLAP is the OLAP server, which sits between a client and a database management systems (DBMS). The OLAP server understands how data is organized in the database and has special functions for analyzing the data. There are OLAP servers available for nearly all the major database systems.

OPEN   Public, as in an open standard or open architecture.

OPEN DATABASE CONNECTIVITY (ODBC)   A programming interface from Microsoft that provides a common language for Windows applications to access databases on a network.

OPEN GROUP   An international consortium of computer and software manufacturers and users dedicated to advancing multi-vendor technologies. The Open Group was formed in February, 1996 by merging two previously independent groups: the Open Software Foundation (OSF) and X/Open Company Ltd. One of the most important technologies fostered by The Open Group is DCE.

OPEN STANDARD ARCHITECTURES   An architecture whose specifications are public. This includes officially approved standards as well as privately designed architectures whose specifications are made public by the designers. The opposite of open is closed or proprietary. The great advantage of open architectures is that anyone can design add-on products for it. By making an architecture public, however, a manufacturer allows others to duplicate its product.

OPEN SYSTEMS INTERCONNECTION (OSI)   An ISO standard for worldwide communications that defines a networking framework for implementing protocols in seven layers. Control is passed from one layer to the next, starting at the application layer in one station, proceeding to the bottom layer, over the channel to the next station and back up the hierarchy. The OSI Model or OSI Reference Model is commonly used to describe the operation of network devices and protocols. It has seven layers as follows:

- *Application (Layer 7):* This layer supports application and end-user processes. Communication partners are identified, quality of service is identified, user authentication and privacy are considered, and any constraints on data syntax are identified. Everything at this layer is application-specific. This layer provides application services for file transfers, e-mail, and other network software services.
- *Presentation (Layer 6):* This layer provides independence from differences in data representation (e.g., encryption) by translating from application to network format, and vice versa. This layer formats and encrypts data to be sent across a network, providing freedom from compatibility problems. It is sometimes called the syntax layer.
- *Session (Layer 5):* This layer establishes, manages and terminates connections between applications. The session layer sets up, coordinates, and terminates conversations, exchanges, and dialogues between the applications at each end. It deals with session and connection coordination.
- *Transport (Layer 4):* This layer provides transparent transfer of data between end systems, or hosts, and is responsible for end-to-end error recovery and flow control. It ensures complete data transfer.
- *Network (Layer 3):* This layer provides switching and routing technologies, creating logical paths, known as virtual circuits, for transmitting data from node to node. Routing and forwarding are functions of this layer, as well as addressing, internetworking, error handling, congestion control and packet sequencing.
- *Data Link (Layer 2):* At this layer, data packets are encoded and decoded into bits. It furnishes transmission protocol knowledge and management and handles errors in the physical layer, flow control and frame synchronization. The data link layer is divided into two sub-layers: The Media Access Control (MAC) layer and the Logical Link Control (LLC) layer. The MAC sub-layer controls how a computer on the network gains access to the data and permission to transmit it. The LLC layer controls frame synchronization, flow control and error checking.
- *Physical (Layer 1):* This layer conveys the bit stream—electrical impulse, light or radio signal—through the network at the electrical and mechanical level. It provides the hardware means of sending and receiving data on a carrier, including defining cables, cards and physical aspects.

OPERATING SYSTEM (OS)   Operating systems provide a software platform on top of which other programs, called application programs, can run. The application programs must be written to use the underlying operating system, which in turn manages the use of resources available on the computer.

OUTSOURCING   The act of hiring an outside source, usually a consultant or service provider, to transfer components or large segments of an organization's internal IT structure, staff, processes and applications for access via a virtual private network or an Internet-based browser.

PACKET   A packet is the unit of data that is routed between an origin and a destination on the Internet or any other packet-switched network. When any file (e-mail message, HTML file, Graphics Interchange Format file, Uniform Resource Locator request, and so forth) is sent from one place to another on the Internet, the Transmission Control Protocol (TCP) layer of TCP/IP divides the file into "chunks" of an efficient size for routing. Each of these packets is separately numbered and includes the Internet address of the destination. The individual packets for a given file may travel different routes through the Internet. When they have all arrived, they are reassembled into the original file (by the TCP layer at the receiving end).

PACKET SWITCHING   A common communications method in which messages are divided into packets and sent individually across a link. In a meshed network, the packets may take different routes and may arrive out of order. The Internet is based on a packet-switching protocol, TCP/IP. Although packet switching is essentially connectionless, a packet switching network can be made connection-oriented by using a higher-level protocol. TCP, for example, makes IP networks connection-oriented.

PERL   Short for Practical Extraction and Report Language, Perl is a programming language developed by Larry Wall, especially designed for processing text. One of the most popular languages for writing CGI scripts, Perl is an interpretive language, which makes it easy to build and test simple programs.

PHP   PHP Hypertext Preprocessor is a server-side, HTML embedded scripting language used to create dynamic Web pages. In an HTML document, PHP script (similar syntax to that of Perl or C) is enclosed within special PHP tags. Because PHP is embedded within tags, the author can jump between HTML and PHP instead of having to rely on heavy amounts of code to output HTML. And, because PHP is executed on the server, the client cannot view the PHP code.

POINT-TO-POINT PROTOCOL (PPP)   A method of connecting a computer to the Internet. PPP is more stable than the older SLIP protocol and provides error checking features.

POINT-TO-POINT TUNNELING PROTOCOL (PPTP) A protocol that allows native network services such as NetBEUI and IPX to be used to create a secure and reliable connection over the Internet.

POINT OF PRESENCE (POP) A telephone number that provides a user with dial-up access. Internet Service Providers (ISPs) generally provide many POPs so that users can make a local call to gain Internet access.

POST OFFICE PROTOCOL (POP3) A protocol used to retrieve e-mail from a mail server.

POTS Telco jargon for Plain Old Telephone System.

PROGRAM An organized list of instructions that, when executed, causes the computer to behave in a predetermined manner. Without programs, computers are useless.

PROGRAMMING LANGUAGE GENERATIONS In the computer industry, these abbreviations are widely used to represent major steps or "generations" in the evolution of programming languages.

- 1GL or first-generation language was (and still is) machine language or the level of instructions and data that the processor is actually given to work on (which in conventional computers is a string of 0s and 1s).
- 2GL or second-generation language is assembler (sometimes called "assembly") language. An assembler converts the assembler language statements into machine language.
- 3GL or third-generation language is a "high-level" programming language, such as PL/I, C, or Java. A compiler converts the statements of a specific high-level programming language into machine language. (In the case of Java, the output is called bytecode, which is converted into appropriate machine language by a Java virtual machine that runs as part of an operating system platform.) A 3GL language requires a considerable amount of programming knowledge.
- 4GL or fourth-generation language is designed to be closer to natural language than a 3GL language. Languages for accessing databases are often described as 4GLs.
- 5GL or fifth-generation language is programming that uses a visual or graphical development interface to create source language that is usually compiled with a 3GL or 4GL language compiler. Microsoft, Borland, IBM, and other companies make 5GL visual programming products for developing applications in Java, for example. Visual programming allows programmers to easily envision object-oriented programming class hierarchies and drag icons to assemble program components.

PROPRIETARY Privately owned and controlled. In the computer industry, proprietary is the opposite of open. A proprietary design or technique is one that is owned by a company. It also implies that the company has not divulged specifications that would allow other companies to duplicate the product. Increasingly, proprietary architectures are seen as a disadvantage for all but their vendors. Open and standardized architectures are preferred because they allow users to mix and match products from different manufacturers.

PROTOCOL An agreed-upon format for transmitting data between two devices.

PROXY SERVER A server that sits between a client application, such as a Web browser, and a real server. It intercepts all requests to the real server to see if it can fulfill the requests itself. If not, it forwards the request to the real server.

PUBLIC KEY ENCRYPTION A cryptographic system that uses two keys—a public key known to everyone and a private or secret key known only to the recipient of the message. An important element to the public key system is that the public and private keys are related in such a way that only the public key can be used to encrypt messages and only the corresponding private key can be used to decrypt them. Moreover, it is virtually impossible to deduce the private key if you know the public key. Public-key systems, such as Pretty Good Privacy (PGP), are becoming popular for transmitting information via the Internet. They are extremely secure and relatively simple to use. The only difficulty with public-key systems is that you need to know the recipient's public key to encrypt a message for him or her. What's needed, therefore, is a global registry of public keys, which is one of the promises of the new LDAP technology.

PUBLIC SWITCHED TELEPHONE NETWORK (PSTN) The public system provided by telephone companies for residential and business telephone and fax services. Consists of exchanges and subexchanges, with calls switched between them as required.

QUALITY OF SERVICE (QOS) A networking term that specifies a guaranteed throughput level. One of the biggest advantages of ATM over competing technologies such as Frame Relay and Fast Ethernet, is that it supports QoS levels. This allows ATM providers to guarantee to their customers that end-to-end latency will not exceed a specified level.

RADIUS Short for Remote Authentication Dial-In User Service, an authentication and accounting system used by many Internet Service Providers (ISPs). When a user dials in to an ISP, he or she must enter a username and password. This information is passed to a RADIUS server, which checks that the information is correct, and then authorizes access to the ISP system. Though not an official standard, the RADIUS specification is maintained by a working group of the IETF

REMOTE DESKTOP PROTOCOL (RDP)   A protocol used by Microsoft in the Terminal Server Edition of its NT and Windows 2000 operating system environments used to extend Windows application user interface to remote Windows clients. RDP is based on International Telecommunications Union's (ITU's) T.120 protocol. The T.120 protocol is an international-standard conferencing protocol that Microsoft uses in its NetMeeting remote-conferencing product. The T.120 protocol supports 64,000 communication channels over the same connection so that data can divide into logical streams.

REMOTE PROCEDURE CALL (RPC)   A type of protocol that allows a program on one computer to execute a program on a server computer. Using RPC, a system developer need not develop specific procedures for the server. The client program sends a message to the server with appropriate arguments and the server returns a message containing the results of the program executed. Sun Microsystems developed the first widely used RPC protocol as part of their Open Network Computing (ONC) architecture in the early 1980s. The specification has been handed off to the Internet Engineering Task Force (IETF) as a step toward making ONC RPC an Internet standard. Two newer object-oriented methods for programs to communicate with each other, CORBA and DCOM, provide the same types of capabilities as traditional RPCs.

REQUEST FOR COMMENT (RFC)   A series of notes about the Internet, started in 1969 (when the Internet was the ARPANET). An RFC can be submitted by anyone. Eventually, if it gains enough interest, it may evolve into an Internet standard. Each RFC is designated by an RFC number that, once published, never changes. Modifications to an original RFC are assigned a new RFC number.

ROSETTANET   Named after the ancient Rosetta stone, which helped decipher hieroglyphics. A non-profit organization (www.rosettanet.org) that seeks to implement standards for supply-chain (manager-supplier) transactions on the Internet. Created in Winter 1998, the group includes companies like American Express, Microsoft, Netscape, and IBM, and is working to standardize labels for elements like product descriptions, part numbers, pricing data, and inventory status. The group hopes to implement many of its goals through XML, a mark-up language that lets programmers classify information with tags.

ROUTER   A device that connects any number of LANs and that uses packet headers and a forwarding table to determine where packets go. Most routers use a specialized protocol to communicate with each other and configure the best route between any two hosts. Very little filtering of data is done through routers.

SCREEN SCRAPING   Screen scraping is programming that translates between legacy application programs (written to communicate with now generally obsolete input/output devices and user interfaces) and new user interfaces so that the logic and data associated with the legacy programs can continue to be used. Screen scraping is sometimes called advanced terminal emulation.

SECURE ELECTRONIC TRANSACTION (SET)   A credit card security and authorization protocol (SET) supported by Visa and MasterCard.

SECURE SOCKET LAYER (SSL)   A protocol developed by Netscape for transmitting private documents via the Internet. SSL works by using a public key to encrypt data that's transferred over the SSL connection. Both Netscape Navigator and Internet Explorer support SSL, and many Web sites use the protocol to obtain confidential user information, such as credit card numbers. By convention, Web pages that require an SSL connection start with https: instead of http:.

SERVER-ATTACHED STORAGE (SAS)   A storage array that is cabled directly to a host bus adapter on a server and is therefore dedicated to that server.

SERVER   A computer or device on a network that manages network resources. For example, a file server is a computer and storage device dedicated to storing files. Any user on the network can store files on the server. A print server is a computer that manages one or more printers, and a network server is a computer that manages network traffic. A database server is a computer system that processes database queries. Servers are often dedicated, meaning that they perform no other tasks besides their server tasks. On multiprocessing operating systems, however, a single computer can execute several programs at once. A server in this case could refer to the program that is managing resources rather than the entire computer.

SERVER FARM   Also referred to as server cluster, compute farm or ranch, a server farm is a group of networked servers that are housed in one location. A server farm streamlines internal processes by distributing the workload between the individual components of the farm and expedites computing processes by harnessing the power of multiple servers. The farms rely on load balancing software that accomplishes such tasks as tracking demand for processing power from different machines, prioritizing the tasks and scheduling and rescheduling them depending on priority and demand that users put on the network. When one server in the farm fails, another can step in as a backup.

SERVICE LEVEL AGREEMENT (SLA)   A contract between the provider and the user that specifies the level of service that is expected during its term. SLAs are used by vendors and customers, as well as internally by IT shops and their end users. They can specify bandwidth availability, response times for routine and ad hoc queries and response time for problem resolution (network down, machine failure, etc.). SLAs can be very general or extremely detailed, including the steps taken in the event of a failure. For example, if the problem persists after 30 minutes, a supervisor is notified; after one hour, the account representative is contacted.

SIMPLE MAIL TRANSPORT PROTOCOL (SMTP)

A protocol for sending e-mail messages between servers. Most e-mail systems that send mail over the Internet use SMTP to send message from server to server.

SOFTWARE   Computer instructions and data.

STANDARD   A definition or format that has been approved by a recognized standards organization or is accepted as a de facto standard by the industry. Standards exist for programming languages, operating systems, data formats, communications protocols, and electrical interfaces.

STORAGE AREA NETWORK (SAN)   A high-speed fabric or subnetwork of shared storage devices and servers.

STORAGE SERVICE PROVIDER (SSP)   A company that provides computer storage space and related management services. SSPs may also offer periodic backup, archiving, and data sharing mechanisms.

SUBSCRIPTION COMPUTING   Providers that supply, not only network access and a foundation suite of applications, but also the complete user environment as a package for a monthly subscription.

SWITCH   In networks, a device that filters and forwards packets between LAN segments. Switches operate at the data link layer (layer 2) of the OSI Reference Model and therefore support any packet protocol. LANs that use switches to join segments are called switched LANs or, in the case of Ethernet networks, switched Ethernet LANs.

T-1   A dedicated phone connection supporting data rates of 1.544Mbits per second. A T-1 line actually consists of 24 individual channels, each of which supports 64Kbits per second. Each 64Kbit/second channel can be configured to carry voice or data traffic. Most telephone companies allow you to buy just some of these individual channels, known as fractional T-1 access. T-1 lines are a popular leased line option for businesses connecting to the Internet and for Internet Service Providers (ISPs) connecting to the Internet backbone. The Internet backbone itself consists of faster T-3 connections. T-1 lines are sometimes referred to as DS1 lines.

T-3   A dedicated phone connection supporting data rates of about 43 Mbps. A T-3 line actually consists of 672 individual channels, each of which supports 64 Kbps. T-3 lines are used mainly by Internet Service Providers (ISPs)

connecting to the Internet backbone and for the backbone itself. T-3 lines are sometimes referred to as DS3 lines.

TCP/IP   The suite of communications protocols used to connect hosts on the Internet. TCP/IP uses several protocols, the two main ones being TCP and IP. TCP/IP is built into the UNIX operating system and is used by the Internet, making it the de facto standard for transmitting data over networks. Even network operating systems that have their own protocols, such as Netware, also support TCP/IP. *See also* INTERNET PROTOCOL.

TERMINAL SERVER   A type of application server software that extends a hosted application's user interface to a remote workstation or PC, treating it as a terminal.

TIMESHARING   A older method of application service provisioning in which the hosting system's operations are shared between multiple customers.

TRANSACTION PROCESSING MONITOR   a program that monitors a transaction as it passes from one stage in a process to another. The TP monitor's purpose is to ensure that the transaction processes completely or, if an error occurs, to take appropriate actions. TP monitors are especially important in three-tier architectures that employ load balancing because a transaction may be forwarded to any of several servers. In fact, many TP monitors handle all load balancing operations, forwarding transactions to different servers based on their availability.

TRUNK   A communications channel between two points. It usually refers to large-bandwidth telephone channels between switching centers that handle many simultaneous voice and data signals. Often used interchangeably (and somewhat confusingly) with line and circuit.

TUNNEL   A technology that enables one network to send its data via another network's connections. Tunneling works by encapsulating a network protocol within packets carried by the second network. For example, Microsoft's PPTP technology enables organizations to use the Internet to transmit data across a virtual private network (VPN). It does this by embedding its own network protocol within the TCP/IP packets carried by the Internet. Tunneling is also called encapsulation.

UNINTERRUPTIBLE POWER SUPPLY (UPS)   A power supply that includes a battery to maintain power in the event of a power outage. Typically, a UPS keeps a computer running for several minutes after a power outage, enabling you to save data that is in RAM and shut down the computer gracefully. Many UPSs now offer a software component that enables the automation of backup and shut down procedures in case there's a power failure while the computer in unattended. There are two basic types of UPS systems: standby power systems (SPSs) and on-line UPS systems. An SPS monitors the power line and switches to battery power as soon as it detects a problem. The switch to battery, however, can require several milliseconds, during which time the computer is not receiving any power. Standby Power Systems are sometimes called Line-interactive UPSes. An on-line UPS avoids these momentary power lapses by constantly providing power from its own inverter, even when the power line is functioning properly.

UNIX A popular multi-user, multitasking operating system originally developed at Bell Labs in the early 1970s to be a small, flexible system used exclusively by programmers. Although it has matured considerably over the years, UNIX still betrays its origins by its cryptic command names and its general lack of user-friendliness. This is changing, however, with graphical user interfaces such as MOTIF. UNIX was one of the first operating systems to be written in a high-level programming language, C. This meant that it could installed on virtually any computer for which a C compiler existed. This natural portability combined with its low price made it a popular choice among universities. (It was inexpensive because antitrust regulations prohibited Bell Labs from marketing it as a full-scale product.) Bell Labs distributed the operating system in its source language form, so anyone who obtained a copy could modify and customize it for his own purposes. By the end of the 1970s, dozens of different versions of UNIX were running at various sites. After its breakup in 1982, AT&T began to market UNIX in earnest. It also began the long and difficult process of defining a standard version of UNIX. To date, there are two main dialects of UNIX; one produced by AT&T known as System V and one developed at Berkeley University and known as BSD4.x, x being a number from 1 to 3. Due to its portability, flexibility, and power, UNIX has become the leading operating system for workstations and servers. Historically, it has been less popular in the personal computer market, but the emergence of a new UNIX-like operating system, Linux, is revitalizing UNIX across all platforms.

VIRTUAL PRIVATE NETWORK (VPN) A network that is constructed by using public wires to connect nodes and that applies encryption and other security mechanisms to ensure that only authorized users can access the network and that the data cannot be intercepted.

VERTICAL APPLICATION An application software package that caters to the unique needs of a particular market segment.

VERTICAL MARKET A vertical market is a particular industry or group of enterprises in which similar products or services are developed and marketed using similar methods (and to whom goods and services can be sold). Broad examples of vertical markets are: insurance, real estate, banking, heavy manufacturing, retail, transportation, hospitals, and government. Vertical market software is software aimed at a particular vertical market and can

be contrasted with horizontal market software (such as word processors and spreadsheet programs) that can be used in a cross-section of industries.

VERTICAL PORTAL A Web site that provides a gateway or portal to information related to a particular industry such as health care, insurance, automobiles, or food manufacturing.

VERTICAL SERVICE PROVIDER (VSP) An ASP catering to the needs of a vertical segment of the market.

W3C Short for World Wide Web Consortium, an international consortium of companies involved with the Internet and the Web. The W3C was founded in 1994 by Tim Berners-Lee, the original architect of the World Wide Web. The organization's purpose is to develop open standards so that the Web evolves in a single direction rather than being splintered among competing factions. The W3C is the chief standards body for HTTP and HTML.

WEB TECHNOLOGY Hardware and software technologies that enable the use of the World Wide Web.

WEBTOP A virtual desktop delivered by an ASP.

WIDE AREA NETWORK (WAN) A computer network that spans a relatively large geographical area. Typically, a WAN consists of two or more local-area networks (LANs). Computers connected to a wide-area network are often connected through public networks, such as the telephone system. They can also be connected through leased lines or satellites. The largest WAN in existence is the Internet.

WINDOWS A family of operating systems from Microsoft Corporation for personal computers and servers. Windows provides a graphical user interface (GUI), virtual memory management, multitasking, and support for many peripheral devices.

WIRELESS APPLICATION PROTOCOL (WAP) An initiative started by Unwired Planet, Motorola, Nokia and Ericsson to develop a standard for wireless content delivery on the next generation of mobile communication devices.

WORLD WIDE WEB (WWW) A system of Internet servers that supports the access to documents specially formatted using a scripting language called HTML (HyperText Markup Language). HTML scripted documents support links to other documents, as well as graphics, audio, and video files. Users can jump from one document to another simply by clicking on "hot spots" embedded in the document. Not all Internet servers are part of the World Wide Web.

X.500 An ISO and ITU standard that defines how global directories should be structured. X.500 directories are hierarchical with different levels for each category of information, such as country, state, and city. X.500 supports X.400 systems.

X-PROTOCOL   The X Protocol was developed in the mid 1980's amid the need to provide a network transparent graphical user interface primarily for the UNIX operating system. X provides for the display and management of graphical information, much in the same manner as Microsoft's Windows and IBM's Presentation Manager. However, X uses a client/server strategy to define the relationship between an application and its display.

X-WINDOWS   A windowing and graphics system developed at the Massachusetts Institute of Technology (MIT). MIT has placed the X-Window source code in the public domain, making it a particularly attractive system for UNIX vendors. Almost all UNIX graphical interfaces, including Motif and OpenLook, are based on X-Window.

Index

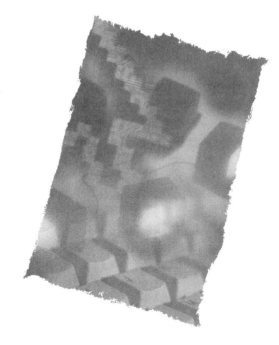